Prosecution of an Insurrection

PROSECUTION OF AN INSURRECTION

THE COMPLETE TRIAL TRANSCRIPT OF THE
SECOND IMPEACHMENT OF DONALD TRUMP

THE HOUSE IMPEACHMENT MANAGERS
AND THE HOUSE DEFENSE

THE
NEW
PRESS

NEW YORK
LONDON

Requests for permission to reproduce selections from this book should be made through our website: https://thenewpress.com/contact.

Published in the United States by The New Press, New York, 2022
Distributed by Two Rivers Distribution

ISBN 978-1-62097-715-6 (pbk)
ISBN 978-1-62097-723-1 (ebook)
CIP data is available

The New Press publishes books that promote and enrich public discussion and understanding of the issues vital to our democracy and to a more equitable world. These books are made possible by the enthusiasm of our readers; the support of a committed group of donors, large and small; the collaboration of our many partners in the independent media and the not-for-profit sector; booksellers, who often hand-sell New Press books; librarians; and above all by our authors.

www.thenewpress.com

Book design and composition by Bookbright Media
This book was set in Times New Roman, Kievit, and Fournier

Printed in the United States of America

10 9 8 7 6 5 4 3 2 1

This manuscript is largely presented as recorded in the Congressional Record. It has been edited for length, clarity, and accuracy. Quotation marks were added where a speaker quoted an individual, but the quotations have not been independently checked for accuracy. Descriptions of video stills have been supplemented for clarity in written format.

CONTENTS

H. Res. 24, Impeaching Donald John Trump, President
    of the United States, for High Crimes and
    Misdemeanors   1

Answer of President Donald John Trump, 45th President of
    the United States, to Article 1: Incitement of
    Insurrection   3

Day One   13

Day Two   73

Day Three   167

Day Four   231

Prosecution of an Insurrection

RESOLUTION

IMPEACHING DONALD JOHN TRUMP, PRESIDENT OF THE UNITED STATES, FOR HIGH crimes and misdemeanors.

Resolved, that Donald John Trump, President of the United States, is impeached for high crimes and misdemeanors and that the following article of impeachment be exhibited to the United States Senate:

Article of impeachment exhibited by the House of Representatives of the United States of America in the name of itself and of the people of the United States of America, against Donald John Trump, President of the United States of America, in maintenance and support of its impeachment against him for high crimes and misdemeanors.

ARTICLE I: INCITEMENT OF INSURRECTION

The Constitution provides that the House of Representatives "shall have the sole Power of Impeachment" and that the President "shall be removed from Office on Impeachment for, and Conviction of, Treason, Bribery, or other high Crimes and Misdemeanors". Further, section 3 of the 14th Amendment to the Constitution prohibits any person who has "engaged in insurrection or rebellion against" the United States from "hold[ing] any office . . . under the United States". In his conduct while President of the United States—and in violation of his constitutional oath faithfully to execute the office of President of the United States and, to the best of his ability, preserve, protect, and defend the Constitution of the United States, and in violation of his constitutional duty to take care that the laws be faithfully executed—Donald John Trump engaged in high Crimes and Misdemeanors by inciting violence against the Government of the United States, in that:

On January 6, 2021, pursuant to the 12th Amendment to the Constitution of the United States, the Vice President of the United States, the House of Representatives, and the Senate met at the United States Capitol for a Joint Session of Congress to count the votes of the Electoral College. In the months preceding the Joint Session, President Trump repeatedly issued false statements asserting that the Presidential election results were the product of widespread fraud and should not be accepted by the American people or certified by State or Federal officials. Shortly before the Joint Session commenced, President Trump addressed a crowd at the Ellipse in Washington, DC. There, he reiterated false claims that "we won this election, and we won it by a landslide". He also willfully made statements that, in context, encouraged—and foreseeably resulted in—lawless action at the Capitol, such as: "if you don't fight like hell you're not going to have a country anymore". Thus incited by President Trump, members of the crowd he had addressed, in an attempt to, among other objectives, interfere with the Joint Session's solemn constitutional duty to certify the results of the 2020 Presidential election, unlawfully breached and vandalized the Capitol, injured and killed law enforcement personnel, menaced Members of Congress, the Vice President, and Congressional personnel, and engaged in other violent, deadly, destructive, and seditious acts.

President Trump's conduct on January 6, 2021, followed his prior efforts to subvert and obstruct the certification of the results of the 2020 Presidential election. Those prior efforts included a phone call on January 2, 2021, during which President Trump urged the secretary of state of Georgia, Brad Raffensperger, to "find" enough votes to overturn the Georgia Presidential election results and threatened Secretary Raffensperger if he failed to do so.

In all this, President Trump gravely endangered the security of the United States and its institutions of Government. He threatened the integrity of the democratic system, interfered with the peaceful transition of power, and imperiled a coequal branch of Government. He thereby betrayed his trust as President, to the manifest injury of the people of the United States.

Wherefore, Donald John Trump, by such conduct, has demonstrated that he will remain a threat to national security, democracy, and the Constitution if allowed to remain in office, and has acted in a manner grossly incompatible with self-governance and the rule of law. Donald John Trump thus warrants impeachment and trial, removal from office, and disqualification to hold and enjoy any office of honor, trust, or profit under the United States.

IN THE SENATE OF THE
UNITED STATES OF AMERICA

ANSWER OF PRESIDENT DONALD JOHN TRUMP, 45TH PRESIDENT OF THE UNITED STATES, TO ARTICLE I: INCITEMENT OF INSURRECTION

To: The Honorable, the Members of the Unites States Senate:

The 45th President of the United States, Donald John Trump, through his counsel Bruce L. Castor, Jr., and David Schoen hereby responds to the Article of Impeachment lodged against him by the United States House of Representatives by breaking the allegations out into 8 Averments and,

Respectfully Represents:

  1. The Constitution provides that the House of Representatives 'shall have the sole Power of Impeachment' and that the President 'shall be removed from Office on Impeachment for, and conviction of, Treason, Bribery, or other high Crimes and Misdemeanors.'

Answer 1:

Admitted in part, denied in part as not relevant to any matter properly before the Senate. It is admitted that the Constitutional provision at Averment 1 is accurately reproduced. It is denied that the quoted provision currently applies to the 45th President of the United States since he is no longer "President." The constitutional provision requires that a person actually hold office to be impeached. Since the 45th President is no longer "President," the clause 'shall be removed from Office on Impeachment for . . .' is impossible for the Senate to accomplish, and thus the current proceeding before the Senate is *void ab initio* as a legal nullity that runs patently contrary to the plain language of the Constitution. Article I, Section 3 of the Constitution states "[j]udgment in cases of impeachment shall not extend further than to removal from office, *and* disqualification to hold and enjoy an office of honor . . ." (emphasis added). Since removal from office by the Senate of the President is *a condition precedent which must occur before*, and jointly with, "disqualification" to hold future office, the fact that the Senate presently is unable to remove from office the 45th President whose term has expired, means that Averment 1 is therefore irrelevant to any matter before the Senate.

2. Further, Section 3 of the 14th Amendment to the Constitution prohibits any person who has 'engaged in insurrection or rebellion against' the United States from 'hold[ing] any office . . . under the United States.'

Answer 2:

Admitted in part, denied in part, and denied as not relevant to any matter properly before the Senate. It is admitted that phrases from Section 3 of the 14th Amendment to the Constitution are correctly replicated in Averment 2. It is denied that the 45th President engaged in insurrection or rebellion against the United States. The 45th President believes and therefore avers that as a private citizen, the Senate has no jurisdiction over his ability to hold office and for the Senate to take action on this averment would constitute a Bill of Attainder in violation of Art. I, Sec. 9. Cl. 3 of the United States Constitution. The 45th President asks the Senate to dismiss Averment 2 relating to the 14th Amendment as moot.

3. In his conduct while President of the United States—and in violation of his constitutional oath faithfully to execute the office of President of the United States and, to the best of his ability, preserve, protect, and defend the Constitution of the United States, and in violation of his constitutional duty to take care that the laws be faithfully executed.

Answer 3:

Denied, and irrelevant to any matter properly before the Senate. It is denied that the 45th President of the United States ever engaged in a violation of his oath of office. To the contrary, at all times, Donald J. Trump fully and faithfully executed his duties as President of the United States, and at all times acted to the best of his ability to preserve, protect and defend the Constitution of the United States, while never engaging in any high Crimes or Misdemeanors. Since the 45th President is no longer "President," the clause 'shall be removed from Office on Impeachment for . . .' referenced at Averment 1 above is impossible, and the current proceeding before the Senate is *void ab initio* as a legal nullity patently contrary to the plain language of the Constitution. As the present proceedings are moot and thus a nullity since the 45th President cannot be removed from an office he no longer occupies, Averment 3 is irrelevant to any matter properly before the Senate.

4. Donald John Trump engaged in high Crimes and Misdemeanors by inciting violence against the Government of the United States, in that:

On January 6, 2021, pursuant to the 12th Amendment to the Constitution of the United States, the Vice President of the United States, the House of Representatives, and the Senate met at the United States Capitol for a joint session of Congress to count the votes of the Electoral College. In the months preceding the Joint Session, President Trump repeatedly issued false statements asserting that the Presidential election results were the product of widespread fraud and should not be accepted by the American people or certified by State or Federal officials.

Answer 4:

Admitted in part, denied in part, and denied as irrelevant to any matter properly before the Senate. It is admitted that on January 6, 2021 a joint session of Congress met with the Vice President, the House and the Senate, to count the votes of the Electoral College. It is admitted that after the November election, the 45th President exercised his First Amendment right under the Constitution to express his belief that the election results were suspect, since with very few exceptions, under the convenient guise of Covid-19 pandemic "safeguards" states' election laws and procedures were changed by local politicians or judges without the necessary approvals from state legislatures. Insufficient evidence exists upon which a reasonable jurist could conclude that the 45th President's statements were accurate or not, and he therefore denies they were false. Like all Americans, the 45th President is protected by the First Amendment. Indeed, he believes, and therefore avers, that the United States is unique on Earth in that its governing documents, the Constitution and Bill of Rights, specifically and intentionally protect unpopular speech from government retaliation. If the First Amendment protected only speech the government deemed popular in current American culture, it would be no protection at all. Since the 45th President is no longer "President," the Constitutional clause at Averment 1 above 'shall be removed from Office on Impeachment for . . .' is impossible since the 45th President does not hold office and the current proceeding before the Senate is *void ab initio* as a legal nullity rendering Averment 4 irrelevant to any matter properly before the Senate.

5. Shortly before the Joint Session commenced, President Trump, addressed a crowd at the Capitol ellipse in Washington DC. There, he re-iterated false claims that "we won this election, and we won it by a landslide."

Answer 5:

Admitted in part, denied in part. It is admitted that President Trump addressed a crowd at the Capitol ellipse on January 6, 2021 as is his right under the First Amendment to the Constitution and expressed his opinion that the election results were suspect, as is contained in the full recording of the speech. To the extent Averment 5 alleges his opinion is factually in error, the 45th President denies this allegation.

6. He also willfully made statements that, in context, encouraged—and foreseeably resulted in—lawless action at the Capitol, such as: "if you don't fight like hell you're not going to have a country anymore." Thus, incited by President Trump, members of the crowd he had addressed, in an attempt to, among other objectives, interfere with the Joint Session's solemn constitutional duty to certify the results of the 2020 Presidential election, unlawfully breached and vandalized the Capitol, injured and killed law enforcement personnel, menaced Members of Congress, the Vice President, and Congressional personnel, and engaged in other violent, deadly, destructive, and seditious acts.

Answer 6:

Admitted in part, denied in part. It is admitted that persons unlawfully breached and vandalized the Capitol, that people were injured and killed, and that law enforcement is currently investigating and prosecuting those who were responsible. "Seditious acts" is a term of art with a legal meaning and the use of that phrase in the article of impeachment is thus denied in the context in which it was used. It is denied that President Trump incited the crowd to engage in destructive behavior. It is denied that the phrase "if you don't fight like hell you're not going to have a country anymore" had anything to do with the action at the Capitol as it was clearly about the need to fight for election security in general, as evidenced by the recording of the speech. It is denied that President Trump intended to interfere with the counting of Electoral votes. As is customary, Members of Congress challenged electoral vote submissions by state under a process written into Congressional rules allowing for the respective Houses of Congress to debate whether a state's submitted electoral votes should be counted. In 2017, Democratic Members of Congress repeatedly challenged the electoral votes submitted from states where President Trump prevailed. In 2021, Republican Members of Congress challenged the electoral votes submitted from states where President Biden prevailed. The purpose of the Joint Sessions of Congress in 2017 and on January 6, 2021 was for Members of Congress to fulfill their duty to be certain the Electoral College votes were properly submitted, and any challenges thereto properly addressed under Congressional rules. Congress' duty, therefore, was *not* just to certify the presidential election. Its duty was to first determine whether certification of the presidential election vote was warranted and permissible under its rules.

7. "President Trump's conduct on January 6, 2021, followed his prior efforts to subvert the certification of the results of the 2020 Presidential Election. Those prior efforts included a phone call on January 2, 2021, during which President Trump urged the secretary of state [of] Georgia, Brad Raffensperger, to "find" enough votes to overturn the Georgia Presidential election results and threatened Secretary Raffensperger if he failed to do so.

Answer 7:

Admitted in part. Denied in part. Denied as irrelevant to any matter properly before the Senate. It is admitted that President Trump spoke on the telephone with Secretary Raffensperger and multiple other parties, including several attorneys for both parties, on January 2, 2021. Secretary Raffensperger or someone at his direction surreptitiously recorded the call and subsequently made it public. The recording accurately reflects the content of the conversation. It is denied President Trump made any effort to subvert the certification of the results of the 2020 Presidential election. It is denied that the word "find" was inappropriate in context, as President Trump was expressing his opinion that if the evidence was carefully examined one would "find that you have many that aren't even signed and you have many that are forgeries." It is denied that President Trump threatened Secretary Raffensperger. It is denied that President Trump acted improperly in that telephone call in any way. Since the 45th President is no longer "President," the Constitutional clause from Averment 1 above 'shall be removed from Office on Impeachment for . . .' is impossible since the 45th President does not hold office rendering the current proceeding before the Senate is *void ab initio* as a legal nullity making Averment 7 irrelevant to any matter properly before the Senate.

8. "In all this, President Trump gravely endangered the security of the United States and its institutions of Government. He threatened the integrity of the democratic system, interfered with the peaceful transition of power, and imperiled a coequal branch Government. He thereby betrayed his trust as President, to the manifest injury of the people of the United States.

Answer 8:

Denied, and denied as irrelevant to any matter properly before the Senate. It is denied that President Trump ever endangered the security of the United States and its institutions of Government. It is denied he threatened the integrity of the democratic system, interfered with the peaceful transition of power, and imperiled a coequal branch Government. It is denied he betrayed his trust as President, to the manifest injury of the people of the United States. Rather, the 45th President of the United States performed admirably in his role as President, at all times doing what he thought was in the best interests of the American people. The 45th President believes and therefore avers that in the United States, the people choose their President, and that he was properly chosen in 2016 and sworn into office in 2017, serving his term to the best of his ability in comportment with his oath of office. Since the 45th President is no longer "President," the Constitutional clause at Averment 1 above 'shall be removed from Office on Impeachment for . . .' is impossible for the Senate to accomplish since the 45th President does not hold office, meaning the current proceeding before the Senate is *void ab initio* as a legal nullity rendering Averment 8 irrelevant to any matter properly before the Senate.

To the extent there are factual allegations made against the 45th President of the United States contained in Article I that are not specifically addressed above, said allegations are **denied** and strict proof at time of hearing is demanded.

Legal Defenses

To: The Honorable, the Members of the United States Senate:

The 45th President of the United States, Donald John Trump, through his counsel Bruce L. Castor, Jr., and David Schoen hereby avers that the Article of Impeachment lodged against him by the United States House of Representatives is facially and substantively flawed, and otherwise unconstitutional, and must be dismissed with prejudice. In support thereof, the 45th President,

Respectfully Represents:

1. The Senate of the United States lacks jurisdiction over the 45th President because he holds no public office from which he can be removed, and the Constitution limits the authority of the Senate in cases of impeachment to removal from office as the prerequisite active remedy allowed the Senate under our Constitution.

2. The Senate of the United States lacks jurisdiction over the 45th President because he holds no public office from which he can be removed rendering the Article of Impeachment moot and a non-justiciable question.

3. Should the Senate act on the Article of Impeachment initiated in the House of Representatives, it will have passed a Bill of Attainder in violation of Article 1, Sec. 9. Cl. 3 of the United States Constitution.

4. The Article of Impeachment misconstrues protected speech and fails to meet the constitutional standard for any impeachable offense.

5. The House of Representatives deprived the 45th President of due process of law in rushing to issue the Article of Impeachment by ignoring it own procedures and precedents going back to the mid-19th century. The lack of due process included, but was not limited to, its failure to conduct any meaningful committee review or other investigation, engage in any full and fair consideration of evidence in support of the Article, as well as the failure to conduct any full and fair discussion by allowing the 45th President's positions to be heard in the House Chamber. No exigent circumstances under the law were present excusing the House of Representatives' rush to judgment. The House of Representatives' action, in depriving the 45th President of due process of law, created a special category of citizenship for a single individual: the 45th President of the United States. Should this body not act in favor of the 45th President, the precedent set by the House of Representatives would become that such persons as the 45th President similarly situated no longer enjoy the rights of all American citizens guaranteed by the Bill of Rights. The actions by the House make clear that in their opinion the 45th President does not enjoy the protections of liberty upon which this great Nation was founded, where free speech, and indeed, free *political* speech form the backbone of all American liberties. None of the traditional reasons permitting the government to act in such haste (i.e. exigent circumstances) were present. The House had no reason to rush its proceedings, disregard its own precedents and procedures, engage in zero committee or other investigation, and fail to grant the accused his "opportunity to be heard" in person or through counsel—all basic tenets of due process of law. There was no exigency, as evidenced by the fact that the House waited until after the end of the President's term to even send the articles over and there was thus no legal or moral reason for the House to act as it did. Political hatred has no place in the administration of justice anywhere in America, especially in the Congress of the United States.

6. The Article of Impeachment violates the 45th President's right to free speech and thought guaranteed under the First Amendment to the United States Constitution.

7. The Article is constitutionally flawed in that it charges multiple instances of allegedly impeachable conduct in a single article. By charging multiple alleged wrongs in one article, the House of Representatives has made it impossible to guarantee compliance with the Constitutional mandate in Article 1, Sec. 3, Cl. 6 that permits a conviction only by at least two thirds of the members. The House charge fails by interweaving differing allegations rather than breaking them out into counts of alleged individual instances of misconduct. Rule XXIII of the *Rules of Procedure and Practice in the Senate When Sitting on Impeachment Trials* provides, in pertinent part, that an article of impeachment shall not be divisible thereon. Because the Article at issue here alleges multiple wrongs in the single article, it would be impossible to know if two thirds of the members agreed on the entire article, or just on parts, as the basis for vote to convict. The House failed to adhere to strict Senate rules and, instead, chose to make the Article as broad as possible intentionally in the hope that some Senators might agree with parts, and other Senators agree with other parts, but that when these groups of Senators were added together, the House might achieve the appearance of two thirds in agreement, when those two thirds of members, in reality, did not concur on the *same* allegations interwoven into an over-broad article designed for just such a purpose. Such behavior on the part of the House of Representatives may have a less nefarious reason, in the alternative, and simply be a by-product of the haste in which the House unnecessarily acted while depriving the 45th President of the United States of his American right to due process of law. The 45th President of the United States believes and therefore avers that the defect in the drafting of the Article requires that Senators be instructed that if two thirds of them fail to find *any* portion of the Article lacking in evidence sufficient for conviction, then the *entire* Article fails and should be dismissed.

8. The Chief Justice of the United States is not set to preside over the proceedings contemplated by the Senate, as he would be constitutionally required to do if the House was seeking to have the president removed from office under Art. I, Sec 3, Cl. 6 of the United States Constitution. Once the 45th President's term expired, and the House chose to allow jurisdiction to lapse on the Article of Impeachment, the constitutional mandate for the Chief Justice to preside at all impeachments involving the President evidently disappeared, and he was replaced by a partisan Senator who will purportedly also act as a juror while ruling on certain issues. The House actions thus were designed to ensure that Chief Justice John Roberts would not preside over the proceedings, which effectively creates the additional appearance of bias with the proceedings now being supervised by a partisan member of the Senate with a long history of public remarks adverse to the 45th President. The 45th President believes and therefore avers that this action of the House of Representatives, additionally, violated his right to due process of law because the House, effectively, maneuvered an ally in the Senate into the judge's chair.

WHEREFORE, Donald John Trump, 45th President of the United States respectfully requests the Honorable Members of the Senate of the United States dismiss Article I: Incitement of Insurrection against him as moot, and thus in violation of the Constitution, because the Senate lacks jurisdiction to remove from office a man who does not hold office. In the alternative, the 45th President respectfully requests the Senate acquit him on the merits of the allegations raised in the article of impeachment.

Respectfully Submitted,
Bruce L. Castor, Jr.
David Schoen
Counsel to the 45th President of the United States

Date: February 2, 2021

DAY ONE

TRIAL OF DONALD J. TRUMP, PRESIDENT OF THE UNITED STATES

Managers' Opening Statements

Mr. Manager RASKIN: Thank you very much, Mr. President, distinguished Members of the Senate. Good afternoon. My name is Jamie Raskin. It is my honor to represent the people of Maryland's Eighth Congressional District in the House and also to serve as the lead House manager. And Mr. President, we will indeed reserve time for rebuttal. Thank you.

Because I have been a professor of constitutional law for three decades, I know there are a lot of people who are dreading endless lectures about the Federalist Papers. Please breathe easy, okay?

I remember well W.H. Auden's line that a professor is someone who speaks while other people are sleeping. You will not be hearing extended lectures from me because our case is based on cold, hard facts. It is all about the facts.

President Trump has sent his lawyers here today to try to stop the Senate from hearing the facts of this case. They want to call the trial over before any evidence is even introduced. Their argument is that if you commit an impeachable offense in your last few weeks in office, you do it with constitutional impunity; you get away with it.

In other words, conduct that would be a high crime and misdemeanor in your first year as President and your second year as President and your third year as President and for the vast majority of your fourth year as President you can suddenly do in your last few weeks in office without facing any constitutional accountability at all.

This would create a brand-new January exception to the Constitution of the United States of America—a January exception. And everyone can see immediately why this is so dangerous. It is an invitation to the President to take his best shot at anything he may want to do on his way out the door, including using violent means to lock that door, to hang onto the Oval Office at all costs, and to block the peaceful transfer of power. In other words, the January exception is an invitation to our Founders' worst nightmare. And if we buy this radical argument that President Trump's lawyers advance, we risk allowing January 6 to become our future. And what will that mean for America? Think about it. What will the January exception mean to future generations if you grant it? I'll show you.

> Mr. TRUMP, at Jan. 6 rally: We will stop the steal. Today I will lay out just some of the evidence proving that we won this election and we won it by a landslide. This was not a close election. And after this, we're going to walk down—and I will be there with you—we're going to walk down—we're gonna walk down to the Capitol.

> (People chanting: Yeah. Let's take the Capitol.)

> Unidentified Males: Take it. Take the Capitol. We are going to the Capitol, where our problems are. It's that direction.

> Unidentified Male as marchers knock down security fencing in front of the Capitol building: Everybody in. This way. This way.

> Mr. TRUMP: Tens of thousands of votes. They came in in duffel bags. Where the hell did they come from?

> (People chanting and pushing through security fencing outside the Capitol: USA.)

> Sergeant at Arms, inside the Capitol: Madam Speaker, the Vice President and the United States Senate.

> Unidentified Officer: Off the sidewalk!

> Unidentified Males: We outnumber you a million to one out here, dude. Take the building. Take the building.

> Unidentified Males, walking up the steps to the Capitol: "Let us in." "Fuck these pigs." "Join us." "Let us in." "That's enough." "There's much more coming."

> Mr. TRUMP: The Constitution says you have to protect our country and you have to protect our Constitution. And you can't vote on fraud. And fraud breaks up everything, doesn't it? When you catch somebody in a fraud, you're allowed to go by very different rules. So I hope Mike has the courage to do what he has to do.

Unidentified Male, marching toward the Capitol: Talking about you, Pence.

Mr. TRUMP: When we fight, we fight like hell. And if you don't fight like hell, you're not going to have a country anymore.

Unidentified Male with others holding Police Lives Matter flag, to police protecting the Capitol building: Fuck D.C. police. Fuck you.

Mr. TRUMP: So we are going to walk down Pennsylvania Avenue. I love Pennsylvania Avenue. And we are going to the Capitol, and we are going to try and give our Republicans—the weak ones, because the strong ones don't need any of our help. We are going to try and give them the kind of pride and boldness that they need to take back our country.

Unidentified Male, to police: Get the fuck out of here, you traitors.

Mr. McCONNELL, inside the Capitol: We are debating a step that has never been taken in American history.

Unidentified Male outside, to police protecting the Capitol, as the crowd pushed through a line of police and security fencing: Fuck you, traitors.

Mr. McCONNELL, inside the building: President Trump claims the election was stolen. The assertions range from specific local allegations to constitutional arguments to sweeping conspiracy theories.

(Outside the building, as members of the crowd fight with police, people chanting: USA.)

Mr. McCONNELL: But my colleagues, nothing before us proves illegality anywhere near the massive scale—the massive scale—that would have tipped the entire election.

Unidentified Female, as crowd breaches two barriers, gains access to the doors of the building, and begins erecting a noose on the Capitol grounds: Our house, our house, our house, our house.

People chanting as they climb stairs and up scaffolding surrounding the Capitol: Fight for Trump.

Unidentified Males: "Fuck you, police." "Let's go. Let's go."

Officer GOODMAN reporting his position to his radio, inside the building, while attempting to divert mob away from the Senate and Vice President: Second floor.

Unidentified Male to GOODMAN: You gonna beat us all? Are you gonna beat us all?

Mr. LANKFORD, inside the Senate chamber: My challenge today is not about the good people of Arizona.

The PRESIDING pro tempore: The Senate will stand in recess until the call of the Chair.

Unidentified Male to LANKFORD: Protestors are in the building.

Mr. LANKFORD: Thank you.

(People chanting as they enter the building: Woot, woot.)

Mr. GOSAR: Madam—Mr. Speaker, can I have order in the Chamber.

The SPEAKER pro tempore: The House will be in order.

Unidentified Male, inside the Capitol: Go, go, go.

The SPEAKER pro tempore: The House will be in order. OK.

(Crowd outside the House chamber: "Stop the steal!" "Traitor Pence." "Break it down." "Treason! Treason!")

Unidentified Male as the crowd breaks a window outside the House chamber where members are evacuated, and where one crowd member is shot trying to climb through: Get down.

Unidentified Male as crowd members enter the evacuated Senate chamber: Let's go. Come on. Where the fuck are they?

(People chanting: No Trump, no peace.) Unidentified Male, as crowd attempts to enter a door sealed by police and sprays police with pepper spray: Let's go. We need fresh patriots to the front. (People chanting: Traitors.) (People chanting: Fight for Trump.)

Mr. TRUMP, in video posted to Twitter over two hours after the Capitol is breached: There has never been a time like this where such a thing happened, where they could take it away from all of us—from me, from you, from our country. This was a fraudulent election, but we can't play into the hands of these people. We have to have peace. So go home. We love you. You're very special. You've seen what happens. You've seen the way others are treated that are so bad and so evil. I know how you feel, but go home, and go home in peace.

(Crowd outside the Capitol chanting: USA.)

Unidentified Male, smashing media equipment: Mobilize in your own cities, your own counties. Storm your own capitol buildings. We take down every one of these corrupt motherfuckers. Hang them!

Mr. TRUMP, in a tweet: These are the things and events that happen when a sacred landslide election victory is so unceremoniously and viciously stripped away from great patriots who have been badly & unfairly treated for so long. Go home with love & in peace. Remember this day forever!

. . .

Mr. Manager RASKIN: Senators, the President was impeached by the U.S. House of Representatives on January 13 for doing that. You ask what a "high crime and misdemeanor" is under our Constitution. That is a high crime and misdemeanor. If that is not an impeachable offense, then there is no such thing.

And if the President's arguments for a January exception are upheld, then even if everyone agrees that he is culpable for these events, even if the evidence proves, as we think it definitively does, that the President incited a violent insurrection on the day Congress met to finalize the Presidential election, he would have you believe there is absolutely nothing the Senate can do about it—no trial, no facts. He wants you to decide that the Senate is powerless at that point. That can't be right.

The transition of power is always the most dangerous moment for democracies. Every historian will tell you that. We just saw it in the most astonishing way. We lived through it. And you know what? The Framers of our Constitution knew it.

That is why they created a Constitution with an oath written into it that binds the President from his very first day in office until his very last day in office and every day in between.

Under that Constitution and under that oath, the President of the United States is forbidden to commit high crimes and misdemeanors against the people at any point that he is in office. Indeed, that is one specific reason the impeachment, conviction, and disqualification of powers exist: to protect us against Presidents who try to overrun the power of the people in their elections and replace the rule of law with the rule of mobs.

These powers must apply even if the President commits his offenses in his final weeks in office. In fact, that is precisely when we need them the most because that is when elections get attacked. Everything that we know about the language of the Constitution, the Framers' original understanding and intent, prior Senate practice, and common sense, confirms this rule. Let's start with the text of the Constitution.

Article I, section 2 gives the House the sole power of impeachment when the President commits high crimes and misdemeanors. We exercised that power on January 13. The President, it is undisputed, committed his offense while he was President, and it is undisputed that we impeached him while he was President. There can be no doubt that this is a valid and legitimate impeachment, and there can be no doubt that the Senate has the power to try this impeachment. We know this because article I, section 3 gives the Senate the sole power to try all impeachments. The Senate has the power, the sole power, to try all impeachments.

"All" means all, and there are no exceptions to the rule. Because the Senate has jurisdiction to try all impeachments, it most certainly has jurisdiction to try this one. It is really that simple. The vast majority of constitutional scholars who studied the question and weighed in on the proposition being advanced by the President, this January exception, heretofore unknown, agree with us, and that includes the Nation's most prominent conservative legal scholars, including former Tenth Circuit Judge Michael McConnell; the cofounder of the Federalist Society, Steven Calabresi; Ronald Reagan's Solicitor General Charles Fried; luminary Washington lawyer Charles Cooper, among hundreds of other constitutional lawyers and professors.

I commend the people I named—their recent writings to you in the newspapers over the last several days, and all of the key precedents, along with detailed explanation of the constitutional history and textual analysis, appear in the trial brief we filed last week and the reply brief that we filed very early this morning. I will spare you a replay, but I want to highlight a few key points from constitutional history that strike me as compelling in foreclosing President Trump's argument that there is a secret January exception hidden away in the Constitution.

The first point comes from English history, which matters because, as Hamilton wrote, England provided "the model from which the idea of this institution has been borrowed." And it would have been immediately obvious to anyone familiar with that history that former officials could be held accountable for their abuses while in office. Every single impeachment of a government official that occurred during the Framers' lifetime concerned a former official—a former official. Indeed, the most famous of these impeachments occurred while the Framers gathered in Philadelphia to write the Constitution. It was the impeachment of Warren Hastings, the former Governor-general of the British colony of Bengal and a corrupt guy.

The Framers knew all about it, and they strongly supported the impeachment. In fact, the Hastings case was invoked by name at the convention. It was the only specific impeachment case that they discussed at the convention. It played a key role in their adoption of the high crimes and misdemeanors standard.

And even though everyone there surely knew that Hastings had left office two years before his impeachment trial began, not a single Framer—not one—raised a concern when Virginian George Mason held up the Hastings impeachment as a model for us in the writing of our Constitution. The early State constitutions supported the idea too. Every single State constitution in the 1780s either specifically said that former officials could be impeached or were entirely consistent with the idea. In contrast, not a single State constitution prohibited trials of former officials. As a result, there was an overwhelming presumption in favor of allowing legislatures to hold former officials accountable in this way.

Any departure from that norm would have been a big deal, and yet there is no sign anywhere that that ever happened. Some States, including Delaware, even confined impeachment only to officials who had already left office. This confirms that removal was never seen as the exclusive purpose of impeachment in America. The goal was always about accountability, protecting society, and deterring official corruption.

Delaware matters for another reason. Writing about impeachment in the Federalist Papers, Hamilton explained that the President of America would stand upon no better ground than a Governor of New York and upon worse ground than the Governors of Maryland and Delaware. He thus emphasized that the President is even more accountable than officials in Delaware, where, as I noted, the constitution clearly allowed impeachment of former officials. And nobody involved in the convention ever said that the Framers meant to reject this widely accepted, deeply rooted understanding of the word "impeachment" when they wrote it into our Constitution.

The convention debates instead confirm this interpretation. There, while discussing impeachment, the Framers repeatedly returned to the threat of Presidential corruption aimed directly to elections, the heart of self-government.

Almost perfectly anticipating President Trump, William Davie of North Carolina explained impeachment was for a President who spared "no effort or means whatever to get himself reelected." Hamilton, in Federalist 1, said the greatest danger to republics and the liberties of the people comes from political opportunists who begin as demagogues and end as tyrants, and the people who are encouraged to follow them.

President Trump may not know a lot about the Framers, but they certainly knew a lot about him. Given the Framers' intense focus on danger to elections and the peaceful transfer of power, it is inconceivable that they designed impeachment to be a dead letter in the President's final days in office when opportunities to interfere with the peaceful transfer of power would be most tempting and most dangerous, as we just saw.

Thus, as a matter of history and original understanding, there is no merit to President Trump's claim that he can incite an insurrection and then insist weeks later that the Senate lacks the power to even hear evidence at a trial, to even hold a trial.

The true rule was stated by former President John Quincy Adams when he categorically declared: "I hold myself, so long as I have the breath of life in my body, amenable to impeachment by [the] House for everything I did during the time I held any public office."

When he comes up in a minute, my colleague Mr. Neguse of Colorado will further pursue the relevant Senate precedents and explain why this body's practice has been supported by the text of the Constitution, and Mr. Cicilline of Rhode Island will then respond to the fallacies presented by the President's counsel. After these gentlemen speak, I will return to discuss the importance—the fundamental importance of the Senate rejecting President Trump's argument for the preservation of democratic self-government and the rule of law in the United States of America. I now turn it over to my colleague, Mr. Neguse of Colorado.

· · ·

Mr. Manager NEGUSE: Mr. President, distinguished Senators, my name is Joe Neguse, and I represent Colorado's Second Congressional District in the United States Congress. Like many of you, I am an attorney. I practiced law before I came to Congress, tried a lot of different cases, some more unique than others, certainly never a case as important as this one, nor a case with such a heavy and weighty constitutional question for you all to decide.

Thankfully, as Lead Manager Raskin so thoroughly explained, the Framers have answered that question for you, for us, and you don't need to be a constitutional scholar to know that the argument President Trump asks you to adopt is not just wrong, it is dangerous. And you don't have to take my word for it. This body, the world's greatest deliberative body, the United States Senate, has reached that

same conclusion in one form or another over the past 200 years on multiple occasions that we will go through.

Over 150 constitutional scholars, experts, judges—conservative, liberal, you name it—they overwhelmingly have reached the same conclusion, that, of course, you can try, convict, and disqualify a former President. And that makes sense because the text of the Constitution makes clear there is no January exception to the impeachment power, that Presidents can't commit grave offenses in their final days and escape any congressional response. That is not how our Constitution works.

Let's start with the precedent, with what has happened in this very Chamber. I would like to focus on just two cases. I will go through them quickly. One of them is the Nation's very first impeachment case, which actually was of a former official. In 1797, about a decade after our country ratified our Constitution, there was a Senator from Tennessee by the name of William Blount, who was caught conspiring with the British to try to sell Florida and Louisiana. Ultimately, President Adams caught him. He turned over the evidence to Congress. Four days later, the House of Representatives impeached him. A day after that, this body, the United States Senate, expelled him from office, so he was very much a former official.

Despite that, the House went forward with its impeachment proceeding in order to disqualify him from ever again holding Federal office. And so the Senate proceeded with the trial with none other than Thomas Jefferson presiding. Now, Blount argued that the Senate couldn't proceed because he had already been expelled. But here is the interesting thing: he expressly disavowed any claim that former officials can't ever be impeached. And unlike President Trump, he was very clear that he respected and understood that he could not even try to argue that ridiculous position.

Even impeached Senator Blount recognized the inherent absurdity of that view. Here is what he said: "I certainly never shall contend that an officer may first commit an offense, and afterwards avoid punishment by resigning his office."

That is the point. And there was no doubt because the Founders were around to confirm that that was their intent and the obvious meaning of what is in the Constitution.

Fast-forward eighty years later—arguably the most important precedent that this body has to consider—the trial of former Secretary of War William Belknap. I am not going to go into all the details, but, in short, in 1876, the House discovered that he was involved in a massive kickback scheme. Hours before the House Committee had discovered this conduct, released its report documenting the scheme, Belknap literally rushed to the White House to resign, tender his resignation to President Ulysses Grant to avoid any further inquiry into his misconduct, and, of course, to avoid being disqualified from holding Federal office in the future.

Later that day, aware of the resignation, what did the House do? The House moved forward and unanimously impeached him, making clear its power to impeach a former official. And when his case reached the Senate—this body— Belknap made the exact same argument that President Trump is making today, that you all lack jurisdiction, any power, to try him because he is a former official.

Now, many Senators at that time, when they heard that argument—literally, they were sitting in the same chair as you all are sitting in today—they were outraged by that argument—outraged. You can read their comments in the Record. They knew it was a dangerous, dangerous argument with dangerous implications. It would literally mean that a President could betray their country, leave office, and avoid impeachment and disqualification entirely.

And that is why, in the end, the United States Senate decisively voted that the Constitution required them to proceed with the trial. The Belknap case is clear precedent that the Senate must proceed with this trial since it rejected pretrial dismissal, affirmed its jurisdiction, and moved to a full consideration of the merits. Now, Belknap ultimately was not convicted but only after a thorough public inquiry into his misconduct, which created a record of his wrongdoing. It ensured his accountability and deterred anyone else from considering such corruption by making clear that it was intolerable. The trial served important constitutional purposes.

Now, given that precedent that I described to you, given all that that precedent imparts, you could imagine my surprise—Lead Manager Raskin's surprise—

when we were reviewing a trial brief filed by the President in which his counsel insists that the Senate actually didn't decide anything in the Belknap case. They say—these are not my words. I will quote from their trial brief: "[It] cannot be read as foreclosing an argument that they never dealt with."

Never dealt with? The Senate didn't debate this question for two hours. The Senate debated this very question for two weeks. The Senate spent an additional two weeks deliberating on the jurisdictional question. And at the end of those deliberations, they decided decisively that the Senate has jurisdiction and that it could proceed, that it must proceed to a full trial.

By the way, unlike Belknap, as we know, President Trump was not impeached for run-of-the-mill corruption, misconduct. He was impeached for inciting a violent insurrection—an insurrection where people died in this building, an insurrection that desecrated our seat of government. And if Congress were just to stand completely aside in the face of such an extraordinary crime against the Republic, it would invite future Presidents to use their power without any fear of accountability. And none of us—I know this—none of us, no matter our party or our politics, wants that.

Now, we have gone through the highlights of the precedent, and I think it is important that you know, as Lead Manager Raskin mentioned, that scholars, overwhelmingly, that reviewed this same precedent have all come to the same conclusion that the Senate must hear this case. Let's go through just a few short examples.

To start, all of us, I know, are familiar with the Federalist Society. Some of you may know Steven Calabresi personally. He is the co-founder of the Federalist Society. Actually, he was the chairman of the board in 2019. He was the first president of the Yale Federalist Society chapter board, a position I understand Senator Hawley later held. Here is what Mr. Calabresi has to say. On January 21, he issued a public letter stating: "Our carefully considered views of the law lead all of us to agree that the Constitution permits the impeachment, conviction, and disqualification of former officers, including presidents."

And by the way, he is not the only one, as Lead Manager Raskin said—President Reagan's former Solicitor General, among many others. Another prominent conservative scholar known to many of you, again, personally is a former Tenth Court of Appeals judge—my circuit—Judge Michael McConnell. He was nominated by President George W. Bush. He was confirmed by this body unanimously. Senator Hatch—many of you served with—he had this to say about Judge McConnell, that he "is an honest man. He calls it as he sees it, and [he] is beholden to no one and no group."

Well, what does Judge McConnell have to say about the question that you are debating this afternoon? He said the following: "Given that the impeachment of

President Trump was legitimate, the text makes clear that the Senate has power to try that impeachment." You heard Lead Manager Raskin mention another lawyer, Chuck Cooper, a prominent conservative lawyer here in Washington. He has represented former Attorney General Jeff Sessions and House Minority Leader Kevin McCarthy. He issued an editorial just two days ago, very powerful, observing that "scholarship on this question has matured substantially" and that, ultimately, arguments that President Trump is championing are beset by "serious weaknesses."

Finally, I have gone through a lot of scholars. I will finish on this one. There is another scholar that I know some of you know and some of you have actually spoken with recently. Up until just a few weeks ago, he was a recognized champion—champion—of the view that the Constitution authorizes the impeachment of former officials. And that is Professor Jonathan Turley. Let me show you what I mean. These are his words.

First, in a very detailed study, thorough study, he explained that the "resignation from office does not prevent trial on articles of impeachment." Those are Professor Turley's words. Same piece. He celebrated the Belknap trial. He described it as "a corrective measure that helped the system regain legitimacy." He wrote another article—he has written several on this topic. This one is actually a 146-page study, very detailed. In that study, he said that the decision in Belknap was "correct in its view that impeachments historically had extended to former officials, such as Warren Hastings," who you heard Lead Manager Raskin describe. In fact, as you can see, Professor Turley argued the House could impeach and the Senate could have tried Richard Nixon after he resigned. His quote on this is very telling: "Future Presidents could not assume that mere resignation would avoid a trial of their conduct" in the United States Senate. Finally, last quote from Professor Turley that "no man in no circumstance, can escape the account, which he owes to the laws of his country."

Not my words, not Lead Manager Raskin's words—Professor Jonathan Turley's words. I agree with him because he is exactly right. Now, a question one might reasonably ask after going through all those quotes from such noted jurists and scholars: Why is there such agreement on this topic? Well, the reason is pretty simple. It is because it is what the Constitution says.

I want to walk you through three provisions of the Constitution that make clear that the Senate must try this case. First, let's start with what the Constitution says about Congress's power in article I. You heard Lead Manager Raskin make this point, but it is worth underscoring. Article I, section 2 gives the House "sole Power of Impeachment." Article I, section 3 gives the Senate the "sole Power to try all Impeachments." Based on President Trump's argument, one would think that language includes caveats, exceptions, but it doesn't. It doesn't say "Impeachment of current civil officers." It doesn't say "Impeachment of those still in office." The Framers didn't mince words. They provided express, absolute, unqualified grants of jurisdictional power to the House to impeach and the Senate to try all impeachments—not some, all.

Former Judge McConnell, the judge that we talked about earlier, he provides very effective textual analysis of this provision. . . . He says, and I will quote, this is Judge McConnell: "Given that the impeachment of Mr. Trump was legitimate, the text makes clear that the Senate has power to try that impeachment."*

Now, again, here is what—it is pretty interesting to me at least—we presented this argument in our trial brief, which we filed over a week ago, where we laid it out step by step so that you could consider it and so that opposing counsel could consider it as well. We received President Trump's response yesterday, and the trial brief offers no rebuttal to this point—none. In fairness, I can't think of any convincing response. I mean, the Constitution is just exceptionally clear on this point. Now, perhaps they will have something to say today about it, but they did not yesterday.

There is another provision worth mentioning here because there has been a lot of confusion about it. I am going to try to clear this up. This is the provision on removal and disqualification. We all know the Senate imposes a judgment only when it convicts. Up on the screen, you will see article I, section 3, clause 7.† With that in mind, the language says that if the Senate convicts, the judgment "shall not extend further than" removal and disqualification. That is it. The meaning is clear. The Senate has the power to impose removal, which only applies to current officials. And, separately, it has the power to impose disqualification, which obviously applies to both current and former officers. But it doesn't have the power to go any further than that.

Now, as I understand President Trump's argument, they believe that this language somehow says that disqualification can only follow the removal of a current officer, but it doesn't. That interpretation essentially rewrites the Constitution. It adds words that aren't there. I mean, after all, the Constitution does not say

---

* The Senators viewed a fuller quote in the visual presentation: "Donald Trump was President of the United States when he was impeached by the House of Representatives. The impeachment was therefore unquestionably permissible (putting aside any disagreement over the nature of the charges) . . . . Given that the impeachment of Mr. Trump was legitimate, the text makes clear that the Senate has the power to try that impeachment."

† "Judgment in cases of Impeachment shall not extend further than to removal from Office, and disqualification to hold and enjoy any Office of honor, Trust or Profit under the United States."

"removal from office and then disqualification." It doesn't say "removal from office followed by disqualification." It simply says the Senate can't do more than two possible sentences: removal and disqualification. This, by the way, is not the first time that this direct question has been debated in this Chamber.

One hundred forty-six years ago, during the Belknap trial, Senator George Edmunds of Vermont was one of the most prestigious Republican Senators of his time. He sat right where Senator Grassley sits today. He zeroed in on this exact point during the Belknap trial. This is his quote: "A prohibition against doing more than two things cannot be turned into a command to do both or neither."

And just imagine the consequences of such an absurd interpretation of the Constitution. If President Trump were right about that language, then officials could commit the most extraordinary, destructive offenses against the American people—high crimes and misdemeanors—they would have total control over whether they could ever be impeached and, if they are, whether the Senate can try the case. If they want to escape any public inquiry into their misconduct or the risk of disqualification from future office, then it is pretty simple. They could just resign one minute before the House impeaches or even one minute before the Senate trial or they could resign during the Senate trial if it is not looking so well. That would effectively erase "disqualification" from the Constitution. It would put wrongdoers in charge of whether the Senate can try them.

The third and final reason why President Trump must stand trial: the provision of article I of the Constitution. You will see here on the screen that the Constitution twice describes the accused in an impeachment trial.* Here is what I want you to focus on. The interesting thing is notice the words. It refers to a "person" and a "party" being impeached. Now, again, we know that the Framers gave a lot of thought to the words that they chose. They even had a style committee during the Constitutional Convention. They could have written "civil officers" here. They did that elsewhere in the Constitution. That would, ultimately, have limited impeachment trials to current officials, but, instead, they used broader language to describe who could be tried by the United States Senate.

So who could be put on trial for impeachment other than civil officers? Who else

---

*   "The Senate shall have the sole Power to try all Impeachments. When sitting for that Purpose, they shall be on Oath or Affirmation. When the President of the United States is tried, the Chief Justice shall preside: And no Person shall be convicted without the Concurrence of two thirds of the Members present.

    Judgment in Cases of Impeachment shall not extend further than to removal from Office, and disqualification to hold and enjoy any Office of honor, Trust or Profit under the United States: but the Party convicted shall nevertheless be liable and subject to Indictment, Trial, Judgment and Punishment, according to Law." U.S. Const. Art. I, § 3, clauses 6 and 7.

could a "person" or a "party" be? Well, really, there is only one possible answer: former officers. And, again, that actually might explain why, during the Belknap trial, Senator Thomas Bayard, of Delaware, who later became the Secretary of State for the United States—he sat right where Senator Carper is sitting now—he found this point so compelling that he felt compelled to speak out on it. During the trial, he concluded that the Constitution must allow the impeachment and trial of people and parties who are not civil officers, and the only group that could possibly encompass was former officials like Belknap and, of course, here, like President Trump.

Just so we are clear, in full disclosure, this is another argument that was not addressed by President Trump in his rebuttal, and we know why they didn't: because their argument doesn't square with the plain text of the Constitution. There is one provision that President Trump relies on almost exclusively, article II, section 4. I am sure you will see it when they present their arguments.

Their argument is that the language you will see on the screen somehow prevents you from holding this trial, by making removal from office an absolute requirement—but, again, where does the language say that? Where does it say anything in that provision about your jurisdiction? In fact, this provision isn't even in the part of the Constitution that addresses your authority. It is in article II, not article I, and it certainly says nothing about former officials. President Trump's interpretation doesn't square with history, originalism, textualism. In fact, even Chuck Cooper, the famous conservative lawyer I mentioned earlier, with clients like the House minority leader, has concluded that this provision of the Constitution that President Trump relies on "cuts against" his position—his words—and that is because, as Cooper says, article II, section 4 means just what it says.

The first half describes what an official must do to be impeached—namely, commit high crimes and misdemeanors—and the second half describes what happens when civil officers of the United States, including the sitting President, are convicted: removal from office. That is it. In Cooper's words: "It simply establishes what is known in criminal law as a 'mandatory minimum' punishment." It says nothing about former officials, nothing at all.

Given all of that, it is not surprising that, in President Trump's legal trial brief—a 75-page brief—they struggled to find any professors to support their position. They did cite one professor, though, Professor Kalt, an expert in this field, who they claim agreed with them that the only purpose of impeachment is removal.

Professor Kalt's position, which they had to have known because it is in the article that they cite in the brief, is that "removal" is "not the sole end of impeachment." Actually, in that same article, he describes the view advocated by President Trump's lawyers as having "deep flaws." Again, you do not have to take my word for it. You can take Professor Kalt's word for it, the professor they cited in their brief, filed yesterday, because he tweeted about it on the screen here.* This is what he had to say.

I am not going to read through it in great detail. I will just simply give you the highlights. "[President] Trump's brief cites my 2001 article on late impeachment a lot. . . . But in several places, they misrepresent what I wrote quite badly. . . .There are multiple examples of such flat-out misrepresentations. . . . They didn't have to be disingenuous and misleading. . . ."

This key constitutional scholar, relied on by President Trump, said it just right. I have explained in great detail the many reasons the argument that President Trump advocates for here today is wrong. I just want to close with a note about why it is dangerous.

Lead Manager Raskin explained that impeachment exists to protect the American people from officials who abuse their power, who betray them. It exists for a case just like this one. Honestly, it is hard to imagine a clearer example of how a President could abuse his office: inciting violence against a coequal branch of government while seeking to remain in power after losing an election—sitting back and watching it unfold. We all know the consequences.

Like every one of you, I was in the Capitol on January 6. I was on the floor with Lead Manager Raskin. Like every one of you, I was evacuated as this violent mob stormed the Capitol's gates. What you experienced that day, what we experienced that day, what our country experienced that day was the Framers' worst nightmare coming to life. Presidents can't inflame insurrection in their final weeks and then walk away like nothing happened. Yet that is the rule that President Trump asks you to adopt. I urge you, we urge you to decline his request, to vindicate the Constitution, to let us try this case.

. . .

Mr. Manager CICILLINE: Mr. President, distinguished Senators, my name is David Cicilline. I have the honor of representing the First Congressional District of Rhode Island. As I hope is now clear from the arguments of Mr. Raskin and Mr. Neguse, impeachment is not merely about removing someone from office. Fundamentally, impeachment exists to protect our constitutional system, to keep each of us safe, to uphold our freedom, to safeguard our democracy. It achieves that

---

* The screen displayed Kalt's tweets: "Trump's brief cites my 2001 article on late impeachment a lot. The article favored late impeachability, but it set out all the evidence I found on both sides—lots for them to use. But in several places, they misrepresent what I wrote quite badly. . . . There are multiple examples of such flat-out misrepresentations. . . . They didn't have to be disingenuous and misleading like this."

by deterring abuse of the extraordinary power that we entrust to our Presidents from the very first day in office to the very last day. It also ensures accountability for Presidents who harm us or our government. In the aftermath of a tragedy, it allows us an opportunity to come together and to heal by working through what happened and reaffirming our constitutional principles, and it authorizes this body and this body alone to disqualify from our political system anybody whose conduct in office proves that they present a danger to the republic.

But impeachment would fail to achieve these purposes if you created, for the first time ever, despite the words of the Framers and the Constitution, a January exception, as Mr. Raskin explained. Now, I was a former defense lawyer for many years, and I can understand why President Trump and his lawyers don't want you to hear this case, why they don't want you to see the evidence, but the argument that you lack jurisdiction rests on a purely fictional loophole—purely fictional—designed to allow the former President to escape all accountability for conduct that is truly indefensible under our Constitution. You saw the consequences of his actions on the video that we played earlier.

I would like to emphasize in still greater detail the extraordinary constitutional offense that the former President thinks you have no power whatsoever to adjudicate. While spreading lies about the election outcome, in a brazen attempt to retain power against the will of the American people, he incited an armed, angry mob to riot—and not just anywhere but here in the seat of our government, in the Capitol, during a joint session of Congress, when the Vice President presided while we carried out a peaceful transfer of power, which was interrupted for the first time in our history. This was a disaster of historic proportion. It was also an unforgivable betrayal of the oath of office of President Trump, the oath he swore, an oath that he sullied and dishonored to advance his own personal interests.

And make no mistake about it, as you think about that day, things could have been much worse. As one Senator said, they could have killed all of us. It was only the bravery and sacrifice of the police, who suffered deaths and injuries as a result of President Trump's actions, that prevented greater tragedy.

At trial, we will prove with overwhelming evidence that President Trump is singularly and directly responsible for inciting the assault on the Capitol. We will also prove that his dereliction of duty, his desire to seek personal advantage from the mayhem, and his decision to issue tweets, further inciting the mob by attacking the Vice President, all compounded the already enormous damage.

Now, virtually every American who saw those events unfold on television was absolutely horrified by the events of January 6, but we also know how President Trump himself felt about the attack. He told us. Here is what he tweeted at 6:01 as the Capitol was in shambles and as dozens of police officers and other law enforcement officers lay battered and bruised and bloodied. Here is what he said:

> These are the things and events that happen when a sacred landslide election victory is so unceremoniously & viciously stripped away from great patriots who have been badly & unfairly treated for so long. Go home with love & in peace. Remember this day forever!

Every time I read that tweet, it chills me to the core. The President of the United States sided with the insurrectionists. He celebrated their cause. He validated their attack. He told them, "Remember this day forever," hours after they marched through these halls looking to assassinate Vice President Pence, the Speaker of the House, and any of us they could find. Given all that, it is no wonder that President Trump would rather talk about jurisdiction and a supposed January exception rather than talk about what happened on January 6.

Make no mistake, his arguments are dead wrong. They are distractions from what really matters. The Senate can and should require President Trump to stand trial. My colleagues have already addressed many of President Trump's efforts to escape trial. I would like to cover the remainder and then address the broader issues at stake in this trial. For starters, in an extension of his mistaken reading of the Constitution, President Trump insists that he cannot face trial in the Senate because he is merely a private citizen. He references here the bill of attainder clause.

But as Mr. Neguse just explained, the Constitution refers to the defendant in an impeachment trial as a "Person" and a "Party," and certainly he counts as one of those. Let's also apply some common sense. There is a reason that he now insists on being called "the 45th President of the United States" rather than "Citizen Trump." He isn't a randomly selected private citizen. He is a former officer of the United States Government. He is a former President of the United States of America. He is treated differently under a law called the Former Presidents Act. For four years, we trusted him with more power than anyone else on Earth.

As a former President, who promised on a Bible to use his power faithfully, he can and should answer for whether he kept that promise while bound by it in office. His insistence otherwise is just wrong, and so is his claim that there is a slippery slope to impeaching private citizens if you proceed. The trial of a former official for abuses he committed as an official, arising from an impeachment that occurred while he was an official, poses absolutely no risk whatsoever of subjecting a private citizen to impeachment for their private conduct.

To emphasize the point, President Trump was impeached while he was in office for conduct in office—period. The alternative, once again, is this January exception, in which our most powerful officials can commit the most terrible abuses and then resign, leave office, and suddenly claim that they are just a private citizen who can't be held accountable at all. In the same vein, President Trump and his lawyers argue that he shouldn't be impeached because it will set a bad precedent for impeaching others.

But that slippery slope argument is also incorrect. For centuries, the prevailing view has been that former officials are subject to impeachment. We just heard a full discussion of that. The House has repeatedly acknowledged that fact. But in the vast majority of cases, the House has rightly recognized that an official's resignation or departure makes the extraordinary step of impeachment unnecessary and maybe even unwise. As a House manager rightly explained in the Belknap case, and I quote: "There is no likelihood that we shall ever unlimber [the] clumsy and bulky monster piece of ordnance to take aim at an object from which all danger has gone by."

President Trump's case, though, is different. The danger has not "gone by." His threat to democracy makes any prior abuse by any government official pale in comparison. Moreover, allowing his conduct to pass without the most decisive response would itself create an extraordinary danger to the Nation, inviting further abuse of power and signaling that the Congress of the United States is unable or unwilling to respond to insurrection incited by the President.

Think about that. To paraphrase Justice Robert Jackson, who said that precedent that I just described would lie about like a loaded weapon, ready for the hand of any future President who decided in his final months to make a play for unlimited power—think of the danger. Here is the rare case in which love of the Constitution and commitment to our democracy required the House to impeach. It is for the same reason the Senate can and must try this case.

Next, President Trump will assert that it somehow is significant or it matters that the Chief Justice isn't presiding over this trial. Let me state this very plainly: it does not matter. It is not significant. Under article I, section 3, "When the President of the United States is tried, the Chief Justice shall preside." There is only one person who is President of the United States at a time. Right now, Joseph R. Biden, Jr., is the 46th President of the United States. As a result, the requirement that the Chief Justice preside isn't triggered. Instead, the normal rules of any impeachment of anyone other than the sitting President apply, and under those rules, the President Pro Tempore, Senator Leahy, can preside.

And, of course, this makes perfect sense. The Chief Justice presides because, when the current President is on trial, if the Chief Justice doesn't preside, the Vice President presides, and it would be a conflict for someone to preside over a trial that would become President if there was a conviction. So there isn't that concern when you have a former President on trial, or, for that matter, when you have anyone on trial other than the current President, which is why the Chief Justice presides only in that single case, and why this is exactly the Presiding Officer the Constitution and the Senate rules require.

As a fallback, President Trump and his lawyers may argue today that he should get a free pass on inciting an armed insurrection against the United States Government and endangering Congress because, as he would put it, this impeachment is somehow unconstitutional. So far as I understand it, from reading the pleadings in this case, this defense involves cobbling together a bunch of meritless legal arguments, all of them attempting to focus on substance rather than jurisdiction and insisting that these kitchen-sink objections lead the Senate to not try the case.

Since they may raise these points, at this juncture I feel obliged, really, to address them. He may argue, for example, that he didn't receive enough process in the House, even though the House proceedings are more like a grand jury action, which is followed later by trial in the Senate, with a full presentation of evidence; even though the evidence of his high crimes and misdemeanors is overwhelming and supported by a huge public record; even though we are going to put that evidence before you at this trial; and even though he had a full and fair opportunity to respond to it before all of you; even though hundreds of others involved in the events of January 6 have already been charged for their role in the attacks that the President incited; and even though we invited him to voluntarily come here and testify and tell his story, a request, as you know, that his lawyers immediately refused, presumably because they understood what would happen if he were to testify under oath.

Regardless, President Trump's process arguments are not only wrong on their own terms, but they are also completely irrelevant to the question of whether you should hold this trial. That question is answered by the Constitution, and the answer is yes. In addition, separate from his due process complaints, President Trump and his counsel—particularly his counsel—have both said on TV that to counter the undisputed evidence of what actually happened in this case, you will see video clips. They will show video clips of other politicians, including Democratic politicians, using what they consider incendiary language. Apparently, they think this will establish some sort of equivalency or that it will show, in contrast, that President Trump's statements at the Save America rally weren't so bad.

Like so much of what President Trump's lawyers might say today, that is a gimmick. It is a parlor game, meant to inflame partisan hostility and play on our divisions. So let me be crystal clear. President Trump was not impeached because the words he used, viewed in isolation, without context, were beyond the pale. Plenty of other politicians have used strong language. But Donald J. Trump was President of the United States. He sought to overturn a Presidential election that had been upheld by every single court to consider it. He spent months insisting to his base that the only way he could lose was a dangerous, wide-ranging conspiracy against them and America itself. He relentlessly attempted to persuade his followers that the peaceful transfer of power that was taking place in the Capitol was an abomination that had to be stopped at all costs. He flirted with groups like the Proud Boys, telling them to "stand back and stand by," while endorsing violence and sparking death threats to his opponents. He summoned an armed, angry, and dangerous crowd that wanted to keep him in power and was widely reported to be poised on a hair trigger for violence at his direction.

He then made his heated statements in circumstances where it was clear, where it was foreseeable, that those statements would spark extraordinary, imminent violence. He then failed to defend the Capitol, the Congress, and the Vice President during the insurrection, engaging in extraordinary dereliction of duty and desertion of duty that was only possible because of the high office he held. He issued statements during the insurrection targeting the Vice President and reiterating the very same lies about the election that had launched the violence in the first place. And he issued a tweet five hours after the Capitol was sacked in which he sided with the bad guys.

We all know that context matters, that office and meaning and intent and consequences matter. Simply put, it matters when and where and how we speak. The oaths we have sworn and the power we hold matter. President Trump was not impeached because he used words that the House decided are forbidden or unpopular. He was impeached for inciting armed violence against the Government of the

United States of America. This leads me to a few final thoughts about why it is so important for you to hear this case, as authorized and as, indeed, required by our history and by the Constitution. President Trump's lawyers will say, I expect, that you should dismiss his case so that the country can "move on." They will assert that this impeachment is partisan, and that the spirit of bipartisanship and bipartisan cooperation requires us to drop the case and march forward in unity.

With all due respect, every premise and every conclusion of that argument is wrong. Just weeks ago—weeks ago—the President of the United States literally incited an armed attack on the Capitol, our seat of government, while seeking to retain power by subverting an election he lost, and then celebrated the attack. People died. People were brutally injured. President Trump's actions endangered every single Member of Congress, his own Vice President, thousands of congressional staffers, and our own Capitol Police and other law enforcement.

This was a national tragedy—a disaster for America's standing in the world—and President Trump is singularly responsible for inciting it. As we will prove, the attack on the Capitol was not solely the work of extremists lurking in the shadows. Indeed, does anyone in this Chamber honestly believe that, but for the conduct of President Trump, that charge in the Article of Impeachment, that that attack at the Capitol would have occurred? Does anybody believe that?

And now his lawyers will come before you and insist, even as the Capitol is still surrounded with barbed wire and fences and soldiers, that we should just move on, let bygones be bygones, and allow President Trump to walk away without any accountability, any reckoning, any consequences. That cannot be right. That is not unity. That is the path to fear of what future Presidents could do.

So there is a good reason why this Article of Impeachment passed the House with bipartisan support. The principles at stake belong to all Americans through all walks of life. We have a common interest in making clear that there are lines nobody can cross, especially the President of the United States, and so we share an interest in this trial where the truth can be shown and where President Trump can be called to account for his offenses. William Faulkner famously wrote that "the past is never dead." But this isn't even the past. This just happened. It is still happening.

Look around as you come to the Capitol and come to work. I really do not believe that our attention span is so short, that our sense of duty so frail, our factional loyalty so all-consuming, that the President can provoke an attack on Congress itself and get away with it just because it occurred near the end of his term. After a betrayal like this, there cannot be unity without accountability. And this is exactly what the Constitution calls for. The Framers' original understanding, this Chamber's own precedent, and the very words used in the Constitution all confirm unquestionably, indisputably, that President Trump must stand trial for his high crimes and misdemeanors against the American people.

We must not, we cannot continue down the path of partisanship and division that has turned the Capitol into an armed fortress. Senators, it now falls to you to bring our country together by holding this trial and, once all the evidence is before you, by delivering justice.

                                    . . .

Mr. Manager RASKIN: Senators, Mr. President, to close, I want to say something personal about the stakes of this decision whether President Trump can stand trial and be held to account for inciting insurrection against us. This trial is personal indeed for every Senator, for every Member of the House, every manager, all of our staff, the Capitol Police, the Washington, DC, Metropolitan Police, the National Guard, the maintenance and custodial crews, the print journalists and TV people who were here, and all of our families and friends. I hope this trial reminds America how personal democracy is and how personal is the loss of democracy too.

Distinguished Members of the Senate, my youngest daughter, Tabitha, was there with me on Wednesday, January 6. It was the day after we buried her brother, our son Tommy, the saddest day of our lives. Also there was my son-in-law Hank, who is married to our oldest daughter, Hannah, and I consider him a son, too, even though he eloped with my daughter and didn't tell us what they were going to do. But it was in the middle of COVID-19.

But the reason they came with me that Wednesday, January 6, was because they wanted to be together with me in the middle of a devastating week for our family, and I told them I had to go back to work because we were counting electoral votes that day on January 6. It was our constitutional duty. And I invited them instead to come with me to witness this historic event, the peaceful transfer of power in America.

And they said they heard that President Trump was calling on his followers to come to Washington to protest, and they asked me directly: Would it be safe? Would it be safe? And I told them: Of course it should be safe. This is the Capitol.

Steny Hoyer, our majority leader, had kindly offered me the use of his office on the House floor because I was one of the managers that day and we were going through our grief. So Tabitha and Hank were with me in Steny's office as colleagues dropped by to console us about the loss of our middle child, Tommy, our beloved Tommy. Mr. Neguse and Mr. Cicilline actually came to see me that day. Dozens of Members—lots of Republicans, lots of Democrats—came to see me, and I felt a sense of being lifted up from the agony, and I won't forget their tenderness.

Through the tears, I was working on a speech to the floor when we would all be together in joint session, and I wanted to focus on unity when we met in the House. I quoted Abraham Lincoln's famous 1878 Lyceum speech, where he said that if division and destruction ever come to America, it won't come from abroad, it will come from within, said Lincoln, and in that same speech, Lincoln passionately deplored mob violence.

This was right after the murder of Elijah Lovejoy, the abolitionist newspaper writer. Lincoln deplored mob violence, and he deplored mob rule, and he said it would lead to tyranny and despotism in America. That was the speech I gave that day after the House very graciously and warmly welcomed me back. Tabitha and Hank came with me to the floor, and they watched it from the Gallery, and when it was over, they went back to that office, Steny's office off of the House floor.

They didn't know that the House had been breached yet and that an insurrection or a riot or a coup had come to Congress, and by the time we learned about it, about what was going on, it was too late. I couldn't get out there to be with them in that office. And all around me, people were calling their wives and their husbands and their loved ones to say goodbye. Members of Congress in the House were removing their congressional pins so they wouldn't be identified by the mob as they tried to escape the violence.

Our new Chaplain got up and said a prayer for us, and we were told to put our gas masks on, and then there was a sound I will never forget, the sound of pounding on the door like a battering ram, the most haunting sound I have ever heard, and I will never forget it.

My chief of staff, Julie Tagen, was with Tabitha and Hank, locked and barricaded in that office, the kids hiding under the desk, placing what they thought were their final texts and whispered phone calls to say their goodbyes. They thought they were going to die. My son-in-law had never even been to the Capitol before. When they were finally rescued over an hour later by Capitol officers and we were together, I hugged them, and I apologized, and I told my daughter Tabitha, who is 24 and a brilliant algebra teacher in Teach for America now, I told her how sorry I was, and I promised her that it would not be like this again the next time she came back to the Capitol with me. And do you know what she said? She said: Dad, I don't want to come back to the Capitol.

Of all the terrible, cruel things I saw and I heard on that day and since then, that one hit me the hardest, that and watching someone use an American flagpole, with the flag still on it, to spear and pummel one of our police officers, ruthlessly, mercilessly tortured by a pole with a flag on it that he was defending with his very life.

People died that day. Officers ended up with head damage and brain damage. People's eyes were gouged. An officer had a heart attack. An officer lost three fingers that day. Two officers have taken their own lives.

Senators, this cannot be our future. This cannot be the future of America. We cannot have Presidents inciting and mobilizing mob violence against our government and our institutions because they refuse to accept the will of the people under the Constitution of the United States. Much less can we create a new January exception in our precious, beloved Constitution that prior generations have died for and fought for, so that corrupt Presidents have several weeks to get away with whatever it is they want to do. History does not support a January exception in any way, so why would we invent one for the future? We close, Mr. President.

. . .

Mr. Counsel CASTOR: Mr. President and Members of the U.S. Senate, thank you for taking the time to hear from me. My name is Bruce Castor. I am the lead prosecutor—lead counsel—for the 45th President of the United States. I was an assistant DA for such a long time, I keep saying "prosecutor," but I do understand the difference, Mr. Raskin.

Before I begin, I want to comment on the outstanding presentation from our opponents and the emotion that certainly welled up in Congressman Raskin about his family being here during that terrible day. You will not hear any member of the team representing former President Trump say anything but, in the strongest possible way, denounce the violence of the rioters and those who breached the Capitol, the very citadel of our democracy—literally, the symbol that flashes on television whenever you are trying to explain that we are talking about the United States; an instant symbol. To have it attacked is repugnant in every sense of the word. The loss of life is horrific. I spent many long years prosecuting homicide cases, catching criminals who committed murders.

I have quite an extensive experience in dealing with the aftermath of those things. Certainly, as an FOP [Fraternal Order of Police] member and a member of many police organizations myself, we mourn the loss of the Capitol Police officer, whom I understand is laying not too far away from here. And, you know, many of you in this room, over your careers, before they reached this summit here in the Senate, would have had times where you represented your local communities as assistant district attorneys, assistant Commonwealth attorneys, assistant State attorneys. And you know this to be true—that when a horrific event occurred in your county or in your jurisdiction, if it was a State jurisdiction, you know that there was a terrible outcry, and the public immediately reacts with a desire that someone pay because something really bad happened.

And that is a natural reaction of human beings. It is a natural reaction of human beings because we are generally a social people. We enjoy being around one another, even in D.C. We recognize that people all the world over, and especially Americans who share that special bond with one another, love the freedoms that this country gives us. And we all feel that if somebody is unsafe when they are walking down the street, that the next person who is unsafe could be you, your spouse, one of your children, some other person that you love and know personally.

So you will never hear anybody representing former President Trump say anything at all other than what happened on January 6 and the storming and breaching of the Capitol should be denounced in the most vigorous terms, nor that those persons responsible should be prosecuted to the fullest extent that our laws allow. Indeed, I have followed some of those cases and those prosecutions, and it seems to me that we are doing a pretty good job of identifying and prosecuting those persons who committed those offenses. And I commend the FBI and the District of Columbia police and the other Agencies for their work. It is natural to recoil. It is an immediate thing. It comes over you without your ability to stop it, the desire for retribution. Who caused this awful thing? How do we make them pay?

We recognize in the law—and I know many of you are lawyers. Probably, lawyers—some of you have been a lawyer for thirty-five years, longer than me— many, longer than me, probably. And we know we have a specific body of law that deals with passion and rage, blinding logic and reason. That is the difference between manslaughter and murder. Manslaughter is the killing of a human being upon sudden and intense provocation. But murder is done with cold blood and reflective thought. We are so understanding of the concept that people's minds can be overpowered with emotion, where logic does not immediately kick in, that we have recognized examples that otherwise would be hearsay, and said that, no, when you are driving down the street and you look over at your wife and you say: "Hey, you know what, that guy is about to drive through the red light and kill that

person," your wife can testify to what you said because, even though it is techni-
cally hearsay, it is an exception because it is the event living through the person.

Why? No opportunity for reflective thought. There are all sorts of examples that
we recognize in the law for why people immediately desire retribution, immediately recognize in the law that people can be overcome by events. And you know,
Senators of the United States, they are not ordinary people. They are extraordinary
people—in the technical sense, extraordinary people. When I was growing up in
suburban Philadelphia, my parents were big fans of Senator Everett Dirksen from
Illinois. Senator Dirksen recorded a series of lectures that my parents had on a
record. We still know what records are, right? The thing you put the needle down
on and you play it. And here is little Bruce—eight, nine, ten years old—listening
to this back in the 1960s. And I would be listening to that voice.

If you ever heard Everett Dirksen's voice, it is the most commanding, gravelly
voice that just oozes belief and sincerity. He must have been a phenomenal U.S.
Senator. He doesn't talk about ordinary people, as we do in the law. We apply the
ordinary person standard. He talks about extraordinary people. He talks about
"Gallant Men," which was the name of the album, and, now, of course, as a sign
of the times, gallant men and women. I would watch television, and I would watch
Senator Goldwater or Senator Byrd or Senator Mansfield or Senator Dole, and I
would be fascinated by these great men. And everybody's parents say this when
they are growing up: you could grow up to be a U.S. Senator. You could do that.
They are just men and women like you are. Well, then, Everett Dirksen tells us that
they are not; they are gallant men and women who do extraordinary things when
their country needs them to do it.

U.S. Senators really are different. I have been around U.S. Senators before. Two
of them in this room from Pennsylvania, I would like to think, are friendly toward
me or at least friends of mine when we are not politically adverse. And I have
been around their predecessors. One thing I have discovered, whether it be Democrats or Republicans, U.S. Senators are patriots first—patriots first. They love their
country. They love their families. They love the States that they represent. There
isn't a Member in this room who has not used the term "I represent the great State
of"—fill in the blank. Why? Because they are all great? Yeah. But you think yours
is greater than others because these are your people. These are the people who sent
you here to do their work. They trusted you with the responsibility of representative government.

You know, I feel proud to know my Senators—Senator Casey, up here in the
back, and Senator Toomey, over to the left. You know, it is funny. This is an aside,
but it is funny. Do you ever notice how, when you are talking or you hear others
talking about you, when you are home in your State, they will say, "You know, I

talked to my Senator" or "I talked to somebody on the staff of my Senator"? It is always "my Senator." Why is it that we say "my Senator"? We say that because the people you represent are proud of their Senators. They absolutely feel that connection of pride because that is not just Pat Toomey of Pennsylvania. That is my Senator from Pennsylvania. Or Bob Casey from Scranton—that is my Senator. And you like that. People like that. The people back home really do.

U.S. Senators have a reputation, and it is deserved. They have a reputation for coolheadedness, being erudite—the men and women who we send from back home to D.C. to look after our interests. We feel a sense of ownership and a sense of pride in our Senators. There is plenty of times I have been around in political gatherings where I hear, "There is no way Senator Toomey is going to allow that"—I don't mean to pick you on, Pat—or "There is no way Senator Casey is going to allow that"—because we feel pride. When something bad is potentially in the wind, we expect our U.S. Senators not reacting to popular will and not reacting to popular emotions. We expect them to do what is right, notwithstanding what is immediately and expedient that the media tells us is the topic of the day.

So Senators are patriots. Senators are family men and women. They are fierce advocates for the great State which they represent. And somewhere far down that list of attributes, way below patriot and way below love of family and country and way below fierce advocates for their States, far down—at least that is what I thought, anyway, and I still think that—somewhere far down that list, Senators have some obligation to be partisans, to represent a group of beliefs that are similar to beliefs shared by other United States Senators. I understand that. And, in fact, I have no problem with that system. It helps us debate and decide what is best for America, the robust debate of different points of view. And I dare say that Senator Schumer and Senator McConnell represent those things in this body and make sure that everything is talked out and robustly debated in this room before United States Senators make a decision of extreme importance to the people they represent. I know you aren't allowed to talk, but I don't see either one of them jumping up and saying I am wrong about that because I think that that is what happens.

I think United States Senators try to listen to each other's views. I think United States Senators try to do what is right for the country, and far down is partisanship. In our system of government, and if you read the Federalist Papers—we are very fortunate because the Federalist Papers were authored as an explanation for why it is the States, the original States, should adopt the Constitution. These were persuasive documents about why the Constitution is a good thing, because if the individual State legislatures didn't adopt the Constitution, we would not have it.

So Mr. Jay and Mr. Madison and Mr. Hamilton, they had an incentive to explain what they were thinking when they wrote it because they are explaining to other erudite people who represent individual States why it is that they feel that this is the right thing to do. And, in fact, as many of you well know, Madison had to promise that there would be a Bill of Rights immediately upon adoption or we wouldn't have a Constitution. Even then there was horse trading going on in the legislative body of the United States.

The other day, when I was down here in Washington—I came down earlier in the week to try to figure out how to find my way around; I worked in this building 40 years ago, I got lost then, and I still do—but in studying the Constitution in all the years I was a prosecutor, where so many things depend on interpretations of phrases in the Constitution, I learned that this body, which one of my worthy colleagues said is the greatest deliberative body in the entire world—and I agree— that was—that particular aspect of our government was intentionally created, if you read the Federalist Papers. The last time a body such as the United States Senate sat at the pinnacle of government with the responsibility that it has today, it was happening in Athens, and it was happening in Rome.

Republicanism, the form of government republicanism, throughout history has always and without exception fallen because of fights from within, because of partisanship from within, because of bickering from within. And in each one of those examples that I mentioned—and there are certainly others, probably, that are smaller countries that lasted for less time that I don't know about off the top of my head—but each one of them, once there was the vacuum created that the greatest deliberative bodies—the Senate of Greece sitting in Athens, the Senate of Rome— the moment that they devolved into such partisanship, it is not as though they ceased to exist; they ceased to exist as representative democracy, both replaced by totalitarianism.

Paraphrasing the famous quote from Benjamin Franklin, who, as a Philadelphian, I feel as though I can do that because he is my Founding Father too: he who would trade liberty for some temporary security deserves neither liberty nor security. If we restrict liberty to attain security, we will lose both. And isn't the way we have enshrined in the Constitution the concepts of liberty that we think are critical, the very concepts of liberty that drove us to separate from Great Britain—and I can't believe these fellas are quoting what happened prerevolution as though that is somehow of value to us.

We left the British system. If we are really going to use prerevolutionary history in Great Britain, then the precedent is we have a Parliament and we have a King. Is that the precedent that we are heading for? Now, it is not an accident that the very first liberty—if you grant me that our liberties are enumerated in the Bill of Rights—it is not an accident that the very first liberty in the first article of the Bill of Rights is the First Amendment, which says: "Congress shall make no law . . . abridging freedom of speech," and et cetera. "Congress shall make no law . . ."—the very first one, the most important one, the ability to have free and robust debate, free and robust political speech.

Something that Mr. Raskin and his team brought up is that it is somehow a suggestion from former President Trump's team that when various public officials were not denouncing the violence that we saw over the summer, that that was somehow the former President equating that speech to his own. Not at all. Exactly backwards. I saw a headline: Representative So-and-So seeks to walk back comments about—I forget what it was—something that bothered her. I was devastated when I saw that she thought it was necessary to go on television yesterday or the day before and say she needs to walk back her comments.

She should be able to comment as much as she wants, and she should be able to say exactly as she feels. And if she feels that the supporters of then-President Trump are not worthy of having their ideas considered, she should be permitted to say that, and anybody who agrees should be permitted to say they agree. That is what we broke away from Great Britain in order to be able to do: to be able to say what we thought in the most robust political debate.

My colleague Mike van der Veen is going to give you a recitation on the First Amendment law of the United States. I commend to your attention the analysis that he is going to give you. I don't expect and I don't believe that the former President expects anybody to walk back any of the language. If that is how they feel about the way things transpired over the last couple of years in this country, they should be allowed to say that, and I will go to court and defend them if anything happens to them as a result. If the government takes action against that State representative or that U.S. Representative who wants to walk back her comments, if the government takes action against her, I have no problem going into court and defending her right to say those things, even though I don't agree with them.

This trial is not about trading liberty for security. It is about trading—it is about suggesting that it is a good idea that we give up those liberties that we have so long fought for. We have sent armies to other parts of the world to convince those governments to implement the freedoms that we enjoy. This trial is about trading liberty for the security from the mob? Honestly, no, it can't be. We can't be thinking about that. We can't possibly be suggesting that we punish people for political speech in this country. And if people go and commit lawless acts as a result of their beliefs and they cross the line, they should be locked up. And, in fact, I have seen quite a number of the complaints that were filed against the people who breached the Capitol. Some of them charged conspiracy. Not a single one I noticed charged conspiracy with the 45th President of the United States, probably because prosecutors have an ethical requirement that they are not allowed to charge people with criminal offenses without probable cause. You might consider that. And if we go down the road that my very worthy adversary here, Mr. Raskin, asks you to go down, the floodgates will open.

I was going to say it will—instead of "floodgates," I was going to say originally it will "release the whirlwind," which is a Biblical reference, but I subsequently learned, since I got here, that that particular phrase has already been taken, so I figured I had better change it to "floodgates." But the political pendulum will shift one day. This Chamber and the Chamber across the way will change one day, and partisan impeachments will become commonplace.

You know, until the impeachment of Bill Clinton, no one alive had ever lived through a Presidential impeachment, not unless some of you are 150 years old. Not a single person alive had lived through a Presidential impeachment. Now most of us have lived through three of them. This is supposed to be the ultimate safety valve, the last thing that happens, the most rare treatment, and a session where this body is sitting as a Court of Impeachment among the most rare things it does. So the slippery-slope principle will have taken hold if we continue to go forward with what is happening today and scheduled to happen later this week.

And after we are long done here and after there has been a shift in the political winds and after there is a change in the makeup of the United States House of Representatives and maybe a change in the makeup of the United States Senate, the pressure from those folks back home, especially for Members of the House, is going to be tremendous because, remember, the Founders recognized that the argument that I started with, that political pressure is driven by the need for immediate action because something under contemporary community standards really horrific happened and the people represented by the Members of the United States House of Representatives become incensed.

And what do you do if a Federal issue—you are back in suburban Philadelphia and something happens that makes the people who live there incensed? You call your Congressman. And your Congressman, elected every two years, with their pulse on the people of their district, 750,000 people, they respond. And, boy, do they respond. The Congressman calls you back, a staffer calls you back, and you get all the information that they have on the issue. Sometimes you even get invited to submit language that would improve whatever the issue is.

Well, when the pendulum swings, perhaps the next person who gets impeached and is sent here for you to consider is Eric Holder during Fast and Furious, the Attorney General of the United States, or any other person whom the other party considers to be a political danger to them down the road because of their avowed abilities and being articulate and having a resume that shows that they are capable.

I picked Eric simply because I think he has a tremendous—he has had a tremendous career, and he might be somebody whom some Republicans somewhere might be worried about.

So maybe the next person they go after is Eric Holder. And, you know, the Republicans might regain the House in two years. History does tend to suggest that the party out of power in the White House does well in the midterm elections. Certainly, the 2020 elections, the House gained—the House majority narrowed, and there was a gain of Republicans. The Members of the House—they have to worry about these consequences because if they don't react to whatever the problem of the day is, somebody in that jurisdiction there—somebody is going to say: if you make me the Congressman, I react to that. And that means that the sitting Member has to worry about it because their terms are short. And it is not just Members of the House of Representatives with their short—with their short terms.

I saw on television the last couple of days the honorable gentleman from Nebraska, Mr. Sasse—I saw that he faced backlash back home because of a vote he made some weeks ago, that the political party was complaining about a decision he made as a United States Senator. You know, it is interesting because I don't want to steal the thunder from the other lawyers, but Nebraska, you are going to hear, is quite a judicial-thinking place, and just maybe Senator Sasse is onto something, and you will hear about what it is that the Nebraska courts have to say about the issue that you all are deciding this week. There seem to be some pretty smart jurists in Nebraska, and I can't believe a United States Senator doesn't know that. A Senator like the gentleman from Nebraska, whose Supreme Court history is ever present in his mind, and rightfully so, he faces the whirlwind even though he knows what the judiciary in his State thinks.

People back home will demand their House Members continue the cycle as political fortunes rise and fall. The only entity that stands between the bitter infighting that led to the downfall of the Greek Republic and the Roman Republic and the American Republic is the Senate of the United States. Shall the business of the Senate and thus the Nation come to a halt, not just for the current weeks while a new President is trying to fill out his administration, but shall the business of the Senate and the Nation come to a halt because impeachment becomes the rule rather than the rare exception?

I know you can see this as a possibility because not a single one of you ever thought that you would be doing a second impeachment inside of thirteen months, and the pressure will be enormous to respond in kind. To quote Everett Dirksen, the gallant men and women of the Senate will not allow that to happen. And this Republic will endure because the top responsibility of the United States Senator and the top characteristic that you all have in common—and, boy, this is a diverse group, but there isn't a single one of you who, A) doesn't consider yourself a patriot of the United States, and 2) there isn't a single one of you who doesn't consider the other ninety-nine to be patriots of the United States. And that is why this attack on the Constitution will not prevail.

The document that is before you is flawed. The rule of the Senate concerning impeachment documents, Articles of Impeachment, rule XXIII, says that such documents cannot be divided. You might have seen that we wrote that in the answer. It might have been a little legalistic or legalese for the newspapers to opine on very much, but there is some significance. The House managers, clever fellows that they are, they cast a broad net. They need to get sixty-seven of you to agree they are right. And that is a good strategy.

I would use the same strategy, except there is a rule that says you can't use that strategy. You see, rule XXIII says that the Article of Impeachment is indivisible, and the reason why that is significant is you have to agree that every single aspect of the entire document warrants impeachment because it is an all-or-nothing document. You can't cut out parts that you agree with that warrant impeachment and parts that don't, because it is not divisible. It flat-out says in the Senate rules it is not divisible.

Now, previous impeachments, like President Clinton's, said the President shall be found guilty of high crimes and misdemeanors for engaging in one or more of the following and then gives a list, so all you had to do was win one, but they didn't do that here. It has to be all or nothing. Some of these things that you are asked to consider might be close calls in your mind, but one of them is not. The argument about the 14th Amendment is absolutely ridiculous. The House managers tell you that the President should be impeached because he violated the 14th Amendment. Here is what the 14th Amendment says: "No person shall be a Senator or Representative in Congress, or elector of President and Vice President, or hold any office, civil or military, under the United States, or [any other] State, who, having previously taken an oath, as a member of Congress, or as an officer of the United States, or [as] a member of any State legislature, or as an executive or judicial officer of any State, to support the Constitution of the United States, [and] shall have engaged in insurrection or rebellion against the same, or given aid or comfort to the enemies thereof. But Congress may vote by two thirds of each House [to] remove such disability."

It doesn't take a constitutional scholar to recognize that that is written for people who fought for the Confederacy or who were previous military officers or were in the government of the Confederacy, and it doesn't take a constitutional scholar to require that they be convicted first in a court, with due process of law. So it never—that question can never be ripe until those things have happened. If you agree with those arguments—and I know you will all get your Constitutions out and you will read it, and if you agree with those arguments, the suggestion that the 14th Amendment applies here is ridiculous. And if you come to that conclusion, then, because the managers have not separated out the counts, any counts within the Article of Impeachment, the whole thing falls. I didn't write that. They are married to that. I wrote it out in individual responses because I didn't know how to respond to the cast-the-wide-net effort.

And fortunately Senators some time in the past realized that you can't do that because you passed a rule that says: Hey, you can't do that. So that is why it is flawed. It is flawed in other ways, too, and my colleague will explain that. I was struck—I thought the House managers who spoke earlier were brilliant speakers, and I made some notes. They will hear about what I think about some of the things they said later when I am closing the case, but I thought they were brilliant speakers, and I loved listening to them. They are smart fellows. But why are the House managers afraid and why is the majority—the House of Representatives—afraid of the American people?

I mean, let's understand why we are really here. We are really here because the majority in the House of Representatives does not want to face Donald Trump as a political rival in the future. That is the real reason we are here. That is why they have to get over the jurisdictional hurdle, which they can't get over, but that is why they have to get over that in order to get to the part of the Constitution that allows removal. So that is the—nobody says it that plainly, but unfortunately I have a way of speaking that way. And the reason that I am having trouble with the argument is, the American people just spoke, and they just changed administrations. So in the light most favorable to my colleagues on the other side of the aisle here, their system works. The people are smart enough—in the light most favorable to them, they are smart enough to pick a new administration if they don't like the old one, and they just did, and he is down there at Pennsylvania Avenue now, probably wondering, how come none of my stuff is happening up at the Capitol?

Why do the Members of the House of Representatives—the majority of the House of Representatives—why are they afraid of the very people who sent them to do this job, the people they hope will continue to send them back here? Why are they afraid that those same people who were smart enough to pick them as their Congressmen aren't smart enough to pick somebody who is a candidate for President of the United States? Why fear that the people will all of a sudden forget how to choose an administration in the next few years?

In fact, this happens all the time when there are changes in administrations from one-term Presidents to others. Well, Nixon was sort of one and a half-term, but Nixon to Ford, Ford to Carter, Carter to Reagan, Bush 41 to Clinton. It happens.

The people get tired of an administration they don't want, and they know how to change it. And they just did.

So why think that they won't know how to do it in 2024 if they want to, or is that what the fear is? Is the fear that the people in 2024, in fact, will want to change and will want to go back to Donald Trump and not the current occupant of the White House, President Biden? Because all of these other times, the people were smart enough to do it, choose who the President should be, and all these other times, they were smart enough to choose who their Members of Congress were—and, by the way, choose you all as well—but they are not smart enough to know how to change the administration, especially since they just did? So it seems pretty evident to me that they do know how. It has worked 100 percent of the time. One hundred percent of the time in the United States, when the people had been fed up with and had enough of the occupant of the White House, they changed the occupant of the White House.

Now, I know that one of the strengths of this body is its deliberative action. I saw Senator Manchin on the TV the other night talking about the filibuster. And the main point was that Senator Manchin was explaining to those of us who don't operate here all the time, that this body has an obligation to try to reach consensus across the aisle to legitimize the decisions it makes. Obviously, he is capable of making his own pronouncements on it, but that is what came across on the television. And I think that that is a good way of saying why the Senate of the United States is different than other places.

You know, the Constitution is a document designed to protect the rights of the minority, not the rights of the majority. Congress shall make no law abridging all of these things. That is because those were the things that were of concern at the time. It is easy to be in favor of liberty and equality and free speech when it is popular. I think that I want to give my colleague Mr. Schoen an opportunity to explain to all of us the legal analysis on jurisdiction. I will be quite frank with you. We changed what we were going to do on account that we thought that the House managers' presentation was well done, and I wanted you to know that we have responses to those things.

I thought that what the first part of the case was, which was the equivalent of a motion to dismiss, was going to be about jurisdiction alone, and one of the fellows who spoke for the House managers—who was a formal criminal defense attorney—seemed to suggest that there was something nefarious that we were discussing jurisdiction in trying to get the case dismissed, but this is where it happens in the case because jurisdiction is the first thing that has to be found. We have counterarguments to everything that they raised, and you will hear them later on in the case from Mr. van der Veen and from myself.

But on the issue of jurisdiction—the scholarly issue of jurisdiction—I will leave you with this before I invite David to come up and give you the erudite explanation. Some of this was shown on the screen, but article I, section 3 says: "Judgment in Cases of Impeachment shall not extend further than to removal from Office, and disqualification to hold . . . any Office of honor, Trust or Profit under the United States: but the Party convicted shall nevertheless be liable and subject to Indictment, Trial, Judgment and Punishment, according to law." So this idea of a January amnesty is nonsense.

If my colleagues on this side of the Chamber actually think that President Trump committed a criminal offense—and let's understand a high crime is a felony and a misdemeanor is a misdemeanor. The words haven't changed that much over time. After he is out of office, you go and arrest him. So there is no opportunity where the President of the United States can run rampant into January, the end of his term, and just go away scot-free. The Department of Justice does know what to do with such people. And so far, I haven't seen any activity in that direction. And not only that, the people who stormed this building and breached it were not accused of conspiring with the President. But the section I read—"Judgment"—in other words, the bad thing that can happen—the "Judgment in Cases of Impeachment"—i.e., what we are doing—"shall not extend further than . . . removal from Office. . . ."

What is so hard about that? Which of those words are unclear? "Shall not extend further than removal . . . from Office . . ." President Trump no longer is in office. The object of the Constitution has been achieved. He was removed by the voters. Mr. Schoen, are you ready—now that I have taken all of his time. Thank you, Mr. President.

. . .

Mr. Counsel SCHOEN: Mr. President, leaders. I stand before you in what I always thought as the hallowed ground of democracy. In this room, American lives have been changed so dramatically in just my lifetime through so many of your legislative initiatives from the Civil Rights Act, when I was a child, through, most recently, the FIRST STEP Act—laws that have provided major opportunities for Americans to move forward and upward and more fully enjoy all of the attributes of what has been the greatest Nation on Earth. I have seen the changes these laws have made to my clients every day for the past thirty-six years. These laws have enabled me to fight for their enjoyment of a fair stake in our American project.

I stand before a group of one hundred United States Senators who have chosen to serve your country from all corners of this great Nation, giving up all sorts of professions, time with family, and perhaps other more lucrative opportunities to serve your country. Mr. President, you are a man who so honorably served this Nation in the Senate and in public service before your tenure here. It is an honor to

appear in this historic hall of democracy. Yet today, that honor is tempered by an overriding feeling of grave concern, grave concern for the danger to the institution of the Presidency that I believe even convening these proceedings indicates.

The joy I believed I would feel if I ever had the great privilege of appearing before this body is replaced by sadness and pain. My overriding emotion is, frankly, wanting to cry for what I believe these proceedings will do to our great, so long-enduring, sacred Constitution and to the American people on both sides of the great divide that now characterizes our Nation. Esteemed Members of the Senate, going forward with this impeachment trial of a former President of the United States is unconstitutional for reasons we have set out in our brief, some of which we will focus on here. And as a matter of policy, it is wrong as wrong can be for all of us as a Nation.

We are told by those who favor having these proceedings that we have to do it for accountability. But anyone truly interested in real accountability for what happened at the Capitol on January 6 would, of course, insist on waiting for a full investigation to be completed. Indeed, one is underway in earnest already, intent on getting to the bottom of what happened.

Anyone interested in ensuring that it is truly the one or ones responsible from whom accountability is sought would more than willingly wait for the actual evidence, especially with new evidence coming in every day about preplanning, about those who were involved, and about their agenda bearing no relationship to the claims made here. They say you need this trial before the Nation can heal, that the Nation cannot heal without it. I say our Nation cannot possibly heal with it. With this trial, you will open up new and bigger wounds across the Nation, for a great many

Americans see this process for exactly what it is: a chance by a group of partisan politicians seeking to eliminate Donald Trump from the American political scene and seeking to disenfranchise 74 million-plus American voters and those who dare to share their political beliefs and vision of America. They hated the results of the 2016 election and want to use this impeachment process to further their political agenda.

These elitists have mocked them for four years. They called their fellow Americans who believe in their country and their Constitution "deplorables." And the latest talk is that they need to deprogram those who supported Donald Trump and the Grand Old Party. But at the end of the day, this is not just about Donald Trump or any individual. This is about our Constitution and abusing the impeachment power for political gain. They tell us that we have to have this impeachment trial, such as it is, to bring about unity, but they don't want unity. And they know this so-called trial will tear the country in half, leaving tens of millions of Americans feeling left out of the Nation's agenda, as dictated by one political party that now holds the power in the White House and in our national legislature. But they are proud Americans who never quit getting back up when they are down, and they don't take dictates from another party based on partisan force-feeding.

This trial will tear this country apart, perhaps like we have only seen once before in our history. And to help the Nation heal, we now learn that the House managers, in their wisdom, have hired a movie company and a large law firm to create, manufacture, and splice for you a package designed by experts to chill and horrify you and our fellow Americans. They want to put you through a sixteen-hour presentation over two days, focusing on this as if it were some sort of blood sport. And to what end? For healing? For unity? For accountability? Not for any of those. For, surely, there are much better ways to achieve each. It is, again, for pure, raw, misguided partisanship that makes them believe playing to our worst instincts somehow is good.

They don't need to show you movies to show you that the riot happened here. We will stipulate that it happened, and you know all about it. This is a process fueled irresponsibly by base hatred by these House managers and those who gave them their charge, and they are willing to sacrifice our national character to advance their hatred and their fear that one day they might not be the party in power. They have a very different view of democracy and freedom from Justice Jackson who once wrote: "Freedom to differ is not limited to things that do not matter much. That would be a mere shadow of freedom. The test of its substance is the right to differ as to things that touch at the heart of the existing order." They have a very different view of democracy and freedom. This is nothing less than the political weaponization of the impeachment process—pure, raw sport, fueled by the misguided idea of party over country when, in fact, both will surely suffer. I can promise you that if these proceedings go forward, everyone will look bad. You will see and hear many Members of our Congress saying and doing things they must surely regret. But, perhaps, far worse than a moment of personal shame in a world in which history passes from our memories in a moment, our great country, a model for all the world, will be far more divided and our standing around the world will be badly broken. Our archenemies who pray each and every day for our downfall will watch with glee, glowing in the moment as they see you at your worst and our country in internal divide.

Let's be perfectly clear. If you vote to proceed with this impeachment trial, future Senators will recognize that you bought into a radical constitutional theory that departs clearly from the language of the Constitution itself and holds—and this is in their brief—that any civil officer who ever dares to want to serve his or her country must know that they will be subject to impeachment long after their service in office has ended, subject only to the political and cultural landscape of the day that is in operation at any future time. This is exactly the position taken by the House managers at page sixty-five of their brief—unprecedented, radical position. They unabashedly say so. Imagine the potential consequences for civil officers you know and who you believed served so honorably but who, in the view of a future Congress, might one day be deemed to be impeachment worthy.

Imagine it now because your imagination is the only limitation. The House managers tell you a correct reading of the impeachment power under the Constitution is that it has no temporal limit and can reach back in time without limitation to target anyone who dared to serve our Nation as a civil officer. Now add that to their demand that you Members put your imprimatur on the snap impeachment they returned in this case and can do again in the future if you endorse it by going forward with this impeachment trial. This is an untenable combination that literally puts the institution of the Presidency directly at risk, nothing less, and it does much more. Under their unsupportable constitutional theory and tortured reading of the text, every civil officer who has served is at risk of impeachment if any given group elected to the House decides that what was thought to be an important service to the country when they served now deserves to be canceled.

They have made clear in public statements that what they really want to accomplish here, in the name of the Constitution, is to bar Donald Trump from ever running for political office again, but this is an affront to the Constitution no matter who they target today. It means nothing less than the denial of the right to vote and the independent right for a candidate to run for elective political office, guaranteed by the 1st and 14th Amendments to the Constitution, using the guise of impeachment as a tool to disenfranchise. Perhaps my friend put the situation simply and sharply into focus last week on his radio show.

My friend is a distinguished lawyer who served as an Ambassador to former President Obama and has friends among you. He described himself to his listeners as a dyed-in-the-wool, lifelong Democrat, but he said the idea of one hundred people in these circumstances deciding that tens of millions of American voters cannot cast their vote for their candidate for President ever again is unthinkable, and it truly should be. I will discuss today several reasons this matter should not and must not proceed; why the Senate lacks jurisdiction to conduct this trial of a former President—a President no longer in office and now a private citizen. Any single reason in our trial memorandum or discussed today suffices, but I want to start with a discussion of the fundamental due process lacking from the start, and that would last through the end if this goes forward because it is this irretrievably flawed process and its product—a dangerous snap impeachment—that brings us here and that threatens to send a message into the future that we will all regret forever and that will stain this body, which up to now our Founding Fathers believed was uniquely suited for the most difficult task of conducting an impeachment trial, as Mr. Hamilton wrote in Federalist No. 65.

These aren't just niceties. I make no apology for demanding in your name, in the name of the Constitution, that the rights to due process guaranteed under the Constitution are adhered to in a process as serious as this in our national lives. The denial of due process in this case, of course, starts with the House of Representatives. In this unprecedented snap impeachment process, the House of Representatives denied every attribute of fundamental constitutional due process that Americans correctly have come to believe is part of what makes this country so great. How and why did that happen? It is a function of the insatiable lust for impeachment in the House for the past four years.

Consider this:

Mr. RASKIN in 2017: I want to say this for Donald Trump, who I may well be voting to impeach . . .

Mr. Keith ELLISON in 2017: Donald Trump has already done a number of things which legitimately raise the question of impeachment . . .

Ms. Maxine WATERS: I don't respect this President, and I will fight every day until he is impeached.

Mr. Joaquin CASTRO: That is grounds to start impeachment proceedings. Those are grounds to start impeachment. Those are grounds to start impeachment proceedings. Yes, I think that's grounds to start impeachment proceedings.

Mr. Al GREEN: I rise today, Mr. Speaker, to call for the impeachment of the President of the United States of America.

Ms. WATERS: I continue to say, Impeach him! Impeach 45! Impeach 45!

Mr. Steve COHEN: So we're calling upon the House to begin impeachment hearings immediately.

Commentator: On the impeachment of Donald Trump, would you vote yes or no?

Ms. Ilhan OMAR: I would vote yes.

Ms. Alexandria OCASIO-CORTEZ: I would vote to impeach.

Ms. Rashida TLAIB: Because we're going to go in there, and we're going to impeach the [bleep bleep]!

Mr. Brad SHERMAN: The fact is I introduced Articles of Impeachment in July of 2017.

Mr. GREEN: If we don't impeach this President, he will get reelected.

Mr. COHEN: My oath requires me to be for impeachment, have impeachment hearings, and leave a scarlet "I" on his chest.

Mr. Cory BOOKER: The Representatives should begin impeachment proceedings against this President.

Ms. Elizabeth WARREN: It is time to bring impeachment charges against him . . . Bring impeachment charges.

Mr. Jerry NADLER: My personal view is that he richly deserves impeachment.

Ms. TLAIB: We are here at an impeachment rally, and we are ready to impeach the— (People chanting: Yeah.)

Counsel SHOEN: The relevant timeline in the House reveals the rush to judgment. On the day following the January 6 riot, the House leadership cynically sensed a political opportunity to score points against the outgoing then-President Trump, and the Speaker demanded that Vice President Pence invoke the 25th Amendment, threatening immediate impeachment for the President if Mr. Pence did not comply with this extraordinary and extraordinarily wrong demand.

Four days later, on January 11, 2021, the instant Article of Impeachment was introduced in the House. Speaker Pelosi then gave the Vice President another ultimatum, threatening to begin impeachment proceedings within twenty-four hours if he did not comply. Vice President Pence rejected Speaker Pelosi's demand, favoring instead adherence to the Constitution and the best interests of the Nation over a politically motivated threat. On January 12, Speaker Pelosi announced who the nine impeachment managers would be, and on January 13, 2021, just days after holding a press conference to announce the launching of an inquiry, the House adopted the Article of Impeachment, completing the fastest impeachment inquiry in history and, according President Trump no due process at all over strong opposition, based in large part on the complete lack of due process.

To say there was a rush to judgment by the House would be a grave understatement. It is not as if the House Members who voted to impeach were not mightily warned about the dangers to the institution of the Presidency and to our system of due process. They were warned in the strongest of terms from within their own ranks adamantly, clearly, and in no uncertain terms not to take this dangerous snap impeachment course. Those warnings were framed in the context of the constitutional due process that was denied here.

Consider the warnings given by one Member during the House proceedings, pleading with the other Members to accord this decision the due process the Constitution demands.

This is Representative Cole of Oklahoma: "With only one week to go in his term, the majority is asking us to consider a resolution impeaching President Trump, and they do so knowing full well that even if the House passes this resolution, the Senate will not be able to begin considering these charges until after President Trump's term ends. I can think of no action the House can take that is more likely to further divide the American people than the action we are contemplating today. Emotions are clearly running high, and political divisions have never been more apparent in my lifetime." Said by Representative Cole.

Mr. Cole's words on the floor emphasizing the care that must be taken with respect to the consideration of the Article of Impeachment echo the concerns by our Founding Fathers on this subject. Listen to this from Mr. Hamilton in Federalist No. 65: "A well constituted court for the trial of impeachments is an object not more to be desired than difficult to be obtained in a government wholly elective. . . . The prosecution of them, for this reason, will seldom fail to agitate the passions of the whole community and to divide it into parties more or less friendly or inimical to the accused. In many cases, it will connect itself with the pre-existing factions, and will enlist all their animosities, partialities, influence and interest on one side or on the other; and in such cases there will always be the greatest danger that the decision will be regulated more by the comparative strength of parties, than by the real demonstrations of innocence or guilt."

Prescient thinking by Mr. Hamilton, as we see often. In what I say to you is a proof of the need for due process, based on the critically serious nature of the singular role the impeachment process has in our government, Mr. Hamilton characterized the consideration of an impeachment in these terms: "The delicacy and magnitude of a trust which so deeply concerns the political reputation and existence of every man engaged in the administration of public affairs, speak for themselves."

This, too, is in Federalist No. 65. Now back to the House and the warnings against this rushed judgment in this case, Mr. Cole of Oklahoma again. In the name of healing, a path forward he said our people so desperately need, he warned that "the House is moving forward erratically with a truncated process that does not comport with the modern practice and that will give members no time to contemplate the serious nature of action before us." Mr. Cole emphasized to his colleagues that such care must be taken with the consideration of an Article of Impeachment "in order to ensure that the American people have confidence in the procedures the House is following" and because "the Presidency itself demands due process in the impeachment proceedings."

Congressman Cole continued: "Unfortunately, the majority has chosen to race to the floor with a new Article of Impeachment, forgoing any investigation, any committee process or any chance for Members to fully contemplate this course of action before proceeding." Mr. Cole complained that "the majority is failing to provide the House with an opportunity to review all the facts—which are still coming to light—to discuss all the evidence, to listen to scholars, to examine the witnesses, and to consider precedents." He noted further: "This is not the type of robust process we have followed for every modern impeachment, and the failure to do so does a great disservice to this institution and to this country."

Mr. Cole complained right on the House floor that "rather than following the appropriate processes the House has used in every modern impeachment, the majority is rushing to the floor, tripping all over themselves in their rush to impeach the President a second time." And in Mr. Cole's words, it was doing so to "settle scores." He warned this snap impeachment approach would cause great division as the country looks ahead to the start of a new administration.

He said to them: "[In] a matter as grave and consequential as impeachment, shouldn't we follow the same process we have used in every modern impeachment rather than rushing to the floor?" And he implored them: "On behalf of generations of Americans to come, we need to think more clearly about the consequences of our action today." Mr. Cole then reached across the aisle and credited a Member of this body, Senator Manchin, having voiced similar sentiments about how ill-advised this rushed process was, suggesting that the underlying events were a matter for the judicial system to investigate, not one for a rushed political process. Finally, Mr. Cole admonished his fellow House Members, telling them: "We need to recognize that we are following a flawed process." The alarm Mr. Cole sounded went unheeded. Now let us consider the process in the House that actually was due. The House managers assert in their memorandum that "[t]he House serves as a grand jury and prosecutor under the Constitution."

They told you that again today. If this is accurate, then they highlight the complete failure to adhere to due process. One should not diminish the significance of impeachment's legal aspects, particularly as they relate to the formalities of the criminal justice process. "It is a hybrid of the political and the legal, a political process moderated by legal formalities . . ."—this is a quote, Richard Broughton. The Fifth Amendment to the United States Constitution provides, in relevant part, that "no person shall be . . . deprived of life, liberty or property, without due process of law." The Supreme Court long ago recognized in *Matthews v. Eldridge* that, at its core, due process is about what we all want, what we all have the right to demand—fundamental fairness.

One scholar, Brian Owsley, has written that "the impeachment process should and does include some of the basic safeguards for the accused that are observed in a criminal process such as fairness, due process, presumption of innocence, and proportionality"—basic American values. And, of course, we know that the Supreme Court has recognized that due process protections attend congressional investigations. While Congress is empowered to make its own rules of proceeding, it may not make rules that ignore constitutional restraints or violate fundamental rights. While the case law is limited in terms of spelling out what due process looks like in impeachment hearings and, of course, in the Nixon case—Walter, not Richard—we know that there is a great deal of leeway afforded Congress with respect to its impeachment rules.

It is clear that the fundamental principles that underlie our understanding of what due process must always look like apply. In *Hastings v. United States*, a D.C. court case vacated on different grounds, they address the matter, clearly concluding that the due process clause applies to impeachment proceedings and that it imposes an independent constitutional constraint on how the Senate exercises its sole power to try all impeachments under article I, section 3, clause 6. The court wrote in *Hastings*: "Impeachment is an extraordinary remedy."

As an essential element of our constitutional system of checks and balances, impeachment must be invoked and carried out with solemn respect and scrupulous attention to fairness. Fairness and due process must be the watchword whenever a branch of the United States Government conducts a trial, whether it be in a criminal case, a civil case, or a case of impeachment. A 1974 Department of Justice memo suggested the same view, opining that "whether or not capable of judicial enforcement, due process standards would seem to be relevant to the manner of conducting an impeachment proceeding." More specifically, as the *Hastings* court described it, "one of the key principles that lies at the heart of our constitutional democracy: fairness." Again, fairness.

The Supreme Court's "precedents establish the general rule that individuals must receive notice and an opportunity to be heard before the government deprives them" of a constitutionally protected interest. It is also true that in any proceeding

that may lead to deprivation of a protected interest, it requires fair procedures com-
mensurate with the interests at stake. Impeachment proceedings plainly involve
deprivations of property and liberty interests protected by the due process clause,
and the House surely seeks to strip Donald Trump of his most highly cherished
constitutional rights, including the right to be eligible to hold public office again,
should he so choose. Due process must apply, and, at a minimum, due process in
the impeachment process must include that the evidence must be disclosed to the
accused, and the accused must be permitted an opportunity to test and confront
the evidence, particularly through "the rights to confront and cross-examine witnesses," which "have long been recognized as essential to due process."

In almost every setting where important decisions turn on questions of fact, due
process requires an opportunity to confront and cross-examine. It is unfathomable
that the Framers, steeped in the history of Anglo-American jurisprudence, would
create a system that would allow the Chief Executive and Commander in Chief of
the Armed Forces to be impeached based on a process that developed evidence
without providing any of the elementary procedures that the common law developed over centuries for ensuring the proper testing of evidence in an adversarial
process. We would never countenance such a system in this country.

Current Members of the House and Senate leadership are themselves on record
repeatedly confirming these procedural due process requirements. Indeed, Congressman Nadler is on record asserting that, in the context of the House impeachment investigation, due process includes the "right to be informed of the law, of
the charges against you, to call your own witnesses, and to have the assistance of
counsel." Then-President Trump was not given any semblance of the due process
Congressman Nadler clearly believes he deserves, based on the Congressman's
description of due process, that must be afforded to an accused in an impeachment
proceeding, as reflected in the statement he made relating to another impeachment
in 1998. No reason was found for the apparent change in the Congressman's point
of view with respect to the two objects of the impeachments at issue.

These fundamental aspects of due process have been honored as required parts
of modern impeachment protocol since at least 1870. It is not seriously debatable,
nor should it be—nor should it be—by any American legislator. In spite of all this,
the House leadership defied all the norms and denied the then-President all of his
basic and constitutionally protected rights. With then-President Donald Trump,
the House impeachment procedure lacked any semblance of due process whatever.
It simply cannot be credibly argued to the contrary, and we do not make special
rules for different targets. It is the very integrity of the institution that suffers when
we do, and that is what the House leadership knowingly has caused.

A review of the House record revealed that the Speaker streamlined the impeachment process—H. Res. 24—to go straight to the floor for a two-hour debate and a

vote, without the ability for amendments. The House record reflects no committee hearing, no witnesses, no presentation or cross-examination of evidence, and no opportunity for the accused to respond or even have counsel present to object. As the *New York Times* recently reported, "there were no witness interviews, no hearings, no committee debates and no real additional fact finding." House managers claim the need for impeachment was so urgent that they had to rush the proceedings, with no time to spare for a more thorough investigation or really, any investigation at all.

But that claim is belied by what happened or didn't happen next. The House leadership unilaterally and by choice waited another twelve days to deliver the Article to this Senate to begin the trial process. In other words, the House leadership spent more time holding the adopted Article than it did on the whole process leading up to the adoption of the Article. That intentional delay, designed to avoid having the trial begin while Mr. Trump was still President, led to yet another egregious denial of due process. Article I, section 3, clause 6 of our Constitution, of course, provides, in pertinent part, that: "The Senate shall have the sole Power to try all impeachments. When sitting for that Purpose, they shall be on Oath or Affirmation. When the President of the United States is tried, the Chief Justice shall preside."

By intentionally waiting until President Trump's term of office expired before delivering the Article of Impeachment to the Senate to initiate trial proceedings, Speaker Pelosi deprived then-President Trump of the express constitutional right—and the right under the Senate's own rule IV—to have the Chief Justice of the United States preside over his trial and wield the considerable power provided for in the Rules of Procedure and Practice in the Senate when sitting on impeachment trials. That power includes, under rule V, the Presiding Officer's exclusive right to make and issue all orders; under rule VII, to make all evidentiary orders subject to objection by a Member of the Senate.

We say, respectfully, that this intentional delay by Speaker Pelosi, such that in the intervening period, President Trump became private citizen Mr. Trump, constitutes a lapse or waiver of jurisdiction here, for Mr. Trump no longer is "the President" described as subject to impeachment in article I, section 3, clause 6 and in article II, section 4, and this body, therefore, has no jurisdiction as a function of that additional due process violation by Speaker Pelosi.

Moreover, with all due respect, then-President Trump suffered a tangible detriment from Speaker Pelosi's actions, which violates not only his rights to due process of law, but also his express constitutional right to have the Chief Justice preside. That tangible detriment includes the loss of the right to a conflict-free, impartial Presiding Officer—with all due respect—the very purpose behind requiring the Chief Justice to preside over the President's impeachment trial, along with the other benefits of having the two branches combined—the Chief Justice from the Judiciary and the Senate—for the impeachment trial of the President, reflected in Federalist 66, one of the reasons the Chief Justice was chosen for that task.

Mr. Trump now faces a situation in which the Presiding Officer will serve as both judge, with all the powers that the rules endow him with, and juror with a vote. And beyond that, the Presiding Officer, although enjoying a lifelong, honorable reputation, of course, has been Mr. Trump's vocal and adamant opponent throughout the Trump administration. And, in fact, in the very matter on trial, the Presiding Officer, respectfully, already has publicly announced his fixed view before hearing any argument or evidence that Mr. Trump must be convicted on the Article of Impeachment before the Senate and, indeed, that Members in both parties have an obligation to vote to convict, as well.[*]

Nowhere in this great country would any American—and, certainly, not this honorable Presiding Officer—consider this scenario to be consistent with any stretch of the American concept of due process and a fair trial and certainly not even the appearance of either. By no stretch of the imagination could any fair minded American be confident that a trial so conducted would or could be the fair trial promised by the leader.

While most procedural aspects of a Senate impeachment trial may be nonjusticiable political questions, this is not an excuse to ignore what law and precedent clearly require. The present situation either presents a violation of the constitutional text found in the articles mentioned above that require the Chief Justice to preside when the President is on trial or it is a clear denial of due process and fair trial rights for Private Citizen Trump to face an impeachment trial so conducted by the Senate.

The impeachment Article should be treated as a nullity and dismissed based on the total lack of due process in the House. It should be dismissed because of Speaker Pelosi's intentional abandonment or waiver of jurisdiction, if the House ever acquired jurisdiction, and the Article should be dismissed because the trial in the Senate of a private citizen is not permitted, let alone with the conflicts just described that attend this proceeding.

Finally, on the subject of due process in this matter, I say the following: this is our Nation's sacred Constitution. It has served us well since it was written, and it has been amended only through a careful process. It is a document unique in all the world. It is a foundational part of what makes the United States a beacon of

---

[*] The screen displayed Senator Patrick Leahy's statement following Trump's second impeachment in the House of Representatives: "We must act together now not just to hold President Trump accountable, but to ensure that no future president, no matter their party, places at risk our democracy in service of their own selfish, illegal, and authoritarian ambitions."

light among the other nations of the world. It not only has room for a tremendous variety of perspectives on the philosophical and political direction our country should take, it encourages the advocacy of our differences. But we have long held that fundamental to its health and well-being and, therefore, to ours as a Nation, is its insistence on due process for every citizen.

The emphasis on the right to due process long ago was recognized as its life breath, a primary guarantor of its eternal viability as our political, civic, and national guiding light. We all well know that there are many systems in other countries around the world that do not offer any semblance of the safeguards our constitutional concept of due process provides. Some of them have chosen their own handbooks, which direct their citizens' conduct on penalty of death. This is one of them.* There can be no room for due process in such a system as this or the system would be lost. Snap decisions are required in a system like this to maintain power for one political philosophy over all others in those kinds of systems. But we as a nation have rejected those systems and the kind of snap decisions they demand to maintain control for one party, for one point of view, and for an imposed way of life. We choose to live freely under a constitution that guarantees our freedom.

Other countries fear those freedoms and seek to ensure adherence to a party line in all civic, political, spiritual, and other affairs and to ensure that the party line is toed. And those systems have no place for due process. Snap decisions that remove political figures are the norm. Maintaining their systems depend on it. That is not our way in America and never must be. We choose in America to live by our Constitution and its amendments and the due process this document demands for every citizen among us.

By putting your imprimatur on the snap judgment made in this matter, to impeach the President of the United States without any semblance of due process at every step along the way, puts the Office of the President of the United States at risk every single day. It is far too dangerous a proposition to countenance, and you must resoundingly reject it by sending the message now that this proceeding, lacking due process from start to finish, must end now with your vote that you lack jurisdiction to conduct an impeachment trial for a former President, whose term in office has expired and who is now a private citizen. So one reason you must send this message here and now is because of the complete lack of due process that brought this Article of Impeachment before this body.

God forbid we should ever lower our vigilance to the principle of due process. An impeachment trial of Private Citizen Trump held before the Senate would be

---

* While making this statement, Shoen held up a copy of *The Little Red Book* containing aphorisms by the late Chinese Communist Party leader Mao Zedong.

nothing more nor less than the trial of a private citizen by a legislative body. An impeachment trial by the Senate of a private citizen violates article I, section 9 of the United States Constitution, which provides that "[n]o bill of attainder . . . shall be passed." The bill of attainder, as this clause is known, prohibits Congress from enacting "a law that legislatively determines guilt and inflicts punishment upon an identifiable individual without provision of the protections of a judicial trial."

A bill of attainder is a legislative act which inflicts punishment without a judicial trial—a *judicial* trial: "The distinguishing characteristic of a bill of attainder is the substitution of a legislative determination of guilt and legislative imposition of punishment for judicial finding and sentence." "[The Bill of Attainder Clause], and the separation of powers doctrine generally, reflect the Framers' concern that trial by a legislature lacks the safeguards necessary to prevent the abuse of power."

As the Supreme Court explained in *United States v. Brown*, "[t]he best available evidence, the writings of the architects of our constitutional system, indicate that the Bill of Attainder Clause was intended not as a narrow, technical (and therefore soon to be outmoded) prohibition, but rather as an implementation of the separation of powers, a general safeguard against legislative exercise of the judicial function, or more simply, trial by legislature." The bill of attainder "reflected the Framers' belief that the Legislative Branch is not so well suited as politically independent judges and juries."

When the Senate undertakes an impeachment trial of a private citizen, as it clearly understands to be the case here, supported by the fact that the Chief Justice is not presiding and Mr. Trump is not "the President," it is acting as a judge and jury rather than a legislative body. And this is exactly the type of situation that the bill of attainder constitutional prohibition was meant to preclude. It is clear that disqualification from holding future office, the punishment the House managers intend to seek here, is a kind of punishment, like banishment and others, that is subject to the constitutional prohibition against the passage of bills of attainder, under which designation bills of pains and penalties are included.

The cases include *Cummings, Ex parte Garland,* and this *Brown* case. The Supreme Court three times has struck down provisions that precluded support of the South or support of communism from holding certain jobs as being in violation of this prohibition. Thus the impeachment of a private citizen in order to disqualify them from holding office is an unconstitutional act constituting a bill of attainder. Moreover, this is the exact type of situation in which the fear would be great that some Members of the Senate might be susceptible to acting in the haste the House acted in when it rushed through the Article of Impeachment in less than forty-eight hours, acting hastily simply to appease the popular clamor of their political base—the very kind of concern expressed by Mr. Hamilton in Federalist 65.

Moreover, as Chief Justice Marshall warned in *Fletcher v. Peck,* "it is not to be disguised that the framers of the Constitution viewed with some apprehension the violent acts that might grow out of the feelings of the moment, and that the people of the United States, in adopting that instrument, have manifested a determination to shield themselves and their property from the effects of those sudden and strong passions to which men and women are exposed. The restrictions on the legislative power of the states are obviously founded in this sentiment, and the Constitution of the United States contains what may be deemed a bill of rights for the people of each state. No state shall pass any bill of attainder. . . . In this form, the power of the legislature over the lives and fortunes of individuals is expressly restrained." So now let's turn to the text of the Constitution.

Turning to the text of the Constitution is, for many, of course, the most appropriate and the most important starting place to trying to answer a Constitution-based question. There are several passages of the United States Constitution that relate to the federal impeachment process. Let's turn to a reading of the text now. A true textual analysis, as the name implies, always begins with the words of the text and only resorts to legislative history or history itself if the meaning of the text is not plain. As the Supreme Court has emphasized, "[s]tatutory interpretation, as we always say, begins with the text." "In interpreting this text, we are guided by the principle that the Constitution was written to be understood by the voters; its words and phrases were used in their normal and ordinary as distinguished from technical meaning." And "[w]e must enforce plain and unambiguous statutory language according to its terms." If a President is impeached, the unambiguous text of the Constitution commands that the Chief Justice of the United States shall preside, as we discussed earlier.

Again, the Chief Justice is disinterested and nonpartisan. His presence brings dignity and solemnity to such a proceeding. In this case, the Chief Justice clearly is not presiding, and the conflict of interest wouldn't necessarily just arise as a substitute for the Vice President. It is the appearance of a conflict of interest and the—and a conflict of interest and the prejudgment that we have discussed. In this case, as we say, the Chief Justice clearly is not presiding. The Senate President pro tempore is presiding. It appears that in the leader's view, undoubtedly joined by other Senators, this is permitted by the Constitution because the subject of the trial is a non-President. As such, it is conceded, as it must be, that for constitutional purposes of the trial, the accused is a non-President. The role of the Senate, though, is to decide whether or not to convict and thereby trigger the application of article II, section 4: "The President, Vice President and all civil Officers of the United States, shall be removed from Office on Impeachment for, and Conviction of, Treason, Bribery, or other high Crimes and Misdemeanors." From which office shall a non-President be removed if convicted? A non-President doesn't hold an office, therefore cannot be impeached under this clause, which provides for the removal from office of the person under the impeachment attack.

The House managers contend that the fact that the Chief Justice is not presiding does not impact the constitutional validity of this trial. Notably, they devote only a single paragraph of their trial memorandum to a development so significant that it prompted multiple Senators to declare the entire proceeding suspect, with one going so far as to say it "crystallized" the unconstitutional nature of this proceeding. And the single paragraph that the House managers do devote to the issue is entirely unpersuasive on the merits. The House managers' position ignores traditional statutory canons of interpretation. It is well established that "[a] term appearing in several places in a statutory text is generally read the same way each time it appears." This presumption is "at its most vigorous when a term is repeated within a given sentence." Additionally, the Court in at least one instance has referred to a broader "established canon" that similar language contained within the same section of a statute be accorded a consistent meaning.

I know this is a lot to listen to at once—a lot of words, but words are what make our Constitution, and the interpretation of that Constitution, as you well know, is a product of words. If the text, "the President of the United States" in the constitutional provision requiring the Chief Justice to preside can refer only to the sitting President, and not to former presidents, then the textual identification of "[t]he President" contained in article II, section 4, which makes the President amenable to impeachment in the first place, also excludes anyone other than the sitting President. In full, that sentence provides that "[t]he President, Vice President and all civil Officers of the United States, shall be removed from Office on

Impeachment for, and Conviction of, Treason, Bribery, or other high Crimes and Misdemeanors."

This is the substantive phrase of the Constitution vesting the conviction and removal power in the Senate, and it contains a clear jurisdictional limitation. The House managers do understand what the word "President" means for the purposes of other constitutional provisions, and so they should understand this limitation as well. Only a sitting President is referred to as the President of the United States in the Constitution. And only a sitting President may be impeached, convicted, and removed upon a trial in the Senate. "The President" in article II, section 4 and "the President" in article I, section 3 identify the same person. If the accused is not "the President" in one, he is not "the President" in the other.

No sound textual interpretation—I emphasize "textual interpretation"—principle permits a contrary reading. In the words of the Supreme Court, it is a "normal rule of statutory construction that identical words used in different parts of the same act are intended to have the same meaning." Unwittingly or unwillingly as it may be, Senate Democrats, in their announcement that Senator Leahy will preside, have already taken their position on this matter. The accused is not the President. The text of the United States Constitution therefore does not vest the Senate with the power to try him and remove him—a factual nullity; he can't be removed—or disqualify him—a legal nullity—as if he was the President.

The House managers contend that the Senate has jurisdiction over this impeachment because despite the fact that he is no longer the President, the conduct that the former President is charged occurred while he was still in office. That argument does not in any way alter the Constitution's clear textual identification of "the President." The House managers justify their strained argument by noting that "[t]he Constitution's impeachment provisions are properly understood by reference to this overarching constitutional plan." But with that very justification in mind, their argument fails once again.

In an impeachment, it is the accused's office that permits the impeachment. Ceasing to hold that office terminates the possibility and the purpose of impeachment. Private persons may not be impeached in America, and so they ask you to look back at the British model. The Constitution, as I see it, does not make private citizens subject to impeachment. The Founders rejected the British model that allowed Parliament to impeach anyone, except for the King, and so they limited impeachment to certain public officials, including Presidents in our country.

Next on the textual front, the primary and, in fact, only required remedy of a conviction is removal. Article II, section 4, states a straightforward rule: whenever a civil officer is impeached and convicted for high crimes and misdemeanors, they shall be removed. It is undeniable that in this instance removal is moot in every possible regard. Removal is a factual and legal impossibility. Yet the Article of Impeachment itself—read it in the wherefore clause; it calls for removal. This is one reason why impeachment proceedings are different from ordinary trials and why the Constitution pointedly separates the two. In ordinary criminal jurisprudence, a person convicted of public crimes committed while he or she was in office may still be punished even though they no longer hold that office.

Not so with impeachment. In a Senate impeachment trial, conviction means and requires removal, and conviction without a removal is no conviction at all. Only upon a valid conviction and its requisite, enforceable removal may the additional judgment of disqualification plausibly be entertained. Presidents are impeachable because Presidents are removable. Former presidents are not because they cannot be removed. The Constitution is clear. Trial by the Senate sitting as a Court of Impeachment is reserved for the President of the United States, not a private citizen who used to be President of the United States. Just as clear, the judgment required upon conviction is removal from office, and a former President can no longer be removed from office.

"The purpose, text and structure of the Constitution's impeachment Clauses confirm this intuitive and common-sense understanding." So wrote Judge Michael Luttig, former judge in the United States Court of Appeals for the Fourth Circuit. And, indeed, there are State court decisions that analyze this very same language and conclude that impeachment can only be entertained against an existing officer subject to removal, in *State v. Hill*, from Nebraska, and *Smith v. Brantley*, a 1981 decision from the Florida supreme court. This is the first time that the United States Senate has ever been asked to apply the Constitution's textual identification of "the President" in the impeachment provisions to anyone other than the sitting President of the United States.

And, of course, most significantly from a textual approach, the term specifically used is "the President" not "a President." And there can only be one "the President"—the incumbent—at a time. Judge Luttig relies on this textual reading for his firm conclusion that a former President cannot be impeached or convicted. Consider the alternative, as Robert Delahunty and John Yoo have: if Mr. Trump can be convicted as "the President," the language the Constitution uses, then why is he still not "the President" under the Commander in Chief clause, for example? They are joined by Professor Alan Dershowitz and University of Chicago Professor Richard Epstein in their focus and conclusion. They point out the dangers of an approach that deviates from a focus on the text. If there is no temporal limitation—that is what they suggested to you—remember, you can go back in time and impeach any civil officer who ever served for anything that occurred during the course of their service, time immemorial. With the House managers' position, the concept necessarily includes all executive officers and judges, including, perhaps, the impeachment now of Jimmy Carter for his handling of the Iran hostage scandal, as one example. That flows logically from their argument without any hesitation. Further, they ask, why not then countenance the broad reading of other terms?

When I say "they ask," I mean the experts who opined on this. Why not then countenance a broad reading of other terms, such that terms like "high crimes and misdemeanors," however broadly construed, are not intended to be exclusively the only kind of conduct intended as impeachable? They conclude—these experts— by writing that a nontextual impeachment power would undermine the Constitution's effort to make the President independent of Congress, a central goal of the Founding Fathers. The authors convincingly argue for textual analysis over non-textual reliance on a presentation of history, suggesting that if one's presentation of history were to control, it would expressly permit conduct contrary to the express language, leading to clearly unintended results.

I must tell you that I have spoken to Judge Ken Starr at some length over this past week about this. This textual approach is something he, too, feels very strongly about. I also happen to be friendly with Chuck Cooper, by the way. He is a fine person. He also happens to be a person who has a strong animus against President Trump. But Chuck Cooper is a fine lawyer and a fine person, as I am sure our friends from Alabama know. As we already have discussed, the risks to the institution of the Presidency and to any and all past officers is limited only by one's imagination. The weakness of the House managers' case is further demonstrated by their reliance on the unproven assertion that if President Trump is not impeached, future officers who are impeached will evade removal by resigning either before impeachment or Senate trial. For example, they contend, citing various law professors, that "[any official] who betrayed the public trust and was impeached could avoid account-ability simply by resigning one minute before the Senate's final conviction vote."

This argument is a complete canard. The Constitution expressly provides in article I, section 3, clause 7 that a convicted party, following impeachment, "shall nevertheless be liable and subject to indictment, trial, judgment, and punish-ment according to law" after removal. Clearly, a former civil officer who is not impeached is subject to the same. We have a judicial process in this country. We have an investigative process in this country to which no former officeholder is immune. That is the process that should be running its course. That is the process the bill of attainder tells us is the appropriate one for investigation, prosecution, and punishment, with all of the attributes of that branch. We are missing it by two articles here that the article III courts provide. They provide that kind of appropri-ate adjudication. That is accountability.

There are appropriate mechanisms in place for full and meaningful account-ability not through the legislature, which does not and cannot offer the safeguards of the judicial system, which every private citizen is constitutionally entitled to. But more to the point here. Their argument does nothing to empower a different reading of the Constitution's plain text; that is, one that reads "the President" in one provision to include former Presidents but reads "the President" in the other provision to mean only the sitting President. Second, this red herring of an argument also fails because the former President did not resign, even amid calls by his opponents that he do so.

As a result, the Senate need not decide whether it possesses the power or juris-diction to try and convict the former President who resigned or how it might best proceed to effectuate justice in such a case. That is not this case. The plain mean-ing of the Constitution's text, faithfully and consistently applied, should govern whether the United States Senate is vested by the Constitution with the power to convict a private citizen of the United States. It is not. The House managers posit in their trial memorandum that despite the fact that the primary and only neces-sary remedy upon conviction, removal, is a legal nullity, this late impeachment trial is appropriate because the other, secondary, optional remedy that the Senate is not even required to consider and which only takes effect upon a later, separate vote—disqualification from future office—can still theoretically be applied to a former President.

The managers contend that "Article II, Section 4 states a straightforward rule: whenever a civil officer is impeached and convicted for high crimes and misde-meanors, they 'shall be removed.' Absolutely nothing about this rule implies, let alone requires, that former officials—who can still face disqualification—are immune from impeachment and conviction." That is what they say. I told you that today. In other words, so the argument goes, a President no longer holding office does not moot the entirety of remedies afforded by impeachment.

This, however, also flies in the face of both the plain meaning of the text and the canons of statutory interpretation. First of all, the managers, once again, simply choose to ignore the text. Even in the passage that the managers cite, the word "shall" does, to put it mildly, imply a requirement, an imperative such that an impeachment in which removal would be impossible is invalid. "'Shall' means shall. The Supreme Court . . . ha[s] made clear that when a statute uses the word 'shall,' Congress has imposed a mandatory duty upon the subject of the command," as in shall remove. Indeed, "the mandatory 'shall' . . . normally creates an obliga-tion impervious to judicial discretion." And "[w]herever the Constitution com-mands, discretion terminates." "Shall" means mandatory, and "shall be removed" is not possible for a former officer no longer in office. Impeachment cannot apply.

Now, here is the "and" argument. You may have heard about it or read about it if you follow such things. This is another one Judge Starr is big on, and many of the textual scholars have written about it. The managers critically ignore this language in article I, section 3, clause 7, which states that "[j]udgment in Cases of Impeachment shall not extend further than to removal from Office, and disqualification to hold and enjoy any Office of honor, Trust or Profit under the United States." Ordinarily, as in everyday English, use of the conjunctive "and" in a list means that all of the listed requirements must be satisfied, while use of the disjunctive "or" means that only one of the list of requirements needs to be satisfied.

Judge Kenneth Starr subscribes strongly to this argument and understands the comma to provide further support for the reading. As Judge Michael Luttig, again, recently argued, "The Constitution links the impeachment remedy of disqualification from future office with the remedy of removal from the office that person currently occupies; the former remedy does not apply in situations where the latter is unavailable." Conviction and removal are inextricably entwined. If removal no longer is possible, neither is an impeachment conviction. Judge Luttig's view is consistent with that of Justice Joseph Story in his famous "Commentaries on the Constitution," wherein Justice Story analyzed "that impeachment is inapplicable to officials who have left their position because removal—a primary remedy that the impeachment process authorizes—is no longer necessary."

Justice Story noted that he is not coming to a firm posit on this. This is his belief, and this is his thought process: "There is also much force in the remark, that an impeachment is a proceeding purely of a political nature. It is not so much designed to punish an offender, as to secure the state against gross official misdemeanors. It touches neither his person, nor his property; but simply divests him of his political capacity." . . . Now, this is—I have to say this is insulting. We heard earlier today we don't cite any scholars. Professor Philip Bobbitt is a distinguished Weschler professor at Columbia University who, along with Professor Charles Black, wrote the handbook on impeachment used for many, many years. He is a constitutional expert on impeachment. He has written that "there is little discussion in the historical record surrounding . . . the precise question of whether a person no longer a civil officer can be impeached—and in light of the clarity of the text, this is hardly surprising," Professor Bobbitt wrote.

Professor Bobbitt, by the way, who has a rich family history in the Democratic Party—LBJ—also asserted the following, as recently as January 27, 2021, arguing against holding this trial. He said: there is no authority granted to Congress to impeach and convict persons who are not "civil officers of the United States." It's as simple as that. But simplicity doesn't mean unimportance. Professor Bobbitt wrote: "Limiting Congress to its specified powers is a crucial element in the central idea of the Constitution: putting the state under law." Professor Bobbitt and former Stanford University Law professor Richard Danzig have remarked that impeachment's principal purpose, as the 66th of the Federalist Papers makes clear, is to check the "encroachments of the executive."

Trial by jury, rules of evidence, and other safeguards are put aside, they write, because of the need to protect the public from further abuse of office. Similarly, yesterday, Professor Eugene Kontorovich wrote: "The Constitution provides that the impeachment process is to be used to remove 'all Civil officers of the United States'—that is, people holding a government position. Yet in the case of Mr. Trump, the House is reading the Constitution as if it said the process applies to 'all Civil officers of the United States, and people who aren't civil officers, but once were.'"

Exactly what it does not say. We have been told by the House managers about missed citations in our brief. I would like to draw your attention to page thirty-seven. This is a substantive misrepresentation to you, I would respectfully suggest, and it reflects to me a very different view of democracy—a fear of democracy. They wrote on page thirty-seven of their brief that the Framers—I am paraphrasing the first part: "The Framers themselves would not have hesitated to convict on these facts. Their worldview was shaped by a study of classical history, as well as a lived experience of resistance and revolution. They were well aware of the danger posed by opportunists who incited mobs to violence for political gain. They drafted the Constitution to avoid such thuggery, which they associated with 'the threat of civil disorder and the early assumption of power by a dictator.'" The citation is "178, Bernard Bailyn, *The Ideological Origins of the American Revolution*." That's this book.*

Professor Bailyn, when he gave his description of the threat of civil disorder and the early assumption of power by a dictator and thuggery, was referring to early colonists' view toward democracy. They feared democracy. That is what they called thuggery, democracy, because it is an elitist's point of view—an elitist's political point of view.

We don't fear democracy. We embrace it. In summing up, let's be crystal clear on where we stand and why we are here. The singular goal of the House managers and House leadership in pursuing the impeachment conviction of Donald J. Trump is to use these proceedings to disenfranchise at least 74 million Americans with whom they viscerally disagree and to ensure that neither they nor any other American ever again can cast a vote for Donald Trump. And if they convince you

---

* Shoen held the book aloft.

to go forward, their ultimate hope is that this will be a shot across the bow of any other candidate for public office who would dare to take up a political message that is very different from their own political point of view as to the direction in which they wish to take our country.

Under our Constitution, this body and the impeachment process must never be permitted to be weaponized for partisan political purposes. This Article of Impeachment must be dismissed for lack of jurisdiction based on what we have discussed here today and what is in our brief. The institution of the Presidency is at risk unless a strong message is sent by the dismissal of the Article of Impeachment.

Before we close, I want to leave you with two thoughts. One was expressed by Abraham Lincoln. He comes to mind first because of the way in which our Nation is now divided. We must learn from his times. He had a simple but important message about the paramount importance of doing what is right. Mr. Lincoln said: "Stand with anybody that stands Right. Stand with him [when] he is right and Part with him when he goes wrong. . . . In both cases you are right. In both cases you oppose the dangerous extremes. In both [cases] you stand on moral ground and hold the ship level and steady. In both you are national and nothing less than national." And the second message is from one of Mr. Lincoln's favorite poets who wrote in 1849, at a time fraught with division and at risk for even more. The message from that other time of division—a call for hope and unity to bring strength—has special meaning today.

A poem Longfellow wrote:

Sail forth into the sea, O ship!
Through wind and wave, right onward steer!
The moistened eye, the trembling lip,
Are not the signs of doubt or fear.
Sail forth into the sea of life,
O gentle, loving, trusting wife,
And safe from all adversity
Upon the bosom of that sea
Thy comings and thy goings be!
For gentleness and love and trust
Prevail o'er angry wave and gust;
And in the wreck of noble lives
Something immortal still survives!
Thou, too, sail on, O Ship of State!
Sail on, O Union, strong and great!
Humanity with all its fears,

With all the hopes of future years,
Is hanging breathless on thy fate!
We know what Master laid thy keel,
What Workmen wrought thy ribs of steel,
Who made each mast, and sail, and rope,
What anvils rang, what hammers beat,
In what a forge and what a heat
Were shaped the anchors of thy hope!
Fear not each sudden sound and shock,
'Tis of the wave and not the rock;
'Tis but the flapping of the sail,
And not a rent made by the gale!
In spite of rock and tempest's roar,
In spite of false lights on the shore,
Sail on, nor fear to breast the sea!
Our hearts, our hopes, are all with thee,
Our hearts, our hopes, our prayers, our tears,
Our faith triumphant o'er our fears,
Are all with thee,—are all with thee!

Mr. Manager RASKIN: Mr. President, it has been a long day. We thank you, and we thank all the Senators for their careful attention to the legal arguments and your courtesy to the managers and to the lawyers here. This has been the most bipartisan impeachment in American history, and we hope it will continue to be so in the days ahead. And nothing could be more bipartisan than the desire to recess.

So the only issue before the Senate today, of course, is whether Donald Trump is subject to the Court of Impeachment that the Senate has convened. We see no need to make any further argument that this body has the power to convict and to disqualify President Trump for his breathtaking constitutional crime of inciting a violent insurrection against our government. Tomorrow, we will address the amazing array of issues suggested by the thoughtful presentations by our colleagues, by including the First Amendment, due process, partisanship under our Constitution, the bill of attainder clause, and many, many more.

But, in the meantime, we waive all further arguments. We waive our thirty-three minutes of rebuttal, and we give those thirty-three minutes, gratefully, back to the Senate of the United States.

(Chorus of "Hear! Hear!")

. . .

The PRESIDENT pro tempore: . . . The question is whether Donald John Trump is subject to the jurisdiction of a Court of Impeachment for acts committed while President of the United States, notwithstanding the expiration of his term in that office?

. . .

Rollcall Vote No. 57

YEAS—56 Baldwin, Bennet, Blumenthal, Booker, Brown, Cantwell, Cardin, Carper, Casey, Cassidy, Collins, Coons, Cortez, Masto, Duckworth, Durbin, Feinstein, Gillibrand, Hassan, Heinrich, Hickenlooper, Hirono, Kaine, Kelly, King, Klobuchar, Leahy, Lujan, Manchin, Markey, Menendez, Merkley, Murkowski, Murphy, Murray, Ossoff, Padilla, Peters, Reed, Romney, Rosen, Sanders, Sasse, Schatz, Schumer, Shaheen, Sinema, Smith, Stabenow, Tester, Toomey, Van Hollen, Warner, Warnock, Warren, Whitehouse, Wyden

NAYS—44 Barrasso, Blackburn, Blunt, Boozman, Braun, Burr, Capito, Cornyn, Cotton, Cramer, Crapo, Cruz, Daines, Ernst, Fischer, Graham, Grassley, Hagerty, Hawley, Hoeven, Hyde-Smith, Inhofe, Johnson, Kennedy, Lankford, Lee, Lummis, Marshall, McConnell, Moran, Paul, Portman, Risch, Rounds, Rubio, Scott (FL), Scott (SC), Shelby, Sullivan, Thune, Tillis, Tuberville, Wicker, Young

. . .

The PRESIDENT pro tempore: On this vote, the yeas are fifty-six, the nays are forty-four. Pursuant to S. Res. 47, the Senate having voted in the affirmative on the foregoing question, the Senate shall proceed with the trial as provided under the provisions of that resolution.

DAY TWO

TRIAL OF DONALD J. TRUMP,
PRESIDENT OF THE UNITED STATES

MR. MANAGER RASKIN: MEMBERS OF THE SENATE, GOOD MORNING, GOOD DAY. Some people think this trial is a contest of lawyers or, even worse, a competition between political parties. It is neither. It is a moment of truth for America.

My late father, Marcus Raskin, once wrote: "Democracy needs a ground to stand upon. And that ground is the truth." America needs the truth about ex-President Trump's role in inciting the insurrection on January 6 because it threatened our government, and it disrupted—it easily could have destroyed—the peaceful transfer of power in the United States for the first time in 233 years.

It was suggested yesterday by President Trump's counsel that this is really like a very bad accident or a natural disaster, where lots of people get injured or killed, and society is just out looking for someone to blame. And that is a natural and normal human reaction, according to the President's counsel. But he says it is totally unfair in this case. President Trump, according to Mr. Castor, is essentially an innocent bystander who got swept up in this catastrophe but did nothing wrong.

In this assertion, Mr. Castor unerringly echoes his client, ex-President Trump, who declared after the insurrection that his conduct in the affair was "totally appropriate," and, therefore, we can only assume he could do and would do the exact same thing again because he said his conduct was totally appropriate.

So now the factual inquiry of the trial is squarely posed for us. The jurisdictional constitutional issue is gone. Whether you were persuaded by the President's constitutional analysis yesterday or not, the Senate voted to reject it. And so the Senate is now properly exercising its jurisdiction and sitting as a Court of Impeachment conducting a trial on the facts. We are having a trial on the facts.

THE FRAMERS OF THE CONSTITUTION REJECTED A JANUARY EXCEPTION

2017	JAN	FEB	MAR	APR	MAY	JUN	JUL	AUG	SEP	OCT	NOV	DEC
						IMPEACHABLE						

2018	JAN	FEB	MAR	APR	MAY	JUN	JUL	AUG	SEP	OCT	NOV	DEC
						IMPEACHABLE						

2019	JAN	FEB	MAR	APR	MAY	JUN	JUL	AUG	SEP	OCT	NOV	DEC
						IMPEACHABLE						

2020	JAN	FEB	MAR	APR	MAY	JUN	JUL	AUG	SEP	OCT	NOV	DEC
						IMPEACHABLE						

2021	JAN	NOT IMPEACHABLE?

The House says ex-President Donald Trump incited a violent insurrection against Congress and the Constitution and the people. The President's lawyers and the President say his conduct was totally appropriate, and he is essentially an innocent victim of circumstances, like the other innocent victims that we will see getting caught up in all of the violence and chaos, over the next several days. The evidence will be for you to see and hear and digest.

The evidence will show you that ex-President Trump was no innocent bystander. The evidence will show that he clearly incited the January 6 insurrection. It will show that Donald Trump surrendered his role as Commander in Chief and became the "inciter in chief" of a dangerous insurrection, and this was, as one of our colleagues put it so cogently on January 6 itself, the greatest betrayal of the presidential oath in the history of the United States. The evidence will show you that he saw it coming and was not remotely surprised by the violence. And when the violence inexorably and inevitably came as predicted and overran this body and the House of Representatives with chaos, we will show you that he completely abdicated his duty as Commander in Chief to stop the violence and protect the government and protect our officers and protect our people. He violated his oath of office to preserve, protect, and defend the Constitution, the government, and the people of the United States.

The evidence will show you that he assembled, inflamed, and incited his followers to descend upon the Capitol to "Stop the Steal," to block Vice President Pence and Congress from finalizing his opponent's election victory over him. It will show that he had been warned that these followers were prepared for a violent attack, targeting us at the Capitol through media reports, law enforcement reports,

and even arrests. In short, we will prove that the impeached President was no innocent bystander whose conduct was totally appropriate and should be a standard for
future Presidents, but that he incited this attack, and he saw it coming.

To us, it may have felt like chaos and madness, but there was method in the
madness that day. This was an organized attack on the counting of the electoral
college votes in joint session of the U.S. Congress under the Twelfth Amendment
and under the Electoral Count Act to prevent Vice President Mike Pence and to
prevent us from counting sufficient electoral college votes to certify Joe Biden's
victory of 306 to 232 in the electoral college—a margin that President Trump had
declared a landslide in 2016.

When my colleague Mr. Neguse speaks after me, he will set forth in detail the
exact roadmap of all the evidence in the case. My fellow House managers and I
will then take you through that evidence step-by-step so everyone can see exactly
how these events unfolded.

But I want to tell you a few key reasons right now that we know this case is
not about blaming an innocent bystander for the horrific violence and harm that
took place on January 6. This is about holding accountable the person singularly
responsible for inciting the attack. Let's start with December 12. You will see during this trial a man who praised and encouraged and cultivated violence. "We have
just begun to fight!" he says more than a month after the election has taken place,
and that is before the second Million MAGA March, a rally that ended in serious
violence and even a burning of a church.

And as the President forecasted, it was only the beginning. On December 19,
eighteen days before January 6, he told his base about where the battle would be
that they would fight next. January 6 would be "wild," he promised. "Be there, will
be wild!" said the President of the United States of America. And that, too, turned
out to be true. You will see in the days that followed, Donald Trump continued to
aggressively promote January 6 to his followers. The event was scheduled at the
precise time that Congress would be meeting in joint session to count the electoral
college votes and to finalize the 2020 Presidential election.

In fact, in the days leading up to the attack, you will learn that there were countless social media posts, news stories, and, most importantly, credible reports from
the FBI and Capitol Police that the thousands gathering for the President's Save
America March were violent, organized with weapons, and were targeting the
Capitol.

This mob got organized so openly because, as they would later scream in these
halls and as they posted on forums before the attack, they were sent here by the
President. They were invited here by the President of the United States of America.
And when they showed up, knowing of these reports that the crowd was angry and

they were armed, here is what Donald Trump told them. President Trump whipped the crowd into a frenzy, exhorting followers: "If you don't fight like hell, you're not going to have a country anymore." And then he aimed straight at the Capitol declaring: "You'll never take back our country with weakness. You have to show strength, and you have to be strong."

He told them to "fight like hell," and they brought us hell on that day. Incited by President Trump, his mob attacked the Capitol. This assault unfolded live on television before a horrified nation. According to those around him at the time, this is how President Trump reportedly responded to the attack that we saw him incite in public: Delight, enthusiasm, confusion as to why others around him weren't as happy as he was.

Trump incited the January 6 attack, and when his mob overran and occupied the Senate and attacked the House and assaulted law enforcement, he watched it on TV like a reality show. He reveled in it, and he did nothing to help us as Commander in Chief. Instead, he served as the "inciter in chief," sending tweets that only further incited the rampaging mob. He made statements lauding and sympathizing with the insurrectionists. At 4:17 p.m.—over three hours after the beginning of the siege—for the very first time, he spoke out loud—not on Twitter. He spoke out loud to the American people.

Here is what he said:

President TRUMP, January 6, 2021: I know your pain. I know your hurt.

So you might be saying: All right, the President is going to console us now. He is going to reassure America. He knows our pain. He knows we are hurt. We have just seen these horrific images of officers being impaled and smashed over the head. We have just been under attack for three hours.

But here is what he actually goes on to say:

President TRUMP: I know your pain. I know your hurt. We had an election that was stolen from us. It was a landslide election, and everyone knows it, especially the other side.

So you would think he is about to decry the mayhem and violence, the unprecedented spectacle of this mob attack on the U.S. Capitol, but he is still promoting the big lie that was responsible for inflaming and inciting the mob in the first place. If anyone ever had a doubt as to his focus that day, it was not to defend us; it was not to console us. It was to praise and sympathize and commiserate with the rampaging mob. It was to continue to act as "inciter in chief," not Commander in Chief, by telling the mob that their election had been stolen from them.

Even then, after that vicious attack, he continued to spread the big lie. And as everyone here knows, Joe Biden won by more than 7 million votes and 306 to 232 in the electoral college. But Donald Trump refused to accept his loss even after this attack, and he celebrated the people who violently interfered with the peaceful transfer of power, for the first time in American history, and did that at his urging.

And when he did, in this video, finally tell them to go home in peace, he added this message: We love you. You're very special.

Distinguished Members of the Senate, this is a day that will live in disgrace in American history; that is, unless you ask Donald Trump, because this is what he tweeted before he went to bed that night at 6:01 p.m.—not consoling the Nation, not reassuring everyone that the government was secure, not a single word that entire day condemning the violent insurrection. This is what he says: "These are the things and events that happen when a sacred landslide election victory is so unceremoniously & viciously stripped away from great patriots who have been badly & unfairly treated for so long. Go home with love & in peace. Remember this day forever!"

"These are the things and events that happen when a sacred landslide election victory is so unceremoniously & viciously stripped away from great patriots. . . ." In other words, this was all perfectly natural and foreseeable to Donald Trump. At the beginning of the day, he told you it was coming. At the end of the day, he basically says: I told you this would happen. And then he adds: "Remember this day forever!" But not as a day of disgrace, a day of horror and trauma, as the rest of us remember it, but as a day of celebration, a day of commemoration. And if we let it be, it will be a day of continuation, a call to action, and a rallying cry for the next rounds of insurrectionary justice because all of this was totally appropriate.

Senators, the stakes of this trial could not be more serious. Every American—young and old and in between—is invited to participate with us in this essential journey to find the facts and share the truth. Trials are public events in a democracy, and no trial is more public or significant than an impeachment trial. Because the insurrection brought shocking violence, bloodshed, and pain to the Nation's Capitol, and we will be showing relevant clips of the mob's attack on police officers and other innocent people, we do urge parents and teachers to exercise close review of what young people are watching here, and please watch along with them if you are allowing them to watch. The impeachment managers will try to give warnings before the most graphic and disturbing violence that took place is shown.

We believe that the managers' comprehensive and meticulous presentation will lead to one powerful and irresistible conclusion: Donald Trump committed a massive crime against our Constitution and our people and the worst violation of the Presidential oath of office in the history of the United States of America. For this, he was impeached by the House of Representatives, and he must be convicted by the United States Senate.

Before I close, I want to address a constitutional issue still lingering from yesterday's argument. The President, obviously, is still exploring ways to change the subject and talk about anything other than his responsibility for inciting the attack. We heard a lot yesterday about his claim that this incitement of the insurrection was perfectly appropriate because it is somehow protected by the First Amendment, and this little diversion caught my eye because I have been a professor of constitutional law and the First Amendment for decades. And as we will demonstrate over the course of the trial, the factual premise and the legal underpinnings of that claim are all wrong.

They present President Trump as merely like a guy at a rally expressing a political opinion that we disagree with, and now we are trying to put him in jail for it. That has nothing to do with the reality of these charges or his constitutional offense. The particular political opinions being expressed are not why we impeached the President and have nothing to do with it. It makes no difference what the ideological content of the mob was, and if we license and forgive incitement to violent insurrection by militant Trump followers this week, you can be sure there will be a whole bunch of new ideological flavors coming soon. As we will demonstrate with overwhelming evidence, portraying Trump as a guy on the street being punished for his ideas is a false description of his actions, his intent, and the role that he played on January 6, when he willfully incited an insurrectionary mob to riot at the Capitol.

Last week, 144 constitutional scholars, including Floyd Abrams, a ferocious defender of free speech; Charles Fried, President Reagan's Solicitor General; Steven Calabresi, the cofounder of the Federalist Society, released a statement calling the President's First Amendment arguments "legally frivolous"—"legally frivolous"—adding: "[W]e all agree that the First Amendment does not prevent the Senate from convicting President Trump and disqualifying him from holding future office." They went on to say: "No reasonable scholar or jurist could conclude that President Trump had a First Amendment right to incite a violent attack on the seat of the legislative branch, or then to sit back and watch on television as Congress was terrorized and the Capitol sacked." Incitement to violence is, of course, not protected by the First Amendment. That is why most Americans have dismissed Donald Trump's First Amendment rhetoric simply by referring to Justice Oliver Wendell Holmes's handy phrase: You can't shout "fire" in a crowded theater.

But even that time-honored principle doesn't begin to capture how off-base the argument is. This case is much worse than someone who falsely shouts "fire" in a crowded theater. It is more like a case where the town fire chief, who is paid to put out fires, sends a mob not to yell "fire" in a crowded theater but to actually set the theater on fire; and who then, when the fire alarms go off and the calls start flooding in to the fire department asking for help, does nothing but sit back, encourage the mob to continue its rampage, and watch the fire spread on TV, with glee and delight.

So then we say this fire chief should never be allowed to hold this public job again, and "you are fired, and you are permanently disqualified"—and he objects. And he says we are violating his free speech rights just because he is pro-mob or pro-fire or whatever it might be. Come on. I mean, you really don't need to go to law school to figure out what is wrong with that argument.

Here is the key. Undoubtedly, a private person can run around on the street expressing his or her support for the enemies of the United States and advocating to overthrow the United States Government. You have got a right to do that under the First Amendment, but if the President spent all of his days doing that, uttering the exact same words, expressing support for the enemies of the United States and for overthrowing the government, is there anyone here who doubts that this would be a violation of his oath of office to preserve, protect, and defend the Constitution of the United States and that he or she could be impeached for doing that?

Look, if you are President of the United States, you have chosen a side with your oath of office, and if you break it, we can impeach, convict, remove, and disqualify you permanently from holding any office of honor, trust, or profit under the United States. As Justice Scalia once said, memorably, "You can't ride with the cops and root for the robbers." And if you become "inciter in chief" to the insurrection, you can't expect to be on the payroll as Commander in Chief for the Union.

Trump was the President of the United States, and he had sworn to preserve, protect, and defend the Constitution. He had an affirmative, binding duty, one that set him apart from everyone else in the country, to take care that the laws be faithfully executed, including all the laws against assaulting Federal officers, destroying Federal property, violently threatening Members of Congress and the Vice President, interfering with Federal elections, and dozens of other Federal laws that are well known to all of you. When he incited insurrection on January 6, he broke that oath. He violated that duty. And that is why we are here today, and that is why he has no credible constitutional defense.

I will tell you a final, sad story in this kaleidoscope of sadness and terror and violence. One of our Capitol officers who defended us that day was a longtime veteran of our force, a brave and honorable public servant who spent several hours battling the mob as part of one of those blue lines defending the Capitol and our democracy. For several hours straight, as the marauders punched and kicked and mauled and spit upon and hit officers with baseball bats and fire extinguishers, cursed the cops and stormed our Capitol, he defended us, and he lived every minute of his oath of office. And afterward, overwhelmed by emotion, he broke down in the Rotunda, and he cried for fifteen minutes, and he shouted out: "I got called an n-word fifteen times today."

And then he reported: "I sat down with one of my buddies, another Black guy, and tears just started streaming down my face. [And] I said, 'What the [F], man? Is this America?'" That is the question before all of you in this trial: Is this America? Can our country and our democracy ever be the same if we don't hold accountable the person responsible for inciting the violent attack against our country, our Capitol, and our democracy and all of those who serve us so faithfully and honorably? Is this America? Mr. Neguse will now provide a roadmap, a roadmap of our evidentiary case.

. . .

Mr. Manager NEGUSE: Mr. President, distinguished Senators, counsel, like several of you, I am a child of immigrants. And as a son of immigrants, I believe firmly in my heart that the United States is the greatest Republic that this world has ever known. A hallmark of our Republic since the days of George Washington has been the peaceful transfer of power. For centuries, we have accepted it as fact.

Unfortunately, sadly, we know now that we can no longer take that for granted because, as Lead Manager Raskin explained, on January 6, the peaceful transition of power was violently interrupted when a mob stormed this Capitol and desecrated this Chamber. As you will see during the course of this trial, that mob was summoned, assembled, and incited by the former President of the United States, Donald Trump, and he did that because he wanted to stop the transfer of power so that he could retain power, even though he had lost the election. And when the violence erupted, when they were here in our building, with weapons, he did nothing to stop it. If we are to protect our Republic and prevent something like this from ever happening again, he must be convicted.

Now, I want to be very clear about what we will show you during the course of this trial. As my fellow managers present our case to you today, tonight, and tomorrow, it will be helpful to think about President Trump's incitement of insurrection in three distinct parts: provocation, the attack, and the harm. Let's start with the provocation. We will show, during the course of this trial, that this attack was provoked by the President, incited by the President, and, as a result, it was predictable, and it was foreseeable. And, of course, that makes sense. This mob was well orchestrated. Their conduct was intentional. They did it all in plain sight—proudly, openly, and loudly—because they believed, they truly believed that they were doing this for him; that this was their patriotic duty. They even predicted that he would protect them. And for the most part, they were right. In his unique role as Commander in Chief of our country and as the one person whom the mob was listening to and following orders from, he had the power to stop it, and he didn't.

Now, some have said that President Trump's remarks, his speech on January 6, was just a speech. Well, let me ask you this: when in our history has a speech led thousands of people to storm our Nation's Capitol with weapons, to scale the walls, break windows, kill a Capitol Police officer? This was not just a speech. It didn't just happen. And as you evaluate the facts that we present to you, it will become clear exactly where that mob came from, because here is the thing: President Trump's words, as you will see, on January 6 in that speech, just like the mob's actions, were carefully chosen. Those words had a very specific meaning to that crowd.

And how do we know this? Because in the weeks prior to, during, and after the election, he used the same words over and over and over again. You will hear over and over three things. . . . First, what Lead Manager Raskin referred to as the "big lie," that the "election was stolen, full of fraud, rigged." You will hear over and over him using that lie to urge his supporters to "never concede" and "stop the steal." Finally, you will hear the call to arms, that it was his supporters' patriotic duty to "fight like hell." To do what? To "stop the steal." To stop the election from being stolen by showing up in this very Chamber. To stop you. To stop us. I respectfully ask that you remember those three phrases as you consider the evidence today—"The election was stolen," "Stop the steal," and "Fight like hell"—because they did not just appear on January 6. Let me show you what I mean.

Let's start with the "big lie." You will see during this trial that the President realized, really by last spring, that he could lose, he might lose the election. So what did he do? He started planting the seeds to get some of his supporters ready by saying that he could only lose the election if it was stolen. In other words, really what he did was create a no-lose scenario: either he won the election, or he would have some angry supporters—not all but some—who believed that if he lost, the election had to be rigged, and they would be angry because he was telling Americans that their vote had been stolen. And in America, our vote is our voice. So his false claims about election fraud, that was the drumbeat being used to inspire, instigate, and ignite them, to anger them. Watch this clip:

> President TRUMP, October 26, 2020: Because we are not going to let this election be taken away from us. That's the only way they are going to win this. We are not going to let it happen.

> President TRUMP, later that same day: It is the only way we can be—it is the only way we can lose, in my opinion, is massive fraud.

We all know what happened after that. He lost. He lost the election. But remember, he had that no-lose scenario that I referenced earlier. He told his base that the election was stolen, as he had forecasted, and then he told them: Your election has been stolen, but you cannot concede. You must stop the steal.

> President TRUMP, December 2, 2020: You can't let another person steal that election from you. All over the country, people are together in holding up signs: Stop the Steal.

> President TRUMP, January 4, 2021: The Democrats are trying to steal the White House. You cannot let them. You just can't let them.

Now, while he is inciting his supporters, he is also simultaneously doing everything he possibly can to overturn the election.

First, he begins with the courts—a legitimate avenue, legitimate avenue—to challenge the election, but he ignores all of their adverse rulings when all of his claims are thrown out. Then he moves on to try to pressure State election officials to block the election results for his opponent even though he had lost in their States. You will hear my fellow managers discuss that in detail.

Then he tries to threaten State election officials to actually change the votes to make him the winner, even threatening criminal penalties if they refused. He had the Justice Department investigate his claims, and even they found no support for those claims. So he tried to persuade some members of his party in Congress to block the certification of his vote with attacks in public forums. When that failed, he tried to intimidate the Vice President of the United States of America to refuse to certify the vote and send it back to the States. None of it worked.

So what does he do, with his back against the wall, when all else has failed? He turned back to his supporters. He had already spent months telling them that the election was stolen, and he amplified it further. He turned it up a notch. He told them that they had to be ready not just to stop the steal but to fight like hell.

President TRUMP, August 17, 2020: We are going to fight for the survival of our nation.

President TRUMP, November 1, 2020: We are going to keep on fighting.

President TRUMP, December 5, 2020: We will never surrender, we will only win. Now is not the time to retreat. Now is the time to fight harder than ever before.

President TRUMP, January 4, 2021: We have to go all the way. We are going to fight like hell, I will tell you right now. We will not bend, we will not break, we will not yield. We will never give in. We will never give up. We will never back down. We will never, ever surrender.

You will see that in the months the President made these statements, people listened. Armed supporters surrounded election officials' homes. The Secretary of State for Georgia got death threats. Officials warned the President that his rhetoric was dangerous, and it was going to result in deadly violence. And that is what makes this so different, because when he saw firsthand the violence that his conduct was creating, he didn't stop it. He didn't condemn the violence. He incited it further, and he got more specific.

He didn't just tell them to fight like hell; he told them how, where, and when. He made sure they had advance notice, eighteen days' advance notice. He sent this "save the date" for January 6. He told them to march to the Capitol and fight like hell on January 6, as Lead Manager Raskin said, the exact same day we were certifying the election results. What time was that rally scheduled for? The exact same time that this Chamber was certifying the election results in joint session.

Haberman, Maggie. "Trump Told Crowd 'You Will Never Take Back Our Country With Weakness,'" *New York Times*, January 6, 2021; Otis, John and Engle, Jeremy. "Weekly News Quiz for Students: Capitol Riot, Senate Runoffs, College Football Champion," *New York Times*, January 12, 2021; Herrera, Allison. "Despite Capitol Violence, Markwayne Mullin Holds Firm in Objecting to Electoral College," KOSU, January 8, 2021; McEvoy, Jemima. "Report: FBI Office Warned of 'War' at U.S. Capitol Despite Claim Attack Was Unknown," *Forbes*, January 12, 2021

When did he conclude his speech? Literally moments before Speaker Pelosi had gaveled us into session.

Many of us were in the House during that joint session of Congress. I was sitting two rows behind Leader Schumer and Leader McConnell. I remember it vividly. And as we were standing there fulfilling our solemn oath to the Constitution, the President was finishing his speech just a couple of miles away. How did he conclude that infamous speech? With a final call to action. He told them to march down Pennsylvania Avenue, to come here; that it was their patriotic duty because the election had been stolen. And when they heard his speech, they understood his words and what they meant because they had heard it before.

Let's take just a minute and really look at his words on January 6 as he spoke at the Save America rally. Remember, I told you, you would hear three phrases: "The election was stolen," "Stop the steal," and "Fight like hell." Let's start with that first phrase.

President TRUMP, January 6, 2021: All of us here today do not want to see our election victory stolen. There has never been anything like this. It is a pure theft in American history. Everybody knows it. Make no mistake, this election was stolen from you, from me, and from the country.

Now, of course, each of you heard those words before. So had the crowd. The President had spent months telling his supporters that the election had been stolen, and he used this speech to incite them further, to inflame them, to stop the steal, to stop the certification of the election results.

President TRUMP, January 6, 2021: We will never give up, we will never concede. It doesn't happen. You don't concede when there's theft involved. And to use a favorite term that all of you people really came up with: We will stop the steal. We must stop the steal.

Finally, the President used the speech as a call to arms. It was not rhetorical. Some of his supporters had been primed for this over many months. As you will learn, days before this speech, as Lead Manager Raskin noted, there were vast reports across all major media outlets that thousands of people would be armed, that they would be violent. You will learn that Capitol Police and the FBI reported in the days leading up to the attack that thousands in the crowd would be targeting the Capitol specifically, that they had arrested people with guns the night before the attack on weapons charges. And this is what our Commander in Chief said to the crowd in the face of those warnings, right before they came here.

President TRUMP, January 6, 2021: We will not let them silence your voices. We're not going to let it happen. Not going let it happen.

(People chanting: Fight for Trump! Fight for Trump! Fight for Trump!)

President TRUMP. Thank you. And you have to get your people to fight because you'll never take back our country with weakness. You have to show strength, and you have to be strong. And we fight. We fight like hell. And if you don't fight like hell, you're not going to have a country anymore.

"You have to get your people to fight," he told them. Senators, this clearly was not just one speech. It didn't just happen. It was part of a carefully planned, months-long effort with a very specific instruction: Show up on January 6 and get your people to fight the certification. He incited it. It was foreseeable. And again, you don't have to take my word for it. The President's former Chief of Staff—he is a retired Marine, four-star general, was confirmed by this body to be the Secretary of Homeland Security, overwhelming vote—that man was John Kelly. On the day after the insurrection, he said this:

Mr. KELLY: You know, the president knows who he's talking to when he tweets or when he makes statements. He knows who he is talking to. He knows what he wants them to do. And the fact that he said the things, he has been saying the things he has been saying since the election, and encouraging people, there is no surprise, again, at what happened yesterday.

"No surprise." Think about that. "No surprise." The President had every reason to know that this would happen because he assembled the mob, he summoned the mob, and he incited the mob. He knew when he took that podium on that fateful morning that those in attendance had heeded the words, and they were waiting for his orders to begin fighting. And that, of course, brings me, my fellow managers, to what happened here in this building.

As Lead Manager Raskin stated, my colleagues are going to walk through the events of January 6 and the evidence in very great detail. They are painful to watch and to recount, and I am not going to repeat the evidence now. But I do want to be clear about what also happened during that terrible attack, and that is this: that President Trump, once again, failed us because when the violence erupted, when we and the law enforcement officials protecting you were under attack, as each of you were being evacuated from this Chamber from a violent mob, as we were being evacuated from the House, he could have immediately and forcefully intervened to stop the violence. It was his duty as Commander in Chief to stop the violence, and he alone had that power, not just because of his unique role as Commander in Chief but because they believed that they were following his orders. They said so.

(video montage featuring members of the January 6, 2021 crowd)

"President Trump! President Trump!" "Fight for Trump! Fight for Trump! Fight for Trump!" "We were invited by the President of the United States!" "I thought I was following my President. I thought I was following what we were called to do." "President Trump requested that we be in DC on the 6th."

You heard it from them. They were doing what he wanted them to do. They wouldn't have listened to you, to me, to the Vice President of the United States who they were attacking. They didn't stop in the face of law enforcement, police officers fighting for their lives to stop them.

They were following the President. He alone, our Commander in Chief, had the power to stop them, and he didn't. You will hear evidence tonight, tomorrow, throughout the trial, about his refusal as Commander in Chief to respond to numerous desperate pleas on the phone, across social media, begging him to stop the attack. And you will see his relentless attack on Vice President Pence, who was at that very moment hiding with his family as armed extremists were chanting, "Hang Mike Pence," calling him a traitor.

You will see that even when he did finally, three and a half hours into the attack, tell these people to go home in peace, he added, as Lead Manager Raskin said, I will quote: "You're very special. We love you."

Think for a moment—just a moment—of the lives lost that day, of the more than 140 wounded police officers, and ask yourself if, as soon as this had started, President Trump had simply gone onto TV, just logged onto Twitter and said "Stop the attack." If he had done so with even half as much force as he said "Stop the steal," how many lives would we have saved? Sadly, he didn't do that. At the end of the day, the President was not successful in stopping the certification. That we know, thanks to the bravery of our law enforcement and to the bravery of the Senators in this room, each of you who still fulfilled your constitutional duty even under the threat of mortal peril.

But there can be no doubt of the grave harm that he caused to our elected leaders; to us, our families; to all who work at the Capitol, our staff, your staff; to our brave Capitol police, who defend us tirelessly with little thanks, who believed that they had a Commander in Chief who would defend and protect them, [but who] instead put them in harm's way; to those killed for heeding his command; to our democracy and the system, which ensures that we have a President elected by the people; to our national security and our standing in the world.

The harm was real. The damage was real. Five people lost their lives on that terrible, tragic day. A woman was shot dead fifty feet from where we later certified the election results. And for those who question just how bad it was, criminal complaints recently unsealed by the Department of Justice are more than revealing. . . .

In the charging affidavit of one of the leaders of the Proud Boys, we learned that members of this group "said that they would have killed . . . Mike Pence if given the chance." In another, we learned of the tweet in real time, while they were in the building, stating: "We broke into the Capitol . . . we got inside, we did our part." . . . "We were looking for Nancy [Pelosi] to shoot her in the friggin' brain but we didn't find her."

And for anyone who suggests otherwise, these defendants themselves have told you exactly why they were here. You will see this in the trial, that in the halls of the Capitol, on social media, in news interviews, and in charging documents, they confirmed they were following the President's orders.*

You can see some of the statements on that screen, one who said: "Trump wants all able-bodied patriots." Another: "President Trump is calling us to FIGHT! . . . This isn't a joke." Another: "I thought I was following my President. I thought I was following what we were called to do. Our President wants us here. We wait and take orders from [the] President."

He made them believe, over many weeks, that the election was stolen and they were following his command to take back their country. As I prepared for today—yesterday, this trial—one memory that I couldn't shake: It was on the night of January 6 and the feeling of walking back onto the House floor and seeing many of you there. I remember us finishing our task at four in the morning, and as I walked off the floor, I was so grateful—so grateful—for the opportunity to thank the Vice President of the United States, Mike Pence, for his actions, for standing before us and asking us to follow our oath and our faith and our duty. We only got a couple of hours of sleep that morning.

Early the next day, I called my dad, who came to this country, as I mentioned, as an immigrant forty years ago, and I told him that the proudest moment, by far, of serving in Congress, for me, was going back on to the floor with each of you to

---

* On the screen, Senators saw clips of an indictment, a criminal complaint, and news stories from people who participated in the riots and stated that they were following Trump's direction.

finish the work that we had started. I am humbled to be back with you today. And just as on January 6, when we overcame that attack on our Capitol, on our country, I am hopeful that at this trial, we can use our resolve and our resilience to, again, uphold our democracy by faithfully applying the law, vindicating the Constitution, and holding President Trump accountable for his actions.

. . .

Mr. Manager RASKIN: Senators, Representatives Joaquin Castro and Eric Swalwell will now show the evidence of President Trump's long campaign to delegitimize his electoral defeat and to galvanize his supporters to help him retain his power at any cost. So we are going to go, at this point, step by step to explain the progression all the way up until the attack.

Mr. Manager CASTRO: Good afternoon, you all. My name is Joaquin Castro. I represent San Antonio in the United States Congress. There is a saying that "[a] lie can travel halfway around the world before the truth has a chance to put on its shoes." That was before the internet. The point of that saying is the lie can do incredible damage and destruction, and that is especially true when that lie is told by the most powerful person on Earth, our Commander in Chief, the President of the United States.

This attack did not come from one speech, and it didn't happen by accident. The evidence shows clearly that this mob was provoked over many months by Donald J. Trump. And if you look at the evidence, his purposeful conduct, you will see that the attack was foreseeable and preventable. I will start by discussing President Trump's actions leading up to the election when he set up his big lie.

Beginning in the spring of 2020, President Trump began to fall behind in the polls, and by July, President Trump had reached a new low. He was running fifteen points behind his opponent, and he was scared. He began to believe that he could legitimately lose the election, so he did something entirely unprecedented in the history of our Nation. He refused to commit to a peaceful transition of power. Here is what he said:

> Mr. Chris WALLACE, July 19, 2020: Can you give a direct answer? You will accept the election?
>
> Mr. TRUMP: I have to see. Look, I have to see. No, I'm not just going to just say yes. I'm not going to say no.
>
> Mr. WALLACE, September 23, 2020: Do you commit to making sure that there is a peaceful transfer of power?
>
> Mr. TRUMP: Get rid of the ballots and you'll have a very peaceful—there won't be a transfer, frankly. There will be a continuation.

Senators, the President of the United States said: "There won't be a transition of power, frankly. There will be a continuation." President Trump was given every opportunity to tell his supporters: "Yes, if I lose, I will peacefully transfer power to the next President." Instead, he told his supporters the only way he could lose the election is if it were stolen. In tweet after tweet, he made sweeping allegations about election fraud that couldn't possibly be true. But that was the point. He didn't care if things were true. He wanted to make sure that his supporters were angry, like the election was being ripped away from them.

On May 24, six months before the election, he tweeted: "It will be the greatest Rigged Election in history." How could he possibly know it would be the greatest rigged election in history six months before the election happened? And, on June 22, more of the same: "RIGGED 2020 ELECTION: IT WILL BE THE SCANDAL OF OUR TIMES!" Again—about an election that had not even happened. On July 30: "2020 will be the most INACCURATE & FRAUDULENT Election in history." Again, just big words with nothing to prove them, but he wanted to make his supporters believe that an election victory would be stolen from him and from them.

This was to rile up his base, to make them angry. Now, these were just a few of the many times President Trump tweeted about this, and he did it in speeches, in rallies, and on television, too.

> President TRUMP, July 31, 2020: This is going to be the greatest election disaster in history.

President TRUMP, August 17, 2020: Because the only way we are going to lose this election is if the election is rigged. Remember that.

President TRUMP, August 24, 2020: The only way they can take this election away from us is if this is a rigged election. We are going to win this election.

President TRUMP, September 24, 2020: It's a rigged election. That's the only way we are going to lose.

President TRUMP, October 8, 2020: But this will be one of the greatest fraudulent—most fraudulent elections ever.

This is clearly a man who refuses to accept the possibility or the reality in our democracy of losing an election, and there are dozens more tweets and speeches of Donald Trump spreading his lie, but you get the point. His supporters got the point as well. They firmly believed that, if he lost, it was because the election was rigged.

Interviewer, September 15, 2020: Will you accept the result if Joe Biden wins?

Unidentified Supporter: No.

Interviewer: Under any circumstances?

Unidentified Supporter: No.

Interviewer: Why is that?

Unidentified Supporter: Because it's lies and deceit and corruption.

Interviewer, September 24, 2020: Do you think that, when you get to election night or in the following days, if Biden winds up somehow becoming the winner—do you think it's rigged?

Second Unidentified Supporter: Oh, yes, very much so.

Interviewer, September 24, 2020: On election night—if it shows up that Joe Biden won—in your opinion, would that be the only way that Trump could lose, that it would be a rigged election? Is that the only way Joe Biden could win?

Third Unidentified Supporter: Absolutely. I agree with that because there's no way in heck our President is going to lose, but, yes, it would be a rigged election. There will be—some type of cheating went on, what have you, and I firmly believe that.

Now, all of us in this room have run for election, and it is no fun to lose. I am a Texas Democrat, and we have lost a few elections over the years, but can you imagine telling your supporters that the only way you could possibly lose is if an American election were rigged and stolen from you? Ask yourself whether you have ever seen anyone at any level of government make the same claim about their own election. But that is exactly what President Trump did.

He truly made his base believe that the only way he could lose was if the election were rigged. Senators, all of us know and all of understand how dangerous that is for our country, because the most combustible thing you can do in a democracy is convince people that an election doesn't count, that their voices and their votes don't count, and that it has all been stolen, especially if what you are saying are lies.

Let us turn now to the election. As you know, the results were not fully reported on election night, which is not unusual in our Nation's history. But by November 7, major news networks, including FOX News, reported that, once the remaining votes were counted, Joe Biden would be the likely victor.

So President Trump began urging his supporters to stop the count. I would imagine that, if we went around this room, there would be folks sitting here who started down on election night and ended up coming back up and winning their races. Perhaps that is why some of you are seated in this room today. But imagine if you were behind, and the results started coming in, and as you started pulling ahead, your opponent said: That's not fair. Stop the count while I am still ahead.

That is what Donald Trump did, but that is not how America works. Here, every vote counts. You don't just stop counting when one person is ahead. We count every vote. And let's be clear: President Trump knew that you just can't stop counting votes, but he wanted to inflame his base. There was a purpose behind this—to truly make them believe that counting votes would result in a stolen, rigged election.

He said at 12:49 a.m. on election night: "They are trying to STEAL the Election. We will never let them do it." A little over an hour later, at, roughly 2:30 in the morning, before all the votes were even close to being counted, he goes even further and actually declares victory. Take a look.

President TRUMP, November 4, 2020: This is a fraud on the American public. This is an embarrassment to our country. We were getting ready to win this election. Frankly, we did win this election.

"Frankly, we did win." Rather than calmly saying: "Let's count the votes. If there are legal issues, we will go to court, and we will resolve them." Instead, he told his supporters that he had actually won the election and that the whole thing was a fraud. He said that on November 4, and he has never renounced that statement since.

Despite President Trump's pressure at the time, election officials around the country continued to carry out their duties, and as votes were counted and his loss became more certain, he riled up his base further.

Take a look at these tweets. On November 5, he tweeted, in all capital letters, as if shouting commands: "STOP THE COUNT! STOP THE FRAUD!"

Senators, this is dangerous. I also want you to remember these tweets for another reason, because that is what it looks like when Donald Trump wants people to stop doing something. Bear in mind, this is not the President saying to his supporters that somebody stole your cup of coffee. This is the Commander in Chief telling his supporters, "Your election is being stolen, and you must stop the counting of American votes," and it worked. His words became their actions. His commands led to their actions.

Take a look at this. The same day as those tweets—the same day as those tweets—around one hundred Trump supporters showed up in front of the Maricopa County elections center in Phoenix, some of them carrying rifles, literally trying to intimidate officials to stop the count just as President Trump had commanded. Arizona Secretary of State Katie Hobbs said that protesters were "causing delay and disruption and preventing those employees from doing their job."

Let's call this what it was. We were facing a global pandemic, and workers were risking their health to ensure the integrity of our elections. President Trump's supporters were encircling them, trying to prevent them from doing their own jobs. This was dangerous, it was scary, and it was a blatant act of political intimidation. In Philadelphia, that same day, police investigated an alleged plot to attack the city's Pennsylvania Convention Center, where votes were being counted. Police took at least one man into custody who was carrying a weapon. This happened all over. In Atlanta, in Detroit, and in Milwaukee, his supporters used armed force to try to disrupt the lawful counting of votes because they bought into Trump's big lie that the election was stolen from them. President Trump's months of inflaming and inciting his supporters had worked. They believed it was their duty to, quite literally, fight to stop the count. So they showed up at election centers across the country to do just that.

> President TRUMP, November 4, 2020: This is a fraud on the American public. This is an embarrassment to our country. We were getting ready to win this election. Frankly, we did win this election.

> (People chanting: Yeah.) (People chanting: Stop the count.) (Unidentified man: They ain't taking it from us.)

> President TRUMP, November 5, 2020: We were winning in all the key locations by a lot, actually, and then our numbers started miraculously getting whittled away in secret.

(Unidentified man to crowd assembled outside Nevada election site: They will pay. They will be destroyed because America is rising.)

(Footage of physical fighting breaking out outside of another election center.)

And there it is. They had bought into his big lie. President Trump told his supporters over and over again, nearly every day, in dozens of tweets, speeches, and rallies, that their most precious right in our democracy—their voice, their vote—was being stripped away, and they had to fight to stop that. They believed him, and so they fought.

You may say: well, he didn't know that they would take up arms. But when he did know, when it was all over the news, President Trump didn't stop. As Mr. Swalwell will show, after Donald Trump lost, he became even more desperate and incited his base even further. He urged them again and again, with increasingly forceful language, to fight to stop the steal. Even as the certification got closer and he grew even more desperate, he gave them specific instructions on how, where, and when to fight to stop the steal. He told them to show up on January 6 and march to the U.S. Capitol to stop the certification of the election results, and he told them to come here and fight like hell. You will see, clearly, that this violent mob that showed up here on January 6 didn't come out of thin air. President Donald John Trump incited this violence, and that is the truth.

. . .

Mr. Manager SWALWELL: Mr. President, distinguished Senators, my name is Eric Swalwell, and I represent California's 15th Congressional District. Manager

Castro just told you about Donald Trump's lies and acts before the election, but to paraphrase Winston Churchill, that wasn't the end of his efforts. That wasn't the beginning of the end, but perhaps it was the end of the beginning. Here is what I mean.

You saw President Trump prime for months his supporters to believe that, if the election were lost, it only could have been so because it was rigged, but that took time, just like, to build a fire, it doesn't just start with the flames. Donald Trump, for months and months, assembled the tinder, the kindling—threw on logs for fuel—to have his supporters believe that the only way their victory would be lost was if it were stolen. So, that way, President Trump was ready, if he lost the election, to light the match. And on November 7, after all the votes were counted, President Trump did lose by seven million votes.

But for Donald Trump, all was not lost. He had a backup plan. Instead of accepting the results or pursuing legitimate claims, he told his base more lies. He doused the flames with kerosene. And this wasn't just some random guy at the neighborhood bar blowing off steam. This was our Commander in Chief. Day after day, he told his supporters false, outlandish lies that the victory—that the election outcome was taken and it was rigged. And he had absolutely no support for his claims, but that wasn't the point. He wanted to make his base angrier and angrier. And to make them angry, he was willing to say anything.

On November 15, he stated: "I concede NOTHING! We have a long way to go. This was a RIGGED ELECTION!" He doesn't say why the election is rigged. November 17, in a Twitter statement: "DEAD PEOPLE VOTED." That is it. No evidence, just "DEAD PEOPLE VOTED." November 28, Twitter statement: "We have found many illegal votes. Stay tuned!" This just wasn't true. He never found illegal votes. He didn't even try to pretend that he had evidence for that. And "stay tuned"? Well, that was all about inciting his base, not about bringing legitimate claims. It was about dramatizing the election to anger his supporters.

December 5, you see here he goes after the Governors of Arizona and Georgia, Governors from his own party, claiming that they weren't with him.* You see, Senators, he is casting this in combat terms; that either you are with him, making sure that he won the election, or you are fighting against him. These are just a few of the hundreds of Twitter statements that President Trump sent. And it wasn't just Twitter statements. As you will see, he was dialing into meetings, holding rallies,

---

* Senators saw Trump's tweet of December 5, 2020: "Between Governor @DougDucey of Arizona and Governor @BrianKempGA of Georgia, the Democrat Party could not be happier. They fight harder against us than do the Radical Left Dems. If they were with us, we would have already won both Arizona and Georgia . . . "

appearing on television, continuing to spread the big lie that his election victory was stolen.

> President TRUMP, November 25, 2020: People that were dead were signing up for ballots. Not only were they jumping in and putting in a ballot, but dead people were requesting ballots, and they were dead for years, and they were requesting ballots.

> President TRUMP, November 26, 2020: Dead people voting all over the place.

> President TRUMP, December 5, 2020: The alleged Biden margin of victory in several states is entirely accounted for by extraordinarily large midnight vote dumps. You saw them going up to the sky.

Massive "midnight vote dumps." "Dead people voting all over the place." He said there were votes "going up to the sky." This was never about pursuing legitimate claims. He was saying anything he could to trigger and anger his base so that they would fight like hell to overturn a legitimate election. And it worked.

Just as Manager Castro showed you, President Trump's supporters were taking up arms to stop the count. His message to "fight like hell" was having real consequences. In Michigan, you will recall that President Trump was attacking that State and its officials. He continued these attacks even after Michigan certified its votes.

> President TRUMP, November 26, 2020: Take a look at Michigan. Take a look at what they did with respect to counties, and then you get to Detroit and it's like more votes than people. Dead people voting all over the place.

> President TRUMP, December 5, 2020: You know I won almost every county in Michigan, almost every district. We should have won that state very easily. We have a similar type of governor, I think, but I'll let you know that in about a week.

He is literally telling them that there were more votes in Detroit than people. About 260 thousand people voted in Detroit. There are roughly 500 thousand registered voters in Detroit. There are approximately 670 thousand people living in the city. So, again, not true. But he needed to make these outlandish claims to truly make his supporters believe that their victory was stolen from them.

And it was working. A few days after these clips, on December 5, his supporters surrounded the Michigan Secretary of State's home.

> Unidentified Speaker, December 5, 2020, with crowd in front of a residential home: I'm just sharing our Secretary of State's house and . . .

> (People chanting repeatedly: "Stop the steal.")

Unidentified Speaker: You are a threat to democracy. You are a threat to free and honest elections.

Nine o'clock at night, the Secretary's family is inside; protestors have surrounded her home; and they are chanting that she is a felon. And, as we saw, when armed protestors showed up to follow President Trump's direction to stop the steal, this was not the first time that President Trump's supporters used threats and intimidation.

President Trump cannot say: "I didn't know what I was inciting." From what Manager Castro showed and what I just showed, there was plenty of evidence that his words had consequences, and if he wanted to stop it, he could stop it. You saw Mr. Castro read statement after statement from our Commander in Chief saying, "Stop the count." "Stop the steal." President Trump was never shy about using his platforms to try and stop something. He could have very easily told his supporters: "Stop threatening officials. Stop going to their homes. Stop it with the threats."

But each time, he didn't. Instead, in the face of escalating violence, he incited them further.

The next phase in the certification of results was the certification on December 14 of the electoral college votes. The night before, President Trump personally issued fourteen Twitter statements, with more false claims about the election being stolen and directing his supporters to make sure that "they cannot be certified."

He states here: "The RINOS"—The RINOS—"that run the state voting apparatus have caused us the problem of allowing the Democrats to so blatantly cheat in their attempt to steal the election, which we won overwhelmingly. We will never give up! In the face of threats to elected officials, this is his message."

And he calls them RINOS—Republicans in name only—and tells them to never give up. President Trump, to him, it was his supporters against anyone who would not overturn the election results so that President Trump could win. But on December 14, despite all of President Trump's efforts to stop, the electors cast their votes according to the will of the American people, and Joe Biden was certified as having won 306 electoral college votes.

The day after this occurred, Leader McConnell recognized this, stating: "Many of us hoped that the presidential election would yield a different result, but our system of government has processes to determine who will be sworn in on January 20. The Electoral College has spoken."

As Manager Castro said, no one here, no one among us wants to lose an election. Sometimes there is a reason to dispute an election. Sometimes the count is close. Sometimes we ask for a recount or we go to court. That is entirely appropriate.

But what President Trump did was different. What President Trump did was the polar opposite of what any of us would do if we lost an election, because once the outcome is clear and a judge rules, we concede. We recognize the will of the American people because we let the people decide. And that is what all of the courts, the Justice Department, and the fifty States that had counted the votes— they said it was time for a peaceful transition of power because that is what our Constitution and rule of law demands.

Except President Trump. He directed all of the rage that he had incited to January 6. That was his last chance to stop the peaceful transition of power. And that brings us to the attack. Manager Castro told you the power of the lie—especially when the lie comes from the most powerful person in the world, the Commander in Chief. It also helps if you spend millions of dollars to amplify that lie. You will see here, in mid-December, President Trump announced the release of ads, including ones entitled "The Evidence is Overwhelming—FRAUD!" "STOP THE STEAL."

He spent $50 million from his legal defense fund on these ads to stop the steal and amplify his message. They were released nationally, played in video ads, online advertising, and targeted text messages. They used the same words and phrases that President Trump had been spreading for months; that the election was full of "fraud," to "stop the steal." But now they had a specific purpose. How do we know that purpose? These ads were designed to run all the way up to January 5, and then they stopped. This was purposeful and deliberate planning to target his base to rally around that day.

And it wasn't just his ads. He continued to use his own platform. He told his supporters, who truly believed their victory had been stolen and were ready to fight, when, where, and how to stop what he believed was a steal. Donald Trump would issue a deliberate call to action, and just like in his ads, that action was centered around January 6. On December 19, at 1:42 in the morning, our Commander in Chief tweeted: "Big protest in D.C. on January 6th. Be there, will be wild!"

We know why he picked this day. It wasn't random. It was his last chance to stop a peaceful transition of power, and he gave his supporters plenty of time to plan. This was the save-the-date sent out eighteen days before the event on January 6, and it wasn't a casual one-off reference or a single invitation. For the next eighteen days, Donald Trump would make sure to remind them over and over and over to show up on January 6. And he would tell them exactly what he wanted them to do.

On December 26, he tweets: "If a Democrat Presidential Candidate had an Election Rigged & Stolen, with proof of such acts at a level never seen before, the Democrat Senators would consider it an act of war, and fight to the death. Mitch & the Republicans do NOTHING, just want to let it pass. NO FIGHT!"

He is saying that the Republicans are doing nothing and have no fight because you are doing your job, taking on the constitutional process of certifying the electoral college results. And he also suggests, President Trump, that if this was the reverse and the Democrats had lost, it would be an act of war—an act of war. That is how Donald Trump prepared his supporters for January 6.

He even stated again, fourteen minutes later, to make sure his supporters understood: "The 'Justice' Department and the FBI have done nothing about the 2020 Presidential Election Voter Fraud, the biggest SCAM"—all caps—"in our nation's history, despite overwhelming evidence. They should be ashamed." And then he adds: "History will remember. Never give up. See everyone in D.C. on January 6th."

That phrase, "history will remember," was the only time—the first time—Donald Trump had used it in his Presidency, and he sent this to 70-plus million Twitter followers the day they needed to show up and be ready to fight. On December 27, he reminds them again: "Don't miss it. Information to follow!"

A few days later, December 30, all caps, "SEE YOU IN DC!" This continues all the way up to January 6. On January 1, he states: "The BIG Protest Rally in Washington . . . will take place at 11:00 A.M. . . . Locational details to follow. StopTheSteal!" You will see that an hour later President Trump retweeted one of his Twitter followers. That follower was Kylie Kremer, executive director of Women for America First, the group organizing the January 6 rally and the creator of the Facebook group Stop the Steal. Kremer tweeted: "The [cavalry] is coming, Mr. President!" referring to the cavalry showing up on January 6. She also added a website for supporters to RSVP and made clear what the message was: "#StopTheSteal."

And what did President Trump say in response to hearing that the cavalry was coming? "A great honor!" he wrote back. This wasn't just a single tweet. He and his organizers would do this over and over repeatedly. On January 3, another supporter tweets: "We have been marching all around the country for you Mr. President. Now we will bring it to DC on Jan 6 and PROUDLY stand beside you! Thank you for fighting for us."

When President Trump reposted her tweet, she wrote back: "BEST DAY EVER!!! Thank you . . . for the retweet! It has been an honor to stand up and fight for you and our nation. We will be standing strong on Jan 6th in DC with you! We are bringing the [cavalry] Mr. President." "We are bringing the cavalry." That was the consistent message. This was not just any old protest. President Trump was inciting something historic. The cavalry was coming, and he was organized. In her post, Ms. Lawrence tagged Kylie Kremer, the organizer of the event, whose post we just saw President Trump retweet. Again, you see this is all connected. I won't show you all the Twitter statements—and there are a lot—but here's one more. President Trump retweeted another of Ms. Kremer's posts, which had all the details of January 6 with the same hashtags: #MarchForTrump, #DoNotCertify, #StopTheSteal.

And in response, President Trump, he writes back: "I will be there. Historic day!"

Before Congress, I prosecuted violent crimes in California as an Alameda County deputy district attorney. And when you investigate and prosecute violent crimes, you have to distinguish: Was this a heat-of-passion crime? Or was it something more deliberate, planned, premeditated? The evidence here on this count is overwhelming. President Trump's conduct leading up to January 6 was deliberate, planned, and premeditated.

This was not one speech, not one tweet. It was dozens in rapid succession with the specific details. He was acting as part of the host committee. In fact, when he had assembled his inflamed mob in D.C., he warned us that he knew what was coming. This was President Trump's statement the night before the attack—I should say this was one of his dozens of statements on Twitter in the hours leading up to the attack: "I hope the Democrats, and even more importantly, the weak and ineffective RINO section of the Republican Party, are looking at the thousands of people pouring into D.C. They won't stand for a landslide . . . victory to be stolen. @senatemajldr @JohnCornyn @SenJohnThune."

"Thousands of people pouring into D.C. [who] won't stand for the landslide election to be stolen"—it's all right there. And he tags Senators to pressure you to stop [the electoral vote certification], and he warns all of us that his thousands of supporters—whom you will see that the FBI had warned were armed and targeting the Capitol—won't stand for us certifying the results of the election.

This was never about one speech. He built this mob over many months with repeated messaging until they believed that they had been robbed of their votes and they would do anything to stop the certification. He made them believe that their victory was stolen and incited them so he could use them to steal the election for himself.

President TRUMP, November 29, 2020: This election was rigged.

Unidentified Supporter at Texas rally for Trump, January 5, 2021: This is tyranny against the people of the United States, and we are not standing for it any more.

President TRUMP, December 2, 2020: If we don't root out the fraud—the tremendous and horrible fraud that has taken place in our 2020 election, we don't have a country anymore.

President TRUMP, December 5, 2020: The Left lies. They cheat, and they steal. They are ruthless, and they are hell-bent on getting power and control by any means necessary.

Footage from pro-Trump rallies in different states: (People chanting and screaming.) (Police: Move back. Move back.) (People chanting: Stop the steal.)

President TRUMP, December 5, 2020: Can't let it happen.

President TRUMP, January 4, 2021: The Democrats are trying to steal the White House. You cannot let them. (People chanting: Fight for Trump.)

"You can't let it happen." "Never concede." "Fight," he told them in speech after speech. These crowds were ready to fight. This is what President Trump was inciting. He foresaw what was coming, and this is what he deliberately led to our doorstep on January 6.

I want to be clear. During this trial, when we talk about the violent mob during the attack, we do not mean every American who showed up at President Trump's rally. Certain Americans came to protest peacefully, as is their right. That is what makes our country so great—to debate freely, openly, and peacefully our differences, just like all of you were attempting to do in this very room on January 6.

But what President Trump did was different. He didn't tell his supporters to fight or be strong in a casual reference. He repeatedly, over months, told them to fight for a specific purpose. He told them their victory was stolen, the election was rigged, and their patriotic duty was to fight to stop the steal. And he repeated this messaging even after he saw the violence it was inciting. And when they were primed and angry and ready to fight, he escalated and channeled their rage with a call to arms: Show up on January 6 at the exact time the votes of the American people were being counted and certified, and then march to the Capitol, and "fight like hell."

He told this to thousands of people who were armed to the teeth, targeting us and determined to stop the electoral college count. What our Commander in Chief did was wildly different from what anyone here in this room did to raise election concerns. This was a deliberate, premeditated incitement to his base to attack our Capitol while the counting was going on. And it was foreseeable, especially to President Trump, who warned us he knew what was coming. This is what the evidence has overwhelmingly shown and will show in this trial, and it is also the truth.

. . .

Ms. Manager MADELEINE DEAN: Mr. President, esteemed Members of the Senate, it is my solemn honor to be before you today. I am Madeleine Dean, Congresswoman from the Fourth Congressional District of Pennsylvania. I am a lawyer. I am a former professor of writing. I am a sister. I am a wife. I am a mother. I

am a grandmother to three, with a fourth on her way. I am a person of faith. And I am an American.

Along with Manager Lieu, I will present the actions of a desperate President, and we will present evidence today of a class of public servants who, standing up to enormous pressure from the President of the United States, did the right thing and upheld their oaths. My colleagues just presented evidence of President Trump's months-long effort to incite his base, leading them to believe the election was stolen, that they needed to fight like hell to stop the steal on January 6.

These weren't President Trump's only efforts to overturn the results. Manager Lieu and I will present evidence of President Trump's relentless, escalating campaign to fabricate an election victory by ignoring adverse court rulings, pressuring and threatening election officials, attacking Senators and Members of Congress, pressuring the Justice Department, and finally bullying his own Vice President. President Trump and his allies filed sixty-two separate lawsuits in Federal courts across more than half a dozen States and the District of Columbia, including Pennsylvania, my home State, as well as Arizona, Georgia, Michigan, Minnesota, Nevada, and Wisconsin. Of the sixty-two postelection legal challenges, he lost sixty-one. Only one was successful, and that case involved ballot curing in Pennsylvania and had no impact on President Biden's 80,555-vote victory in our Commonwealth.

To be clear, not a single court, not a single judge agreed that the election results were invalid or should be invalidated. Instead, court after court reviewing these challenges said these cases were "not credible," "without merit," "based on nothing but speculation," and "flat out wrong." The judiciary resoundingly rejected Trump's fraud allegations and upheld the election results, but it was more than that.

The court said these cases were different; they were dangerous to our democracy. For an example, in an opinion by United States District Court Judge Matthew Brann from Pennsylvania, he said: "[T]his Court has been presented with strained legal arguments without merit and speculative accusations. . . . In the United States of America, this cannot justify the disenfranchisement of a single voter, let alone all the voters of its sixth most populated state. Our people, [and] laws, and institutions demand more. Because this Court has no authority to take away the right to vote of even a single person, let alone millions of citizens, it cannot grant Plaintiff's requested relief."

That decision by Judge Brann was affirmed on appeal by Judge Stephanos Bibas, a Trump appointee who agreed and wrote: "The Campaign's claims have no merit. The number of ballots it specifically challenges is far smaller than the roughly 81,000-vote margin of victory. And it never claims fraud or that any of the votes were cast by illegal voters. Plus, tossing out millions of mail-in ballots would be drastic and unprecedented, disfranchising a huge swath of the electorate and upsetting all down-ballot races."

Similarly, as Judge Linda Parker of the Eastern District of Michigan framed it—she said: "[S]tunning in its scope and breathtaking in its reach. If granted, the relief would disenfranchise the votes of . . . more than 5.5 million Michigan citizens who, with dignity, [and] hope, and a promise of a [vote], participated in the 2020 General Election."

Donald Trump told his supporters: "They are stealing the election. They took away your vote. It is rigged." That was not true. According to judge after judge, the truth was exactly the opposite. Trump was not suing to ensure election integrity; he was pursuing lawsuits that would, in effect, strip away American votes so that he could win. In other words, Donald Trump was asking the judiciary to take away votes from Americans so that he could steal the election for himself.

Then, after losing in all the courts, Trump turned to another tactic: pressuring and threatening election officials. You saw what happened in Michigan after Trump attacked the State and its election officials. His supporters surrounded the secretary of state's home, as you saw in the earlier slide, chanting, calling her a felon. On November 17, the Board of Canvassers for Wayne County, Michigan, home to Detroit, unanimously certified the election results for Biden. That same night, after their vote to certify the results, Trump called the two Republican members of that board, pressuring them to change their minds.

The call worked. The next day, both Monica Palmer and William Heartmann, the Republican board members, attempted to rescind their vote to certify Michigan's election results, but they simply couldn't. President Trump didn't stop there. He then contacted majority leader of the Michigan Senate, Mike Shirkey, and the speaker of the Michigan House, Lee Chatfield, to lobby them to overturn Michigan's results. Trump invited Mr. Chatfield and Mr. Shirkey to Washington to meet with him at the White House, where the President lobbied them further. Let's be clear. Donald Trump was calling officials, hosting them at the White House, urging them to defy the voters in their State and instead award votes to Trump.

The officials held strong, and so Trump moved on to a different State, my home State of Pennsylvania. I am certain my Senators, Casey and Toomey, remember what happened there. In early December, as he did in Michigan, he began calling election officials, including my former colleagues in the Pennsylvania Legislature, Republicans, Majority Leader Kim Ward and Speaker of the House Bryan Cutler. Majority Leader Ward said the President called her to "declare there was a fraud in the voting." Then, on November 25, President Trump phoned in to a Republican state senate policy hearing, trying to convince the Republican legislators, senators, and house members there had been a fraud in the vote. He even had his lawyer hold a phone up to the microphone in that hearing room so the committee could hear him. Here is what he said:

President TRUMP, to attendees at a Pennsylvania Republican state senate policy hearing: We can't let that happen. We can't let it happen for our country. And this election has to be turned around because we won Pennsylvania by a lot, and we won all of these swing States by a lot.

This was a gathering—I have attended many, I have to tell you, as a former State legislator, a lot of policy hearings. I have to say with some confidence, that was likely the first time a President of the United States of America called in to a State legislative policy hearing. And, remember, here is the President saying he won Pennsylvania, and Pennsylvania had been certified, that Biden had won by more than 80,000 votes. Less than a week after calling in to that meeting, he invited multiple Republican members of the Pennsylvania Legislature to the White House—the same scheme he had used on the Michigan legislators. It didn't work with those public servants either.

Think about it. The President of the United States was calling public officials, calling from the White House, inviting them into the Oval Office, telling them to disenfranchise voters of their State, telling them to overturn the will of the American people. All so he could take the election for himself. And then in Georgia, a State Trump had counted on for victory, his conduct was perhaps the most egregious. On November 11, Republican Secretary of State Brad Raffensperger confirmed that he believed ballots were accurately counted for Biden. Trump went on a relentless attack.

Here are just a few examples. In all, Trump tweeted at Raffensperger seventeen times in the coming weeks—there are just a few—calling him a "disaster," "obstinate," not having a clue, being played for a fool, and being a "so-called Republican," all because Raffensperger was doing his job, ensuring the integrity of our elections. And these attacks had consequences. Mr. Raffensperger and his family received death threats: "Your husband deserves to face a firing squad." "You better not botch this recount." "Your life depends [upon] it." "The Raffenspergers should be put on trial for treason and face execution." Just some of the threats they received.

After these death threats, on November 25, Mr. Raffensperger wrote an op-ed, where he said: "My family voted for [Trump], donated to him and are now being thrown under the bus by him." But he also noted: "Elections are the bedrock of our democracy. They need to be run fairly and, perhaps more [importantly], impartially. That's not partisan. That's just American."

It is important to remember that this wasn't just a random attack. Trump wasn't just criticizing a politician over policy or saying he didn't agree. Donald Trump was savagely attacking a Secretary of State because the official did his job and certified the State according to how the people in that State voted. Donald Trump was trying to undermine our elections by taking votes away from the American people so that he could remain President, and he was willing to blame and betray anyone—anyone—even his own supporters, if they got in the way.

Remember, Senators, those threats were to Mr. Raffensperger's family. So some may say Trump didn't know his attacks against Mr. Raffensperger would result in death threats—except that all of this was very public. The Secretary published his op-ed in *USA Today*, and major networks, including FOX, covered the threats against the Raffenspergers. What did Trump do? Did he stop? Did he say: "No, no, supporters; that isn't what I meant"? No. He doubled down. Let's see the evidence.

President TRUMP, November 26, 2020: This was a massive fraud. This should never take place in this country. We're like a third world country. Look at—look at Georgia. But I understand the secretary of state who is really, uh, he's an enemy of the people. The secretary of state—and whether he's Republican or not, this man, what he's done. . . .

President TRUMP, November 29, 2020: . . . this character in Georgia, who is a disaster.

Let that sink in. A Republican public servant doing his job, whose family had just received death threats, and the President of the United States labeled him "an enemy of the people." And that is why this is different, because this was not just one attack or one comment. This was attack after attack in the face of clear threats of violence. And on December 1, another official, Gabriel Sterling, a Republican who voted for Trump, made this point and appealed directly to our President to stop his dangerous conduct:

> Mr. STERLING, December 1, 2020: Mr. President, it looks like you likely lost the State of Georgia. We're investigating. There's always a possibility—I get it—and you have the right to go through the courts. What you don't have the ability to do—and you need to step up and say this—is stop inspiring people to commit potential acts of violence. Someone's going to get hurt, someone's going to get shot, someone's going to get killed.

Mr. Sterling put this perfectly. In this country, we can appropriately challenge a close count or go to the courts or disagree with others or make bold statements, but what Trump was doing was different. Someone's going to get hurt, someone's going to get shot, someone's going to get killed.

Mr. Sterling saw what Trump's conduct was fomenting. He warned him on live TV that violence was already happening and that more violence was foreseeable and inevitable. Sterling's pleas were played over and over on every network. Rather than heed that warning, Trump escalated again. In early December, Trump called Brian Kemp, the Governor of Georgia, and pressured him to hold a special session of the State legislature to overturn the election results and to appoint electors who would vote for Trump.

A few weeks later, on December 23, Trump called the chief investigator for the Georgia Bureau of Investigation, who was conducting an audit, an audit of the signature-matching procedures for absentee ballots. Trump urged him, "[F]ind the fraud," and claimed the official would be a "national hero" if he did.

Let's call this what it is. He was asking the official to say there was evidence of fraud when there wasn't any. The official refused, and the investigation was completed. And on December 29, Raffensperger announced that the audit found "no fraudulent absentee ballots" with a "99 percent confidence" level.

On January 3, Trump tweeted about a call he had with Georgia election officials the day before. He said: "I spoke to Secretary of State Brad Raffensperger yesterday about Fulton County and voter fraud in Georgia. He was unwilling, or unable, to answer questions such as the 'ballots under the table' scam, ballot destruction, out of state 'voters', dead voters, and more. He has no clue!"

On January 5, the *Washington Post* released a recording of that call which had occurred on January 2—remember, just four days before the attack on the Capitol. Here is what President Trump said:

President TRUMP, January 2, 2020: It's more illegal for you than it is for them because you know what they did and you're not reporting it. That's the—you know, that's a criminal—that's a criminal offense. And you know, you can't let that happen. That's—that's a big risk to you and to Ryan, your lawyer. That's a big risk.

Let's be clear. This is the President of the United States telling a Secretary of State that if he does not find votes, he will face criminal penalties. And not just any number of votes. Donald Trump was asking the Secretary of State to somehow find the exact number of votes Donald Trump lost the State by.

Remember, President Biden won Georgia by 11,779 votes. In his own words, Trump said: "All I want to do is this. I just want to find 11,780 votes." He wanted the Secretary of State to somehow find the precise number, plus one, so that he could win. Here is what he said.

President TRUMP, January 2, 2020: So, look, all I want to do is this. I just want to find 11,780 votes, which is one more than we have.

He says it right there, the President of the United States, telling a public official to manufacture the exact votes needed so he can win.

Senators, we must not become numb to this.

Trump did this across State after State, so often, so loudly, so publicly. Public officials like you and me received death threats and calls threatening criminal penalties, all because Trump wanted to remain in power. These public officials exercised great political and personal courage in the face of unprecedented pressure from a President of the United States. Senators, ours is a dialogue with history, a conversation with the past, with a hope for the future. Senators, I thank you today for your kind attention.

. . .

Mr. Manager LIEU: Good afternoon. I am Congressman Ted Lieu. My colleague Congresswoman Dean went through President Trump's efforts to overturn the election through the courts and, when that started failing, his deeply disturbing attacks on State and local officials. I am going to walk through President Trump's extraordinary efforts remaining until January 6, when he tried again to overturn the election.

I first want to highlight Representative Raskin's question to all of you today: Is this America? Like all of you, I love this country. I am an immigrant. My parents came to Ohio, and we started off living in the basement of a person's home. We were poor, and they went to flea markets to sell gifts to make ends meet. Over many years, they built a small business, opened six gift stores, and achieved

the American dream. That is one reason I joined the United States Air Force on Active Duty.

I believe America is an exceptional country. I was trained as a prosecutor at Maxwell Air Force Base in Alabama, and I remain in the Reserves because we are the greatest country in the world. But how did our exceptional country get to the point where a violent mob attacked our Capitol, murdering a police officer, assaulting over 140 other officers? How did we get to the point where rioters desecrated, defiled, and dishonored your Senate Chamber, where the very place in which you sit became a crime scene, and where National Guard troops still patrol outside wearing body armor? I will show you how we got here.

President Donald J. Trump ran out of nonviolent options to maintain power. After his efforts in courts and threatening officials failed, he turned to privately and publicly attacking Members of his own party in the House and in the Senate. He would publicly bait Senators, naming them in social media.

For example, on December 18, President Trump named "@senatemajldr and Republican Senators," telling them they "have to get tougher" or they "won't have a Republican Party anymore. We won the Presidential Election, by a lot. FIGHT FOR IT. Don't let them take it away!" President Trump was suggesting to Members of this Senate that if they didn't help him try to overturn the election, there would be consequences.

On December 24, President Trump wrote: "I saved at least 8 Republican Senators, including Mitch, from losing in the last Rigged (for President) Election. Now they (almost all) sit back and watch me fight against a crooked and vicious foe, the Radical Left Democrats. I will"—and in all capital letters he wrote—"NEVER FORGET!"

President Trump was telling you that you owe him; that if you don't help him fight to overturn the results, he will never forget and that there will be consequences. These are threats, just like the threats he made to State and local officials.

And it continued. On December 29, President Trump tweeted: "Can you imagine if the Republicans stole a Presidential Election from the Democrats—All hell would break out. Republican leadership only wants the path of least resistance. Our leaders (not me, of course!) are pathetic. They only know how to lose! P.S. I got MANY Senators and Congressmen/Congresswomen Elected. I do believe they forgot!"

President Trump targeted Senators and Members of Congress on social media, calling them pathetic for letting the election get "stolen" from them. On January 4, two days before the attack, President Trump tweeted: "The 'Surrender Caucus' within the Republican Party will go down in infamy as weak and ineffective 'guardians' of our Nation, who were willing to accept the certification of fraudulent presidential numbers!" Now he is mocking some Republican Members as the "Surrender Caucus," calling them "weak and ineffective guardians of our Nation" because they would not pretend that he had won when, in fact, he had not. And then, the very day before the attack, President Trump's threats were even more heated and specific toward Republicans that he considered to be part of that "Surrender Caucus."

Now, we have shown you this tweet before, but I want to draw your attention to how the President was not just inciting his base but how he was also calling out specific Senate Republicans at the end of this tweet.* This is a specific warning to anyone who won't help him overturn the results. Anyone who was against the President became an enemy.

And let me be very clear. The President wasn't just coming for one or two people or Democrats like me; he was coming for you, for Democratic and Republican Senators. He was coming for all of us, just as the mob did at his direction. In addition to going after Senators and Members of Congress, President Trump also pressured our Justice Department to investigate the false claims that the election was stolen. At the President's direction, Attorney General William Barr, a loyal member of the President's Cabinet, authorized Federal prosecutors to pursue "substantial allegations of voting and vote tabulation irregularities."

Bill Barr pursuing these allegations sparked an outcry. Sixteen assistant U.S.

---

* On the screen was Trump's January 5, 2021 tweet: "I hope the Democrats, and even more importantly, the weak and ineffective RINO section of the Republican Party, are looking at the thousands of people pouring into D.C. They won't stand for a landslide election victory to be stolen. @senatemajldr @JohnCornyn @SenJohnThune"

attorneys in the Trump administration urged the Attorney General to cease investigations because they had not seen evidence of any substantial anomalies. That means they did not find any evidence of real fraud. Attorney General Barr pursued the investigation anyway, and after his investigation, this is what he found: "[W]e have not seen fraud on a scale that could have effected a different outcome in the election."

Two weeks later, on December 14, the electors voted to give Joe Biden 306 electoral votes and ensured his victory. The following day, Bill Barr resigned. Attorney General Barr had loyally served President Trump. He had never publicly come out against the President. But for Bill Barr, making up election fraud claims and saying the election was stolen was a bridge too far. Bill Barr made clear that attempting to overturn election results crossed a line. According to a news report, Bill Barr, the highest law enforcement official in the land, told President Donald Trump to his face that his theories of election fraud were "bullshit."

When Bill Barr resigned, his former deputy Jeff Rosen took his place. President Trump initially tweeted about Mr. Rosen that he was "an outstanding person" when he announced that he would become Acting Attorney General, but when Rosen took over, President Trump put the same pressure on him that he had done with State officials and Members of Congress, U.S. Senators, and his former Attorney General. President Trump reportedly summoned Acting Attorney General Rosen to the Oval Office the next day and pressured Rosen to appoint special counsels to keep investigating the election, including unfounded accusations of widespread voter fraud, and also to investigate Dominion, the voting machines firm.

According to reports, Mr. Rosen refused. He maintained that he would make decisions based on the facts and the law and reminded President Trump what he had already been told by Attorney General Bill Barr that the Department had already investigated and "found no evidence of widespread fraud." But President Trump refused to follow the facts and the law, so the President turned to someone he knew would do his bidding.

He turned to Jeffrey Clark, another Justice Department lawyer, who had allegedly expressed support for using the Department of Justice to investigate the election results. Shortly after Acting Attorney General Rosen followed his duty—and the law—to refuse to reopen investigations, President Trump intended to replace Mr. Rosen with Mr. Clark, who could then try to stop Congress from certifying the electoral college results.

According to reports, White House Counsel Pat Cipollone advised President Trump not to fire Acting Attorney General Rosen. Department officials had also threatened to resign en masse if he had fired Rosen. President Trump's actions time and time again made clear that he would do anything and pressure anyone if it meant overturning the election results. We watched President Trump use any means necessary to pursue this aim, feverishly grasping for straws at retaining his hold on the Presidency, but all his efforts prior to January 6 kept failing.

Finally, in his desperation, he turned on his own Vice President. He pressured Mike Pence to violate his constitutional oath and to refuse to certify the vote. President Trump had decided that Vice President Pence, who presided over the certification, could somehow stop it. As Pence later confirmed, the Vice President does not have that power in the Constitution. And President Trump never tried to explain why he thought the Vice President could block the certification of the election results; he just began relentlessly attacking the Vice President.

Publicly, President Trump attacked Pence on social media and at rallies, getting his supporters to believe that Mike Pence could stop the certification on January 6. Here is what President Trump said in Georgia on January 4.

> President TRUMP, January 4, 2020: And I hope Mike Pence comes through for us, I have to tell you. I hope that our great Vice President, our great Vice President comes through for us. He's a great guy. Of course, if he doesn't come through, I won't like him quite as much.

Behind closed doors, President Trump applied significant pressure to his second-in-command. Multiple reports confirmed that President Trump used his personal attorneys and other officials to pressure the Vice President. Trump reportedly told almost anyone who called him to also call the Vice President. According to reports, when Mike Pence was in the Oval Office, President Trump would call people to try to get them to convince the Vice President to help him.

And President Trump kept repeating the myth that Pence could stop the certification to his base to anger them, hoping to intimidate Mike Pence. On the morning of the rally on January 6, President Trump tweeted: "All Mike Pence has to do is send them back to the States, AND WE WIN. Do it Mike, this is a time for extreme courage!" President Trump later went on to attack Pence nearly a dozen times in his speech at the Save America March.

Privately, in person, before Pence headed to oversee the joint session on January 6, President Trump again threatened Pence. "You can either go down in history as a patriot," Mr. Trump told him, according to two people briefed on the conversation, "or you can go down in history as a pussy."

As a veteran, I find it deeply dishonorable that our former President and Commander in Chief equated patriotism with violating the Constitution and overturning the election. You will see and hear the consequences of President Trump's repeated attacks on the Vice President, the chants of "Traitor" and the chants of "Hang Mike Pence."

Thankfully, Vice President Mike Pence stood his ground, like our other brave officials stood their ground. He refused the President and fulfilled his duty on January 6. Even after the Capitol was attacked, even after he was personally targeted, even after his family was targeted, Vice President Pence stood strong and certified the election. Vice President Pence showed us what it means to be an American, what it means to show courage. He put his country, his oath, his values, and his morals above the will of one man. The President had tried everything in his power to seize the—everything in his attempt to seize power from the rightful victor of the election.

President Trump's extraordinary actions grew increasingly more desperate. You saw him go from pursuing claims in the courts to threatening State and local election officials, to then attacking Members of Congress in the Senate, to compromising our Justice Department, and then to attacking the Republican Vice President. These great public servants were being pressured by our Commander in Chief to overturn the results. Some of them and their families got death threats. Thankfully, at every turn, our democratic processes prevailed, and the rule of law prevailed. It is only because all of these people stayed strong and refused President Trump that our Republic held fast and the will of the electorate was seen through.

And at this point, President Donald J. Trump ran out of nonviolent options to maintain power. I began today by raising the question of how we got here. What you saw was a man so desperate to cling to power that he tried everything he could to keep it, and when he ran out of nonviolent measures, he turned to the violent mob that attacked your Senate Chamber on January 6. As you cast your vote after this trial, I hope each of you will think of the bravery of all of these people who said no to President Trump because they knew that this was not right, that this was not America.

. . .

Ms. Manager PLASKETT: I am Stacey Plaskett, and I represent the people of the Virgin Islands of the United States. Over this past weekend, my eleven-year-old daughter—I overheard her telling one of my sons: "Mommy doesn't seem really nervous about the impeachment trial," to which that son, sounding like an older brother, said: "Taliah, you will learn that most of the time, Mommy really seems to have it under control."

We know as parents that is not always the case, but I have learned throughout my life that preparation and truth can carry far, can allow you to speak truth to power. I have learned that as a young Black girl growing up in the projects in Brooklyn, a housing community on St. Croix, sent to the most unlikeliest of settings, and now, as an adult woman representing an island territory, speaking to the U.S. Senate. And because of truth, I am confident today speaking before you because truth and fact are overwhelming that our President, the President of the United States, incited a mob to storm the Capitol to attempt to stop the certification of a Presidential election.

My fellow managers have shown and will continue to show clear evidence that President Trump incited a violent mob to storm our Capitol when he ran out of nonviolent means to stop the election. Once assembled, that mob, at the President's direction, erupted into the bloodiest attack on this Capitol since 1814. Some of you have said there is no way the President could have known how violent the mob would be. That is false because the violence—it was foreseeable. I want to show you why this violence was foreseeable and why Donald Trump was different than any other politician just telling their fighters, their supporters to fight for something. The violence that occurred on January 6, like the attack itself, did not just appear. You will see that Donald Trump knew the people he was inciting, he saw the violence that they were capable of, and he had a pattern and practice of praising and encouraging that violence, never ever condemning it. And you will see that this violent attack was not planned in secret.

The insurgents believed that they were doing the duty of their President. They were following his orders. And so they publicized openly, loudly, proudly exact blueprints of how the attack would be made. Law enforcement saw these postings and reported that these insurgents would violently attack the Capitol itself. This was months of cultivating a base of people who were violent, praising that violence, then leading that violence—that rage—straight at our door. The point is this: by the time he called the cavalry of his thousands of supporters on January 6, at an event he had invited them to, he had every reason to know that they were armed, that they were violent, and that they would actually fight. He knew who he was calling and the violence they were capable of, and he still gave the marching orders to go to the Capitol and "Fight like hell" to "Stop the Steal."

Make no mistake, the violence was not just foreseeable to President Trump; the violence was what he deliberately encouraged. As early as September, Trump set the precedent that, when asked to denounce violence, he would do the opposite and encourage it. Now, if the President had only said something once about fighting to stop the steal, and violence erupted, there would be no way to know he intended to incite it or saw it coming. But just as the President spent months spreading his big lie of the election, he also spent months cultivating groups of people who, following his command, repeatedly engaged in real, dangerous violence. And when they did, when the violence erupted as a response to his calls to fight against the stolen election, he did not walk it back. He did not tell them no. He did the opposite—the opposite. He praised and encouraged the violence so that it would continue. He fanned the flame of violence, and it worked.

You will see this over time. These very groups and individuals whose violence the President praised helped lead the attack on January 6. And that is how we know clearly that President Trump deliberately incited this and how we know he saw it coming. There are many examples where the President engaged in this pattern. I am just going to walk you through a few of them.

Let's start with President Trump's incitement of the Proud Boys. Many of you have heard of this group, which since 2018 has been classified by the FBI as an extremist organization. Since that classification, the group has repeatedly engaged in serious acts of violence, including at pro-Trump rallies. In one such act on September 7, the Proud Boys attacked a man with a baseball bat and then punched him while he was down on the ground. On September 29, during a Presidential debate, President Trump was asked specifically if he was willing to condemn White supremacy and militia groups, if he was willing to tell them to stand down and stop the violence. Let's watch.

Mr. WALLACE, September 29, 2020: Are you willing tonight to condemn White supremacists and militia groups—

President TRUMP: Sure.

Mr. WALLACE: And to say that they need to stand down and not add to the violence at a number of these cities as we saw in Kenosha and as we've seen in Portland?

President TRUMP: Sure. I'm willing to do that.

Mr. WALLACE: Will you say that specifically?

President TRUMP: I would say—

Mr. WALLACE: Then go ahead, sir. Do it. Say it.

President TRUMP: I would say—

Let's hear now the President's response:

Mr. Chris WALLACE: Do it, sir. Say it. Do it.

President TRUMP: Say it. Do it. Say it. You want to call them—what do you want to call them? Give me a name. Give me a name. Go ahead.

Mr. Chris WALLACE: White supremacists and White proud—

President TRUMP: Who do you want me to condemn? Proud Boys, stand back and stand by.

When asked to condemn the Proud Boys and white supremacists, what did our President say? He said: "Stand back and stand by." His message was heard loud and clear. The group adopted that phrase, "Stand back and stand by" as their official slogan. They created merchandise with their new slogan, which they wore proudly across their backs at Trump's rallies, and they followed the President's orders. You will see more about this later in the trial, but you will see in these photos to the left, Dominic Pezzola, and to the right, William Pepe, two of the leaders of the group heading to the Capitol on January 6. They were later charged with working together to obstruct law enforcement.

As we go through this evidence, I want you to keep in mind these words by President Trump when asked to condemn violence: "Stand back and stand by." And see example after example of the kinds of people, like the Proud Boys, who he had standing by on January 6. By October, as my colleagues Mr. Castro and Mr. Swalwell showed you, Donald Trump was escalating his big lie that the only way he could lose the election was if it was rigged. So as election day neared, his supporters were frustrated, and they were angry. They were prepared to ensure his victory by any means necessary.

One of these violent acts was on October 30. Sometime after 12:30 p.m., a caravan of more than fifty trucks covered in pro-Trump campaign gear confronted and surrounded cars carrying Biden-Harris campaign workers and a Biden-Harris campaign bus as they were traveling down Interstate 35 from San Antonio to Austin.

(Footage of a caravan of trucks and cars flying Trump flags and surrounding Biden-Harris vehicles on the interstate.)

According to witnesses, this caravan repeatedly tried to force the bus you saw, and you see in that video, to slow down in the middle of the highway and then to run it off the road. What that video you just saw does not show is that the bus that they tried to run off the road was filled with young campaign staff, volunteers, supporters, surrogates—people.

As the Trump supporters closed in on the bus, a large black pickup truck adorned with Trump flags suddenly and intentionally swerved and crashed into a car driven by a Biden-Harris volunteer. News of the event went viral on social media.

The President of the United States, in a campaign, saw his own supporters trying to run a bus carrying his opponents' campaign workers off the highway, to physically intimidate people in this country campaigning. Here was his response the next day.

(Footage of Donald Trump's tweet of a video of protestors attempting to run Biden-Harris campaign vehicles off of the highway, with a Republican fight song, "Red Kingdom," playing in the background.)

The President of the United States tweeted a video of his supporters trying to drive a bus off of the road. You will recall in that first video that I showed you there was no sound. Well, the one that he tweeted had a fight theme song placed to it that the President—the President—put that music to that video and he added at the top: "I LOVE TEXAS!"

By the next evening, that tweet that he did had been viewed 12.6 million times. And it wasn't just the tweet. On November 1, at a Michigan rally with a sea of supporters, the President talked about that incident again. Here it is.

President TRUMP, November 1, 2020: You see the way our people, you know, they were protecting his bus yesterday because they're nice. So his bus—they had hundreds of cars, "Trump," "Trump," "Trump," "Trump" and the American flag. You see "Trump" and the American flag.

The President made a public joke of violence against campaigners in an American election. He made light of it. This was not a joke. In fact, it was so violent, it put so many people in harm's way that the FBI investigated the incident and the criminal responsibility of those who attacked these campaign workers.

Now, our President, Donald Trump, could have said: "Okay, I didn't realize how bad that was. This was very violent. Please stop." But he didn't. He saw the investigation and made a statement in defense of his supporters' attack on the bus, writing: "In my opinion, these patriots did nothing wrong."

Engaging in violence for him made them patriots to Donald Trump. For anyone who says Donald Trump didn't know the violence he was inciting, I ask you to consider: his supporters tried to drive a bus off a highway in the middle of the day to intimidate his opponents' campaign workers, and his response was to tweet the video of the incident that had fight music, joke about it, and call those individuals in that incident "patriots." And once again, Donald Trump's praise worked to incite them further. Emboldened by that praise, they remained ready to fight, ready to "Stand back and stand by."

This link is not hypothetical. Just like we saw the Proud Boys showing up in full force on January 6, Donald Trump's encouragement of this attack made sure his supporters were ready for the next one. The caravan bus attack had been organized by a Trump supporter named Keith Lee. Leading up to the attack on our Capitol of January 6, Mr. Lee teamed up with other supporters to fundraise to help to bring people to Washington, D.C., for that date. The morning of the attack, he filmed footage of the Capitol, pointed out the flimsiness of the fencing, and then addressed his supporters before the attack, saying: "As soon as you all get done hearing the President, y'all get to the Capitol, we need to surround this place." During the attack, he used the bullhorn to call out for the mob to rush in. He later went to the Rotunda, himself, and then back outside to urge the crowd to come inside. These are the people that President Trump cultivated, who were standing by.

I would like to look at another example. After the election on December 12, Trump supporters gathered in mass to protest the "stolen" election in D.C. It was billed by his loyalists as the second Million MAGA March. The rally was organized by Women for America First, the same group that you will see later secured the permit for the January 6 rally. And who else was there? The Proud Boys, standing by. Donald Trump did not attend that rally, but he made sure to make clear to his supporters, throughout the day, how he felt about the event. At 8:47 a.m., he sent out a tweet: "WE HAVE JUST BEGUN TO FIGHT!!!" And then the rally began.

And Donald Trump's allies who spoke at the rally carried on his message of the stolen election and the importance of fighting to stop the steal. Here is Nicholas Fuentes, a commentator who had organized a "stop the steal rally" in Michigan with Trump supporters.

Mr. FUENTES, December 12, 2020: In the first Million MAGA March, we promised that if the GOP would not do everything in their power to keep Trump in office that we would destroy the GOP.

Mr. FUENTES: And as we gather here in Washington, D.C., for a second Million MAGA March, we're done making promises. It has to happen now. We are going to destroy the GOP!

(People chanting: Yeah. Yeah. Let's go. Let's go. Destroy the GOP. Destroy the GOP. Destroy the GOP.)

Those words—that was Trump's message: destroy anyone who won't listen, who won't help them take the election for Trump. And, as you will see, this was just the preview for Fuentes, who, like the Proud Boys and the Trump caravan organizers, would later heed the President's call and come to Washington and be there on January 6.

Later in the rally, a former Trump campaign spokeswoman, Katrina Pierson, also spoke. During her speech, she stated: "This isn't over. This is just beginning," referring to the fight to stop the steal. Then she added: "We knew that both Republican and Democrats were against we the people. We are the cavalry. No one's coming for us." It is clear that Trump and some of his supporters saw this as war—a fight against anyone who was unwilling to do whatever it took to keep Donald Trump in power. "We are the cavalry."

President Trump continued to reinforce the support of these messages throughout the day. At 1:48 p.m., after both speeches, he retweeted his Deputy Chief of Staff's tweet, showing his crowd that he had flown over on Marine One, and he tweeted: "Thank you, Patriots." These people were, as you can see, gathered en masse and being told by the President's allies that their election had been stolen, and they were told they were the cavalry; that no one else could do it. After hearing these speeches and seeing the President's support, this is what Donald Trump's cavalry was capable of.

(Video footage of violence at the Million MAGA March on December 12, 2020.)

What you just saw was the violence that ensued after that rally. The Proud Boys, after that rally, engaged in serious acts of violence in downtown D.C. Some Trump supporters and self-identified Proud Boys vandalized churches after that rally. If we look at these events, it is clear how we got here because what did the President do after that? He turned right around, and a little over a week later, he began coordinating the January 6 Save America rally with the same people who had planned the second Million MAGA March.

You will recall that the Women for America First had organized that second Million MAGA March. They had originally planned rallies for January 22 and January 23, after the inauguration, but Donald Trump had other plans. On December 19, President Trump tweeted his save the date for January 6. He told his supporters to come to D.C. for a "big protest" that day, billing it as "wild." Just days later, Women for America First amended their permit to hold their rally on

January 6, pursuant to the President's save the date, instead of after the inauguration. This was deliberate.

Reports confirm that the President himself, President Trump, became directly involved with the planning of the event, including the speaking lineup and even the music to be played, just as he chose the music of his retweet of the caravan, driving the Biden-Harris bus off the road, with a fight song. He brought in the same people who spoke at the second Million MAGA rally to help as well. Trump's campaign adviser, Katrina Pierson, who you will recall said on December 12 that this is only the beginning—"we are the cavalry"—also became directly involved in planning the event.

They even sent out invitations together. This is Amy Kremer, one of the Founders of Women for America First, tweeting the invitation, tagging Donald Trump and other organizers, inviting the same supporters who had just engaged in serious violence at the second Million MAGA rally to show up to the largest rally to stop the steal. President Trump seemed to have other plans for what was going to happen at that rally too. Women for America First had initially planned for the rally goers to remain at the Ellipse until the counting of the State electoral slates was completed, just like they had remained at the Freedom Plaza after the second Million MAGA March. In fact, the permit stated, in no uncertain terms, that the march from the Ellipse was not permitted.

PERMIT FOR SAVE AMERICA MARCH

PERMIT #21-0278 (AMENDED)
PERMITTEE: WOMEN FOR AMERICA FIRST
LOCATION: ELLIPSE, SOUTHWEST QUADRANT, AND SOUTHEAST QUADRANT; SOUTH OF TREE LIGHTING SITE
DATE: JANUARY 2-8, 2021 (06:30 AM – 7:30 PM)

Additional Conditions

    A. This permit authorizes the use of the Ellipse southwest quadrant, west of the vista site line and south of the tree lighting site starting on Saturday, January 2 at 6:30 am until Wednesday, January 8, 2021 at 7:30 pm. This permit does not authorize a march from the Ellipse.

https://www.nps.gov/aboutus/foia/upload/21-0278-Women-for-America-First-Ellispse-permit_REDACTED.pdf

It was not until after President Trump and his team became involved in the planning that the march from the Ellipse to the Capitol came about in direct contravention of the original permit. This was not a coincidence. None of this was. Donald

Trump, over many months, cultivated violence, praised it, and then, when he saw the violence his supporters were capable of, he channeled it to his big, wild, historic event. He organized January 6 with the same people who had just organized the rally resulting in substantial violence, and he made absolutely sure, this time, these violent rally-goers wouldn't just remain in place. He made sure that those violent people would literally march right here, to our steps, from the Ellipse to the Capitol, to stop the steal—his cavalry.

This was deliberate. Because the President of the United States incited this, because he was orchestrating this, because he was inviting them, the insurgents were not shy about their planning. They believed they were following the orders of the Commander in Chief. They were, as with the tweet we just saw, quite literally, his cavalry. So they posted exact blueprints of the attack openly, loudly, proudly, and they did this all over public forums.

They were not just hidden posts on dark websites that Trump would not have seen. Quite the opposite. We know that President Trump's team monitored these websites. We know this because his advisers confirmed it. An "ex-White House and campaign insider," as you will read, "who has known both Scavino and the president for years, said there was no way that Scavino and the Trump social media operation would not have been aware of the plans circulating online to storm the Capitol" because the Trump "operation closely monitored the web's darkest corners, ranging from mainstream sites such as Twitter, Facebook, and Reddit, to fringe message boards like 4chan and 8cha (now called 8kun) to TheDonald.win, an offshoot from a banned Reddit community dedicated to rabidly supporting all things Trump."

They actively monitored the exact sites, like TheDonald.win, on which these insurrectionists wrote their posts. So what would Trump and his team have seen when they were monitoring these sites? What would his supporters have said? They would have seen a clear roadmap of exactly what happened. This is an example of a post that was captured from one of the sites dedicated to Donald Trump, that we just talked about, shortly before the site was taken down. The meme reads: "The Capitol is our goal. Everything else is a distraction. Every corrupt Member of Congress locked in one room and surrounded by real Americans is an opportunity that will never present itself again."

Let that sink in. Think about that. The exact thing that happened on January 6— that was their goal, and they said it out loud on sites that the Trump administration was actively monitoring. A third-party site captured a post on TheDonald.win, where one user posted: "This cannot simply be a protest. It has to be the establishment of the MAGA militia with command offices set up, with all further militia tactical missions spreading from there." Another user said in response: "We will have to achieve an actual tactical victory like storming and occupying [the Capitol] to have the intended effect." That is what they understood Donald Trump to want—there it is in black and white—and they explained why they felt justified in this.

Another poster on the forum TheDonald.win wrote on January 4: "If Congress illegally certifies Biden . . . Trump would have absolutely no choice but to demand us to storm Congress and kill/beat them up for it." Donald Trump will have no choice. That was what he made them believe to the point his supporters felt justified even in carrying weapons and storming our Capitol. This was in post after post. Here's another. When discussing how to carry guns into D.C., one noted: "Yes, it's illegal, but this is war, and we're clearly in a post-legal phase of our society." What?

They treated it as a war, and they meant it. On the morning of the attack, under a thread titled "Today, I told my kids goodbye," one poster wrote: "Today I had the very difficult conversation with my children, that daddy might not come home from DC." Within a matter of hours, that post amassed 4,000 "likes." President Trump had truly made them believe that their election had been stolen and that it was their patriotic duty to fight to steal it back—"patriotic," a term he gave those who use violence for him—and they were willing to say goodbye to their children for this fight.

These supporters didn't just rely on entering the Capitol with guns haphazardly. They had maps of this building. They talked through which tunnels to use and how to get to the Senate Chamber. Some posted specific floor plan layouts of the Capitol alongside hopes of overwhelming law enforcement to "find the tunnels; arrest the worst traitors." Posters also fixated on what they saw as their ability to easily overwhelm the Capitol Police as "there are only around 2k of them," and, again, they urged "the capitol is our goal. Everything else is a distraction."

There were hundreds of these posts—hundreds—monitored by the Trump administration, and these posts were chillingly accurate right down to communication devices. A new affidavit, filed by the FBI, described preparations by the rightwing group, the Proud Boys, to storm the Capitol, including using earpieces and walkie-talkies to direct movements throughout the building. This happened. That is the level of planning in advance that occurred. They had earpieces. On the slide, you will see Proud Boy member Dominic Pezzola has an earpiece in his right ear, consistent with the affidavit.

And in addition to these detailed posts, they made clear why they thought they should do this. Why they thought they *could* do this. It wasn't just that they were doing it following the President's orders; they thought he would help them. A third-party site captured a post on TheDonald.win—again, the site monitored by

Trump's team. "He [meaning Donald Trump in this instance] can order the NAT guard to stand down if needed. Unfortunately he has no control over the Capitol Police . . . but there are only around 2k of them and a lot are useless fat asses or girls." It is all right there—the overall goal, maps of the Capitol, the weapons, communications devices. They even said publicly, openly, proudly that President Trump will help them to commandeer the National Guard so all they have to do is overwhelm the 2,000 Capitol Police officers.

This was reported in the NBC News and the *Washington Post*, with headlines like: "Violent threats ripple through far-right internet forums ahead of protest." "Pro-Trump forums erupt with violent threats ahead of Wednesday's rally against the 2020 election." FOX News also reported that the Proud Boys would come to the January 6 rally prepared for violent action, even quoting a Proud Boy member who said they would be "incognito" and "spread across downtown DC in smaller numbers."

City officials, seeing these same warnings, also publicly warned about the violence and unlawful weapons at the event. D.C. Mayor Muriel Bowser cautioned residents of the District of Columbia to avoid the downtown area while the rally attendees were in town. Federal law enforcement warned of these threats also. On January 3, a Capitol Police intelligence report warned of a violent scenario in which "Congress itself" could be the target of the angry supporters of President Trump on January 6.

According to that report, obtained by the *Washington Post*: "Supporters of the current president see January 6, 2021, as the last opportunity to overturn the results of presidential election. . . . This sense of desperation and disappointment may lead to more . . . incentive to become violent. Unlike previous post-election protests, the targets of the pro-Trump supporters are not necessarily the counter-protesters as they were previously, but rather Congress itself is the target [for January 6]."

The day before the rioters stormed the Congress, an FBI office in Virginia also issued an explicit warning that extremists were preparing to travel to Washington to commit violence and "war," according to internal reports. The FBI report cited to an online post where the user declared that Trump supporters should go to Washington and get violent. The supporter said: "Stop calling this a march, or rally, or a protest. Go there ready for war. We get our President or we die." These threat warnings were not just hypothetical. Actual arrests occurred in the days leading to the attack.

On January 4, two days before the rally, one extremely well-publicized arrest was of a Proud Boy leader who destroyed a church's Black Lives Matter banner a month earlier during the December 12, second Million MAGA March. The report emphasized that when he was arrested, he was carrying high-capacity firearms magazines, which he claimed were meant to be supplied to another rally attendee for January 6. By the night before the January 6 attack, D.C. police had already made six arrests in connection with the planned protests on charges of carrying weapons, ammunitions, assault, assaulting police.

This is all in public view—all of it. The truth is usually seen and rarely heard. Truth is truth, whether denied or not, and the truth is, President Trump had spent months calling his supporters to a march on a specific day, at a specific time, in specific places to stop the certification. And leading up to the event, there were hundreds—hundreds—of posts online showing that his supporters took this as a call to arms to attack the Capitol. There were detailed posts of the plan to attack online. Law enforcement warned that these posts were real threats and even made arrests days leading up to the attack.

And yet, in the face of all this—these credible warnings of serious, dangerous threats to our Capitol—when those thousands of people were standing in front of President Trump, ready to take orders and attack, this is what he said: "We're going to the Capitol. And we fight. We fight like hell. And if you don't fight like hell, you're not going to have a country anymore." And that is why this is different. That is why he must be convicted and disqualified.

. . .

Ms. Manager DEAN: For me and for many Americans, January 6 is forever etched in our memories. I went to work with a sense of excitement—the start of my second term in Congress and the first time I would participate in the certification of a Presidential election. And then we all know what happened.

I know many of us have similar experiences from that day, but I will briefly share mine. I stood with colleagues in the Gallery above the House floor to observe the Arizona challenge. Moments later, police radios reported a breach of the Capitol grounds. Someone shouted up to us, "Duck"; then, "Lie down"; then, "Ready your gas masks."

Shortly after, there was a terrifying banging on the Chamber doors. I will never forget that sound. Shouts and panicked calls to my husband and to my sons, instructions to flee, and then the constant whirring of the gas masks filtering the air—the Chamber of the United States House of Representatives turned to chaos.

For Donald Trump, it was a very different day. Earlier, I showed you Donald Trump's desperate attempts to maintain power: ignoring adverse court rulings, attacking elected officials, pressuring his Justice Department, even attacking his own Vice President. You saw a man who refused to lose, who was desperate to retain power by any means necessary. You saw a man willing to attack anyone and everyone who got in his way, and you saw a man who thought he could play by different rules. He told his supporters, as my colleague Ms. Plaskett just showed you, exactly what he thought those different rules were—combat, fight, violence.

This was not just one speech. This was weeks and weeks of deliberate effort by Donald Trump to overturn the election results so that he didn't have to give up the Presidency. The speech on January 6 builds on, refers to, and amplifies that same pattern—the pattern Trump had used and broadcasted for months: he refused to lose, his attacks on others, and his different rules.

The only thing different about his speech on January 6 from all these other times that we went through was that he was no longer telling his base just that they had to fight to stop the steal. He was finally telling them: Now is the time to do it. Here is the place, and here is how. For weeks, he had urged his supporters to show up at a specific time and place, and when they got there, he told them exactly what he wanted.

Let's start with his desperation. You saw how much planning went into January 6, and when the day arrived, Donald Trump's desperation was in full force. Between the time he woke up on January 5 and the start of the Save America March that next day, he had tweeted thirty-four times. When Donald Trump wants to get his message across, he is not shy, as you all know. These tweets were relentless.

And these tweets all centered on his singular focus—his drumbeat to motivate, anger, and incite his supporters—his big lie: the Presidential election had been rigged. It had been stolen from him, and they had to fight to stop it. And the timing was no coincidence. He sent thirty-four tweets because this was his last chance to rile up his supporters before the big, historic, wild event he had planned. Now, I won't go through all of these tweets, but let me just highlight a few. At one in the morning, he tweeted: "If Vice President [Mike Pence] comes through for us, we will win the Presidency. . . . Mike can send it back."

This will look familiar to you because Mr. Lieu just showed you how Trump had privately been pressuring and publicly attacking his Vice President to stop the certification. And when Vice President Pence refused, when he explained that the Constitution simply does not allow him to stop certification, Donald Trump provoked his base to attack him. The late-in-the-evening tweet was no different. It just got more forceful.

Let's be clear. What Donald Trump was saying—that Vice President Pence could send back the certification—was not true. For one thing, all fifty States had ratified this election. And for another, Vice President Pence explained to him that he does not have the power to unilaterally overturn States' votes and just send certification back. And Donald Trump knew this, but this was his last chance to get his Vice President to stop the certification, and so he was willing to say or do just about anything. These tweets—attacking the election as fraudulent, attacking his Vice President, and urging his supporters to fight—continued throughout the morning. Here is another example. At 8:17 a.m. he tweeted: "All Mike Pence has to do is send it back to the States, AND WE WIN."

"And we win." That is what he said, even though by then he had clearly lost. As Trump continued tweeting, the Save America March at the White House was now in full swing. The speakers who warmed up the crowd for Trump were members of his inner circle—family members, his personal attorney, people President Trump had deputized to speak on his behalf. Some of the speakers also spoke at the second Million MAGA March, which resulted in serious violence.

The warmup acts on January 6 focused on promoting Donald Trump's big lie. They stoked the same fears—a stolen election, of fraud, of ripping victory away from them. And the speakers told them what to do about it. As the crowd erupted in "fight for Trump" chants throughout that morning, Donald Trump Jr. urged: "That's the message! These guys better fight for Trump!" The speakers lasted three hours, repeating President Trump's message.

And, finally, at about noon, Donald Trump took the stage with the seal of the Presidency on his podium and the White House as his backdrop. President Trump spoke for more than seventy minutes. His narrative was familiar. It was the same message he had spent months spreading to his supporters: the big lie, the election was stolen; that they should never concede; and that his supporters should be patriots and fight much harder to stop the steal, to "take back our country"—the same phrases he had spread for weeks.

But now the message was immediate. Now it was . . . no longer just fight; it was "fight right now."

President TRUMP, January 6, 2021: All of us here today do not want to see our election victory stolen by emboldened radical-left Democrats, which is what they're doing. And stolen by the fake news media. That is what they've done and what they're doing. We will never give up. We will never concede. It doesn't happen. You don't concede where there's theft involved. Our country has had enough. We will not take it anymore, and that's what this is all about. And to use a favorite term that all of you people really came up with: We will stop the steal.

That set the tone. "Our country has had enough." And "[w]e will not take it anymore." He told them and us, right at the beginning, that the only way to take back the country was to fight. Let's look at what he said next.

President TRUMP, January 6, 2021, 12:05 p.m.: And, Rudy, you did a great job. He's got guts. You know what? He's got guts, unlike a lot of people in the Republican Party. He's got guts. He fights.

Ms. Plaskett showed you example after example of Donald Trump, when confronted with violence, praising it. We saw him instruct the Proud Boys, a violent extremist group, to stand back and stand by. That group was there on January 6. We saw him praise a caravan of his supporters after they tried to drive a bus belonging to the Biden campaign off the road. The organizer of that attack was there on January 6. And we saw him team up with the organizers of the violent second MAGA Million March to plan his rally on January 6. What does he do at that rally? He tells Giuliani he is doing a great job addressing the crowd, saying he has "guts" to call for fighting. And to be clear, this is what he was praising.

Mr. GUILIANI, January 6, 2021, 10:50 a.m.: So let's have trial by combat.

"Trial by combat." Donald Trump praised Rudy, said he did a good job, had guts for telling the crowd that we need trial by combat. Next, more attacks.

President TRUMP, January 6, 2021, 12:06 p.m.: All Vice President Pence has to do is send it back to the States to recertify, and we become President and you are the happiest people.

This attack, like the tweets he sent that morning, had a purpose: convincing his supporters that the future of our country, of our democracy, hinged on whether Vice President Pence would overturn the election—something he knew Pence could not and would not do. He called out Vice President Pence nine times that day, and each time, he got more forceful. Here is what he said at 12:15.

President TRUMP, January 6, 2021, 12:15 p.m.: And we're going to have to fight much harder. And Mike Pence is going to have to come through for us. And if he doesn't, that will be a sad day for our country, because you're sworn to uphold our Constitution.

Now it is up to Congress to confront this egregious assault on our democracy. And after this, we are going to walk down—and I'll be there with you. We are going to walk down. We are going to walk down any one you want, but I think right here, we're going to walk down to the Capitol.

And we're going to cheer on our brave Senators and Congressmen and women, and we are probably not going to be cheering so much for some of them. Because you'll never take back our country with weakness. You have to show strength and you have to be strong.

"We're going to have to fight much harder. And Mike Pence will have to come through for us." That's what he said, and he told the crowd what he meant and exactly what to do, literally commanding them to confront us at the Capitol. He even told them he would walk there with them, which, of course, was not true, and then he told them exactly what to do when they got to the Capitol. "You'll never take [your] country back with weakness. You have to show strength."

And don't forget who is standing there, the same people Ms. Plaskett described to you: many people, violent—violent people law enforcement had warned would be armed and would be targeting us. One of President Trump's key defenses focused on what he said for a few seconds, fifteen minutes into the speech.

President TRUMP, January 6, 2021, 12:16 p.m.: I know that everyone here will soon be marching over to the Capitol building, to peacefully and patriotically make your voices heard.

In a speech spanning almost eleven thousand words—yes, we did check—that was the one time, the only time President Trump used the word "peaceful" or any suggestion of nonviolence.

The implication of the President's tweets, the rally, and the speeches were clear. President Trump used the word "fight" or "fighting" twenty times, including telling the crowd they needed to "fight like hell" to save our democracy. We know how the crowd responded to Donald Trump's words, and he knew how they responded to his speech. Here is the evidence of how the crowd reacted.

President TRUMP, January 6, 2021, 12:15 p.m., as heard from the assembled crowd: We are going down to the Capitol—

(People cheering.)

President TRUMP:.... weakness, you have to show strength—

Unidentified Speaker: Yes. Right.

(People chanting: Take the Capitol. Taking the Capitol right now. Invade the Capitol building. Storm the Capitol.)

President TRUMP: Make your voices heard.

Crowd: Storm the Capitol. Invade the Capitol. Fight, fight, fight. Take the Capitol right now.

These were the words of the crowd. Trump was telling them to fight, and he would keep telling them to fight throughout the rest of his speech. These are not only words of aggression, they are words of insurrection, and if you have any doubt, listen to what he says next.

President TRUMP, January 6, 2021, 12:20 p.m.: Today we see a very important event though, because right over there, right there, we see the events that will take place. And I am going to be watching, because history is going to be made. We are going to see whether or not we have great and courageous leaders or whether or not we have leaders that should be ashamed of themselves throughout history. Throughout eternity they will be ashamed. And you know what? If they do the wrong thing, we should never ever forget that they did. Never forget. We should never ever forget.

The Commander in Chief points to Congress and tells those assembled: "I am going to be watching . . . history is going to be made." This was clearly not just some rally or march or protest; this was about Donald Trump trying to steal the election for himself, claiming that the election was fraudulent, illegitimate, so that his supporters would fight to take it back.

In fact, after stoking the crowd's anger for nearly forty minutes, after repeating false election conspiracy after false election conspiracy, he said this in no uncertain terms:

President TRUMP, January 6, 2021, 12:39 p.m.: You will have an illegitimate President, that is what you'll have.

Any outcome besides him keeping the Presidency would be illegitimate. This was building on the big lie of a rigged and stolen election. And here is what he said a little later in his speech.

President TRUMP, January 6, 1:02 p.m.: When you catch somebody in a fraud, you are allowed to go by very different rules. So I hope Mike has the courage to do what he has to do.

"When you catch somebody in a fraud, you are allowed to go by very different rules." We told you that context matters. Here is the context: this was not just one reference or a message to supporters by a politician to fight for a cause. He had assembled thousands of violent people, people he knew were capable of violence, people he had seen be violent. They were standing now in front of him. And then he pointed to us, lit the fuse, and sent an angry mob to fight the perceived enemy—his own Vice President and the Members of Congress as we certified an election.

President TRUMP, January 6, 2021: But I said, something's wrong here. Something's really wrong. Can't have happened. And we fight. We fight like hell. And if you don't fight like hell, you're not going to have a country anymore. Our exciting adventures and boldest endeavors have not yet begun. My fellow Americans, for our world, for our children, and for our beloved country—and I say this despite all that's happened—the best is yet to come.

So we're going to—we're going to walk down Pennsylvania Avenue. I love Pennsylvania Avenue. And we're going to the Capitol, and we are going to try and give—the Democrats are hopeless. They never voted for anything—not even one vote. But we are going to try and give our Republicans—the weak ones, because the strong ones don't need any of our help. We are going to try and give them the kind of pride and boldness that they need to take back our country. So let's walk down Pennsylvania Avenue.

(Cheers and applause.)

President TRUMP: I want to thank you all. God bless you and God bless America. Thank you all for being here. This is incredible. Thank you very much.

(Cheers and applause.)

People chanting outside the Capitol building: Fight for Trump. Who are we here for? Donald Trump!

"If you don't fight like hell, you're not going to have a country anymore." And there was only one fight left, and it was a mile up the road.

Donald Trump, the President of the United States, ordered the crowd to march on Congress, and so the crowd marched. "This is incredible," we heard him say. That is how President Trump ended his speech.

I would like to close with a very brief timeline of what was happening in parallel alongside the President as he spoke on the 6th of January. A little after noon, President Trump began his speech with a fiery refusal to concede. He commanded the crowd to fight and march down Pennsylvania Avenue, and around 12:20, some rallygoers, some attendees, began marching. By 12:30, as President Trump continued to incite his supporters, large segments of the rally crowd had amassed at the Capitol.

At 12:53, as the President's speech was playing on cell phone broadcasts, the outermost barricades of the northwest side of the Capitol were breached, and Capitol Police were forced back to the steps of the Capitol. At 1:10, the President ended his speech with a final call to fight and a final order to march to the Capitol. At 1:45, the President's followers surged past Capitol Police, shouting: "This is a revolution."

Just after 2:10, an hour after President Trump ended his speech, the insurrectionist mob overwhelmed Capitol security and made it inside the Halls of Congress, because the truth is, this attack never would have happened but for Donald Trump. And so they came, draped in Trump's flag and used our flag, the American flag, to batter and to bludgeon. And at 2:30, I heard that terrifying banging on the House Chamber doors. For the first time in more than 200 years, the seat of our government was ransacked on our watch.

. . .

Ms. Manager PLASKETT: Mr. President, Senators, almost all of us were here on January 6, and we all have our individual experiences: what we felt, what we saw, what we heard. We have seen clips and reports in the media, but I have to tell you, it was not until preparing for this trial that I understood the full scope and learned the information that you are going to see that I understood the effort to attack our seat of government in order to carry out President Trump's mission to prevent the certification of a Presidential election. It was an attack to our Republic, to our democratic process.

My colleagues, Manager Swalwell, and I are going to walk you through the attack on the Capitol that day and the danger that it posed to the Vice President, to the Speaker of the House, to you all as Senators, my colleagues in the House, Capitol Police, and everyone who works in and around this Capitol. As you have heard, President Trump had been telling his supporters and his millions of Twitter followers that Pence had the ability to secure the Presidency for Trump; that Mike Pence alone had the power to overturn the election results if he would just do it.

But at 12:55 p.m., on January 6, Vice President Pence formally refused the President's demand. He wrote, and I quote: "It is my considered judgment that my oath to support and defend the Constitution constrains me from claiming unilateral authority to determine which electoral votes should be counted and which should not." Pence ended his letter with a passage including the words: "I will do my duty." Even though the count resulted in the defeat of his party and his own candidacy, Vice President Pence had the courage to stand against the President, tell the American public the truth, and uphold our Constitution. That is patriotism. That patriotism is also what put the Vice President in so much danger on January 6 by the mob sent by our President. To the President and the mob he incited, that duty to our Constitution was an all-out betrayal, and the Vice President was the direct target of that rage.

At 12:53 p.m., Senators, Members of Congress, Vice President Pence were in their respective Chambers. Outside, rioters, including some linked to the Proud Boys, broke through the outer barricade surrounding the lawn of the Capitol.

(Crowd members outside the Capitol building beginning to fight police and destroy police fencing. People chanting: USA.)

Unidentified Speakers: Whoa, whoa, whoa. Hey, hey, hey. Way to go. Break it down.

Twelve minutes later, Vice President Pence began presiding over the joint session of Congress to certify the results of the Presidential election. You can see Vice President Pence gaveling in the joint session here.

The VICE PRESIDENT: Madam President, Members of Congress, pursuant to the Constitution and the laws of the United States, the Senate and House of Representatives are meeting in joint session to verify the certificates and count the votes of the electors of the several States for President and Vice President of the United States.

While Vice President Pence presided over the joint session, Trump supporters began their assault on our Capitol. Radio communications from the Metropolitan Police Department highlight how, during and following President Trump's speech, Trump supporters descended on the Capitol and became increasingly violent. What you are about to hear has not been made public before.

Officer, January 6, 2021: Multiple Capitol injuries. Multiple Capitol injuries.

Dispatcher: 1318.

Officer: Twelve to 50, we're coming around from the south side.

Dispatcher: Be advised, the speech has ended.

Dispatcher: Intel 1, be advised you've got a group of about fifty up the hill on the west front just north of the stairs. They are approaching the wall now.

Officer: They're starting to dismantle the reviewing stand. They're throwing metal poles at us.

Officer: Cruiser 50, give me DSO up here now.

DSO: Multiple law enforcement injuries. DSO, get up here.

Officer: All right. We're thirty seconds out.

Officer: We need some reinforcements up here now. They're starting to pull the gates down. They're throwing metal poles at us.

Officer: Cruiser 50, DSO, get up here.

Officer: OK. We're here.

Officer: Twelve to 50, we're here.

Officer: We just had an explosion go on up here. I don't know if they're fireworks or what, but they're starting to throw explosives, fireworks material.

After attempting to dismantle the outermost perimeter, the rioters did every-thing in their power to storm past the police and into the Capitol. They coordi-nated, moving metal barricades the police were using to maintain distance. Listen to the yelling of "pull them this way" as they grabbed the barriers and attacked officers trying to hold the line.

Unidentified Trump Supporter, as crowd outside Capitol fights with police and pulls on police fencing: Pull. Pull this way. Pull forward.

At about 1:10 and 1:23 p.m., respectively, Capitol Police sent out the first evacua-tion alerts of the day, telling people to evacuate the Madison Building and the Can-non Building, respectively. Shortly after, at 1:45 p.m., Trump supporters surged past Capitol Police protecting the Capitol's west steps, the side that is facing the White House. In another radio communication between Metropolitan Police offi-cers, you can hear an officer declare that there is a riot at the Capitol at 1:49 p.m.

Officer: Cruiser 50, we're going to give riot warnings as soon as the LRAD is here. We're going to give riot warnings. We're going to try to get compliance, but this now is effectively a riot.

Dispatcher: 1349 hours. Declaring it a riot.

The next video, as well as several videos that follow, have a model of the Capitol Complex. The video is from the west front of the Capitol on the Senate side, the side facing the White House. Watch the red dot, which moves up the lower steps of the Capitol, indicating the approximate location of the rioters as they surge past the police.

Unidentified Speakers: This is our fucking house. This is a revolution. Let's go. Push! Go. Fuck you. Fuck you.

While the mob that Donald Trump sent to stop the certification came closer and closer to breaching the Capitol, just one floor below where we are now, Vice President Pence continued to preside over the session in the Senate Chamber above. At about 2:12 p.m., Secret Service quickly and suddenly evacuated Vice President Pence from the Senate floor. Here is the immediate reaction to that evacuation.

https://projects.propublica.org/parler-capitol-videos/?id=zOZaCgfNUl5Y

Speaker 1 on MSNBC: No audio. They just cut out. It looks like they—and sometimes the Senate—

Speaker 2: It seemed like they just ushered Mike Pence out really quickly.

Speaker 1: Yes, they did. That's exactly what just happened there. They ushered Mike Pence out. They moved him fast. They were—yeah, I saw the motions too.

While Vice President Pence was being evacuated from the Senate Chamber, rioters were at that time breaking into the Capitol. This next video shows their approach and the initial breach of the Capitol Complex. Remember to watch the red dot, which has been tracking throughout this incident.

Unidentified Speaker 1 banging on the door as others smash through a window: Let us in.

Unidentified Speaker 2: Break the window, bro.

Unidentified Speaker 3, as people begin entering the building through the broken window: Let's go!

Now we are going to show you, through security footage that has not been made public before, what that same breach looked like from the inside. Now, because this is security footage, there is no sound.

(Security footage of rioters entering the building after breaking windows.)

Note, as the video begins, we are seeing the inside view as the mob approaches from outside and beats the windows and doors. You can see that the rioters first break the window with the wooden beam that you saw previously, and a lone police officer inside responds and begins to spray the first man who enters but is quickly overwhelmed. I want you to pay attention to the first group of assailants as they break into the building. The second man through the window is wearing full tactical body armor and is carrying a baseball bat. Others are carrying riot shields. Among this group are members of the Proud Boys—some of whom, like Dominic Pezzola, who was recently indicted on Federal conspiracy charges—we will discuss later. You can watch where they are coming on our model as well.

When I first saw this model that was created for this, I thought back to September 11. I know a lot of you Senators were here. Some of you might have been Members on the House side. I was also here on September 11. I was a staffer at that time. My office was on the west front of the Capitol. I worked in the Capitol, and I was on the House side.

This year is twenty years since the attacks of September 11, and almost every day I remember that forty-four Americans gave their lives to stop the plane that was headed to this Capitol Building. I thank them every day for saving my life and the life of so many others. Those Americans sacrificed their lives for love of country, honor, duty—all the things that America means. The Capitol stands because of people like that—this Capitol that was conceived by our Founding Fathers, that was built by slaves, that remains through the sacrifice of servicemen and women around the world. And when I think of that, I think of these insurgents, these images, incited by our own President of the United States, attacking this Capitol to stop the certification of a Presidential election, our democracy, our Republic.

At the same time that that breach on this Capitol Building occurred, at approximately 2:13 p.m., just one floor up, while Senator Lankford was speaking on the Senate floor, Senator Grassley, who had taken over for Vice President Pence, called an unscheduled immediate recess of the Senate. A Senate aide approached Senator Lankford and informed him that the Capitol had been breached. Senator Grassley is immediately escorted out of the Senate Chamber.

Unidentified Speaker to Mr. LANKFORD: "Protesters are in the building."

Mr. LANKFORD: "Thank you."

Now, while this was going on, Officer Eugene Goodman responded to the initial breach. You all may have seen footage of Officer Goodman previously, but there is more to his heroic story. In this security footage, you can see Officer Goodman running to respond to the initial breach.

(Video of Officer Goodman sprinting down the hallway toward Senator Romney and directing him to turn around.)

Officer Goodman passes Senator Mitt Romney and directs him to turn around in order to get to safety. On the first floor, just beneath them, the mob had already started to search for the Senate Chamber. Officer Goodman made his way down to the first floor, where he encountered the same insurrectionists we just saw—watched—breach the Capitol.

In this video, we can see the rioters surge toward Officer Goodman. Recall that the rioters are in red, and Officer Goodman, in this model, is in blue.

Watch Officer Goodman, who backs up the stairs.

(People entering the Capitol chanting: USA.)

Unidentified Speakers: You work for us. Where is the meeting at? Hey, where do they count the fucking votes? You work for us! Where are they counting the votes? Where are they counting the votes? Right there. Hey. We have no weapons. We have no fucking weapons.

Officer GOODMAN: Back up!

Unidentified Speaker: He's one person, we're thousands!

Although they were shouting that they did not have any weapons, we know from the earlier video that that's not true. The second assailant through that breach was the one carrying a metal baseball bat. We know there were other weapons there that day. Did you hear the other shouts? "We're here for you." "He's one person, we're thousands." And—"Where do they count the votes?"

They were coming at the urging of Donald Trump to keep Congress—a separate branch of government—from certifying the results of a Presidential election. As the rioters reached the top of the stairs, they were within one hundred feet of where the Vice President was sheltering with his family. And they were just feet away from one of the doors to this Chamber, where many of you remained at that time. I also want to show you a different angle from the security footage of Officer Goodman's acts.

This video is on the second floor of the Senate wing of the Capitol. The red dot, as you recall, represents the insurrectionists. The blue dot is Officer Goodman, who led the mob away from the Chamber, just minutes earlier.

(Video showing Officer Goodman directing rioters away from the Senate chamber.)

On the left-hand side of the video, just inside the hallway is the door to the Senate Chamber. And watch how Officer Goodman provoked the rioters and purpose-fully draws them away from the door to the Senate Chamber and toward the other officers waiting down the hall. The rioter seen carrying a baseball bat in this video is the same one we saw moments ago breaching the window on the first floor.

While all of this was going on, Vice President Pence was still in the room near the Senate Chamber. It was not until 2:26 that he was evacuated to a secure location.

This next security video shows that evacuation. His movements are depicted by the orange dot in our model. The red and blue dots represent the location where the mob and Officer Goodman were and where Officer Goodman led the mob away from the Chamber just moments ago.

(Video of Pence evacuating.)

You can see Vice President Pence and his family quickly moved down the stairs. The Vice President turns around briefly as he is headed down.

As Pence was being evacuated, rioters started to spread throughout the Capi-tol. Those inside helped other rioters break in through doors in several locations around this entire building. And the mob was looking for Vice President Pence because of his patriotism, because the Vice President had refused to do what the President demanded and overturn the election results. During the assault on the Capitol, extremists reportedly coordinated online and discussed how they could hunt down the Vice President.

Journalists in the Capitol reported they heard rioters say they were looking for Pence in order to execute him. Trump supporters had erected a gallows on the lawn in front of the Capitol Building.[*]

Another group of rioters chanted: "Hang Mike Pence," as they stood in the open door of the Capitol Building. You can hear the security alarm through the door in the background. And you can hear the mob calling for the death of the Vice President of the United States.

(Video of people entering the Capitol as security alarms beep chanting: "Hang Mike Pence.")

This wasn't an isolated area or incident where that was being said. It was going on everywhere. Here is another example of the crowd outside yelling: "Bring out Pence, bring him out."

---

[*] A photo of the gallows was displayed.

(People outside the Capitol chanting: Bring him out.) (People chanting: Bring out Pence.)

After President Trump had primed his followers for months and inflamed the rally-goers that morning, it is no wonder that the Vice President of the United States was the target of their wrath after Pence refused to overturn the election results. Listen to this man explain.

> Unidentified Speaker wearing Trump hat, in self-filmed video: While Congress, cowards, hid in their—inside, and were escorted away because of fear of the people. Of course they are cowards. They can't face the people. They can't do the right thing. Pence lied to us. He is a total treasonous pig. And his name will be mud forever. Now the real battle begins. And it looks like the American people are very pissed. So good luck with that. Peace out.

"Peace out." Several insurrectionists described what they had planned to do if they encountered the Vice President or other lawmakers. One of them, Dominic Pezzola, also known as Spaz, is a member of the Proud Boys, as we discussed. Pezzola came to the Capitol on January 6 with deadly intentions. He commandeered a Capitol Police shield, used it to smash a glass window, entered the Capitol, and paved the way for dozens of insurrectionists. As you recall from an earlier video, Pezzola was one of the first wave of rioters to breach the building. On the left, you can see a screen shot from the video of the break-in we showed earlier.* And on the right, you can see Pezzola in the mob chase Capitol Police Officer Eugene Goodman through the building. Pezzola is the man in the center of the photo with the gray beard.

Pezzola has since been charged with eight Federal crimes for his conduct related to January 6. According to an FBI Agent's affidavit submitted to the court, the group that was with him during the sack of the Capitol confirmed that they were out to murder "anyone they got their hands on."

Here is what the FBI said: other members of the group talked about things they had done that day, and they said that anyone they got their hands on they would have killed, including Nancy Pelosi. And, I quote: "[T]hey would have killed [Vice President] Mike Pence if given the chance." They were talking about assassinating the Vice President of the United States.

During the course of the attack, the Vice President never left the Capitol, remained locked down with his family—with his family—inside the building. Remember that as you think about these images and the sounds of the attack. The Vice President, our second in command, was always at the center of it. Vice President Pence was threatened with death by the President's supporters because he rejected President Trump's demand that he overturn the election. The mob also went after the Speaker of the House, who alongside the Vice President, was presiding over the joint session of the certification in the House Chamber.

The chilling evidence shows that on January 6, armed and organized insurrectionists trained their sights on Speaker Pelosi. They sought out the Speaker on the floor and in her office, publicly declared their intent to harm or kill her, ransacked her office, and terrorized her staff. And they did it because Donald Trump sent them on this mission. As the insurrectionists got closer, Capitol Police rushed the Speaker from the House floor at 2:15 p.m., mere minutes after the Capitol was first breached. They recognized immediately that she was in danger.

The Speaker was not just rushed from the floor; the Capitol Police deemed the threat so dangerous that they evacuated her entirely from the Capitol Complex, rushing her to a secure offsite location. The insurrectionists' intent to murder the Speaker of the House is well documented in charging documents that are now available.

We know from the rioters themselves that if they had found Speaker Pelosi, they would have killed her. I have already discussed Proud Boys member Dominic Pezzola, who has since been charged with eight Federal crimes for his conduct on January 6. As you will recall, according to the FBI agent's affidavit submitted to the court, the group he attacked the Capitol with confirmed that "anyone they got their hands on they would have killed, including Nancy Pelosi."

William Calhoun, a lawyer, from Georgia, also participated in the insurrection

---

* Images of Pezzola were displayed.

that day. And he, too, has been charged for his actions. This insurrectionist detailed his criminal activity at the Capitol online. Calhoun wrote about his involvement on his own Facebook page. Here is the post.

Calhoun stated: And get this—"the first of us who got upstairs kicked in Nancy Pelosi's door and pushed down the hall towards her inner sanctum, the mob howling with rage—Crazy Nancy probably would have been torn into little pieces, but she was nowhere to be seen."

"Crazy Nancy"—that is Trump's nickname for the Speaker of the House. Then he explains that he and his group only abandoned their claim to the Speaker's office when "a SWAT team showed up." He writes: "Then a SWAT team showed and we retreated back to the rotunda and continued our hostile takeover of the Capitol Building."

"Retreated," "hostile takeover." He is using military terms for this attack.

The mob continued to look for Nancy Pelosi throughout the time they occupied the Capitol, including invading her offices. Watch now how the mob searches for Speaker Pelosi's office, which is marked in red, and the House Chamber itself.

(Video of rioters searching for Pelosi in the Capitol building.)

Unidentified Speakers: Where are you, Nancy? We are looking for you. Naaaaancy! Oh, Naaaaancy! Nan-cy! Where are you, Nancy?

During the siege, the Speaker's staff took cover in her office, hiding in fear for their lives for hours, as rioters broke in and ransacked her office.

As the rioters were breaking into the Capitol, her staff retreated into an interior room. Eight of them gathered in a conference room. About the same time, Capitol Police announced the Capitol had been breached, Speaker Pelosi's staff heeded the call to shelter in place. On our model, you can see the rioters in the Rotunda in red and the Speaker's office, again, in orange.

(Video of Pelosi's staff entering a conference room and barricading themselves inside as rioters get closer.)

As you can see, the staff moves from their offices through the halls and then enters a door on the right-hand side. That is the outer door of a conference room, which also has an inner door that they barricaded with furniture. The staff then hid under a conference room table in that inner room. This is the last staffer going in and then barricading themselves inside the inner office.

After just seven minutes of them barricading themselves and the last staffer entering the door on the right, a group of rioters entered the hallway outside and, once inside, the rioters have free rein in the Speaker of the House's offices. In this security video, pay attention to the door that we saw those staffers leaning into and going into.

(Video of rioters successfully breaking open the outer door of Pelosi's conference room.)

One of the rioters, you can see, is throwing his body against the door three times until he breaks open that outer door. Luckily, when faced with the inner door, he moves on. Another rioter later tried unsuccessfully to break through that inner door. At this point, the mob had already broken into the Speaker's formal conference room that is in the back of the hall at the top of the video.

I want to play some audio we have of the Speaker's staff with the rioters at the door that day. You can hear the terror in their voices as they describe what is happening to them as they are barricaded in that conference room. Please listen carefully because the staffer is whispering into a phone as he hides from the rioters that are outside the door.

Staffer to police as rioters approach: They're in the hall. We need the Capitol Police to come into the hallway. They're pounding on doors trying to find her now.

You can hear the pounding in the background as that staffer is speaking.

One of those staffers explained later that they could hear the mob going through her offices, breaking down the door and yelling: "Where are you, Nancy?" The

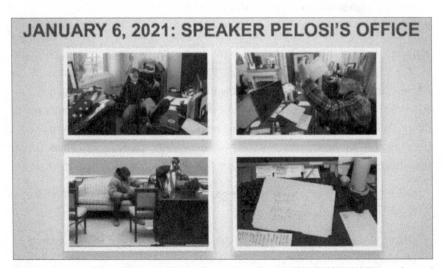

JANUARY 6, 2021: SPEAKER PELOSI'S OFFICE

Clockwise from top left: https://www.npr.org/sections/insurrection-at-the-capitol/2021/01/08/954940681/man-who-posed-for-photos-sitting-at-desk-in-pelosis-office-has-been-arrested; https://www.dailydot.com/debug/letter-guy-pelosi-ppp-loan; https://abcnews.go.com/US/rioter-accused-stealing-nancy-pelosis-laptop-house-arrest/story?id=75403067; https://www.businessinsider.com/trump-supporters-leave-threatening-note-in-pelosis-office-2021-1

mob also pillaged and vandalized the Speaker's office and documented their crimes on social media. They stole objects, desecrated the office of the Speaker of the House of Representatives of the United States. As you can see in these photos, rioters broke down a door. They also shattered a mirror.

At 2:50 p.m., several rioters, including Richard "Bigo" Barnett, entered Speaker Pelosi's office. The world is all now too familiar with the images from these slides. If you look closely, however, at the now-infamous pictures of Barnett with his feet on the desk, you might see something that you didn't notice previously. Here is a better look.

As this photo highlights, he is carrying a stun gun tucked into his waistband.[*] The FBI identified the device as a 950,000-volt stun gun walking stick. The weapon could have caused serious pain and incapacitated anyone Barnett had used it against. Richard Barnett bragged about his actions. He was proud of the way he desecrated the Speaker of the House's office. He left a note: "WE WILL NOT BACK DOWN."

Here is Barnett in his own words.

> Unidentified Man to Barnett about a letter he stole from Pelosi's office: How'd you get it?
>
> Mr. BARNETT: I didn't steal it. I bled on it. And they were fucking macing me, and I couldn't fucking see. And so I figure: Well, I'm in her office. I got blood in her office. I put a quarter on her desk even though she ain't fucking worth it. And I left her a note on her desk that says: Nancy, Bigo was here, you bitch.

Trump's mob ransacked the Speaker of the House's office. They terrorized her staff. Again, that is a mob that was sent by the President of the United States to stop the certification of an election. The Vice President, the Speaker of the House—the first and second in line to the Presidency—were performing their constitutional duties, presiding over the election certification. And they were put in danger because President Trump put his own desires—his own need for power—over his duty to the Constitution and our democratic process. President Trump put a target on their backs, and his mob broke into the Capitol to hunt them down.

> Officer: We're talking projectiles. Let's go. We need units outside on the terrace ASAP. We need units. We're surrounded.
>
> Officer: Cruiser 50, they've breached the scaffolds. Let Capitol know they have breached the scaffolds. They're behind our lines.

---

[*] A photo of Barnett sitting at Pelosi's desk with a stun gun on his waist was displayed.

. . .

Mr. Manager SWALWELL: Shortly after 2 p.m., the Capitol Police and Metropolitan Police were overwhelmed by President Trump's mob. Perimeters were broken. The Capitol had been breached. Those officers kept fighting back for hours and hours to hold the line. They fought to defend the Capitol Building and all of us within it. But they weren't there just to protect us—and they did—and our staff and the custodial staff and all the people who work so hard in this building. They were there to protect the votes of the American people that were being counted that day. I will show you more later about what that day was like for those brave officers.

But first, let's go back to what was happening where Manager Plaskett left off in the House Chamber. Rioters who had entered the building through the Senate quickly spread out through the Capitol. Many headed toward the House and Senate Chambers. After Speaker Pelosi was ushered out, Chairman McGovern was presiding in the House, attempting to keep the counting process going. On our phones, Members were receiving security updates and watching social media to see the horror that was going on outside. We never thought it would make its way in.

By 2:25 p.m., rioters who were already in the building opened the east side doors of the Capitol Rotunda to let more of the mob in. They quickly flooded through the doors, overwhelming the officers. This is new security footage of those doors, and, as before, the mob is identified with the red dot on the model of the Capitol. If you look closely, you will see the first person through the door is holding the Trump flag.

At the same time, just one floor below, the mob finally pushed through a line of Capitol Police officers and overtook the area. We all know that area in the Capitol as the Crypt. This is directly beneath the Rotunda at the very center of the Capitol.

(People chanting: Open up.)

Officer: No harm. No harm.

Inside the House Chamber, a security officer suspended the floor debate to update Members.

Officer to House members: We have a person with tear gas in the Rotunda. Please stand by. There are masks under your seats. Please grab a mask. Place it in your lap, and be prepared to don your mask in the event the room is breached.

We were told there were tear gas masks underneath our seats and to be prepared to grab them. Determined to keep the count going, Chairman McGovern called the House back into session, but only four minutes later, at 2:30 p.m., the House abruptly recessed. A new security announcement was made.

> Officer to House members: Be prepared to get down under your chairs, if necessary. So we have folks entering the Rotunda and coming down this way. So we'll update you as soon as we can, but just be prepared. Stay calm.

As I heard that announcement on the floor, I saw the new House Chaplain, on just her fourth day on the job, walk to the front podium unannounced, and, amidst the chaos, she started to recite a prayer for peace.

Uncertain what would happen next, I sent a text message to my wife: "I love you and the babies, please hug them for me." I imagine many of you sent a similar message. What we could not see from inside the Chamber was that outside, the mob was growing larger and larger and approaching our doors. But we could hear them.

This security footage shows a closeup of Trump's mob as they move toward the second floor of the House Chamber to stop the counting of votes.

> (Video of hundreds of rioters approaching the House chamber.)

In the back of the group, you see one individual carrying a "Stop the Steal" sign. They get within footsteps of the House door.

The next video is the viewpoint of the insurrectionists. It begins with the mob amassing and cuts ahead to show you their surge to the House door.

> (People chanting repeatedly: We want Trump.)

> Unidentified Man to Capitol police officers: It's a mob. They're going. Just stop. Whoa, whoa. Dude, dude, dude, dude—you're not helping. You're not helping. You are going to get me hurt and other people.

> (People chanting: Stop the steal.)

> Unidentified Man: All right, no violence.

> Unidentified Man: It's too late for that. They don't listen without that shit.

> (People chanting: Stop the steal.)

Those doors, to orient you at home, are the doors that the President of the United States walks through when he or she gives the State of the Union Address. You may have heard one man yell "no violence" and another respond: "It's too late for that. They don't listen without that." They were there to stop the certification of the election.

At this point, inside the House Chamber, we can now hear the pounding on the doors. At 2:35 p.m., Members on the House floor were told that an evacuation route was secure, and it was time to leave. This video shows Members of Congress exiting to the side of the podium where we would go through the House Lobby and downstairs.

(Video of House members evacuating.)

Because of coronavirus restrictions, congressional Members had been waiting in the Gallery for their time to speak, just one level above the House floor. Representatives, staff, journalists all took cover under their chairs, helped each other put on their gas masks, and held hands as rioters gathered outside. Here, on this slide, you see Representative Jason Crow comforting our colleague Representative Susan Wild.*

As told to Minutaglio, Rose. "Rep. Susan Wild on the 'Sheer Panic' She Felt in That Viral Photo," *Elle*, January 7, 2021, via Tom Williams

(Video of security footage.)

The rioters continued to surround the House Chamber, flooding the halls and kicking on the doors as they passed them.

---

* An image of Crow aiding Wild was displayed.

(Video of security footage showing rioters directing others toward the location where House members were evacuating.)

This security video shows Ashli Babbitt, followed by others in the mob, turning the corner to the House Lobby doors where the Members were leaving.

Chairman McGovern was one of the last Members to leave the floor. As he left through the House Lobby, just after 2:40 p.m., he was spotted by the mob.

(Video of rioters hitting police officers and punching and breaking glass in an attempt to access evacuating representatives.)

Minutes later, at 2:44 p.m., Ashli Babbitt attempted to climb through a shattered window into the House Lobby. To protect the Members in the Lobby, an officer discharged his weapon, and she was killed. I want to warn everyone that the next video, which shows her death, is graphic.

(Video of a crowd of rioters attempting to break down a door that would permit access to the House lobby, and of an officer fatally shooting Ashli Babbitt as she attempts to breach the doors by climbing through the glass.)

Unidentified speaker: He has a gun! He has a gun! He's got a gun!

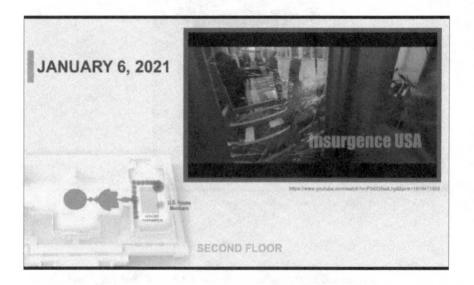

Inside the Chamber, Representatives, staff, and journalists remained trapped in the Gallery, one floor above the House floor, and heard the gunshot.

My colleague Representative Dan Kildee produced this recording.

> Speaker inside the Gallery: Take your pins off. (A gunshot is heard.) What the fuck? Take your pins off. Pins off!

Out of fear that they would be seen or taken by the mob, my colleagues were telling each other to take off their congressional pins.

That buzzing sound that you hear in the background of these videos was the sound of the gas masks. It was not until approximately 2:50 p.m., about six minutes after the shooting, remaining Members, staff, and journalists in the Gallery were finally able to flee. In this security footage video, you can see them exiting. Many Members are still wearing their gas masks. They walk just feet away from where the Capitol Police are holding an insurrectionist at gunpoint. Just minutes earlier, that insurrectionist had tried to open the Gallery door and, thankfully, was stopped by a tactical team.

(Video of people from the Gallery evacuating past a rioter being held at gunpoint.)

Although Members were now being moved to another location, the mob continued to fight—to stop the count, to find the Members, to engage with the police. The building was not yet secure. This security video from 2:56 p.m. shows the mob in the House of Representatives' wing on the second floor of the Capitol. Insurrectionists who are still inside the building are fighting with the police, who are overwhelmed in trying to get them out.

(Video of rioters inside the Capitol fighting the police.)

Throughout this presentation, we have been very careful to not share where Members of Congress were taken on the paths they followed to get out and off the floors, but that very issue was under discussion by the insurrectionists themselves. One example comes from an FBI affidavit, which stated that a leader of a militia group known as the Oath Keepers received messages while he was at the Capitol. The leader was given directions to where Representatives were thought to be sheltering and instructions to "Turn on gas; seal them in."

As you know, the threat to the Senate was no less than that of the Members of the House. The mob approached the Senate with the same purpose: fulfilling President Trump's goal of stopping the count; delaying the certification of the electoral college votes of the American people. As you heard from Manager Plaskett, Vice President Pence was moved away from the area near the Senate Chamber at around 2:25 p.m. By that time, rioters had breached several areas close to this Chamber, and they were flooding the hallways just outside and nearby. The Senate Chamber was not evacuated until 2:30 p.m. The mob had been in the building for more than fifteen minutes. This new security footage of the Senators and staff leaving the Chamber will be displayed on the screens.

(Video of Senators evacuating.)

You cannot see it in this footage, but quick-thinking Senate floor staff grabbed and protected the electoral ballots that the mob was after. Those of you who were here that day will recall that, once you left the Senate floor, you moved through a hallway to get to safety. That hallway was near where Officer Goodman had encountered a mob and led them upstairs and away from the Senate Chamber. You know how close you came to the mob.

Some of you, I understand, could hear them, but most of the public does not know how close these rioters came to you. As you were moving through that hallway—I paced it off—you were just fifty-eight steps away from where the mob was amassing and where police were rushing to stop them. They were yelling. In this security video, you can see how the Capitol Police created a line and blocked the hallway with their bodies to prevent rioters at the end of the hall from reaching you and your staff.

(Video of Senators and Senate staff evacuating as police block the rioters' passage.)

Because this is security footage that you have not seen before, I want to play it again. The top of the screen is the other end of that hallway where the mob has amassed and the officers are rushing to protect you.*

Additional security footage shows how Leader Schumer and the members of his protective detail had a near-miss with the mob. They came within just yards of rioters and had to turn around. Here, in this new video, you see Leader Schumer walking up a ramp. In going up the ramp with his detail, he will soon go out of view.

(Video of Schumer evacuating up a ramp, only to turn around and run the other way. The door to the ramp is sealed after he passes back through them.)

Seconds later, they return and run back down the hallway, and officers immediately shut the door and use their bodies to keep them safe.

At 2:45 p.m., shortly after Senators were ushered to safety from the Senate floor,

---

* The same video was replayed.

insurrectionists reached the Senate Galleries. The following video was filmed by a *New Yorker* reporter.

Unidentified Speakers: Knooock-knoooock! We're here! Where the fuck are they?

Minutes later, the insurrectionists invaded and desecrated the Senate floor. These vandals shouted and rifled through the desks of this room. They took pictures of documents and of themselves, celebrating that they had taken over the floor and stopped the counting of the electoral college votes.

Unidentified Speaker 1: Look at this. Take a picture.

Unidentified Speaker 2: Here. Look. Ted Cruz's objections. He was going to sell us out all along.

Unidentified Speaker 1: Really?

Unidentified Speaker 2: Objection to counting the electoral votes of the State of Arizona.

Unidentified Speaker 1: No, no, that's a good thing.

Unidentified Speaker 3 rifling through documents: There's got to be something in here we can use against these scum bags.

Unidentified Speaker 4: What happened to the phone?

Larry Brock, who was arrested for his role in the insurrection, was photographed on the Senate floor, wearing a helmet, tactical gear, and carrying flex cuffs.

Eric Gavelek Munchel, January 6, 2021, via Getty Images

This man, also in the Senate Galleries, is Eric Munchel. Like Brock, he was dressed in what appears to be tactical gear, also holding up flex cuffs.[*]

If the doors to this Chamber had been breached just minutes earlier, imagine what they could have done with those cuffs. After insurrectionists occupied the Capitol and stopped the joint session from counting the votes, the Capitol was in lockdown for five hours. As long as it took to get back to the Capitol, to get back to the certification of the election, it could have been so much longer, or we might not have been able to resume at all.

As horrific as it was—140 officers injured, three officers who ultimately lost their lives—we all know that awful day could have been so much worse. The only reason it was not was because of the extraordinary bravery of the men and women of the Capitol Police and the Metropolitan Police Departments. For hours and hours, these insurrectionists were in hand-to-hand combat with these brave men and women.

Like some of you, I come from a law enforcement family. My dad was a cop. My two brothers—my little brothers are cops who walk the beat today. I am proud of them. And like in every law enforcement family, when we hang up the phone, we don't only say "I love you," we say, "Be safe." So let's focus now on the attack and what it was like for the officers defending the Capitol that day. And, again, I want to warn you that the following audio and videos are graphic and are unsettling, but it is important that we understand the extent of what occurred. Here is an audio recording from the radio traffic of the D.C. Metropolitan Police Department describing the violence.

> Cruiser 50, I copy. We're still talking rocks, bottles, and pieces of flag and metal pole.

> Cruiser 50, the crowd is using munitions against us. They have bear spray in the crowd. Bear spray in the crowd. 1328. Multiple deployments U.S. Capitol with pepper spray. DSO, DSO, I need a re-up. I need a re-up up here.

You hear the officer describe they are "using munitions"—they, the rioters, are "using munitions against us." This video shows how the sprays that were described were used against the officers.

In a separate Metropolitan Police Department radio traffic recording, you can hear an officer when he realizes that the insurrectionists had overtaken the police line.

> Cruiser 50. We lost the line. We've lost the line. All MPD, pull back. All MPD, pull back up to the upper deck. All MPD, pull back to the upper deck ASAP. All

---

[*]   Images of Brock and Munchel were displayed.

MPD, come back to the upper deck. Upper deck. Cruiser 50, we're flanked. 10-33. I repeat 10-33 west front of the Capitol. We have been flanked and we've lost the line.

The MPD officer calls out "10-33." That is the code for emergency, officer in need of assistance; his words, "We've lost the line."

Hours after Members of the House and Senate had left this area on the west front of the building, the mob continued to grow, continued to beat the officers, as they tried to get in. In this new security video, you can see the mob attacking officers with a crutch, a hockey stick, a bull horn, and a Trump flag.

(Video of rioters attacking police.)

I want to show you that same attack from the officer's perspective, from his body camera footage.

(Body camera footage from an officer who was being attacked.)

This body camera footage is from 4:27 p.m., over two hours from when the Capitol was first breached. The attack on police that afternoon was constant. Metropolitan Police Officer Michael Fanone, a twenty-year police veteran with four daughters, was part of a line of officers protecting the Capitol. He was one of three officers whom the mob dragged down the stairs. When they dragged him, they stole his badge, his radio, his ammunition magazine, and they tased him, triggered a heart attack. Here he describes his experience.

Officer FANONE: It looked like a medieval battle scene. It was some of the most brutal combat, you know, I have ever—ever encountered. At one point I got tased. People were yelling at me, "We got one. We got one."

Officer Christina Laury, who regularly serves in MPD's Narcotics and Specialized Investigation Division, also protected the front Capitol entrance. Here is her experience.

Officer LAURY: I mean, I can't say enough about the officers that were there, the officers that were on the frontline. And when I say "the frontline," I mean, literally, officers that were in a line, stopping these people that were beating them with metal poles. They were spraying them with bear mace. I mean, they did everything in their power to not let those people in. And this was going on for hours.

Around 4:30 p.m., hours into the Capitol riots, Officer Daniel Hodges was protecting a west side Capitol entrance when rioters who were trying to stop the certification trapped him between two doors. When Officer Hodges was interviewed later, this is how he described what was happening.

Officer HODGES: They threw down a huge metal object that hit me on the head. I was also knocked down. The medical mask I was wearing at the time got pulled up over my eyes, so I was on the ground and blinded, and they started attacking me from all sides.

Rioters crushed Officer Hodges. He was wedged in the doorway, blood dripping from his mouth. He was struggling to breathe, all while the insurrectionists hit him.

Officer Hodges' experience reminds you of what he and many other officers experienced that day, what they went through. We are also reminded of three officers who lost their lives: Capitol Hill Police Officers Sicknick, Liebengood, and Metropolitan Police Officer Smith. In many law enforcement families, we pray for our loved ones, and we know the scripture of Matthew 5:9, "Blessed are the peacemakers, for they shall be called the children of God."

I am sorry I have to show you the next video, but in it you will see how blessed we were that on that hellish day, we had a peacemaker like Officer Hodges protecting our lives, our staffs' lives, this Capitol, and the certification process. May we do all we can in this Chamber to make sure that never happens again.

(Video of Officer Hodges being attacked and then crushed as officers attempted to keep doors sealed against hundreds of rioters pushing on the doors and repeatedly yelling, "Heave-ho!")

. . .

Mr. Manager CICILLINE: Mr. President, distinguished Senators, you just heard from my colleagues about the harrowing events that happened here at the Capitol on January 6 and saw that very disturbing video, and now I would like to turn your attention to what was happening on the other end of Pennsylvania Avenue at the White House.

The truth is, the facts are, that on January 6, Donald Trump did not once condemn this attack. He did not once condemn the attackers. In fact, on January 6, the only person he condemned was his own Vice President, Mike Pence, who was hiding in this building with his family in fear for his life. In the first crucial hours of this violent attack, he did nothing to stop it, nothing to help us. By all accounts, from the people that were around him, he was delighted. And here is the last thing

Donald Trump said that day, and you might remember this from my motions presentation earlier in the week.

At 6 p.m. on January 6, after all the destruction that you just saw, Capitol Police and the National Guard fighting to secure this building, here is what Donald Trump tweeted: "These are the things and events that happen when a sacred landslide election victory is so unceremoniously & viciously stripped away from great patriots who have been badly & unfairly treated for so long. Go home with love & in peace. Remember this day forever!"

He got what he incited, and according to Donald Trump, we got what we deserve. Donald Trump's incitement of this insurrection, including his dereliction of his duty as Commander in Chief to defend the Capitol and the people in it, his complete refusal to condemn the attack while it was going on, and his continuing to incite the violence during the attack require impeachment.

Now, let's turn to then-President Trump's conduct that day. I want to start at the beginning, when he addressed his thousands of great patriots, as he called them that morning. Around noon, Donald Trump began speaking at his rally just down Pennsylvania Avenue. Even before Donald Trump finished speaking, his supporters began to walk down toward the Capitol, and they were already starting to chant "Stop the steal" and "Storm the Capitol" and "Invade the Capitol" and "Fight for Trump." And by 12:53 p.m., they had violently forced their way through the barricades here at the Capitol.

Now, about one o'clock that day, with this chaos just starting, Speaker Pelosi, as the Constitution requires, formally commenced the process by which this Chamber certifies election results. Within ten minutes, at 1:11 p.m., as if almost on cue, Donald Trump concluded his speech with his final reminder to the thousands gathered there: It was time to go to the Capitol. Let's watch.

President TRUMP, January 6, 2021, 1:10 p.m.: We're going to the Capitol, and we're going to try and give—and we're going to try and give our Republicans—the weak ones because the strong ones don't need any of our help—we're going to try and give them the kind of pride and boldness that they need to take back our country. So let's walk down Pennsylvania Avenue. I want to thank you all. God bless you, and God bless America. Thank you all for being here. This is incredible. Thank you very much.

(A crowd of rioters chanting outside the Capitol, 1:17 p.m.: Fight for Trump.)

Now, you have seen what happened when these supporters, following his orders, arrived here at the Capitol. But we want to look at what happened next. Now, you will recall, during the speech, President Trump said, "We're going to the Capitol," sort of suggesting he was going to go with this crowd. Of course, that was not true. But let's hear what he said.

President TRUMP, 12:15 p.m.: Now it is up to Congress to confront this egregious assault on our democracy. And after this, we're going to walk down, and I'll be there with you. We're going to walk down. We're going to walk down. Any one you want, but I think right here. We're going to walk down to the Capitol.

This, of course, was not true. He did not go with them to the Capitol. He left and went back to the White House, and while he was en route to the White House, violence began to grow here at the Capitol. And within minutes of Donald Trump's speech ending, there were significant reports of escalating violence that began to surface. Buildings around the Capitol were starting to be evacuated, and by 1:15, an explosive device had been found at the DNC, and a pipe bomb had been found at the RNC about fifteen minutes earlier. The House Sergeant at Arms had called for immediate assistance.

At 1:34 p.m., the mayor of Washington, D.C. called for additional National Guard troops. I won't go through all of the details of violence that unfolded here. You just saw that. But as we walk through what our Commander in Chief did that day, I want to be very clear about exactly what was happening here at the same time. For forty minutes—while buildings were being cleared, pipe bombs were being found, and his supporters were literally breaching the perimeter of the Capitol and overwhelming law enforcement, you saw the violence that was occurring—we heard nothing from the President of the United States. We didn't hear anything from Donald Trump until 1:49 p.m., when, while all of this is unfolding, President Trump sent out a tweet. This was the first thing he did when he learned the U.S. Capitol, with all the Members of Congress and his own Vice President, was under violent attack. What was that tweet? Nearly an hour after the rioters breached the Capitol perimeter at 1:49, Donald Trump released a propaganda reel of his "Save America" speech that he had given an hour before.

I want to be clear. The events I just described—the rioters breaching the Capitol, attacking law enforcement, the violence that is being broadcast all over the television for the whole world to see, including the President of the United States—I want to show you: this is what is happening right before Donald Trump sends that video out again and as he does it.

President TRUMP, January 6, 2021 at 1:49 p.m., in video he posted to Twitter featuring highlights of his speech from earlier: Our country has had enough. We will not take it anymore and that's what this is all about. And to use a favorite term that all of you people really came up with: We will stop the steal. Because you'll never take back our country with weakness. You have to show strength, and you have to be strong.*

Even if President Trump claims he didn't know the extent of the violence that would follow his speech, it was now happening in plain view, broadcast on television. His supporters were attacking law enforcement. The mayor and the police chief were calling for help. Members of Congress and the Vice President were inside scared for their lives. He doesn't send help, and he doesn't try to stop it. He doesn't even acknowledge the attack. Instead, our Commander in Chief tweeted the video of the speech that he had given before, that included language like "our country has had enough. We will not take it anymore and that's what this is all about. . . . You have to be strong."

Those around Donald Trump—this was later reported—were disgusted. His close aides, his advisers, those working for him, former officials, and even his family were begging him to do something. Kellyanne Conway, the President's close adviser, called to "add her name" to the chorus of aides urging Donald Trump to take action. Ivanka Trump, the President's own daughter, went to the Oval Office "as soon as" the rioting escalated, and as was confirmed by Senator Graham, "trying to get [Trump] to speak out, to tell everyone to leave."

Minority Leader Kevin McCarthy called Jared Kushner, "pleading with him to persuade Trump to issue a statement" or to do something. And Kushner, too, went down to the White House after that call. And it wasn't just the people at the White House. Members of Congress from both parties, who were trapped here, were calling the White House to ask for help. Some Members even appealed directly to Donald Trump. These Members who had "been loyal Trump supporters and were even willing to vote against the electoral college results, were now scared for their lives."

Minority Leader Kevin McCarthy [reportedly] even got into a screaming match as the attack was under way, demanding that Mr. Trump do something, issue a statement denouncing the mob. I imagine many of you sitting here today picked up your phone and tried to reach somebody at the White House to ask for help. This wasn't partisan politics. These were Americans from all sides trying to force our Commander in Chief to protect and defend our country. He was required to do that.

Now, the extent of how many people tried to reach the President to get him to act

---

* This video was juxtaposed on screen with live footage from Fox News that was broadcast as Trump posted to Twitter, showing the violent mob outside the Capitol.

is not known. But what is clear, what we know without any doubt, is that from the very beginning, the people around Donald Trump lobbied him to take command. What is also clear is what Donald Trump, our Commander in Chief, did in those initial hours to protect us. Nothing. Not a thing. He knew it was happening. The attack was on TV. We all know that President Trump had the power to stop these attacks.

He was our Commander in Chief. He had the power to assess the security situation, send backup, and send help. He also had incited these violent attacks. They were listening to him. He could have commanded them to leave, but he didn't. The first critical hour and a half of this bloody attack, Donald Trump tweeted his rally speech and did nothing else. And we know why. We know his state of mind that prompted his utter, complete refusal to defend us. It was reported by those around him.

The President, as reported by sources at the time, was delighted. As he watched the violence unfold on television, President Trump was reportedly "borderline enthusiastic because it meant the certification was being derailed." Senator Ben Sasse relayed a conversation with senior White House officials that President Trump was "walking around the White House confused about why other people on his team weren't as excited as he was."

Mr. Trump's reaction to this attack, reportedly, genuinely freaked people out. I understand why. We just suffered a very serious attack, an attack on our country. And we saw them—the people around him—do it. But when Donald Trump saw it, he was delighted. Now, what President Trump did next confirms why he was so delighted, why he wanted this, because it shows that his singular focus that day— the day we were attacked—was not protecting us, was not protecting you, was not protecting the Capitol, but it was stopping the certification of the election results. The evidence is clear.

Shortly after 2 p.m., as the siege was fully under way, then-President Trump made a call. This is the first call that we are aware he made to anyone inside the Capitol during the attack. He didn't call the Vice President to ask how he could help defend the Capitol. He didn't call the next two in line to succession of the Presidency to check on their safety or well-being. Instead, he attempted to call Senator Tuberville. He dialed Senator Lee by accident.

Let's be clear. At roughly 2 p.m., when Donald Trump was walking around the White House watching the TV delighted and spent five to ten minutes talking to Senator Tuberville, urging him to delay the election results, this is what was happening in the Capitol.

(Video of rioters breaking windows in order to enter the Capitol building as Members and Senators began evacuating.)

You saw Senator Lankford stop speaking and leave the floor quickly in that clip because the insurgents had broken through the barricades and entered the building. And as these armed insurrectionists banged on the doors, Members of Congress were told to put on their gas masks, to put bags over their heads for safety, and prepare to evacuate. And Donald Trump was calling to ask the Senator to delay the certification process. Let that sink in. Donald Trump didn't get to finish that call. It was cut off because the Senators had to move to another location, for your security. And thank God they did because as the call was occurring, the rioters got closer to the Senate Chamber, and as we all know now, but for the heroism of Capitol Police Officer Eugene Goodman and other law enforcement officers who took them in a different direction to the police line, they very likely would have gotten here.

Think about that. Armed insurrectionists with guns, weapons, zip ties, brass knuckles, they were coming for us. They were inside the United States Capitol, trying to stop the certification process. The police were outnumbered. And but for the grace of God, they would have gotten us, all of us. And our Commander in Chief makes a call about an hour after the siege began, not to preserve, protect, and defend you and our country and the Capitol but to join forces with the mob and pressure a Senator to stop certification.

We just can't get numb to this kind of behavior. There can be no doubt as to the purpose of Donald Trump's call, that he was not calling to assess the security threats or to check on the well-being of you or anyone else. Indeed, later on that evening, while all of the destruction and damage still continued, dozens of officers were being treated for serious injuries. Deaths were confirmed. About 7 p.m., the President's personal lawyer, Rudy Giuliani, made a call, and just in case you don't think there was some coordination, he also called Senator Lee's phone trying to reach Senator Tuberville. We don't have to guess as to what Rudy Giuliani said in that voicemail because we have it recorded. So let's listen to what the President's personal lawyer said on the night of this attack.

Mr. GIULIANI: Senator Tuberville—or I should say Coach Tuberville, this is Rudy Giuliani, the President's lawyer. I'm calling you because I want to discuss with you how they're trying to rush this hearing and how we need you, our Republican friends, to try to just slow it down.

This was the singular focus of Donald Trump during this bloody, violent attack on the Capitol: stopping the certification. Look, as I mentioned, I was a trial lawyer for sixteen years. Sometimes, you have to ask a jury to use reasonable inferences to piece together a defendant's state of mind. We don't have to do this here. While our country was violently attacked by an armed mob, President Trump not only refused to stop the attack or even address the attack at all, he made clear his focus was on the same goal of the attackers he incited: to stop the certification process and prevent the peaceful transition of power.

The only action we know that he took an hour into this attack was to call Senator Tuberville to ask him to delay the certification. This is as clear evidence as I have ever seen of what Donald Trump really cared about that day. Now, look, the certification process, as we all know, includes debate and objections. Some of us disagreed, but we came here on January 6 to formally administer the certification process pursuant to our constitutional duties. At the end of it, Congress certified the results to ensure that we continue to be a country with leaders who are elected by the people for the people.

Donald Trump's objections to the certification are not on trial, but what is on trial is, while we were under armed attack and being evacuated, while our law enforcement officers were fighting for their lives, our Commander in Chief was calling not to determine how to best secure the building and the people in it but to continue to pressure Senators to stop the certification process and a peaceful transfer of power, just as he incited the mob to do earlier in the day. This was a breathtaking dereliction of his duty and a violation of his oath as our Commander in Chief.

Senators, before I hand this over to Manager Castro to walk through the rest of the day, please let me make one final point. These attackers stood right where you are. They went through that rostrum. They rifled through your desks, and they desecrated this place. And literally, the President sat delighted, doing nothing to help us, calling one of you to pressure you to stop the certification. It can't be that the Commander in Chief can incite a lawless, bloody insurrection and then utterly fail in his duty as Commander in Chief to defend us from the attack, to defend our law enforcement officers from that attack, and just get away with it. Donald Trump abdicated his duty to us all. We have to make this right, and you can make it right.

. . .

Mr. Manager CASTRO of Texas: My fellow manager David Cicilline showed you what President Trump did and did not do in those first critical hours of the attack. He sent a tweet at 1:49 p.m., where he reposted a video of the speech that incited the attack, and he called a Senator to ask him to delay the certification as the Senator was being evacuated for his own safety. We left off around 2:15 p.m.

At this point, insurgents were inside the Senate and the House, and the Senate had been evacuated for everyone's safety. As you saw, Vice President Mike Pence and his family even had to be evacuated for their safety. Now, you will recall Donald Trump had made Vice President Pence a target. He attacked the Vice President at the rallies, in speeches, and on Twitter. And during President Trump's speech that morning of the attack, he ramped it up again. After privately pressuring Mike Pence in front of thousands in the crowd, he called Mike Pence out eleven times, including saying:

> Mike Pence, I hope you're going to stand up for the good of our Constitution and for the good of your country. And if you're not, I'm [going] to be . . . disappointed in you. I will tell you right now.

And this was the crowd's response to Donald Trump's days of relentless attacks on his own Vice President:

(People chanting just outside the Capitol: Hang Mike Pence.)

By 2:15 p.m., the crowd was chanting in unison "Hang Mike Pence" outside the very building he had been evacuated from with his family. Now, even if President Trump didn't know that his inflammatory remarks about his Vice President would result in chants of "Hang Mike Pence," by 2:15 p.m., he surely knew. The attack was all over television. They were doing this out in the open. This was a Vice President whose life, whose family's life, was being threatened by people whom the President had summoned to the Capitol. And what did President Trump do in response? Did he stop? Did he tell his base: "No, don't attack my Vice President." Even when President Trump knew what his words were causing, he didn't do any of those things to stop the crowd.

In fact, he did the opposite. He fueled the fire. At 2:24 p.m., he tweeted: "Mike Pence didn't have the courage to do what should have been done to protect our country and our Constitution. . . . USA demands the truth." Over an hour and a half into the attack, and this is what he tweeted. And he still, even at this point, did not acknowledge the attack on the Capitol, let alone condemn it. Instead, he further incites the mob against his own Vice President, whose life was being threatened.

"Well," some of you may say: "Well, who was paying attention anyway?" Well, that mob was paying attention.

Unidentified Speakers: Mike Pence didn't have the courage to do what should have been done to protect our country and our Constitution, giving States a chance to certify or correct a set of facts, not the fraudulent or inaccurate ones, which they were asked to previously certify. U.S. demands the truth. Mike Pence is a bitch! Mike Pence is a bitch! Can I speak to Pelosi? Yeah, we're coming, bitch. Oh, Mike Pence, we're coming for you, too, fucking traitor. Donald J. Trump sent a tweet out saying that Mike Pence let us down. If you wanna get something done, you're gonna have to do it yourself.

The insurgents amplified President Trump's tweet attacking the Vice President with a bullhorn. They were paying attention, and they also followed instructions. In fact, the insurgents were at one point, as you saw, sixty feet away from the Vice President and the Vice President's family. Some of these insurgents were heard saying that they "hoped to find Vice President Mike Pence and execute him by hanging him from a Capitol Hill tree as a traitor." And then, they erected a gallows with a noose.

This is what Donald Trump incited.* Please take a close look at that picture. It hearkens back to our Nation's worst history of lynching. A President's words have the power to move people to action, and these were the results. And why did the President incite such rage against the Vice President? He was fulfilling his constitutional duty, as we all were that day. Vice Presidents in this country have been carrying out this constitutional duty—overseeing the certification of election results—without incident, without contest, without a word, for the entirety of our Nation. It is part of our peaceful transition of power in the United States.

The Vice President said he reviewed the Constitution, and he could not block certification, as President Trump wanted him and was pressuring him to do. He told the President in a letter that morning, a few hours before President Trump's tweet: "[I will] approach this moment with [a] sense of duty and an open mind, setting politics and personal interests aside, and do [my] part to faithfully discharge our duties under the Constitution. I also pray that we will do so with humility and faith."

And the President's response to that statement was to attack Mike Pence while he was with his family under the threat of a violent mob. The Vice President was following his faith, his duty, and his oath to our Nation. The Vice President and I don't agree on too much in politics, but he is a man who upholds his oath, his faith, his duty, and most of all upholds the Constitution. And Mike Pence is not a traitor to this country. He is a patriot. And he and his family, who was with him that day, didn't deserve this, didn't deserve a President unleashing a mob on them, especially because he was just doing his job.

---

* A photo of the gallows was displayed.

As this was unfolding and the crowd grew more violent, the President, of course, was not alone at the White House, and the people closest to him—his family and advisers—who saw this unfolding in real-time, begged him, implored him to stop the attack. An aide to Mark Meadows, the President's Chief of Staff, urged his boss to go see the President, saying: "They are going to kill people." "They are going to kill people."

Trump, Donald J. (@realdonaldtrump). Jan. 6, 2021, 2:38 PM. *The Daily Briefing with Dana Perino*, Fox News, January 6, 2021; Capitol security footage, January 6, 2021; Groeger, Lena V. et al. "What Parler Saw During the Attack on the Capitol," January 17, 2021; YouTube post; "Lawmakers Evacuate Congress as Trump Supporters Storm Capitol Building," *VOA News*, January 6, 2021

That is what those around President Trump feared, and still nothing. It wasn't until 2:38 p.m., nearly two hours after the start of the siege, that Donald Trump even acknowledged the attack. And when he finally did acknowledge the attack, here is what he said. On the right you will see what had been happening prior to that tweet and as he sent the tweet, and on the left you will see exactly what he tweeted.*

> Unidentified Reporter: I'm going to stop you there for just one moment because we do have some breaking news. We want to bring in congressional correspondent Chad Pergram as this is all developing right now. Chad, I understand the Capitol is now on lockdown?
>
> (Video of rioters violently breaking into the Capitol building as Members and Senators are evacuated.)

---

* Senators saw a 2:38 p.m. tweet from Trump: "Please support our Capitol Police and Law Enforcement. They are truly on the side of our country!" juxtaposed against images of rioters breaking into the building.

Reporter: They're definitely fired up. The chant I heard the most today was "fight for Trump," and that's clearly what many of them feel they're doing.

Unidentified Speaker: Hold the line.

(Rioters singing as they collectively push on Capitol doors with broken glass: O'er the land of the free.)

That is what our President saw unfolding in real time, broadcast all over television, and this is what he tweeted at 2:38 p.m.: "Please support our Capitol Police and Law Enforcement. They are truly on the side of our Country. Stay peaceful!"

Much has been made of the fact that in this tweet he says, "Stay peaceful." Senators, "stay peaceful"? Think about that for a second.

These folks were not peaceful. They were breaking windows, pushing through law enforcement officers, waving the flag as they invaded this Capitol Building. This was a violent, armed attack. "Stay peaceful"? How about: Stop the attack. Stop the violence. "Stay peaceful"? How about you say: Immediately leave. Stop. And he said: "Please support our Law Enforcement." How about he actually support our law enforcement by telling these insurgents to leave the Capitol immediately, which he never did. He didn't because, the truth is, he didn't want it to stop. He wanted them to stay and to stop the certification.

And his failure had grave and deadly consequences. By 2:45 p.m., the warnings were tragically proven correct. Ashli Babbitt was shot by an officer as she tried to break through a glass door to reach the Speaker's Lobby. At this point, the pleas to Donald Trump, publicly and privately, grew even more desperate. At 2:54 p.m., Alyssa Farah, a former strategic communications director, begged the President: "Condemn this now. You are the only one they will listen to. For our country!"

Mick Mulvaney, the President's former Chief of Staff, his right-hand man at one point, tweeted at 3:01: "The President's tweet is not enough. He can stop this now and needs to do exactly that. Tell these folks to go home. He can stop this now. Tell these folks to go home."

At 3:06 p.m., Representative McCarthy appeared on FOX News. Here is what he said.

Mr. McCARTHY: I could not be sadder or more disappointed with the way our country looks at this very moment. People are getting hurt. Anyone involved in this, if you're hearing me, hear me very loud and clear: This is not the American way.

He is saying on FOX News, which the President watches: This is not the American way. Stop the attack. Representative Gallagher, at 3:11 p.m., while secured in his own office, posted a video to Twitter.

> Mr. GALLAGHER: Mr. President, you have got to stop this. You are the only person who can call this off. Call it off.

And then, when the President didn't answer his pleas on Twitter, Representative Gallagher went on live television.

> Mr. GALLAGHER: I mean, this is insane. I mean—I—I have not seen anything like this since I deployed to Iraq in 2007 and 2008. I mean, this is America, and this is what is happening right now. We need—the President needs to call it off. Like, call it off. Call it off.

Representative Gallagher, you see there, said he had not seen anything like this since he was deployed in Iraq. The message around the President was clear, from everyone: You need to call this off. Stop it. But does he? No. His next tweet was not until about 3:13 p.m. Once again, it is important to consider what was happening between Donald Trump's 2:38 p.m. tweet and his next tweet at 3:13 p.m. You will see footage from the attack during that time on the right and Donald Trump's tweet on the left.*

> Unidentified Speaker on Fox News: We've been informed that protesters have penetrated the Capitol.
>
> Unidentified Rioter: This is my fucking building.
>
> Unidentified Speaker on Fox News: I tell ya, the sentiment in the streets is really getting to a different level. This is spinning out of control. This is turning violent. This is getting dangerous.
>
> Unidentified Rioter: Stand up for America.
>
> (Footage of rioters trying to break down the doors into the lower levels of the Capitol building.)

This isn't ten minutes into the insurrection. This isn't just after his speech earlier that day. That is what our Commander in Chief saw happening, and that was

---

* Trump's next tweet, sent at 3:13 p.m., read: "I am asking for everyone at the Capitol to remain peaceful. No violence! Remember, WE are the Party of Law & Order—respect the Law and our great men & women in Blue. Thank you!" Senators saw this tweet next to broadcasts that were being played on TV contemporaneously.

his response. You will notice one of the things he says to his mob, to these insur-rectionists, rather than to stop or to leave, was to say thank you.

Thank you. Thank you for what? Thank you for shattering the windows and destroying property? Thank you for injuring more than 140 police officers? Thank you for putting in danger all of our lives and the lives of our families? How about, instead of "thank you," Donald Trump, on that day, acted like our Commander in Chief and stopped this, as only he could, and told those people to leave. Here is what former Governor Chris Christie, his very good friend, said after that tweet.

> Mr. CHRISTIE, on ABC News: It's pretty simple. The President caused this protest to occur. He is the only one who can make it stop. What the President said is not good enough. The President has to come out and tell his supporters to leave the Capitol grounds and to allow the Congress to do their business peacefully, and anything short of that is an abrogation of his responsibility.

He is right. Chris Christie is right.

We know how Donald Trump acts on Twitter and otherwise when he has a mes-sage to convey. In fact, I asked you to remember those tweets earlier this morn-ing when he yelled on Twitter: "STOP THE COUNT." When he wanted to incite his supporters to show up on January 6, President Trump tweeted sixteen times between midnight on January 5 and his noon rally/speech the next day—sixteen times to get them to do something he wanted. And his message in those sixteen times was clear: "Fight." "Stay strong." "Be strong."

But when the violence started, he never once said the one thing everyone around him was begging him to say: "Stop the attack." He refused to stop it. And as Gov-ernor Christie and Representative Kinzinger and others made clear, only Donald Trump could have stopped that attack.

> Mr. KINZINGER on NewsNation Now: You know, a guy who knows how to tweet very aggressively on Twitter, you know, puts out one of the weakest statements on one of the saddest days in American history because his ego won't let him, you know, admit defeat.

He was not just our Commander in Chief. He had incited the attack. The insur-gents were following his commands, as we saw when they read aloud the tweet attacking the Vice President. They confirmed this during the attack too.

> Unidentified Speaker inside the Capitol to Police: Stand down, you're outnumbered. There's a fucking million of us out there. And we are listening to Trump, your boss!

Senators, ask yourselves this: How easy would it have been for the President to give a simple command, a simple instruction, just telling them: "Stop. Leave." This was a dereliction of duty, plain and simple, and it would have been for any President who had done that. And that brings me to my next point. You heard from my colleagues that when planning this attack, the insurgents predicted that Donald Trump would command the National Guard to help them.

There is a lot that we don't know yet about what happened that day, but here is what we do know: Donald Trump did not send help to these officers who were badly outnumbered, overwhelmed, and being beaten down. Two hours into the insurrection, by 3 p.m., President Trump had not deployed the National Guard or any other law enforcement to help, despite multiple pleas to do so. President Donald Trump was at the time our Commander in Chief of the United States of America. He took a solemn oath to preserve, protect, and defend this country, and he failed to uphold that oath. In fact, there is no indication that President Trump ever made a call to have the Guard deployed or had anything to do with the Guard being deployed when it ultimately was.

Shortly after 3:04 p.m., the Acting Defense Secretary announced that the Guard had been activated and listed the people he spoke with prior to this activation, including Vice President Mike Pence, Speaker Pelosi, Leader McConnell, Senator Schumer, and Representative Hoyer. But that list did not include the President. This omission of his name was reportedly not accidental. According to reports, "Trump initially rebuffed requests to mobilize the National Guard and required interference by other officials," including his own White House Counsel. And later, "as a mob of Trump supporters breached police barricades and seized the Capitol," Trump reportedly was "disengaged in discussions with Pentagon leaders about deploying the National Guard to aid the overwhelmed U.S. Capitol Police." President Trump was reportedly "completely, totally out of it. He made no attempt to reach [the National Guard.]" And it was Vice President Pence, still under threat for his life, who reportedly spoke to the Guard.

President Trump's conduct confirms this too. At no point on January 6 did Donald Trump even reference the National Guard. The only thing that we heard connecting the President to the Guard was from his Press Secretary, who tweeted about the Guard being deployed at the President's direction over half an hour later, at 3:36 p.m. We have seen what Donald Trump does when he tries to take credit for something, and yet, even when the National Guard was finally deployed, he didn't even acknowledge it. In fact, he didn't say a word about the National Guard the entire day.

Think about that: the bloodiest attack we have seen on our Capitol since 1812, and our President couldn't be bothered to even mention that help was on its way.

These insurgents had been attacking our government for over four hours by that point. And we may have been the target, but it was the brave men and women who protect our Capitol who were out there combating thousands of armed insurgents in a fight for their lives, and that is who Donald Trump left entirely unprotected.

(Video montage of rioters violently clashing with police outside the Capitol.)

This is hard to watch, but I think it is important to understand what the Capitol Police were facing, how severely they were outnumbered while our Commander in Chief, whose job it was to protect and defend them, was just watching, doing nothing for hours, refusing to send help. If he wanted to protect these officers, if he cared about their safety, as he tweeted about, he would have told his supporters to leave. He would have sent help right away.

One brave officer was killed. Others took their lives after the attack. More than 140 police officers were injured, including cracked ribs, smashed spinal discs. One officer will lose an eye. Another was stabbed with a metal fence stake. They were completely and violently overwhelmed by a mob and needed help, and our Commander in Chief, President Trump, refused to send it. Senators, you have seen all the evidence so far, and this is clear: On January 6, President Trump left everyone in this Capitol for dead. For the next hour after President Trump's 3 p.m. tweet, he still did nothing. Not until 4:17 p.m., over three and a half hours after the violence started, did our President send a message finally asking the insurgents to go home. On the right, you will see what happened that day in the hours leading up to his prerecorded video. On the left, you will see his message. Let's watch.*

President TRUMP, in prerecorded video posted to Twitter: I know your pain, I know your hurt, we had an election that was stolen from us. It was a landslide election, and everyone knows it, especially the other side. But you have to go home now. We have to have peace. We have to have law and order. We have to respect our great people in law and order. We don't want anybody hurt. It's a very tough period of time. There's never been a time like this, where such a thing happened, where they could take it away from all of us. From me, from you, from our country. This was a fraudulent election, but we can't play into the hands of these people. We have to have peace. So go home. We love you, you're very special. We've seen what happens, you see the way others are treated that are so bad and so evil. I know how you feel. But go home and go home in peace.

---

* As Trump's video played, Senators were also shown a montage of videos displaying the violence that took place during the hours preceding Trump's message.

This is the first time our Commander in Chief spoke publicly at all since the attack began, over three and a half hours after it started, and these are the entirety of the words the President spoke out loud to the American people or to the attackers that entire day. Nowhere in that video, not once did he say: "I condemn this insurrection. I condemn what you did today." Nowhere did he say: "I am sending help immediately. Stop this."

Here is what he said instead: "I know your pain, I know you're hurt. We had an election that was stolen." Even after all the things we witnessed, even after all of that carnage, he goes out and tells the same big lie, the same big lie that enraged and incited the attack. He repeated this while the attack was ongoing and while we were still under threat. And here is what else he said: "Go home in peace. We love you, you're very special."

Senators, you were here. You saw this with your own eyes. You faced that danger. And when President Trump had an opportunity to confront them as the leader of us all, as our Commander in Chief, what did he tell them? "We love you, you're very special." This was not a condemnation; this was a message of consolation, of support, of praise. And if there is any doubt that his supporters, these insurgents, took this as a message of support and praise, watch for yourselves.

Mr. ANGELI: Donald Trump asked everybody to go home. He just said—he just put out a tweet. It's a minute long. He asked everybody to go home.

Unidentified Speaker: Why do you think so?

Mr. ANGELI: Because, dude, we won the fucking day. We fucking won.

Unidentified Speaker: How did we win?

Mr. ANGELI: Well, we won by sending a message to the Senators and the Congressmen, we won by sending a message to Pence, okay, that if they don't do as—as it is their oath do, if they don't uphold the Constitution, then we will remove them from office, one way or another.

I suspect you recognize that man. You will hear him say that "we won the day." Who won the day? We know that at least five people lost their lives that day. The House and the Senate were in life-threatening danger, and so was the Vice President, and think of everyone else here as well. Who won on January 6? That is not a win for America, but it is a win for Donald Trump unless we hold him accountable.

Now, a little over an hour after that video, the brave members of law enforcement secured the Capitol, and we as a Congress got ready to continue certifying the results of our free and fair election. A half hour after that, President Trump issued another tweet. In case there was any doubt as to whether he was happy with the people who did this, as to whether he had incited this, he commemorated what happened on January 6.

At 6:01 p.m. on January 6, he tweeted: "These are the things and events that happen when a sacred landslide election victory is so unceremoniously & viciously stripped away from great patriots who have been badly & unfairly treated for so long." Ending with: "Remember this day forever!"

My colleague Manager Cicilline started with this tweet because this tweet shows exactly how Donald Trump felt about what happened on January 6. "These are the things . . . that happen." He is saying this was foreseeable. He is saying: "I told you this was going to happen if you certified the election for anyone else, and you got what you deserved for trying to take my power away." "[G]reat patriots. . . . Go home with love & in peace. Remember this day forever!" He is saying to them: "You did good." He is not regretful. He is not grieving. He is not sad. He is not angry about the attack. He is celebrating it. He is commemorating it.

This is the entirety of what President Trump said to the public once the attack began—five tweets and a prerecorded video. On the day of the most bloody insurrection we faced in generations, our Commander in Chief, who is known for sending 108 tweets in a normal day, sent five tweets and a prerecorded video. That is the entirety of President Trump's public statements from when the attack began until he went to bed on January 6. That is all he did despite all the people we know who begged him to preserve, protect, and defend. That was our Commander in Chief's response.

He began the day with "Our country has had enough, we will not take it anymore, and that's what this is all about," and he ended the attack with letting us know that we got what he forewarned that morning. We will, of course, each of us, remember that day forever, but not in the way that President Trump intended, not because of the actions of these violent, unpatriotic insurrectionists. I will remember that day forever because despite President Trump's vicious attempts throughout the day to encourage the siege and block the certification, he failed. At 8:06 p.m., the Senate gaveled into session, and the counting of the electoral votes continued. About an hour later, the House followed suit. And close to 4 a.m., after spending a significant part of the day evacuated or on the floor or hiding, this great body fulfilled the will of the people and certified the electoral college vote.

And I am proud to be part of Congress. I am proud that we ensured that the will of the American people finally prevailed on that day. And I am proud that I and everyone in this room abided by our oath of office even if the President didn't abide by his. President Trump, too, took an oath as President. He swore on a Bible to preserve, protect, and defend. And who among us can honestly say they believe that he upheld that oath? Who among us will let his utter dereliction of duty stand?

DAY THREE

TRIAL OF DONALD J. TRUMP,
PRESIDENT OF THE UNITED STATES

Ms. MANAGER DeGETTE: MY FRIENDS AND COLLEAGUES, YESTERDAY WAS AN emotionally wrenching day. As I watched the footage of the violence in the Capitol Building, my own experience flooded back to me. I was one of the unlucky Members who was stuck in the House Gallery along with Congresswoman Dean. As the House floor was cleared beneath us of Members and staff, we could see the mob pounding on the door to the House Chamber. We could see the Capitol Police officers inside the Chamber pull their guns and point them at the intruders. Then we heard gunshots on the other side, and we flung ourselves down on the floor and removed our Member pins. Then we heard pounding on the very flimsy Gallery doors right up above us. Finally, after that situation for some time, we were told to run out of the door at the end of the Gallery.

As we ran through a line of police toward the staircase, this is what I saw: the SWAT team pointing automatic weapons at marauders on the floor. Looking at these people makes you wonder: Who sent them here? In the next few minutes, I want to step back from the horrors of the attack itself and look at January 6 from a totally different perspective—the perspective of the insurrectionists themselves. Their own statements before, during, and after the attack make clear the attack was done for Donald Trump, at his instructions and to fulfill his wishes. Donald Trump had sent them there. They truly believed that the whole intrusion was at the President's orders, and we know that because they said so. Many of them actually posed for pictures, bragging about it on social media, and they tagged Mr. Trump in tweets.

Folks, this was not a hidden crime. The President told them to be there, and so they actually believed they would face no punishment. The defense argued in their briefs, and they argued again here on Tuesday that the insurrectionists were acting on their own, that they were not incited by President Trump or acting at his direction. This is in their brief: they did so of their own accord and for their own reasons and are being criminally prosecuted. But that is just not the case. It is not what the insurrectionists actually said. They said they came here because the President instructed them to do so. Leading up to the attack, the insurrectionists said they were coming to D.C. for President Trump. He invited them with clear instructions for a specific time and place and with clear orders: stop to fight—or to fight to stop the certification in Congress by any means necessary.

The crowd at Donald Trump's speech echoed and chanted his words, and when people in the crowd followed his direction and marched to the Capitol, they chanted the same words as they breached this building. Now, let's return to the speech for a moment. During the rally, President Trump led the crowd in a "Stop the steal" chant. Here is what that chant sounded like from the crowd's perspective:

President TRUMP, at the January 6, 2021 rally, from the crowd's perspective, with extremely loud chanting from a sea of people: And to use a favorite term that all of you people really came up with: We will stop the steal.

(People chanting: Yeah.) (People chanting: Stop the steal.)

Soon after, the President basked as the crowd chanted, "Fight for Trump." And when he incited the crowd to show strength, people responded: "Storm the Capitol." "Invade the Capitol."

Here are both of those moments but from the crowd's perspective:

(People repeatedly chanting: Fight for Trump.)

President TRUMP: Thank you.

President TRUMP: You have to show strength.

Unidentified Speakers: Yes. Invade the Capitol Building!

We also have another perspective from this moment: online extremist chatter.

At the same time as the people in the crowd shouted, "Take the Capitol Building," as President Trump said, "Show strength," a person posted to Parler saying: "Time to fight. Civil war is upon us."

Another user said: "We are going to have a civil war. Get ready!"

An analysis found that members of "Civil War" quadrupled on Parler in the hour after Donald Trump said, "Show strength." When the insurrectionists got to the Capitol, they continued those rally cries. Insurrectionists holding Confederate flags and brandishing weapons cheered the President's very words:

Unidentified Speaker as rioters fight with police and approach doors to the Capitol building.

(People repeatedly chanting. Stop the steal.)

You heard them chanting "Stop the steal," and as the crowd chanted at the rally, the crowd at the Capitol made clear who they were doing this for. They also chanted "Fight for Trump."

(People chanting outside the Capitol doors: Fight for Trump.)

And it wasn't just that they were doing this for Mr. Trump. They were following his instructions. They said he had invited them, and, in fact, as we heard, he had invited them. As one man explained on a livestream he taped from inside the Capitol, "Our president wants us here. . . . We wait and take orders from our president." Footage from inside the Capitol shows when the insurrectionists first got into the building and confronted police, the mob screamed at the officers that they were listening to President Trump.

Unidentified Speaker: Stand down. You're outnumbered. There's a fucking million of us out there, and we are listening to Trump, your boss.

The insurrectionists argued with law enforcement that they shouldn't even be fighting them because they believed that the Commander in Chief was ordering this. This was the person's understanding. When President-Elect Biden went on television that day to demand an end to the siege, one woman asked this:

> Unidentified Speaker: Does he not realize President Trump called us to siege the place?

The examples of these types of comments are endless. Don't worry. I won't play all of them. But it wasn't just the words of the insurrectionists that proved that they did this in response to orders from their Commander in Chief. We can see this in the fact that they were not hiding. One rioter, in a livestream at the Capitol said: "He'll be happy. We're fighting for Trump."

> Unidentified Speakers: Let's call Trump, yes. Dude, dude, let's tell Trump what's up. Trump would be very upset. They'd be like, no. Just say we love them. We love you, bro. No, he'll be happy. What do you mean? We're fighting for Trump.

And, again, this was not an isolated incident. The individuals in this slide posted photos of themselves committing these crimes. Trump supporters who had broken into the Capitol were taking selfies, streaming live videos, and posing.

Social media posts via Balsamo, Michael et al. "'THIS IS ME': Rioters Flaunt Involvement in Capitol Siege," Associated Press, January 26, 2021

In fact, they wanted the President to know: "This is me!" In fact, you can see the person wrote on his own posting: "This is me!" And if there were any remaining doubt, after hours of prompting, when President Trump finally told the insurrectionists to go home, only then did some of them begin to listen.

As you previously saw, at 4:17 p.m., Mr. Trump released a prerecorded video saying to the mob: "Go home. We love you. You're very special." Shortly after he tweeted this video, a few of the insurrectionists who had seen it could be claiming victory—heard claiming victory—and telling people to go home because of Donald Trump's message and instructions. You saw earlier the insurrectionist Jacob Chansley, who told someone: "We won the day."

A little before that video of Chansley, he said the same thing to the crowd through a bullhorn and instructed them to go home because of the video that President Trump had tweeted. Let's watch.

> Unidentified Speaker: Today is ours, ladies and gentlemen. We won the day. Today is ours. We won the day. That's right. Donald Trump has asked everybody to just go home. You can look it up on his Twitter. He just did a video. It's a minute long. He asked everybody to go home.

Even after the attack, the insurrectionists made clear to law enforcement that they were just following President Trump's orders. They didn't shy away from their crimes because they thought they were following orders from the Commander in Chief and so they would not be punished.

They were wrong. After the attack, there were dozens of arrests. These were Federal offenses, including assaulting the police. When law enforcement interviewed the people who were at the Capitol on January 6, they, once again, said it was because the President told them to be there. Robert Sanford was seen in this widely circulated video throwing a fire extinguisher that struck a Capitol Police officer outside the building.

> (Video of man throwing a fire extinguisher and hitting an officer.)

A witness told the FBI that Sanford said he had traveled to Washington, D.C., on a bus with a group of people. The group had gone to the White House and listened to Donald J. Trump's speech and then had followed the President's instructions and gone to the Capitol.

Folks, the insurrectionists didn't just make this up. As Sanford's lawyer explained: "You're being told, 'You gotta fight like hell.' Does 'fight like hell' mean you throw things at people? Maybe." The lawyer added that his client "wouldn't have been there if it wasn't for the president.'"

Now, Sanford wasn't the exception; he was the rule. In their statements after the attack, insurrectionists routinely echoed what they had said before and during the attack: they were there because the President told them to be. Now, look, the lawyers who are saying that their clients were told to commit these acts by Mr. Trump, well, they know that putting the blame on the President doesn't exonerate their clients. They are just saying it, frankly, because that is exactly what happened.

Another Trump supporter who has been federally charged is Texas real estate agent Jennifer Ryan. Now, Ms. Ryan has given many TV interviews in which she says she was only doing what the President asked her and others to do. She also recorded video before the rally talking about the mob's plans for violence, and here is what she said.

> Ms. RYAN: Personally, I do not feel a sense of shame or guilt from my heart for what I was doing. I thought I was following my President. I thought I was follow-ing what we were called to do. He asked us to fly there. He asked us to be there. So I was doing what he asked us to do. Ultimately, yes, we were going in solidarity with President Trump. President Trump requested that we be in D.C. on the 6th, so this was our way of going and stopping the steal. If it comes down to work—guess what—I'm going to be there. We're all going to be up here, and we're going to be breaking those windows.

Yet another Trump supporter who was arrested after breaching the Capitol, Douglas Sweet, explained in a media interview why he did it. Referring to Donald Trump, Mr. Sweet said: "He said, 'Hey, I need my digital soldiers to show up on January 6.' And we all did."

Some of these individuals who joined in the attack on our Capitol did so as part of violent, racist groups, which have been officially condemned by our government.

Daniel Goodwyn is a self-proclaimed member of the Proud Boys. He was one of many. On November 7, Goodwyn tweeted a picture showing a Proud Boys logo surrounded by "Stand Back" and "Stand By" and, again, "Stand back and stand by!" and "Await orders from our Commander in Chief." Look closely at this slide.[*] You are looking at an image of Goodwyn's own tweet. He was such a loyal fol-lower of President Trump that he used the President's photo as his own profile picture on Twitter.

Now, remember, President Trump told them to "Stand back and stand by" at the debate. They took it as a call to arms. And when he called them to arms, they were all ready to act. They were waiting for their orders, which they got on January 6. And Goodwyn followed those orders. He stood ready as others broke into the win-

---

[*] Senators saw a screenshot of a tweet by Goodwyn from November 7, 2020 that featured the Proud Boys logo, the words "Stand Back and Stand By," and instructions to Goodwyn's followers to show up at their state capitols at noon local time to "await orders from our Com-mander in Chief."

dows of the Capitol and climbed inside. Here he is on another of the insurrectionist live streams in one of the first floor hallways of the building. When it became clear that Donald Trump was not going to save these folks from prosecution, when it became clear that the Commander in Chief had given false commands that went against this country, some of his supporters even expressed regret, and they said they felt duped.

Here is Jacob Chansley again, whom we saw in a video claiming victory after the President told the rioters to go home. Earlier in the afternoon, as you will recall, Chansley carried a spear as he breached the Capitol, entered the Senate through the Gallery, and went right here, onto the Senate floor. Chansley left a threatening note for Vice President Pence, right there on the Senate dais. It read: "It's only a matter of time. Justice is coming."

On January 7, Chansley spoke to the FBI, and he said that he came as part of a group effort with other "patriots" from Arizona at the request of the President that all "patriots" come to D.C. on January 6, 2021. On January 14, Chansley's lawyer gave an interview to Chris Cuomo, in which he said that Chansley was there "at the invitation of our President, who said [he would] walk down Pennsylvania Avenue with him." In fact, Chansley's lawyer now says that Chansley felt duped by the President, and he regrets what the President brought him to do.

This man, who ran through our halls, who ran into this Chamber, who sat right there on the dais, and who wrote a note for Vice President Pence that he was coming for him—he and those with him declared they would remove us from office if we went against Donald Trump. Now he is saying he would not have done any of that if Mr. Trump had told him not to.

Chansley is not alone in his post-arrest confession that he was following the directions of Donald Trump. As more and more of these people have been charged, the confession and the regret simply cascades. More and more insurrectionists are admitting that they came at Trump's direction. When Riley June Williams, known for allegedly helping steal a laptop from Speaker Pelosi's office, appeared in court on January 21, her lawyer said to the judge: "It is regrettable that Ms. Williams took the President's bait and went inside the Capitol." Troy Smocks, who was in the Capitol riot on January 6, posted online that day: "[T]oday President Trump told Us to 'fight like hell.'" He also posted that the President "said that Our cause was a matter of national security."

Samuel Fisher was charged with disorderly conduct and illegally being in the Capitol on January 6. That day, before the attack on this building, he wrote on his website: "Trump just needs to fire the bat signal . . . and then the pain comes." The lawyer for Dominic Pezzola, a leader of the Proud Boys, who was the first person to break inside the Capitol, said that President Trump effectively told his client and others: "'People of the country, come on down, let people know what you think.' [The] logical thinking was, 'He invited us down.'" Pezzola's lawyer went on: "These were people acting in a way they have never acted before, and it begs the question, 'Who lit the fuse?'"

On January 6, we know who lit the fuse. Donald Trump told these insurrectionists to come to the Capitol and stop the steal. And they did come to the Capitol, and they tried to stop the certification. They came because he told them to. And they did stop our proceedings, but only temporarily, because he told them to.

Have you noticed, throughout this presentation, the uncanny similarity, over and over and over again, of what all these people are saying? They said what Donald Trump said, and they echo each other: "Stand back and stand by." "Stop the steal." "Fight like hell." "Trump sent us." "We are listening to Trump."

The riots that day left at least seven people dead; more than 150 people injured; Members, Senators, and our staffs all traumatized to this day; damage and pain to our Capitol; damage and pain to Americans; damage to our police force; and damage to other nations who have always seen us as a bastion of democracy. All of these people who have been arrested and charged, they are being held accountable for their actions. Their leader, the man who incited them, must be held accountable as well. But, as I said earlier, you don't have to take my word for it that the insurrectionists acted at Donald Trump's direction. They said so. They were invited here. They were invited by the President of the United States.

> Unidentified rioter outside the Capitol, screaming: We were invited here. We were invited. Hey, we were invited here. We were invited by the President of the United States.

. . .

Mr. Manager RASKIN: Senators, Representative DeGette just showed how the insurrectionists believed and understood themselves to be following President Trump's marching orders. She explained in chilling detail how they were acting in perfect alignment with his political instructions and his explicit strategy to retain power. They did what he told them to do.

This pro-Trump insurrection did not spring into life out of thin air. We saw how Trump spent months cultivating America's most dangerous extremist groups. We saw how he riled them up with corrosive lies and violent rhetoric, so much so that they were ready and eager for their most dangerous mission, invalidating the will of the people to keep Donald Trump in office. We must remember that this was not the first time Donald Trump had inflamed and incited a mob. Trump knew that his incitement would result in violence not only because of the thousands of violent messages that were posted all over the forums and the widespread news of preparations for violence among extremist groups and his communications on Twitter with the insurrectionists themselves; he knew it also because he had seen many of the exact same groups he was mobilizing participate in extremist violence before. Moreover, he had seen clearly how his own incitement of violence in praise after the violence took place galvanized, encouraged, and electrified these extremist followers.

These tactics were road-tested. January 6 was a culmination of the President's actions, not an aberration from them. The insurrection was the most violent and dangerous episode—so far—in Donald Trump's continuing pattern and practice of inciting violence. But I emphasize "so far." Earlier, Congresswoman Plaskett showed several episodes of Trump's incitement that took place during the Presidential election. But his encouragement of violence against other public officials who he thought had crossed him long predates the 2020 campaign. The incitement of violence is always dangerous, but it is uniquely intolerable when done by the President of the United States of America.

But that became the norm. On President Trump's watch, white supremacists and extremist groups have spread like wildfire across the land. His own Department of Homeland Security called homegrown terrorism the No. 1 threat facing Americans today. But no matter how many people inside and outside government begged him to condemn extreme elements promoting violence and, indeed, civil war in America and race war in America, he just wouldn't do it, and that is because he wanted to incite and provoke their violence for his own political gain and for his own strategic objectives. Ever since he became President, Trump revealed what he thought of political violence for his side. He praised it, and he encouraged it. Right now, I am going to play for you just a few clips from over the years when the President's words successfully incited his supporters into assaulting his opponents.

(Footage from an October 23, 2015 Trump rally.)

(Footage of a person being beaten by a crowd yelling: USA! USA!)

TRUMP, at the rally: See, the first group, I was nice: Oh, take your time. The second group, I was pretty nice. The third group, I'll be a little more violent. And the fourth group, I'll say: Get the hell out of here.

(Footage of a rally from November 21, 2015.)

(Footage of a person being beaten by a crowd.)

TRUMP, at the rally: Yeah, get him the hell out of here, will you, please? Get him out of here. Throw him out.

TRUMP, at a February 1, 2016 rally: I get a little notice—in case you see the security guys, they are wonderful security guys. They said: "Mr. Trump, there may be somebody with tomatoes in the audience." So if you see somebody getting ready to throw a tomato, knock the crap out of them, would you? Seriously, OK? Just knock the hell—I promise you, I will pay for the legal fees. I promise.

Well, we have seen these clips and many, many more like them before, but think about the brutal power and effectiveness of his words with his followers. You heard him. He told his supporters to be a little more violent, and they responded to his command by literally dragging a protester across the floor at one of his campaign rallies. He cried: "Get him the hell out of here. Throw him out." His supporters punched and kicked another protester as he was escorted from the hall. He told his supporters to knock the hell out of people who opposed him and promised to pay the legal fees of the assailants.

Time after time, he encouraged violence. His supporters listened, and they got the message. But it wasn't just Trump's encouragement of violence that conditioned his supporters to participate in this insurrection on January 6; it was also his explicit sanctioning of the violence after it took place. Let's watch some of those incidents, beginning with Trump praising supporters who assaulted a black protester.

(Footage from March 9, 2016 rally where a member of the crowd is seen throwing the first punch at a black protestor in the crowd as Trump talks.)

President TRUMP, discussing the beating later: But we've had a couple that were really violent. And the particular one, when I said I would like to bang 'em, that was a very vicious—you know, it was a guy who was swinging—very loud and then started swinging at the audience. And you know what? The audience swung back. And I thought it was very, very appropriate. He was swinging, he was hitting people, and the audience hit back. And that's what we need a little bit more of.

Congressional candidate Greg Gianforte, to a reporter, at a campaign event: We will talk to you about that later.

Reporter: Yep, but, there's not going to be time.

(Crashing sounds as reporter is assaulted.)

GIANFORTE: I am sick and tired of you guys. The last time you came here you did the same thing. Get the hell out of here. Get the hell out of here. The last guy did the same thing. Are you *The Guardian*?

Reporter: Yes, and you just broke my glasses.

GIANFORTE: The last guy did the same damn thing.

Reporter: You just body-slammed me and broke my glasses.

President TRUMP: Greg [Gianforte] is smart. And, by the way, never wrestle him. (Crowd laughs.) Do you understand that? Never. Any guy that can do a body slam, he is my kind—(Crowd laughs and cheers.)

(White supremacists marching in Charlottesville: Jews will not replace us.) (People chanting: Fuck you, faggots.)

(Members of the Charlottesville crowd attack counter-protestors.)

Unidentified Speaker: I am not even saying we are not violent. I'm saying that we fucking didn't aggress. We did not initiate force against anybody. We are not non-violent. We will fucking kill these people if we have to.

(Footage of a car driving into a crowd of counter-protestors in Charlottesville, fatally injuring Heather Heyer, as the crowd of counter-protestors screams.)

President TRUMP, after Heyer's murder, at a press conference: I do think there's blame, yes. I think there is blame on both sides. You look at—you look at both sides. I think there is blame on both sides. You also had people that were very fine people on both sides.

Just in case you didn't catch all of that, the President praised a Republican candidate who assaulted a journalist as "my kind" of guy. He said there were "very fine people on both sides" when the neo-Nazis, the Klansmen, and Proud Boys invaded the city—the great city of Charlottesville—and killed Heather Heyer. And he said that an attack on a black protester at one of his rallies was very, very appropriate. Does that sound familiar? Listen to how President Trump responded when asked about his own conduct on January 6.

Reporter to Trump: What is your personal responsibility?

President TRUMP: So if you read my speech—and many people have done it—it has been analyzed, and people thought that what I said was totally appropriate.

So there the pattern is, staring us in the face. Very, very "appropriate," he said after a man was assaulted at one of his rallies. "Totally appropriate" was how he characterized his incitement on January 6, meaning that, of course, if given the chance, he would gladly do it again because why would he not engage in totally appropriate conduct?

An examination of his past statements makes it clear that when Donald Trump tells a crowd, as he did on January 6, "fight like hell or you won't have a country anymore," he meant for them to fight like hell. On January 6, that became clear to all of America.

Now, let's consider the events, Senators, that took place last year in Michigan where President Trump demonstrated his willingness and his ability to incite violence against government officials who he thought were getting in his way. When responding to extremist plots in Michigan, Trump showed he knew how to use the power of a mob to advance his political objectives. Beginning in March, Trump leveled attacks on Michigan Governor Gretchen Whitmer for the coronavirus policies in her State.

On March 17, the day after Governor Whitmer pushed the Federal Government to better support the States on COVID-19, Trump criticized her handling of the pandemic, tweeting: "Failing Michigan Governor must work harder and be much more proactive. We are pushing her to get the job done. I stand with Michigan!"

On March 27, he added: "I love Michigan, one of the reasons we are doing such a GREAT job for them during this horrible Pandemic. Yet your Governor, Gretchen 'Half' Whitmer is way in over her ahead, she doesn't have a clue. Likes blaming everyone for her own ineptitude! #MAGA."

By April, Trump's rhetorical attacks and name-calling turned to calls for mass mobilization of his supporters. This was a sign of things to come. On April 17, 2020, he tweeted: "LIBERATE MICHIGAN"

Not even two weeks later, on April 30, his supporters marched on the Michigan State capitol in Lansing. They stormed the building. Trump's marching orders were followed by aggressive action on the ground.

Unidentified crowd member: We have a right. Let us in.

(People chanting: Let us in. No more Whitmer!)

Unidentified Speakers: Heil, Heil Hitler! Heil Hitler to Whitmer! You policemen are all cowards. You betrayed us. The police have betrayed the people.

(People chanting: Lock her up.)

As the video shows, these militant protesters showed up ready to take a violent stand. They came armed and tightly packed themselves into the building with no regard, of course, for social distancing. This Trump-inspired mob may indeed look familiar to you: Confederate battle flags, MAGA hats, weapons, camo Army gear—just like the insurrectionists who showed up and invaded this Chamber on January 6.

Matthew Dae Smith, *Lansing State Journal*; Seth Herald, Reuters; Jeff Kowalsky, AFP via Getty Images; Win McNamee, Getty Images; Saul Loweb, AFP via Getty Images; Shannon Stapleton, Reuters

The siege of the Michigan State House was effectively a State-level dress rehearsal for the siege of the U.S. Capitol that Trump incited on January 6. It was a preview of the coming insurrection. President Trump's response to these two events was strikingly similar.

Following the armed siege in Lansing, President Trump refused to condemn the attacks on the Michigan capitol or denounce the violent lawbreakers. Instead, he did just the opposite. He upheld the righteousness of his violent followers' cause, and he put pressure on the victim of the attack to listen to his supporters. The day after the mob attack in Lansing, Trump told Governor Whitmer to negotiate with extremists, tweeting that the Governor should just "give a little" to the violent men who had stormed the Capitol, threatening not only the stability of the Michigan government but her own life.

As you can see, he tweeted: "The Governor of Michigan should give a little, and put out the fire. These are very good people, but they are angry. They want their lives back again, safely! See them, talk to them, make a deal." The President said heavily armed extremists carrying Confederate battle flags and pushing past police to overtake the Michigan State House chamber are "very good people" and just negotiate with them. It is clear he doesn't think that they are at fault in any way at all.

But April 30 wasn't the only time Trump supporters stormed the Michigan capitol. Emboldened by the praise and his encouragement and support, they escalated again. Governor Whitmer refused to capitulate to the President's demand to negotiate with them. Two weeks later, on May 14, Trump's mob again stormed the

State capitol. This time, as you can see here,* one man brought a doll with a noose around the neck, foreshadowing the appearance of the large gallows erected outside of this building, downstairs from here, on January 6, as the crowd chanted—and I still can hear the words ringing in my ear—"Hang Mike Pence. Hang Mike Pence. Hang Mike Pence."

Over the coming months, even after a crowd threatening Governor Whitmer stormed the capitol, Trump continued to assail her in public. At a rally in Michigan on September 10, Trump whipped up the crowd against Governor Whitmer, saying she doesn't have a clue about reopening her own state's economy. The crowd cheered.

Then, on October 8, the precise consequences of the President's incitement to violence were revealed to the whole world. Thirteen men were arrested by the FBI for plotting to storm the Michigan State capitol building, launch a civil war, kidnap Governor Whitmer, transport her to Wisconsin, and then try and execute her. This was an assassination conspiracy, a kidnapping conspiracy. Look at the language that they used. In the charging document, the FBI reported that one of the conspirators said he needed "200 men" to storm the capitol building and take political hostages, including the Governor. The suspect called it a "snatch and grab, man. Grab the [f'ing] Governor."

One of those men already pled guilty to this conspiracy. The plot was well organized, just like the one that was coming on January 6. The men in Michigan even considered building Molotov cocktails to disarm police vehicles and attempted to construct their own IEDs—something that actually happened here on January 6. Police authorities arrested extremists who had weapons and materials to build explosive devices, including one man found with an assault rifle and enough materials to make eleven Molotov cocktails. On September 17, 2020, one of the Michigan conspiracists posted, "When the time comes there will be no need to try and strike fear through presence. The fear will be manifested through bullets."

And what did Donald Trump do as President of the United States to defend one of our Nation's Governors against a plotted kidnapping by violent insurrections? Did he publicly condemn violent domestic extremists who hoped and planned to launch a civil war in America? No, not at all. He further inflamed them by continuing to attack the Governor who was the object of their hatred in this kidnapping conspiracy. The very night this conspiracy became public and that Governor Whitmer learned that there were thirteen men who were planning to kidnap and likely kill her, Trump did not condemn the violence. He did not criticize the extremists. He didn't even check on Governor Whitmer's safety.

---

* The Senators viewed a photo of a doll hanging from a makeshift noose.

He chose to vilify Governor Whitmer again and then, amazingly, took credit for foiling the plot against her, demanding her gratitude, and then quickly, of course, changed the subject to Antifa. He tweeted: "Governor Whitmer . . . has done a terrible job." He demanded that she thank him for the law enforcement operation that had foiled the kidnapping conspiracy that had been encouraged by his rhetoric.

On October 17, a little over a week after these people were arrested for preparing to kidnap Gretchen Whitmer, Donald Trump riled up the boisterous crowd in Muskegon with more personal attacks on Whitmer, driving the crowd to chant "Lock her up. Lock her up." He had now seen that some of his followers were prepared to engage in criminal violence with orchestrated attacks, deadly weapons, and willing bodies to storm a State capitol building and to attack his perceived political enemies, and so as the crowd chanted "Lock her up," he pivoted to his next goal. He told them they couldn't trust the Governor to administer fair elections in Michigan. He used the crowd that he knew would readily engage in violence to prepare his followers for his next and, of course, his paramount political objective: claiming the election was stolen and inciting insurrectionary action.

He did it again on October 27 during a preelection rally speech in Lansing, MI, where the capitol had been stormed. Trump openly joked with the crowd about critics saying his words had provoked the violent plot against Governor Whitmer. Check it out. It is telling.

President TRUMP, October 27, 2020: We got to get her going. I don't think she likes me too much.

(People chanting: Lock her up.)

President TRUMP: See, I don't comment to that because every time, if I make just even a little bit of a nod, they say: "The President led them on." No, I don't have to lead you on. Even a little nod, they say: "The President said." Your Governor, at the urging of her husband, who has abused our system very badly—the only man allowed in the State of Michigan—the only man allowed to go sailing is her husband. Now, your Governor—I don't think she likes me too much. Hey, hey, hey, hey, I'm the one. It was our people that helped her out with her problem. I mean, we have to see if it is a problem, right? People are entitled to say maybe it was a problem, maybe it wasn't. It was our people—my people—our people that helped her out.

So President Trump offered them a little winking inside joke about his constant incitement of the mob and how much can actually be communicated by him with just a little nod—just a little nod. He presided over another pounding, rhythmic rendition of his trademark chant: "Lock her up. Lock her up." Then, referring to the FBI's foiling of the kidnapping conspiracy, which was deadly serious, he said that he helped her out with a problem. "Maybe it was a problem; maybe it wasn't." We will "have to see." "Maybe it was a problem; maybe it wasn't."

The President of the United States of America—he could not bring himself to publicly oppose a kidnapping and potential assassination conspiracy plot against a sitting Governor of one of our fifty States? Trump knew exactly what he was doing in inciting the January 6 mob—exactly.

He had just seen how easily his words and actions inspired riots in Michigan. He sent a clear message to his supporters. He encouraged planning and conspiracies to take over capitol buildings and threaten public officials who refused to bow down to his political will. Is there any chance Donald Trump was surprised by the results of his own incitement? Let's do what Tom Paine told us to do, use our common sense, the sense we have in common as citizens.

If we don't draw the line here, what is next? What makes you think the nightmare with Donald Trump and his lawmaking and violent mobs is over? If we let him get away with it, and then it comes to your State capital or it comes back here again, what are we going to say? These prior acts of incitement cast a harsh light on Trump's obvious intent—obvious intent—his unavoidable knowledge of the consequences of his incitement, the unavoidable knowledge of the consequences of his incitement, and the clear foreseeability of the violent harm that he unleashed on our people and our Republic.

January 6 was not some unexpected, radical break from his normal law-abiding and peaceful disposition. This was his state of mind. This was his essential M.O. He knew that, egged on by his tweets, his lies, and his promise of a wild time in Washington to guarantee his grip on power, his most extreme followers would show up bright and early, ready to attack, ready to engage in violence, ready to fight like hell for their hero, just like they answered his call in Michigan.

President Trump has said over and over his supporters are loyal. In his own words, his supporters are the "most loyal" we have seen in our country's history. He knew that his most hardcore supporters were willing to direct violence at elected officials—indeed, to attack and lay siege to a capitol building—and he knew they would be ready to heed his call on January 6 to stop the steal by using violence to block the peaceful transfer of power in the United States. He knew they were coming. He brought them here, and he welcomed them with open arms: We hear you (and love you) from the Oval Office.

My dear colleagues, is there any political leader in this room who believes that if he is ever allowed by the Senate to get back into the Oval Office, Donald Trump would stop at inciting violence to get his way? Would you bet the lives of more police officers on that? Would you bet the safety of your family on that? Would you bet the future of your democracy on that? President Trump declared his conduct totally appropriate, so if he gets back into office and it happens again, we will have no one to blame but ourselves.

. . .

Mr. Manager LIEU: Good afternoon. My colleagues walked you through President Trump's actions leading up to January 6 and then the horrific events on January 6, and we saw both during the attack as well as in the days after the attack that this was a President who showed no remorse and took no accountability—in fact, quite the opposite. As Representative Raskin showed you, President Trump claimed that his actions were "totally appropriate."

The assertion that everyone thought Donald Trump's actions were totally appropriate, including people in this room, is, of course, untrue. It is also dangerous. That is why Members of Congress and U.S. Senators, former and current administration officials, State and local officials, all unequivocally confirm what we witnessed with our own eyes—that Donald Trump's conduct was wrong, it was destructive, dishonorable, and un-American.

President Trump's lack of remorse and refusal to take accountability during the attack shows his state of mind. It shows that he intended the events of January 6 to happen, and when it did, he delighted in it. President Trump's lack of remorse and refusal to take accountability after the attack poses its own unique and continuing danger. It sends the message that it is acceptable to incite a violent insurrection to overthrow the will of the people and that a President of the United States can do that and get away with it. That is why we have to hold President Trump accountable, to send a message that it is never patriotic to incite a violent attack against our Nation's Capitol and that future Presidents will know that they cannot follow in Donald Trump's footsteps and get away with it.

So let's start with the day of the attack. On insurrection day, January 6, President Trump did not once condemn the attack, not even once. Even when he finally asked the violent extremists to go home, which was three hours after the attack began, he sends this video, and he ends it with "You're very special. We love you." That was his message to people who perpetrated this violent, gruesome attack—"We love you"—and then two hours later, he tweets "Remember this day forever."

This is not a man who showed remorse, but it is worse than that. After that tweet, it took him another full day to even condemn the attack itself. The very next day, President Trump was eerily silent, and then at 7:01 p.m., he releases a prerecorded video, and there, President Trump for the first time, nearly thirty hours after the attack began, acknowledges and condemns the violent mayhem that occurred. He said the demonstrators "defiled the seat of American democracy." He said that these demonstrators didn't represent this country and if they broke the law, they would pay. But even in that video, he says more lies. He says in that

Donald J. Trump ✔
@realDonaldTrump

These are the things and events that happen when a sacred landslide election victory is so unceremoniously & viciously stripped away from great patriots who have been badly & unfairly treated for so long. Go home with love & in peace. Remember this day forever!

6:01 PM · Jan 6, 2021

very same video that he immediately deployed the National Guard. That, again, is not true. The National Guard was not deployed until over two hours after the attack began at around 3 p.m. Because of this late deployment, the National Guard did not arrive until after 5 p.m. When the Guard was deployed, the Pentagon had released a statement that showed the list of people—and you saw that list—of folks that were consulted before deploying the National Guard. Several people were on their list, including the Vice President. President Trump was not on that list.

You know, as a veteran, I find it deeply dishonorable that our Commander in Chief did not protect us. Then, later, he tried to take credit for something he failed to do. Shameful. Also, in that video, you should note what it did not say. Absent from that entire video was any actual acceptance of responsibility for his actions. Absent from that video was a call to his most fervent supporters to never do this again. And here was his final message in that so-called condemnation-of-attack video.

Here is what he actually said:

President TRUMP: And to all of my wonderful supporters, I know you are disappointed, but I also want you to know that our incredible journey is only just beginning.

President Trump not only failed to show remorse or take accountability, he made clear he is just beginning. For days, he did not address the Nation after this attack. We needed our Commander in Chief to lead, to unite a grieving country, to comfort us. But what did President Trump do? Nothing. Silence.

We are all aware that a violent mob murdered a police officer. It took President Trump three days before he lowered the flag of the United States of America—three days—and President Trump, who was Commander in Chief at the time, did not attend and pay respects to the officer who lay in state in the very building that he died defending.

Now, some people have argued that President Trump made a mistake, that he gets a mulligan. But we know President Trump didn't make a mistake because, you see, if you or I make a mistake when something very bad happens, we would show remorse; we would accept responsibility. President Trump didn't do any of that. Why not? Because he intended for what happened on January 6. And how do we know that? He told us. On January 12, as President Trump was boarding Air Force One, headed to Texas—and you saw this video before, and I am going to show it again—he was asked by a reporter: What is your role in what happened at the Capitol? What is your personal responsibility?

This was his response:

President TRUMP: But they've analyzed my speech and my words and my final paragraph, my final sentence, and everybody, to the T, thought it was totally appropriate.

On January 12, President Trump had seen the violent attack on the Capitol. He knew people had died, and his message to all of us was that his conduct was totally appropriate. I am a former prosecutor, and we are trained to recognize lack of remorse, but it doesn't take a prosecutor to understand that President Trump was not showing remorse; he was showing defiance. He was telling us that he would do this again; that he could do this again; that he and future Presidents can run for national election, lose an election, inflame their supporters for months, and then incite an insurrection and that that would be totally appropriate.

One week after the attack, on January 13, President Trump, in response to continuing bipartisan criticism, released another video.

Here is part of what he said:

President TRUMP: I want to be very clear. I unequivocally condemn the violence that we saw last week. Violence and vandalism have absolutely no place in our country and no place in our movement.

President Trump, of course, needed to make that statement. He needed to unequivocally condemn that attack, but he also needed to mean those words. You saw Donald Trump tweet endless attacks—sometimes 108 tweets in a day—and in public speeches and across rallies, repeating words of "Fight" and "Stop the steal" and "Never surrender."

You know what it looks like when President Trump wants to convey a message.

Forcefully, loudly, and repeatedly he does that. This video, sent after a week of the attack, was not that. We know this because, in this video, he again does not show remorse and does not take responsibility. He again does not acknowledge his role in the insurrection. He does not say in that video, for example, "Everything I said in the months prior went too far," and he does not say the one sentence that matters. He does not say the one sentence that would stop future political violence: "The election was not stolen." He still hasn't said that sentence.

That is why National Guard troops, in full body armor, still patrol outside. Reports from the White House also confirm that President Trump believed he was "forced by the bipartisan furor after the insurrection to acknowledge the new administration." We know he did not stand behind his belated condemnation because those around him confirmed it. Behind closed doors, sources confirmed that President Trump still refused to directly acknowledge his election loss to Joe Biden. He refused to even attend the peaceful transition of power—the first President in modern history.

President Trump even, reportedly, while watching the impeachment vote, "focused his ire" on the Republicans who voted for his impeachment, peppering aides with questions about "what he could do to exact revenge." President Trump has made clear that, if he is not held accountable, he will not be accountable. He will not stop.

Now, President Trump would have his base and the world believe that his conduct was totally appropriate. It is important to impeach that falsehood, to make clear to his supporters and everyone watching that what Donald Trump did was not acceptable—in fact, quite the opposite. People in his own party—State officials, former officials, current officials, Members of Congress—have, unambiguously and passionately, said that what Donald Trump did was "disgraceful," "shameful," and have called his behavior "existential" and "wrong," and they have said that his actions gave rise to one of the darkest chapters in United States' history. Let's hear what some of these officials had to say. Here are Governors Spencer Cox, Charlie Baker, Mike DeWine, Larry Hogan, and Phil Scott.

> Mr. COX: And people have to be held accountable. And yes, that includes the President.

> . . .

> Mr. BAKER: It's important to remember that they were the culmination of months of President Trump repeating over and over again that the American electoral system is a fraud. After he stoked the flames of outrage for weeks leading up to the events of yesterday, he refused to adequately prepare the U.S. Capitol for the possibility of

violence and left it nearly defenseless. His remarks during and after the travesty of the attack on the Capitol were disgraceful.

. . .

Mr. DEWINE: President Trump's continued refusal to accept the election results without producing credible evidence of a rigged election has stirred the fire that has threatened to burn down our democracy. This incendiary speech yesterday, the one he gave preceding the march, that he gave to the protesters, served only to fan those flames.

. . .

Mr. HOGAN: I proudly stood by my father's side at age 12 on the floor of the House Chamber as we both took the oath of office, an oath to support and defend the Constitution of the United States. It's clear to me that President Trump has abandoned this sacred oath.

. . .

Mr. SCOTT: Seeing our Capitol, a symbol of democracy around the world, stormed by an angry mob was heartbreaking. And let me be clear: These actions were not patriotic, and these people are not patriots. The fact that these flames of hate and insurrection were lit by the President of the United States will be remembered as one of the darkest chapters in our Nation's history.

"One of the darkest chapters in our Nation's history." Former members of the Trump administration, longstanding Republicans, also made clear that President Trump incited this insurrection and that it went against our democracy. The President's former Secretary of Defense, James Mattis, declared: "[T]oday's violent assault on our Capitol, an effort to subjugate American democracy by mob rule, was fomented by Mr. Trump." Former White House Chief of Staff John Kelly spoke on this as well, and I would like to play an audio clip of what he said.

Mr. KELLY: What happened on Capitol Hill yesterday was a direct result of him poisoning the minds of people with the lies and the frauds.

Former Speaker of the House John Boehner declared: "[T]he invasion of our Capitol by a mob, incited by lies from some entrusted with power, is a disgrace to all who sacrificed to build our Republic." This was echoed by former Trump official after former Trump official. Here is what former National Security Advisors John Bolton and H.R. McMaster, former White House Communications Director Alyssa Farah, and former Chief of Staff Mick Mulvaney said:

Mr. TAPPER: Let me just ask you: Do you think President Trump has blood on his hands?

Mr. BOLTON: I think he does. Look, I agree with Bill Barr. I think he did incite this mob with the clear intention of having them disrupt the electoral college certification and delay it to give him more time. I don't think there's any question about it.

. . .

Mr. McMASTER: There are many reasons for this assault on the Capitol, but foremost among them was the President's exhortations, was the President's sustained disinformation. . . . We've seen a President stoking fears amidst these crises.

. . .

Ms. FARAH: First and foremost, I want to say that what happened at the Capitol was unacceptable, un-American, undemocratic.

. . .

Mr. MULVANEY: I think everybody recognizes that what happened on Wednesday is different. You can go down the long litany of things that people complained about with Donald Trump, and I could probably defend almost all of them. Many of them were policy differences; many of them were stylistic differences, but Wednesday was different. Wednesday was existential. Wednesday is one of those things that struck to the very heart of what it means to be an American, and it was wrong.

Mick Mulvaney, President Trump's former Chief of Staff, is clearly saying what we all felt—that January 6 was different. It was existential. It was wrong. It was un-American. This sentiment was echoed not just from people outside the administration but from people inside the Trump administration. Perhaps the most telling was the flood of resignations from people inside President Trump's administration with firsthand access to President Trump. His own officials felt so betrayed by his conduct that numerous officials resigned in protest days before the end of President Trump's term.

Sixteen officials resigned in protest—sixteen. They all took this dramatic action of resigning because they saw the clear link between President Trump's conduct and the violent insurrection. Here is some of what they said. Secretary DeVos, who was in the administration the entire term, told President Trump in her resignation letter: "[T]here is no mistaking the impact your rhetoric had on the situation, and it is an inflection point for me."

Secretary Chao, who was in the administration the entire term, explained: "[Y]esterday, our country experienced a traumatic and entirely avoidable event as supporters of the President stormed the Capitol building following a rally he addressed. As I'm sure is the case with many of you, it has deeply troubled me in a way I simply cannot set aside." Deputy Costello told his associates the attack was his "breaking point" and, he hoped, "a wake-up call."

These rebukes and resignations from President Trump's own administration make clear that President Trump's conduct was anything but totally appropriate. They also remind us that this can and must be a wake-up call. As Representative Fred Upton so eloquently put it, "[President Trump] expressed no regrets for last week's violent insurrection at the U.S. Capitol. This sends exactly the wrong signal to those of us who support the very core of our democratic principles and took a solemn oath to the Constitution. . . . It is time to say: Enough is enough."

Now, no one is saying here that President Trump cannot contest the election. Of course, he can. But what President Trump did, as his former Chief of Staff explained, was different. It was dishonorable, it was un-American, and it resulted in fatalities. President Trump spent months inflaming his supporters, spread lies to incite a violent attack on our Capitol, on our law enforcement, and on all of us. And then he lied again to his base to tell them that this was all okay, that this was all acceptable. And that is why President Trump is so dangerous—because he would have all of us, all Americans, believe that any President who comes after him can do exactly the same thing.

That is why lack of remorse is an important factor in impeachment, because impeachment, conviction, and disqualification is not just about the past. It is about the future. It is making sure that no future official, no future President does the same exact thing President Trump does. President Trump's lack of remorse shows that he will undoubtedly cause future harm if allowed, because he still refuses to account for his previous grave crime against our government. You know, I am not afraid of Donald Trump running again in four years. I am afraid he is going to run again and lose because he can do this again.

We are in an unusual situation because, despite President Trump's claim that everyone thinks what he did was fine, so many have come out and spoken so strongly and passionately about what happened here. I would like to highlight a statement by Representative Anthony Gonzalez. He said, "The Vice President and both chambers of Congress had their lives put in grave danger as a result of the President's actions in the events leading up to and on January 6th. During the attack itself, the President abandoned his post while many members asked for help, thus further endangering all present. These are fundamental threats not just to people's lives but to the very foundation of our Republic."

And now I would like to show what Members of Congress said leading up to the most bipartisan impeachment vote in U.S. history, because I do want everyone watching, especially President Trump's supporters, to see firsthand what I believe we all feel—that what President Trump did was not appropriate, that it was not American, and that it absolutely cannot stand.

Ms. CHENEY: What he has done and what he has caused here is something that we've never seen before in our history.

Mr. KINZINGER: All indications are that the President has become unmoored not just from his duty or even his oath but from reality itself.

Mr. KATKO: The President's role in this insurrection is undeniable. Both on social media ahead of January 6 and in his speech that day, he deliberately promoted baseless theories creating a combustible environment of misinformation and division. To allow the President of the United States to incite this attack without consequences is a direct threat to the future of [this] democracy.

After this trial, I hope you will come together and cast your vote and make absolutely clear how we, as a Congress and as a nation, feel about what Donald Trump did by convicting him, and to prevent this from being "only the beginning," as President Trump said, and to deter future Presidents who do not like the outcome of a national election from believing they can follow in President Trump's footsteps. It is what our Constitution requires. It is what our country deserves.

. . .

Ms. Manager DeGETTE: My colleagues have showed you the overwhelming evidence of how President Trump's conduct assembled, incited, and inflamed the mob. We showed how and why this attack, this violence, was not only foreseeable but preventable. We showed that President Trump knew his conduct could and would result in violence, and that when the attack occurred, he did not fulfill his duty as Commander in Chief and defend us. Instead, he was delighted. Donald Trump incited a violent insurrection, and he failed to defend our Nation, our Capitol, this Congress, and our law enforcement from the attack he incited.

Now I want to turn to the impact, the long-term harm of this conduct. My colleagues and I will walk through the breadth and gravity of this harm. I would like to start with the effect President Trump's conduct had on our domestic security. We saw firsthand how Donald Trump's conduct emboldened and escalated domestic violence extremists. These folks are known in the law enforcement community as DVEs. These threats were and are made worse by President Trump's refusal to take accountability and his refusal to forcibly denounce what his own FBI identified as some of the most dangerous elements of our country. Even as the attack was underway, he tweeted words of support to his violent supporters, and then, in the aftermath on January 7, President Trump made it clear this was only the beginning.

> President TRUMP: And to all of my wonderful supporters, I know you are disappointed, but I also want you to know that our incredible journey is only just beginning.

And he was right. Unless we take action, the violence is only just beginning. In the aftermath of the attack, we saw a huge rise in threats from domestic violence extremists, including specific threats to the inauguration in D.C., and also to all fifty State capitols. Our intelligence agencies confirmed that, in addition to these specific threats, President Trump's conduct emboldened the very same violent groups who initiated the attack and sparked new violent coalitions.

These groups believe that they are following his orders. They believe that their acts of insurrection and violence are patriotic. Violence is never patriotic, and it is never American. It is not the Democratic way, and it is not the Republican way. After the attack, the Nation's top defense and law enforcement Agencies reported an increase in credible threats to the inauguration from Donald Trump's supporters.

On January 13, 2021, a joint intelligence bulletin issued by the Department of Homeland Security, the FBI, and the National Counterterrorism Center found: since the 6 January event, violent online rhetoric regarding the 20 January Presidential Inauguration has increased, with some calling for unspecified "justice" for the 6 January fatal shooting by law enforcement of a participant who had illegally entered the Capitol Building, and another posting that "many" armed individuals would return on 19 January.

The Agencies also made clear why these threats were escalating, especially regarding the inauguration. The report explained that a primary motivating factor was the shared false narrative of a "stolen" election, and opposition to the change in control of the executive and legislative branches of the Federal Government may lead some individuals to adopt the belief that there is no political solution to address their grievances and that violent action is necessary.

In other words, President Trump's spreading of inflammatory disinformation about the election incited the insurrection on January 6 and may lead to further violence. Online, just as they did prior to the January 6 attack, Trump supporters took to the internet to organize and document their desire and plans for future violence at President Biden's inauguration. And indeed, in the days shortly after the attack, several posters on extremist social media websites made further plans for violence.

They posted:* "Many of us will return on January 19, 2021, carrying our weapons, in support of our nation's resolve, to which [sic] the world will never forget!!! We will come in numbers that no standing army or police agency can match." "We took the building once [and] we can take it again."

Other users, eager to participate in additional attacks, confirmed that they were waiting on President Trump's instructions about what to do next. Referring to a future planned attack, a user on the online platform known as Gab posted: I'd like to come do this, but want to know, does our President want us there? Awaiting instructions.

In fact, in the days leading up to the inauguration, multiple individuals—many, potentially, in an attempt to carry out the plots that I just previewed—were arrested in Washington, D.C., including on serious weapons charges. One of those men was Couy Griffin, the founder of Cowboys for Trump, who took part in the Capitol attack and was also arrested on January 17. Here is what he said about his plans for violence.

> Mr. GRIFFIN: You know, you want to say that that was a mob? You want to say that was violence? No, sir. No, ma'am. No. We could have a Second Amendment rally on those same steps that we had that rally yesterday. You know, and if we do, then it's going to be a sad day, because there is going to be blood running out of that building. But at the end of the day, you mark my word, we will plant our flag on the desk of Nancy Pelosi and Chuck Schumer.

"Blood running out of that building"—this building, the Capitol, where all of us are right now. Now, the name Couy Griffin may sound familiar because he previously faced controversy for a May 2020 video, where he said, the only good Democrat is a dead Democrat. Hear it from him yourself.

> Mr. GRIFFIN: What I've come to the conclusion is, the only good Democrat is a dead Democrat.

Now, when he said this, President Trump actually retweeted Griffin and thanked him for that sentiment. When Donald Trump retweeted this, he was no stranger to Griffin. In fact, in March 2019, over a year earlier, Griffin and Trump had spo-

---

ken on the phone for nearly thirty minutes. President Trump's conduct, without a doubt, made it clear that he supported Griffin. In fact, Griffin even said so himself. As Griffin later said about President Trump retweeting his inflammatory comment about the dead Democrats: "It really means a lot to me, because I know that the President of the United States has my back."

Remember, this is a man who was here on January 6, who was arrested after threatening to come back here to make blood come running out of this building. Threats like Griffin's have triggered a deployment of forces the likes of which we have never seen. There were approximately 25,000 National Guard troops brought in from around the country to protect D.C. leading up to and on Inauguration Day. As you know, many of those troops are still here. Take a look at that.* These were scenes that played out all over the country.

Five days following the siege on the Capitol, on January 11, 2021, the FBI warned: Armed protests are being planned at all fifty State capitols from 16 January through at least 20 January, and at the U.S. Capitol from 17 January through 20 January. As a result, at least twenty-one States activated their National Guards in preparation for potential attacks. President Trump's incitement has reverberated around the country, prompting massive law enforcement mobilization in several State capitols, including in Washington, Illinois, Michigan, and Georgia.

Look at these photos.† This is what Donald Trump has done to America. This massive deployment of law enforcement has cost the taxpayers dearly. The National Guard deployment to D.C. alone is expected to cost at least $480 million. The bills are also racking up in the States. North Carolina, South Carolina, Pennsylvania, Utah, and Wisconsin have each spent about half a million dollars to safeguard their capitols in the run up to the inauguration. Ohio spent $1.2 million over this same two-week period.

And, remember, this is at a time when State budgets are already suffering under the weight of the pandemic. Our brave servicemembers showed up. Thanks to their dedication and their vigilance, the inauguration and the days leading up to it mercifully proceeded without incident. In fact, after news broke of law enforcement's preparedness for further attacks, leaders of the Proud Boys and the Three Percenters militia, the organizers of the Million MAGA March, they all now told their followers to avoid protests at or leading up to the inauguration for fear that law enforcement would crush them and arrest rioters who showed up.

---

* Senators saw a photo of members of the military guarding the Capitol building behind tall metal barriers topped with barbed wire.

† Senators were shown photos of members of the military guarding four different state capitols.

Thank God there wasn't an insurrection sequel here on January 20, but look at the price we have paid—the price that we are still paying. It is not just dollars and cents. This Capitol has become a fortress, as State capitols have all across the country. Our constituents no longer have access to their elected representatives. Every Democrat and Republican, including people who came here on January 6 peacefully, is paying the price. And it is not just a loss of access; it is a dimming of their freedom. It is a dimming of all of our freedom. We must uphold our oaths, as the tens of thousands of law enforcement officers have done in the wake of January 6, because if we do not, President Trump's mob stands ready for more attacks.

Now, this should be no surprise. Having a Commander in Chief who incites violence has given life to the existing violent groups he spent years cultivating and has inspired new coalitions among extremist groups who actually view January as a success. According to the FBI, President Trump's assemblage of his mob was particularly dangerous because "in-person engagement between DVEs of differing ideological goals during the Capitol breach likely served to foster connections, which may increase DVEs' willingness, capability, and motivation to attack and undermine a government they view as illegitimate." In other words, they all got to talking to each other.

This bulletin by our own Intelligence Committee was also confirmed by concrete evidence. Rioters celebrated their roles in the January 6 attack on social media. They boasted about their success in breaching the Capitol and forcing Members of Congress and the Vice President to evacuate. Take, for example, rightwing provocateur Nick Fuentes. The day before the Capitol insurrection, Fuentes said this on his internet show:

> Mr. FUENTES: What can you and I do to a State legislator besides kill them? Although we should not kill them—I am not advising that. But, I mean, what else can you do, right?

Fuentes was at the Capitol on January 6 and praised the insurrection on a live stream as "glorious" and "awe-inspiring." He later said: "We forced a joint session of Congress and the vice president to evacuate because Trump supporters were banging down and then successfully burst through the doors."

Fuentes was not the only provocateur to revel in the violence. According to Mike Dunn, a member of the Boogaloo Bois—an anti-government movement whose adherents helped lead multiple groups in storming the Capitol—the Boogaloo Bois will be "working overtime" to capitalize on the January 6 riots and hope it will lead to more action. They said: "Just know there is more to come."

Proud Boys members were bragging about the attack on the Capitol. One post on the Proud Boys telegram channel said: "People saw what we can do, they know what's up, they want in." The leader of the Proud Boys himself sent the same message. Enrique Tarrio said the Proud Boys would be active during Biden's Presidency. Tarrio stated: "You're definitely going to see more of us."

Extremist groups are also boasting that the attack on our Capitol is a boon for their recruitment efforts. Three Percent Security Force leader Chris Hill says he has been contacted by several people interested in joining since the insurrection. As one expert who focuses on domestic extremism, Jared Holt, explained: "By all measurable effects this was for far-right extremists one of the most successful attacks that they've ever launched. . . . They're talking about this as the first stab in a greater revolution."

As indicated by Mr. Holt, their perceived success has given them encouragement to continue and to escalate attacks. Intelligence agencies have also noted that these extremist groups will unfortunately be targeting vulnerable minority communities in the U.S. A January 27, 2021 DHS bulletin warned "long-standing racial and ethnic tension" of the sort that led to a man killing twenty-three people at an El Paso Walmart in 2019 would continue to grow and motivate further attacks.

The January 13 Joint Intelligence Bulletin report stated that in addition to the other types of violence listed, "DVEs may be inspired to carry out more violence, including violence against racial, ethnic, and religious minorities and associated institutions, journalists, members of the LGBTQ+ community, and other targets common among some DVEs."

These prejudiced elements could be seen, visibly, in the crowd that attacked the Capitol. Pictured here is Robert Packer. Robert Packer is an avowed White supremacist and Holocaust denier who proudly wore that sweatshirt, which states "Camp Auschwitz." These prejudiced elements could also be heard from the crowds. As you have heard, the insurrectionists that attacked the Capitol on January 6 hurled racial slurs, including at Black police officers. One officer described the trauma he experienced when the rioters seized the Capitol. He said, "I'm a Black officer. There was a lot of racism that day. I was called racial slurs, and in the moment, I didn't process this as traumatic. I was just trying to survive. I just wanted to get home, to see my daughter again. I couldn't show weakness. I finally reached a safe place, surrounded by officers, I was able to cry. To let it out. To attempt to process it."

These extremist groups were emboldened because President Trump told them repeatedly that their insurrectionist activities were the pinnacle of patriotism. Well, let today be the day that we reclaim the definition of patriotism. Impeachment is not to punish but to prevent. We are not here to punish Donald Trump. We are here to prevent the seeds of hatred that he planted from bearing any more fruit.

As my colleagues showed, this is not the first time that President Trump inspired violence, but it must be the last time that he is given a platform to do so. This must be our wake-up call. We must condemn it because the threat is not over. President Trump refused to condemn this type of violence. Instead, over and over again, he has encouraged it. Our response must be different this time.

We simply cannot sweep this under the rug. We must take a united stand, all of us, that this is not American. Think back to August 2017, when a young woman was murdered during a White supremacist rally in Charlottesville, VA. Her name was Heather Heyer. Her mother's name is Susan Bro. Ms. Bro has been a steadfast advocate for her daughter's memory. In a 2018 interview, she expressed concern that people had rushed too quickly to reconciliation without accountability.

> Ms. BRO: If you rush to heal, if you rush to "everybody grab each other and sing Kumbaya," we've accomplished nothing, and we will be right back here in a few years.

"We will be right back here in a few years." Those were her words in 2018, three years ago. Her daughter's murderer, he was held to account, but our Nation did not impose any meaningful accountability on a President who, at the time, said that there were "very fine people on both sides." And, now, where are we, three years later?

I would argue we are not just back where we were. I would argue things are worse. In 2017, it was unfathomable to most of us to think that Charlottesville could happen, just as it was unfathomable to most of us that the Capitol could have been breached on January 6. Frankly, what unfathomable horrors await us if we do not stand up now and say: no, this is not America, and we will not just express condolences and denunciations. We won't just close the book and try to move on. We will act to make sure this never happens again.

. . .

Mr. Manager CICILLINE: Mr. President, distinguished Senators, you just heard from my colleague Manager DeGette how the conduct of Donald Trump dramatically increased the threats to our security and emboldened violent domestic extremists. I would like to now turn to the harm that was caused here, inside these walls, as a result of the conduct on January 6—the harm to us, to Congress, to those who serve our country, and to the constitutional processes as the Trump mob tried to stop the election certification process.

The attack on January 6 is one of the bloodiest intrusions of the Capitol since the British invaded in the War of 1812 and burned it to the ground. And you have heard in painstaking detail the President's mob posed an immediate and serious threat to the continuity and constitutional succession of the United States Government with the first, second, and third in line to the Presidency. The Vice President, the Speaker of the House, and the President pro tempore were all together and faced a common threat in the same location, and we have seen the first and the second were purposely targeted by these attackers. These were not idle threats. The mob, as you recall, chanted: "Hang Mike Pence."

(People chanting: Hang Mike Pence.)

The charging documents show that the rioters said they would have killed Vice President Pence and Speaker Pelosi had they found them. Dawn Bancroft and Diana Santos-Smith, two of the rioters charged in the attack, were caught on tape discussing the brutal violence that they hoped to inflict on Speaker Pelosi had she not been rushed out to safety. They said: "We broke into the Capitol. . . . We got inside, we did our part. We were looking for Nancy to shoot her in the friggin' brain but we didn't find her."

Senators, simply put, this mob was trying to overthrow our government, and it came perilously close to reaching the first three people in line to the Presidency. It wasn't just the Vice President and the Speaker; rioters were prepared to attack any Member of Congress they found. Thomas Edward Caldwell, Donovan Ray Crowl, and Jessica Marie Watkins, three militia members, were also charged for their role in the attack. They discussed trapping us inside the underground tunnels. The indictment quotes social media chatter with Caldwell: "All members are in the tunnels under [the] capitol. Seal them in. Turn on gas. All legislators are down in the tunnels 3 floors down. Do like we had to do when I was in the Corps, start tearing out floors, go from top to bottom."

Never did any of us imagine that we or our colleagues would face mortal peril by a mob riled up by the President of the United States, the leader of the free world, but we did, all because Donald Trump could not accept his election defeat. Trump chose himself above the people, above our institutions, above our democracy, above all of you. You know, we have heard Trump espouse for years now his "America First" policy.

But his true North Star isn't America's well-being. It is not "Country First" like our dear departed colleague John McCain. No, his directive is Trump first, no matter the cost, no matter the threat to our democracy. But each and every one of us in this room must agree on one thing: we can never allow the kind of violent attack that occurred on January 6 to ever happen again in this country.

In the immediate aftermath, we heard many disturbing accounts from many Members of Congress about what they experienced that day. Here are some of the reactions. Following the attack, Representative Dusty Johnson expressed concerns that we had gotten to the point where so many of us had sown the seeds of anger and division.

> Mr. JOHNSON: We were barricaded, and there was some fear, to be sure, but overwhelmingly the emotion that I experienced was one of anger. I just could not believe that this was happening. I could not believe that we had gotten to this point where so many of us had sown these seeds of anger and of division, and we had built this powder keg, and literally we were starting to see this powder keg light up, and it was—frankly, I was furious.

Representative Jason Crow compared the events of this day to his time in Afghanistan as an Army Ranger, something Senator Reed knows something about.

> Mr. CROW: What I felt in the Capitol behind us is something that I haven't felt since I was in Afghanistan when I was an Army Ranger. And to think that as a Member of Congress, in 2021, in the U.S. Capitol on the House floor, that I was preparing to fight my way out of the people's House against a mob is just beyond troubling.

Representative Pat Fallon was humbled by his experience on January 6. He described the events as "surreal" as they unfolded here in the Capitol.

> Mr. FALLON: It was something that I just never thought—I just never thought I'd see this in our Nation's Capitol and particularly in the House Chamber. It was surreal when it was unfolding. Well, you know, what was interesting was the bravery and the courage of some of my fellow Members. When we got to a point where the mob was banging on the doors, and then all that kept them from breaching that, the Chamber itself, was the doors and then some furniture that we had moved and some Capitol Police. And they needed to be augmented, and so Tony Gonzales, a new Representative from Texas, and Ronny Jackson and Troy Nehls and Markwayne Mullin stepped in, and we broke off furniture. Some of the hand sanitizer stations are on these big giant poles, wooden poles, and we turned them upside down, and we were ready to actually have to street fight in the House Chamber. It was unbelievable.

Many Members that day wondered if they would ever see their families again as the rioters breached the Capitol and they were outnumbered and trapped inside. They were calling loved ones to say goodbye. Representative Dan Kildee was one of them. Listen to how he described the impact of the riot on him.

Mr. KILDEE: I was laying on the floor trying to, you know, protect myself sort of behind this little wall, and, you know, we all took our pins off because we were concerned that if this mob were to come in we would be easily identified Members of Congress. And I called my wife, and, you know, it wasn't 'till I heard her voice that I thought, wow, this is like one of those calls you hear about.

While most coverage focused on the extreme danger posed to Members and the Capitol Police, who were targets of this attack, there were lots of other people in the Capitol working on January 6 as well, from personal aides to floor employees, cleaning staff, food service workers. We can't forget all the people who were in harm's way that day. These employees experienced trauma. Some cowered, hiding places just a few feet away from where this rabid crowd had assembled. Many were just kids, twenty-somethings who came here to work because they believed in their country, and they believed in working to make it better. Others were dedicated food and service workers, all working incredibly hard to make sure that we can come here to do our job. These workers are the lifeblood of the legislative branch. They deserve better.

You already heard from Speaker Pelosi's staff—staff that was hiding under the conference table, cowering in the dark, making sure that the attackers couldn't hear them. I would like to share with you what some other staffers went through. Listen as two staffers recall what they experienced that day.

Unidentified Staff Members: But then we were seeing on Twitter, on our phones, and hearing from some of the police officers on the floor that the building had been breached, you know. "Building breached"—those are two words I had never heard. That was particularly stressful, being in a room close to where things are happening and not really knowing what was happening and seeing it come in live and getting texts from people, you know, "Are you OK?" And, truthfully, I didn't know what was happening. I heard: "Shots fired. Shots fired. Shots fired. Show me your hands. Show me your hands." Then I did not know if they were right outside, if there were lots of people with weapons, if there were one shooter, if they had—you know, I didn't know what it looked like. I just knew that there were shots fired outside of the House Chamber.

According to reports, one Republican Senate staffer whose office was not far from the floor "took a steel rod and barricaded his door as the rioters banged on his door trying to break in." The *New York Times* also reported that a senior black staffer was under lockdown for six hours during the insurrection and was so disturbed about these events that she quit her job. Another staffer who was on the floor of the House that day described that what happened on January 6 still echoes in his mind. Listen to him describe the moments just before this indelible image.

> Unidentified Speaker: I heard blasts, and I could see the window panes on the House main door sort of pop, and I figured that, you know, obviously I knew they were at the door, and they figured out a way to break the glass. And the last thing I remember before I walked off the floor was several police officers had drawn their guns and had their guns trained on the door. Clearly, it was—I didn't think there was anything else I could do, and I didn't want to be there for what was about to occur. So I got to the top of the stairs. The stairway was pretty packed, and right about that point, I don't know whether it was a police officer or somebody else said, "They are right behind us. Run." For me, what I keep thinking about—and, again, there isn't a day that has gone by since January 6 that at some point in the day I haven't kind of gone back and picked up some little thing—but the sound of those window panes popping, I won't forget that sound.

"I won't forget that sound." How long will the sound of window panes breaking haunt this staffer? And he isn't alone. There are countless people still living with the trauma of what happened that day. This includes, by the way, another group of people who were with us in the Capitol that day, and that is the press. They were in danger, particularly after years of being derided by President Trump as fake news.

Kristin Wilson, a reporter for CNN, recently tweeted about her experience. She said: "I have fourteen people on my team. We were scattered everywhere. Two of them were on crutches and couldn't have run if they had to. They had to anyway. One was trapped in the House Chamber and had to crawl out to hide. Four of us barricaded ourselves in a room off the Senate Chamber. Every bang on the door of them trying to come through I can still hear in my head."

The janitorial and custodial staff in the Capitol, the people who day after day tend to our home away from home, were also traumatized, but we don't talk about them and the harm they suffered often enough. One janitorial worker recounts how he was so scared, he had to hide in the closet during the attack. He said: "I was all by myself. I didn't know what was going on." Another employee, a mother of three, said: "The insurrection shattered all my sense of security at work." An employee of the Capitol said: "I hope nothing else happens because these people were talking about killing us, killing Federal employees, killing the police." Another employee was afraid to work on Inauguration Day, saying: "I honestly fear for my life. I've got two children at home."

For many of the black and brown staff, the trauma was made worse by the many painful symbols of hate that were on full display that day. Insurrectionists waved

Confederate flags and hurled the most disgusting racial slurs at dedicated Capitol workers. Then, after all of that, these same workers, many of them people of color, were forced to clean up the mess left by mobs of white nationalists. One member of the janitorial staff reflected how terrible he felt when he had to clean up feces that had been smeared on the wall, blood of the rioter who had died, broken glass, and other objects strewn all over the floor.

He said, "I felt bad. I felt degraded." Let's also not forget that this violent attack happened in the middle of a global pandemic. Social distancing was impossible because we were hiding for our lives in cramped quarters for long periods of time. Since January 6, at least seven Members who hid with other Members of Congress have tested positive for COVID-19. At least thirty-eight Capitol Police officers have either tested positive or been exposed, and nearly 200 National Guard troops, who were deployed to our Nation's Capital to provide all of us protection, have tested positive. The Capitol Police and the National Guard came here to keep us safe, to serve. They put their lives in danger. They deserve better than this. We all did.

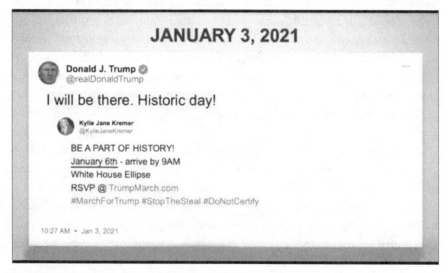

Trump, Donald J. (@realdonaldtrump). Jan. 3, 2021, 10:27 AM

That brings me to the next harm. Now, all of us in this room made it out alive, but not everyone was so lucky. Three law enforcement officers tragically lost their lives as a result of the riot on January 6. These officers were Capitol Police Officer Brian Sicknick, Capitol Police Officer Howard Liebengood, and Metropolitan Police Officer Jeffrey Smith. All honorably served to protect and defend. My colleague Mr. Swalwell told you about Officer Sicknick, who was a forty-two-year-old military veteran who dedicated his entire life to public service. On January 6, he fought a mob of rioters as they streamed into the Capitol and ultimately lost his life protecting us.

Officer Liebengood was a fifteen-year veteran of the Capitol Police. His father served as Sergeant at Arms here in the Senate, and Officer Liebengood followed his extraordinary example of public service. Officer Smith served twelve years with the Metropolitan Police Department. He heeded the call of January 6 by coming to stand with Capitol Police to help secure our democracy. Earlier, my colleague Manager Swalwell showed you terrible videos of the police being physically abused and injured.

You remember what happened to Officer Fanone and Officer Hodges of the MPD, but there were scores of other officers whose names we don't know who were also brutalized that day. Injuries to the U.S. Capitol Police and the Metropolitan Police Department were concussions, irritated lungs, and serious injuries caused by repeated blows from bats, poles, and clubs. Capitol Police officers also sustained injuries that will be with them for the rest of their lives. One officer lost the tip of a right index finger. In a statement issued on January 7, the chairman of the Capitol Police Officers' Union said: "I have officers who were not issued helmets prior to the attack who have sustained brain injuries." One officer has two cracked ribs and two smashed spinal discs. One officer is going to lose his eye, and another was stabbed with a metal fence stake. In total, at least eighty-one members of Capitol Police and sixty-five members of the Metropolitan Police Department were injured during the attack on January 6.

Former Capitol Police Chief Sund described the insurrection as violent, unlike anything he had seen in his thirty-year career in law enforcement. D.C. Police Chief Robert J. Contee III, who had spoken with an officer who had been beaten and injured with a stun gun, said: "I've talked to officers who have done two tours of Iraq who said this was scarier to them than their time in combat." Of course, the physical violence is not the only thing that will have a lasting effect on our brave sworn officers. Trump's mob verbally denigrated their patriotism, questioned their loyalty, and yelled racial slurs. They called them "traitors," "Nazis," "un-American" for protecting us.

For example, in our next clip, a rioter wearing a hunting jacket accosts a police officer.

Unidentified Speaker to Officer: Are you an American? Act like one. You have no idea what the fuck you're doing. You guys have no idea what the fuck you're doing. Stand up for America, goddamnit.

(Rioter punches and hits police officer.)

Unidentified Speaker: They work for us. Fuck them.

Listen to how the Trump mob talked to these officers. You heard that with your own ears.

Unidentified Speakers: Fuck you. Fuck you, bitch. Fuck you. Fucking traitors. You're a fucking traitor. You come here, motherfucker. You are a fucking traitor to your country. You are a fucking traitor. Yeah, traitor.

"F'ing traitor"—so much for backing the blue. Just a couple more examples.

Unidentified Speaker: Hand over your paycheck. Fuck you guys. You can't even call yourself American. You broke your fucking oath today. 1776, bitch.

(People chanting: Traitor. Go home. Fight for Trump. Traitor.)

They called law enforcement officers "traitors." You have to wonder, who are these rioters sworn to? To whom do they believe the police owe their loyalty? To the people? To the Constitution? To our democracy? Or to Donald Trump? Even those who were not outwardly injured, the mental toll has been significant. Several Capitol Police officers have reportedly threatened self-harm in the days following the riot. And in one case, an officer voluntarily turned in her gun because she was afraid of what might happen.

Black police officers were also met with racist vitriol. You heard Lead Manager Raskin reference a black police officer who was weary from racialized violence that he had experienced that day, saying: "Tears just started streaming down my face. I said, 'What the eff, man? Is this America?' 'Is this America?'" Lead Manager Raskin asked: "Is this America?"

What is your answer to that question? Is this okay? If not, what are we going to do about it? These people matter—these matter who risked their lives for us. So I ask you, respectfully, to consider them—the police officers, the staff of this building—when you cast your vote. These people are in deep pain because they showed up here to serve, to serve the American people, to serve their government, to serve all of us. And I ask each of you when you cast your vote to remember them and honor them and act in service of them, as they deserve.

I also want to recognize that four individuals—four insurrectionists—also lost their lives during the attack. These people were led here by the words and actions of an individual who made them believe that they were patriots.

The loss of human life is, of course, the most consequential, but that was not the only damage brought that day. The Trump mob also damaged this building. They defiled some of the most sacred places: Statuary Hall, the Rotunda, where some of America's greatest champions, Presidents, Supreme Court Justices, civil rights heroes, and other defenders are honored after their death. Trump's violent mob had little respect for this place. This video shows the wreckage left in the Senate Parliamentarian's office by the insurrectionists.

(Video showing ransacked office.)

A bust of President Zachary Taylor was smeared with what appeared to be blood. An empty picture frame presumably robbed of its content was found on the floor. And videos of the insurrection captured one man stealing a framed photo, another one tearing a scroll from the wall and ripping it up and throwing those pieces on the floor.

A sign paying tribute to John Lewis was also shamefully destroyed, and only a broken piece of the memorial was found on the ground next to a trash can. The photo of Mr. Lewis was gone. The damage done to this building is a stain on all of us and on the dignity of our democracy. The attack we saw had a purpose: stop the certification. Stop our democratic process.

Fortunately, they did not prevail. Newspapers across America on January 21, the day after the inauguration, proclaimed: democracy has prevailed. President-Elect Biden said that in his inauguration speech. The headline was in so many places because the world's oldest constitutional democracy and the principles underlying it had been attacked and challenged. This wasn't just an attack on the Capitol Building and the dedicated people inside. It was an attack on what we were elected to preserve—our democracy. This attack on our elections, on the peaceful transfer of power from one President to the next didn't even happen during the Civil War.

But it did just happen because of the cold, calculated, and conspiratorial acts of our former President Donald J. Trump. We showed you that the insurrectionists were deliberate, that they came looking for Vice President Pence and Speaker Pelosi, ready to kill.

When President Trump incited a lawless mob to attack our process, he was attacking our democracy. He was trying to become King and rule over us, against the will of the people and the valid results of the election. For the first time ever in our history, a sitting President actively instigated his supporters to violently disrupt the process that provides for the peaceful transfer of power from one President to the next.

Think about that for a moment. What if President Trump had been successful? What if he had succeeded in overturning the will of the people and our constitutional processes? Who among us is willing to risk that outcome by letting Trump's constitutional crimes go unanswered? The Founders included impeachment in our Constitution, not as a punishment, but to prevent. We have to prevent every President—today, tomorrow, or any time in the future—from believing that this conduct is acceptable. Today, we have to stand up for our democracy and ensure we remain a country governed by the people, for the people, by telling Donald Trump and people all across this country and all across the world that his crimes will not and cannot stand.

. . .

Mr. Manager CASTRO of Texas: My colleagues discussed with you the many harms to our Nation as a result of President Trump's conduct. Now I would like to spend some time talking about the harm to our national security and our standing in the world. On January 6, when President Trump incited a mob to march to the Capitol, he led them to a building that houses some of our Nation's most sensitive information.

Consider who was part of that mob. Some of the individuals were on the FBI watch list. The past behavior of some individuals led here by President Trump so alarmed investigators that their names had been added to the national Terrorist Screening Database, and at least one of the insurrectionists may have intended to steal information and give it to a foreign adversary. According to charging documents, Riley Williams allegedly helped steal a laptop from Speaker Pelosi's office to "send the computer device to a friend in Russia, who then planned to sell the device to SVR, Russia's foreign intelligence service."

While we can't be certain if or how many foreign spies infiltrated the crowd or at least coordinated with those who did, we can be sure that any enemy who wanted access to our secrets would have wanted to be part of that mob inside these halls. The point is this: many of the insurrectionists that President Trump incited to invade this Chamber were dangerous—people on the FBI watch list, violent extremists, white supremacists.

And these insurrectionists incited by President Trump threatened our national security: stealing laptops, again, from Speaker Pelosi's office; taking documents from Leader McConnell's desk; snapping photographs, as you saw in the videos earlier, in sensitive areas; ransacking your offices; rifling through your desks. The President of the United States, the Commander in Chief, knew the risk of anyone reaching the Capitol. He swore an oath to preserve, protect, and defend this country. And yet, he incited them here to break into the Capitol. Senators, as you all know, we have spent trillions of dollars building the strongest military in the world and billions of dollars on the most sophisticated weaponry on the planet to prevent the kind of attack that occurred at this Capitol on January 6. Here is what the insurrectionists incited by President Trump did.

Unidentified Speakers after entering the Senate chamber: Hey, let's take a seat, people. Let's take a seat. You be Nancy Pelosi. Let's vote on some shit. Oh, my God.

We did this shit. We took this shit. She's in the House. The House is on the other side. I want to just get a snap of that. Yeah, take a picture.

In many ways, this room is sacred, and so are the traditions that it represents. They have been carried on for centuries. Congress has declared war eleven times on this floor, including entering World War II. Where Congress passed the Civil Rights Act and expanded the right to vote to ensure that no matter your race or your gender, you have a voice in our Nation: this floor is where history has been made. And now, our intelligence agencies and law enforcement agencies have the burden to figure out exactly what was stolen, taken, ransacked, and compromised.

As acting U.S. Attorney Michael Sherwin explained, "Materials were stolen, and we have to identify what was done, mitigate that, and it could have potential national security equities." These investigations are necessary now because of the actions of President Trump. And it wasn't just the people that he led here the intelligence agencies have to look into, it is also what they took and what they gathered, and it was the very fact that this building, with so much sensitive information and some classified information, that this Capitol was breached.

Think about it. Every foreign adversary considering attacking this building got to watch a dress rehearsal, and they saw that this Capitol could be overtaken. As Elizabeth Neumann, a former Trump administration official, stated, "[Y]ou have terrorists who would love to destroy the Capitol. They just saw how easy it was to penetrate. We just exposed a huge vulnerability." And it is not just the Capitol, this attack has implications for all government buildings. Senator Rubio made this point well.

Mr. RUBIO: If you're a terrorist right now and you're sitting out there watching this, you're saying to yourself, hey, it's not that hard to get into the Capitol. Maybe it's not hard to get into the White House or the Supreme Court building or somewhere else.

Our government, our intelligence agencies, and our law enforcement have implemented additional safety measures since the attack on January 6, but while we secure this physical space, what message will we send the rest of the world?

We already know what message our adversaries took from January 6. This is how some of them responded after the attack. For America's adversaries, there was no greater proof of the fallibility of Western democracy than the sight of the U.S. Capitol shrouded in smoke and besieged by a mob whipped up by their unwillingly outgoing president. To make matters worse, our adversaries are even using the events of January 6 not only to denigrate America but to justify their own anti-democratic behavior, calling America hypocritical.

Here is what the Chinese Government is saying. The spokesperson for China's Ministry of Foreign Affairs said the Capitol riots "should spark 'deep reflection' among U.S. lawmakers regarding how they discuss the pro-democracy movement in Hong Kong, suggesting that the U.S. is hypocritical in denouncing Beijing's crackdown in the city while it struggles with its own unrest at home." The *Global Times*, an outlet affiliated with the Chinese Communist Party, even tweeted a series of side-by-side photos of two events: the siege of the U.S. Capitol and a July 2019 incident in which pro-democracy protesters in Hong Kong broke into the city's Legislative Council building.

Think about that. President Trump gave the Chinese Government an opening to create a false equivalency between Hongkongers protesting for democracy and violent insurrections trying to overthrow it. As Representative Gallagher described in real time:

> Mr. GALLAGHER: If we don't think other countries around the world are watching this happen right now, if we don't think the Chinese Communist Party is sitting back and laughing, then we're deluding ourselves. So call it off, Mr. President. We need you to call this off.

Russia has also seized on this violent attack against our government, decrying that democracy is "over." The chairman of the Russian upper house of Parliament's International Affairs Committee said: "The celebration of democracy is over. This is, alas, actually the bottom. I say this without a hint of gloating. America is no longer charting the course, and therefore has lost all its rights to set it. And especially to impose it on others." They are using President Trump's incitement of an insurrection to declare that democracy is over. In Iran, the Supreme Leader is using President Trump's incitement of an insurrection to mock America. He said of the situation in the United States: "This is their democracy and human rights, this is their election scandal, these are their values. These values are being mocked by the whole world. Even their friends are laughing at them."

These statements are serious and pervasive. According to a joint threat assessment bulletin from the Department of Homeland Security, the FBI, and eight other law enforcement entities, "Since the incident at the U.S. Capitol on 6 January, Russian, Iranian, and Chinese influence actors have seized the opportunity to amplify narratives in furtherance of their policy interest amid the presidential transition."

We cannot let them use what happened on January 6 to define us, who we are, and what we stand for. We get to define ourselves by how we respond to the attack of January 6. Some might be tempted to say and point out that our adversaries are always going to be critical of the United States. But following the insurrection on January 6, even our allies are speaking up. Canadian Prime Minister Justin Trudeau said: "What we witnessed was an assault on democracy by violent rioters, incited by the current president and other politicians. As shocking, deeply disturbing and frankly saddening as that event remains—we have also seen this week that democracy is resilient in America, our closest ally and neighbor. "

The German Foreign Minister said: "This closing of ranks begins with holding those accountable who are responsible for such escalations. That includes the violent rioters and also includes their instigators."

The world is watching and wondering whether we are who we say we are because when other countries have known chaos, our Constitution has helped keep order in America. This is why we have a Constitution. We must stand up for the rule of law because the rule of law doesn't just stand up by itself.

After the insurrection, my colleagues on the House Foreign Affairs Committee, the chairman and the ranking member, issued a bipartisan statement that said: "America has always been a beacon of freedom to the world; proof that free and fair elections are achievable, and that democracy works. But what happened at the Capitol today has scarred our reputation and has damaged our standing in the world. Today's violence—an inevitable result when leaders in positions of power misled the public—will certainly empower dictators and damage struggling democracies."

And that is true. For generations, the United States has been a North Star in the world for freedom, democracy, and human rights because America is not only a

---

JANUARY 6, 2021

Donald J. Trump ✔
@realDonaldTrump

Mike Pence didn't have the courage to do what should have been done to protect our Country and our Constitution, giving States a chance to certify a corrected set of facts, not the fraudulent or inaccurate ones which they were asked to previously certify. USA demands the truth!

2:24 PM • Jan 6, 2021

Trump, Donald J. (@realdonaldtrump). Jan. 6, 2021, 2:24 PM

nation for many, it is also an idea. It is the light that gives hope to people struggling for democracy in autocratic regimes, the light that inspires people fighting across the world for fundamental human rights, and the light that inspires us to believe in something larger than ourselves. This trial is an opportunity to respond and to send a message back to the world.

I say this as somebody who loves my country, our country, just as all of you do. There is a lot of courage in this room, a lot of courage that has been demonstrated in the lives of the people in this room. Some folks have stood up for the civil rights of fellow Americans and risked their careers and their reputations, their livelihoods and their safety in standing up for civil rights.

Many Members of Congress have risked their lives in service to our country, in uniform: in fighting in the jungles of Vietnam, in patrolling the mountains of Afghanistan. You served our country because you were willing to sacrifice to defend our Nation as we know it and as the world knows it. Although most of you have traded in your uniforms for public service, your country needs you one more time. The world watched President Trump tell his big lie. The world watched his supporters come to Washington at his invitation, and the world watched as he told his supporters to march here to the Capitol. President Trump, our Commander in Chief at the time, failed to take any action to defend us as he utterly failed in his duty to preserve, protect, and defend.

Now the world is watching us, wondering whether our constitutional Republic is going to respond the way it should, the way it is supposed to—whether the rule of law will prevail over mob rule. The answer to that question has consequences far beyond our own borders. Think of the consequences to our diplomats and negotiators as they sit at tables around the world to enforce our agenda on trade, the economy, and human rights.

To fail to convict a President of the United States who incited a deadly insurrection, who acted in concert with a violent mob, who interfered with the certification of the electoral college votes, who abdicated his duty as Commander in Chief, would be to forfeit the power of our example as a North Star for freedom, democracy, human rights, and most of all, the rule of law. To convict Donald Trump would mean that America stands for the rule of law no matter who violates it. Let us show the world that January 6 was not America, and let us remind the world that we are truly their North Star.

. . .

Mr. Manager NEGUSE: Mr. President, distinguished Senators, good afternoon. You have heard over the course of the last several days that President Trump incited an insurrection, but, as Lead Manager Raskin mentioned, as we prepare to close, we would be remiss if we didn't just briefly address, apparently, the principal defense the President will offer to excuse his conduct, and that is this notion that he can't be held accountable for what happened on January 6 because his actions are somehow protected by the First Amendment.

Now, let's stop for a moment and try to really understand the argument they are making. According to President Trump, everything he did—everything we showed you that he did—was perfectly okay for him to do and for a future President to do again, and the Constitution, apparently, in their view, forbids you from doing anything to stop it. That can't be right. It can't be, and it isn't right. Their argument is meant as a distraction. They are concerned not with the facts that actually occurred, the facts that we have proven, but with an alternative set of facts where President Trump did nothing but deliver a controversial speech at a rally.

Of course, that is not what we have charged in the Article of Impeachment, and it is not what happened. You will hear from my colleague Lead Manager Raskin of the many myriad reasons why this argument that they make is wrong on the law completely, not just around the edges. They make major, fundamental mistakes of constitutional law, the kind that Lead Manager Raskin tells me wouldn't cut it in his first-year law course, which, of course, he certainly would know, as he has taught this subject for decades.

That explains why so many lawyers who have dedicated their lives to protecting free speech, including many of the Nation's most prominent conservative free speech lawyers, have described President Trump's First Amendment claims as "legally frivolous." Here is another quote from a recent letter from prominent free speech lawyers: "The First Amendment is no bar to the Senate convicting former President Trump and disqualifying him from holding future office. Their argument is wrong on the facts, wrong on the law, and would flip the Constitution upside down."

Let's start with the facts because, as you will see, his free speech claim depends on an account of what he did, of why we are here, that has no basis in the evidence. To hear his lawyers tell it, he was just some guy at a rally, expressing unpopular opinions. They would have you believe that this whole impeachment is because he said things that one may disagree with. Really? Make no mistake, they will do anything to avoid talking about the facts of this case. That, I can assure you. Instead, we expect they will talk about a lot of other speeches, including some given by Democratic officials, and they will insist, with indignation, that the First Amendment protects all of this as though it were exactly the same. We trust you to know the difference because you have seen the evidence that we have seen.

You have seen, as we have proven over the last three days, that his arguments completely misdescribe the reality of what happened on January 6. They leave out everything that matters about why we are here and what he did. President Trump wasn't just some guy with political opinions who showed up at a rally on January 6 and delivered controversial remarks. He was the President of the United States, and he had spent months—months—using the unique power of that office, of his bully pulpit, to spread that big lie that the election had been stolen; to convince his followers to stop the steal; to assemble just blocks away from here on January 6 at the very moment that we were meeting to count the electoral college votes, where he knew—where it had been widely reported—that they were primed and eager and ready for violence at his signal.

Then, standing in the middle of that explosive situation, in that powder keg that he had created over the course of months, before a crowd filled with people who were poised for violence at his signal, he struck a match, and he aimed it straight at this building, at us. You have seen all of that evidence. There is no denying it. That is why the House impeached him. That is why he is on trial.

No President, no matter the politics or the politics of the followers—conservative, liberal, or anything else—can do what President Trump did because this isn't about politics; it is about his refusal to accept the outcome of the election and his decision to incite an insurrection. There is no serious argument that the First Amendment protects that, and it would be extraordinarily dangerous for the United States Senate to conclude otherwise, to tell future Presidents that they can do exactly what President Trump did and get away with it, to set the precedent that this is acceptable, that now this is a constitutionally protected way to respond to losing an election.

You will notice something that Lead Manager Raskin and I noticed, which is that, by all accounts, it doesn't appear that President Trump's lawyers disagree. I mean, they don't insist that if the facts we have charged, the facts that we have proven, the facts supported by overwhelming evidence are true, as, of course, you now know they are, that there is nothing you can do. They are not arguing that it is okay for a person to incite a mob to violence—at least I don't think they are arguing that.

Instead, what they are doing is offering a radically different version of what happened that day, totally inconsistent with the evidence. Then they insist that if that fictional version of events, if that alternate reality were true, well then he may be protected by the First Amendment. That is their argument, but you are here to adjudicate real evidence, real facts, not hypothetical ones, and for that reason alone, you should reject their argument because it has been advanced to defend a situation that bears no resemblance to the actual facts of this case. With that, I want to turn it over to my colleague Lead Manager Raskin to address the many legal flaws, as I mentioned, in President Trump's position.

. . .

Mr. Manager RASKIN: Mr. Neguse has explained why President Trump's last-ditch First Amendment argument has got nothing to do with the actual facts of the case. He has been impeached for inciting a violent insurrection against the government. Inciting a violent insurrection is not protected by free speech. There is no First Amendment defense to impeachment for high crimes and misdemeanors. The idea itself is absurd.

The whole First Amendment smokescreen is a completely irrelevant distraction from the standard of high crimes and misdemeanors governing a President who has violated his oath of office. Yet President Trump, we know, has a good way of treating up as down and wrong as right. He tried to pull off the biggest election fraud in American history by overturning the results of the 2020 election even as he insisted that his own fraud was, in fact, an effort to stop the steal, to stop a fraud—a vast conspiracy that he blamed on local and State officials of both political parties, the media, election officials, the judiciary—Federal, State—and Members of Congress. Anybody who wouldn't go along with him was part of the conspiracy. He violated his oath of office by inciting mob violence to prevent Congress from counting electoral college votes as we were assigned to do by the 12th Amendment and the Electoral Count Act. He even attacked Vice President Pence at a rally for [not] violating his oath of office and going along with an egregious assault on democracy.

Now he argues that the Congress is violating his free speech rights when it was Donald Trump who incited an insurrection as an attack against us, that halted speech and debate on the floor of the House and Senate during the peaceful transfer of power, and that imperiled the very constitutional order that protects freedom of speech in the first place along with all of our other fundamental rights. As a matter of law, it is a matter of logic.

President Trump's brazen attempt to invoke the First Amendment now won't hold up in any way. The basic flaw, of course, is that it completely ignores the fact that he was the President of the United States—a public official. He swears an oath as President that nobody else swears. In exchange, he is given greater powers than anyone else in the entire country—maybe on Earth. He or she promises to preserve, protect, and defend the Constitution of the United States and our government institutions and our people. And, as we all know, the power we entrust to people in public office, in government office—especially, our Presidents—comes with special obligations to uphold the laws and the integrity of our Republic, and we all support that.

Now, what if a President publicly—say a President publicly and on a daily basis advocated replacing the Constitution with a totalitarian form of government and urged States to secede from the Union and swore an oath of loyalty to a foreign leader or a foreign government. Well, as a private citizen, you couldn't do anything about people using those words to advocate totalitarianism, to advocate secession from the Union, to swear an oath of personal loyalty to a foreign leader or foreign government or country. You couldn't. That is totally protected. If you tried to prosecute somebody for that, as a prosecutor, you would lose. But it is simply inconceivable, unthinkable that a President could do any of these things—get up and swear an oath to foreign governments or leaders, advocate totalitarianism, advocate secession, and not be impeached for it. It is just unthinkable that that could happen. Would that violate their First Amendment rights?

The opposite view pressed here by President Trump's counsel would leave the Nation powerless to respond to a President who would use his unmatched power, privilege, and prestige of his or her office—the famous bully pulpit—in ways that risk the ruin of the Republic, all for his or her own ambition and corruption and lust for power.

Everyone should be clear: there is nothing remotely exotic about what we are saying. It should be common sense to everybody—common sense—about this understanding of the First Amendment as it applies to public servants—cops, firefighters, teachers, everybody across the land. My daughter, who I mentioned early in the trial, she is a teacher in a public school. The courts have said teachers teach, but if they go off script and they start advocating totalitarianism, treason, or what have you, they are not living up to the duties of their office as teacher. They can be fired.

Everybody knows that, and it happens all the time, by the way, including to cops and firefighters and people on the frontlines. It happens all the time. In fact, it happened countless times to people fired by President Trump for their statements or ideas about things, including on election fraud, not long ago. There are people in the government who lost their jobs because the President didn't like what they said or what they wrote. Now, as I mentioned yesterday—and I can't help but repeat it—Justice Scalia got it exactly right on this. He wrote on these cases about how the First Amendment affects people who take on a public office, who take on public employment, and he summed it up like this. He said: "you can't ride with the cops but root for the robbers." You can't ride with the cops but root for the robbers. That is what Justice Scalia said, and when it comes to the peaceful transfer of power, to the rule of law, to respecting election outcomes, our President, whoever he or she is, must choose the side of the Constitution—must—and not the side of the insurrection or the coup or anybody who is coming against us. And if he or she chooses the wrong side, I am sorry, there is nothing in this First Amendment or anywhere else in the Constitution that can excuse your betrayal of your oath of office. It is not a free speech question.

But there is more. Let's play make-believe and pretend that President Trump was just a run-of-the-mill private citizen—as my colleague Mr. Neguse said, just another guy at the rally—who is just expressing a deeply unpopular opinion, because we shouldn't overlook the fact that, while there were thousands of people in that violent mob, they represent a tiny, tiny, tiny part of less than one percent of the population, and the vast majority of the American people reject the kind of seditious mob violence that we saw on January 6.

But let's say that he was just another guy in the crowd that day. It is a bedrock principle that nobody—nobody—can incite a riot. The First Amendment doesn't protect it. Key case? *Brandenburg v. Ohio*. There is no First Amendment protection for speech directed to inciting and producing imminent lawless action and likely to produce such action. And for all the reasons you have heard, based on the voluminous, comprehensive, totally unrefuted—and we think irrefutable, but we are eager to hear our colleagues—based on all the evidence you have heard, and for all the reasons you have heard, that definition of proscribable speech fits President Trump's conduct perfectly. This is a classic case of incitement. And you don't have to take my word for it. The 144 free speech lawyers, which Mr. Neguse mentioned, who include many of the Nation's most dedicated, most uncompromising free speech advocates—unlike Mr. Trump, of course—but these people agree that there is a powerful case for conviction under the *Brandenburg* standard, even if the President of the United States were just to be treated like some guy in the crowd. And they add: "The First Amendment is no defense to the article of impeachment leveled against the former President." And I mention the *Brandenburg* standard not because it applies here. Of course it doesn't. This is an impeachment. It is not a criminal trial, and there is no risk of jail time. Let's be clear about that. The President doesn't go to jail for one week, one day, one hour, or one minute based on impeachment and conviction and disqualification from further office.

Rather, I mention it to emphasize that absolutely nobody in America would be protected by the First Amendment if they did all the things that Donald Trump did. Nobody made Donald Trump run for President and swear an oath to preserve, protect, and defend the Constitution on January 20, 2017. But when he did, by virtue of swearing that oath and entering this high office, he took upon himself a duty to affirm and take care that our laws would be faithfully execute under his leadership—all of the laws, the laws against Federal destruction of property, all of the laws. We expected him in everything he said and everything he did to protect and preserve and defend our constitutional system, including the separation of powers.

But, instead, he betrayed us, and as Representative Cheney said, it was the greatest betrayal of a Presidential oath in the history of the United States of America—

the greatest. As I mentioned yesterday, President Trump is not even close to the proverbial citizen who falsely shouts "fire" in a crowded theater. He is like the now proverbial municipal fire chief who incites a mob to go set the theater on fire, and not only refuses to put out the fire but encourages the mob to keep going as the blaze spreads. We would hold that fire chief accountable. We would forbid him from that job ever again, and that is exactly what must happen here. There are hundreds of millions of citizens who can be President.

Donald Trump has disqualified himself, and you must disqualify him too. Just like the fire chief who sends the mob, President Trump perverted his office by attacking the very Constitution he was sworn to uphold. In fact, that is one reason why this free speech rhetoric at this trial is so insidious. His conduct represented the most devastating and dangerous assault by a government official on our Constitution, including the First Amendment, in living memory. We wouldn't have free speech or any of the rights if we didn't have the rule of law and peaceful transfer of power and a democracy where the outcome of the election is accepted by the candidate who lost.

We had it all the way up until 2020. And the central purposes of the First Amendment are democratic self- government and civic truth seeking—two purposes that President Trump sought to undermine, not advance, in the course of his conduct as we have definitively demonstrated at this trial. The violence he incited threatened all of our freedoms. It threatened the very constitutional order that protects free speech, due process, religious free exercise, the right to vote, equal protection, and the many other fundamental rights that we all treasure and cherish as citizens of the United States.

The First Amendment does not create some superpower immunity from impeachment for a President who attacks the Constitution in word, in deed, while rejecting the outcome of an election he happened to lose. If anything, President Trump's conduct was an assault on the First Amendment and equal protection rights that millions of Americans exercised when they voted last year, often under extraordinarily difficult and arduous circumstances. Remember, the First Amendment protects the right of the people to speak about the great issues of our day, to debate during elections, and then to participate in politics by selecting the people who will be our leaders. And remember, in American democracy those of us who aspire [to] and attain the public office are nothing but the servants of the people—nothing. Not the masters of the people—we have no kings here. We have no czars.

Here, the people govern, President Ford said—the people. The most important words of the Constitution are the first three—"We the People." But all this—all this—means little if a President who dislikes the election results can incite violence to try to replace and usurp the will of the people as expressed in the States, ignore the judicial branch of government, and then run over the legislative branch of government with a mob. President Trump's high crimes and misdemeanors sought to nullify the political rights and sovereignty of the American people—our right as a people to deliberate, to form opinions, to persuade each other to vote, and then to decide who our President will be—the sovereignty of the people. That is an attack on the First Amendment, I would say.

In addition, President Trump's actions were a direct attack on our own freedom of speech here in the Capitol. Members of Congress are sent here to speak for their constituents. That is why we have our own little "mini free speech" clause—the speech and debate clause. That is literally our job when we come here and represent the views of our people. The attack that President Trump incited forced Members of Congress to stop speaking and to literally flee for our lives and the lives of our staffs and our families. The man whose statements and actions halted the speech in Congress—speech related to the peaceful transfer of power—has no right, no right, to claim that free speech principles prevent this body from exercising its constitutional power to hold him accountable for his offense against us.

You know, Voltaire said famously, and our Founders knew it: "I may disagree with everything you say, but I will defend with my life your right to say it." President Trump says: "Because I disagree with everything you say, I will overturn your popular election and incite insurrection against the government." And we might take a moment to consider another Voltaire insight, which a high school teacher of mine told me when her student asked: "When was the beginning of the

Enlightenment?" And she said: "I think it was when Voltaire said: anyone who can make you believe absurdities can make you commit atrocities."

There is no merit whatsoever to any of the free speech rhetoric—the empty free speech rhetoric—you may hear from President Trump's lawyers. He attacked the First Amendment. He attacked the Constitution. He betrayed his oath of office. Presidents don't have any right to do that. It is forbidden so that our Republic may survive. The people are far more important than that.

The precedent he asks you to create, which would allow any future President to do precisely what he did, is self-evidently dangerous, and so there can be no doubt—none at all—that the President lacks any First Amendment excuse or defense or immunity. He incited a violent insurrection against our government. He must be convicted.

. . .

Mr. Manager LIEU: Thank you for your time and your attention. We all heard President Trump's attorneys on Tuesday, and as part of President Trump's efforts to avoid talking about his own conduct, to avoid talking about anything related to this constitutional crime, we expect that President Trump will raise due process objections. His due process claims are without merit. Under the Constitution, the House has "the sole Power of Impeachment." That provision confirms that the House functions as a grand jury or a prosecutor. The House decides whether to bring charges.

Now, on other impeachment cases, the House can provide certain deliberative and procedural privileges to the person being impeached, but those are exactly that—privileges. They are discretionary. The House has the power to decide its own rules, how it wants to pass the Article of Impeachment, and in this case, the House debated the Article of Impeachment and passed it on a bipartisan vote. I am a former prosecutor. I just want to add that I have had opportunities to decide whether to bring charges, and when you see a crime committed in plain view, prosecutors don't have to spend months investigating before they bring charges.

I know that in this case, in fact, hundreds of people have been arrested and charged by prosecutors for the violence on January 6. There was no reason for the House to wait to impeach the man at the very top that incited the violence. I would also like to emphasize that the House had good reason to move quickly. This was an exigent circumstance. This was not a case where there was hidden conduct or some conspiracy that required months and maybe years of investigation.

This case has not raised very complicated legal issues. The gravity of the President's conduct demanded the clearest of responses from the legislature, particularly given that the President was still in office at the time the House approved this Article and rumors of further violence echoed around the country. They still do.

There must be absolutely no doubt that Congress will act decisively against a President who incites violence against us. That is why the House moved quickly here, and President Trump, who created that emergency, cannot be here to complain that the House impeached him too quickly for the emergency he caused.

Another point on the due process question: earlier in this trial, President Trump's attorneys suggested that the House somehow deliberately delayed the transmission of this Article of Impeachment. That is simply not accurate. When the House adopted this Article of Impeachment on a bipartisan vote, we were ready to begin trial, but the Senate was not in session at the time. And when we inquired as to our options, Senate officials told us, clearly, and in no uncertain terms, that if the Clerk of the House attempted to deliver the Article of Impeachment to the Secretary of the Senate before the Senate reconvened, that the Clerk of the House would have been turned back at the door. That is why the trial did not begin then—another reason why the President's objections of due process are meritless.

Finally, let me just conclude that you all are going to see and have seen a full presentation of evidence by the House, and you are going to hear a full presentation by the President's attorneys. You are going to be able to ask questions. The Senate has the sole power to try all impeachments. President Trump is receiving any and all process that he is due right here in this Chamber.

. . .

Mr. Manager RASKIN: Mr. President, Senators, in just a moment, my colleague, Mr. Neguse, will return to show that we have established, with overwhelming evidence, that President Trump engaged in high crimes and misdemeanors. Before Mr. Neguse comes up, though, I would like to emphasize what should be an uncontroversial point but is really key to understand. If we have proven to you the conduct that we have alleged in this Article, then President Trump has indeed committed a high crime and misdemeanor under the Constitution.

Incitement of insurrection under these circumstances is, undoubtedly, in the words of George Mason from the Constitutional Convention, a "great and dangerous" offense against the Republic. Indeed, it is hard to think of a greater or more dangerous offense against the Republic than this one. So to be very precise about this, I hope we all can agree today that if a President does incite a violent insurrection against the government, he can be impeached for it. I hope we all can agree that that is a constitutional crime.

Another key point: while President Trump's lawyers may be arguing otherwise, the question here is not whether President Trump committed a crime under the Federal Code or D.C. law or the law of any State. Impeachment does not result in criminal penalties, as we keep emphasizing. No one spends a day in jail. There are not even criminal or civil fines. Centuries of history, not to mention the constitutional text, structure, and original intent and understanding, all confirm the teaching of James Wilson, another Framer, who wrote "that impeachments and offenses come not within the sphere of ordinary jurisprudence."

Simply put, impeachment was created for a purpose separate and distinct from criminal punishment. It was created to prevent and deter elected officials who swear an oath to represent America but then commit dangerous offense against our Republic. That is a constitutional crime. And Senators, what greater offense could one commit than to incite the violent insurrection at our seat of government during the peaceful transfer of power—in circumstances where violence is foreseeable, where a crowd is poised for violence, to provoke a mob of thousands to attack us with weapons and sticks and poles, to bludgeon and beat our law enforcement officers and to deface these sacred walls and to trash the place and to do so while seeking to stop us from fulfilling our own oaths, our own duties to uphold the Constitution by counting the votes from our free and fair elections and then to sit back and watch in delight as insurrectionists attack us, violating a sacred oath and engaging in a profound dereliction and desertion of duty?

How can we assure that our Commander in Chief will protect, preserve, and defend our Constitution if we don't hold a President accountable in a circumstance like this? What is impeachable conduct, if not this? I challenge you all to think about it. If you think this is not impeachable, what is? What would be? If President Trump's lawyers endorse his breathtaking assertion that his conduct in inciting these events was totally appropriate and the Senate acquits Donald Trump, then any President could incite and provoke insurrectionary violence against us again. If you don't find this a high crime and misdemeanor today, you have set a new, terrible standard for Presidential misconduct in the United States of America.

The only real question here is the factual one. Did we prove that Donald Trump, while President of the United States, incited a violent insurrection against the government? Incitement, of course, is an inherently fact-based and fact-intensive judgment, which is why we commend you all for your scrupulous attention to everything that took place, but we believe that we have shown you overwhelming evidence in this case that would convince anyone using their common sense that this was indeed incitement—meaning that Donald Trump's conduct encouraged violence; the violence was foreseeable; and he acted willfully in the actions that incurred violence.

Mr. Neguse will take you through that evidence again—not the whole thing. We are almost done. We are almost done, but we don't want it to be said that they never proved this or they never proved that because my magnificent team of managers has stayed up night after night after night, through weeks, to compile all of the factual evidence, and we have put it before you and we have put it before all of you in this public trial because we love our country that much. Mr. Neguse will show you that we have proven our case and that President Trump committed this impeachable offense that we impeached him for on January 13 and that you should convict him.

. . .

Mr. Manager NEGUSE: Mr. President, distinguished Senators, good afternoon, again. As my colleague, Lead Manager Raskin, has mentioned, I know it has been a long few days, and I want to say thank you. We are very grateful for your patience, for your attention, and the attention that you have paid to every one of our managers as they presented our case. As Lead Manager Raskin mentioned, I hope, I trust, that we could all agree that if a President incites a violent insurrection against our government, that that is impeachable conduct.

So what I would like to do as we close our case is just walk you through why our evidence overwhelmingly establishes that President Trump committed that offense. Now, as you consider that question, that question as to whether the President incited insurrection, there are three questions that reasonably come to mind: Was violence foreseeable; did he encourage violence; and did he act willfully? I am going to show you why the answer to every one of those questions has to be yes.

First, let's start with foreseeability. Was it foreseeable that violence would erupt on January 6 if President Trump lit a spark? Was it predictable that the crowd at the Save America rally was poised on a hair trigger for violence, that they would fight, literally, if provoked to do so? Of course, it was. When President Trump stood up to that podium on January 6, he knew that many in that crowd were inflamed, were armed, were ready for violence. It was an explosive situation, and he knew it. We have shown you the evidence on this point. You have seen it—the images, the videos, the articles, and the pattern which showed that the violence on that terrible day was entirely foreseeable. We have showed you how this all began with the big lie, the claim that the election was rigged, and that President Trump and his supporters were the victims of a massive fraud, a massive conspiracy to rip away their votes. We have showed you how President Trump spread that lie, and how, over the course of months, with his support and encouragement, it inflamed part of his base, resulting in death threats, real-world violence, and increasingly extreme calls to stop the steal.

We established that after he lost the election, the President was willing to do just about anything to prevent the peaceful transfer of power; that he tried everything he could do to stop it. You will recall the evidence on the screen: him pressuring and threatening State election officials, attacking them to the point of literally calling them enemies of the state, threatening at least one of them with criminal penalties; then, attacking Senators, Members of Congress, all across the media;

pressuring the Justice Department, prompting outcries from assistant U.S. attorneys, not to mention his own Attorney General, reportedly telling him that the stolen election claims were "BS"—not my phrase, his. And then, as January 6 approached, he moved on to attacking his own Vice President openly and savagely. We have recounted, throughout that entire period, all the ways in which President Trump inflamed his supporters with lies that the election was stolen. As every single one of us knows, nothing in this country is more sacred—nothing—than our right to vote, our voice, and here you have the President of the United States telling his supporters that their voice, that their rights as Americans were being stolen from them, ripped away. That made them angry, angry enough to stop the steal, to fight like hell to stop the steal. And we showed you this. You saw the endless tweets, the rallies, and the statements encouraging and spreading that big lie. You saw that he did this over and over again, with the same message each time: you must fight to win it back. You must never surrender, no matter what. And remember, each time, his supporters along the way showed violence. He endorsed it, encouraged it, and praised it. It was all part of that same demand to stop the steal and fight like hell.

Remember the video that Manager Plaskett showed you from Texas? Some of his supporters encircling a bus of campaign workers on a highway? People easily could have been killed—easily. What did he do? He tweeted and made a joke about it at a rally, called them patriots and held them out as an example of what it means to stop the steal. When he told his supporters to stop the steal, they took up arms to literally intimidate officials to overturn the election results. You saw the evidence, and so did he, and he welcomed it.

Trump, Donald J. (@realdonaldtrump). Oct. 31, 2021, 8:41 PM

When President Trump attacked Georgia's Secretary of State for certifying the results, his supporters sent death threats. You saw those in great detail from Manager Dean. What did he do? He attacked the election officials further. When his supporters gathered together to have a second Million MAGA rally—that is the rally that Manager Plaskett showed you, a rally about the stolen election—he tweeted that the fight had just begun.

What happened next? It is not rocket science. Fights broke out, stabbings, serious violence. Now, President Trump, like all of us, he saw what happened at that rally. He saw all the violence, the burning, and chaos. How did he respond? He tweeted praise of the event, and then—see it on the screen—he bought $50 million—$50 million worth of ads to further promote his message to those exact same people. He immediately joined forces with that very same group. He joined forces with the same people who had just erupted into violence. Was violence predictable? Was it obvious that the crowd on January 6 was poised for violence, prepared for it? Absolutely.

And this isn't just clear looking back in time; it was widely recognized at the time. In the days leading up to January 6, there were dozens, hundreds of warnings. And he knew it. He knew the rally would explode if provoked. He knew all it would take was a slight push. Remember, you heard from Manager Plaskett the chatter on social media websites that the Trump administration monitored and were known to the Trump operation. It showed that the people he invited to the January 6 rally took this as a serious call to arms, that this was not just any attack, it was to storm the Capitol, if necessary, to stop the steal.

And it wasn't just clear on these websites that the Trump administration was monitoring; the FBI issued reports about this credible threat, a threat to target us. Law enforcement made six arrests the night before. Six arrests. Newspapers across the city warned of the risk of violence. There can be no doubt that the risk of violence was foreseeable. What did he do in the days leading up to the rally? Did he calm the situation? Ask yourself, I mean, did he call for peace? No. He didn't do that. He spread his big lie, the most dangerous lie, as I mentioned, that Americans' votes were being stolen and that the final act of theft would occur here in the Capitol. Then he assembled all of those supporters. He invited them to an organized event on a specific day at a specific time matched perfectly to coincide with the joint session of Congress, to coincide with the steal that he had told them to stop by any and all means. Again, he was told by law enforcement and all over the news that these people were armed and ready for real violence. He knew it. He knew it perfectly well, that he had created this powder keg at his rally. He knew just how combustible that situation was. He knew there were people before him who had prepared, who were armed and armored. He knew they would jump to violence at any signal, at any sign from him that he needed them to fight, that he needed them to stop the steal, and we all know what happened next.

Second question. Did he encourage the violence? Standing in that powder keg, did he light a match? Everyone knows the answer to that question. The hours of video you all have watched leave no doubt. Just remember what he said on January 6.

> President TRUMP: All of us here today do not want to see our election victory stolen. There's never been anything like this. It's a pure theft in American history. Everybody knows it. Make no mistake, this election was stolen from you, from me, from the country.

> We will never give up. We will never concede. It doesn't happen. You don't concede when there's theft involved. And to use a favorite term that all of you people really came up with: "We will stop the steal. We will stop the steal." We will not let them silence your voices. We're not going to let it happen. Not going to let it happen.

> (People chanting: Fight for Trump.)

> President TRUMP: Thank you.

> (People chanting: Fight for Trump.)

> President TRUMP: You have to get your people to fight because you'll never take back our country with weakness. You have to show strength, and you have to be strong. And we fight. We fight like hell. And if you don't fight like hell, you're not going to have a country anymore.

You may remember at the outset of this trial, I told you would hear three phrases over and over and over again: The big lie that the election had been stolen, "stop the steal and never concede," and "fight like hell to stop that steal." You heard those phrases throughout the course of this trial, video after video, statement after statement, telling his supporters that they should be patriots, to fight hard, stop the steal. On that day, that day, where did he direct the crowd's ire? He directed them here to Congress. He quite literally in one part of that speech pointed at us. He told them to "fight like hell. And if you don't fight like hell, you're not going to have a country anymore."

And here is the thing. That wasn't metaphorical. It wasn't rhetorical. He already made it perfectly clear that when he said "fight," he meant it. And when followers, in fact, fought, when they engaged in violence, he praised and honored them as patriots. He implied that it was OK to break the law because the election was being stolen. You heard it. You remember the clip that Manager Dean showed you earlier in this trial. He told them—the quote is on the screen—"When you catch somebody in a fraud, you're allowed to go by very different rules."

Remember how all of his supporters—some of his supporters across social media were treating this as a war, talking about bringing in the cavalry? Well, President Trump made clear what those different rules were. He had been making it clear for months.

Mr. GIULIANI at the Stop the Steal rally, January 6, 2021: So let's have trial by combat.

President TRUMP, at the rally later that morning: And, Rudy, you did a great job. He's got guts. You know what? He's got guts, unlike a lot of people in the Republican Party. He's got guts. He fights.

His message was crystal clear, and it was understood immediately, instantly by his followers. And we don't have to guess. We don't have to guess as to how they reacted. We can look at how people reacted to what he said. You saw them, and you saw the violence. It is pretty simple: he said it, and they did it. And we know this because they told us. They told us in real time during the attack. You saw the affidavits, the interviews on social media and on live TV. They were doing this for him because he asked them to.

It wasn't just insurrectionists who confirmed this. Many, many people, including current and former officials, immediately recognized that the President had incited the crowd, that he alone was capable of stopping the violence, that he did this, and he had to call it off because he was the only one who could.

Let's see what Representative McCarthy, Representative Gallagher, Chris Christie, Representative Kinzinger, and Representative Katko had to say.

Mr. McCARTHY: I could not be sadder or more disappointed with the way our country looks at this very moment. People are getting hurt. Anyone involved in this, if you're hearing me, hear me loud and clear: this is not the American way.

Mr. GALLAGHER: Mr. President, you have got to stop this. You are the only person who can call this off. Call it off.

Mr. CHRISTIE: It's pretty simple. The President caused this protest to occur. He's the only one who could make it stop. What the President says is not good enough. The President has to come out and tell his supporters to leave the Capitol grounds and to allow the Congress to do their business peacefully, and anything short of that is an abrogation of his responsibility.

Mr. KINZINGER: You know, a guy that knows how to tweet very aggressively on Twitter, you know, puts out one of the weakest statements on one of the saddest days in American history.

Mr. KATKO: The President's role in this insurrection is undeniable, both on social media ahead of January 6 and in his speech that day. He deliberately promoted baseless theories, creating a combustible environment of disinformation and division. To allow the President of the United States to incite this attack without consequences is a direct threat to the future of this democracy.

Did the President encourage violence? Yes, no doubt that he did.

Final question: did the President act willfully in his actions that encouraged violence? Well, let's look at the facts. He stood before an armed, angry crowd known to be ready for violence at his provocation. And what did he do? He provoked them. He aimed them here, told them to "fight like hell." And that is exactly what they did. And his conduct throughout the rest of that terrible day really only confirms that he acted willfully, that he incited the crowd and then engaged in the dereliction of duty while he continued inflaming the violence. And, again, we don't have to guess what he thought because he told us.

Remember the video he released at 4:17 p.m.? Lead Manager Raskin showed that to you yesterday, the one where he said: we had an election that was stolen from us.

Remember the tweet that he put out just a couple hours later, 6:01 p.m., on January 6? You have seen it many times. You could see it on the slide: "These are the things that happen when a sacred landslide election victory is so unceremoniously & viciously stripped away." That is what he was focused on, spreading the big lie and praising the mob that attacked us and our government.

You heard Manager Cicilline describe reports that the President was delighted, enthusiastic, confused that others didn't share his excitement as he watched the attack unfold on TV. He cared more about pressing his efforts to overturn the election than he did about saving lives, our lives.

Look at what President Trump did that day after the rally. It is important. He did virtually nothing. We have seen—Manager Castro mentioned this—that when President Trump wants to stop something, he does so simply, easily, quickly. But aside from four tweets and a short clip during the over five-hour long attack, he did nothing. On January 6, he didn't condemn the attack, didn't condemn the attackers, didn't say that he would send help to defend us or defend law enforcement. He didn't react to the violence with shock or horror or dismay, as we did. He didn't immediately rush to Twitter and demand in the clearest possible terms that the mob disperse, that they stop it, that they retreat. Instead, he issued messages in the afternoon that sided with them, the insurrectionists who had left police officers battered and bloodied. He reacted exactly the way someone would react if they were delighted and exactly unlike how a person would react if they were angry at how their followers were acting.

Again, ask yourself how many lives would have been saved, how much pain and trauma would have been avoided if he had reacted the way that a President of the United States is supposed to act. There are two parts of President Trump's failure here—his dereliction of duty—that I just have to emphasize for a moment. First is what he did to Vice President Mike Pence, the Vice President of the United States of America. His own Vice President was in this building with an armed mob shouting "Hang him," the same armed mob that set up gallows outside. You saw those pictures. And what did President Trump do? He attacked him more. He singled him out by name. It is honestly hard to fathom.

Second, our law enforcement—the brave officers who were sacrificing their lives to defend us, who could not evacuate or seek cover because they were pro- tecting us. I am not going to go through again what my fellow managers showed you yesterday, but let me just say this: those officers serve us faithfully and duti- fully, and they follow their oaths. They deserve a President who upholds his, who would not risk their lives and safety to retain power, a President who would pre- serve, protect, and defend them. But that is not what he did. When they, the police, still barricaded and being attacked with poles—he said in his video to the people attacking them: "We love you. You're very special."

What more could we possibly need to know about President Trump's state of mind? Senators, the evidence is clear. We showed you statements, videos, affi- davits that prove President Trump incited an insurrection—an insurrection that he alone had the power to stop. And the fact that he didn't stop it, the fact that he incited a lawless attack and abdicated his duty to defend us from it, the fact that he actually further inflamed the mob—further inflamed that mob attacking his Vice President while assassins were pursuing him in this Capitol—more than requires conviction and disqualification. We humbly—humbly ask you to convict President Trump for the crime for which he is overwhelmingly guilty because if you don't, if we pretend this didn't happen or, worse, if we let it go unanswered, who is to say it won't happen again?

. . .

Mr. Manager RASKIN: Mr. President, Members of the Senate, first of all, thank you for your close attention and seriousness of purpose that you have demonstrated over the last few days. Thank you also for your courtesy to the House managers as we have come over here, strangers in a strange land, to make our case before this distinguished and august body. We are about to close. And I am proud that our managers have been so disciplined and so focused. I think we are closing some-where between five and six hours under the time that you have allotted to us, but we think we have been able to tell you everything we need to say.

We will, obviously, have the opportunity to address your questions and then to do a final closing when we get there. I just wanted to leave you with a few thoughts. And, again, I am not going to retraumatize you by going through the evidence once again. I just wanted to leave you with a few thoughts to consider as you enter upon this very high and difficult duty that you have to render impartial justice in this case, as you have all sworn to do. And I wanted to start simply by saying that, in the history of humanity, democracy is an extremely rare and fragile and precarious and transitory thing.

Abraham Lincoln knew that when he spoke from the battlefield and vowed that "government of the people, by the people, [and] for the people shall not perish from the earth." He was speaking not long after the Republic was created, and he was trying to prove that point, that we would not allow it to perish from the Earth.

For most of history, the norm has been dictators, autocrats, bullies, despots, tyrants, cowards who take over our government—for most of the history of the world—and that is why America is such a miracle. We were founded on the extraordinary principles of the inalienable rights of the people and the consent of the governed and the fundamental equality of all of us. You know, when Lincoln said "government of the people, by the people, [and] for the people" and he hear-kened back to the Declaration of Independence, when he said, "Four score and seven years ago," he knew that that wasn't how we started.

We started imperfectly. We started as a slave republic. Lincoln knew that. But he was struggling to make the country better. And however flawed the Founders were as men in their times, they inscribed in the Declaration of Independence and the Constitution all the beautiful principles that we needed to open America up to successive waves of political struggle and constitutional change and trans-formation in the country so we really would become something much more like Lincoln's beautiful vision of "government of the people, by the people, [and] for the people"—the world's greatest, multiracial, multireligious, multiethnic con-stitutional democracy, the envy of the world, as Tom Paine said, an asylum for humanity where people would come. Think about the preamble, those first three words pregnant with such meaning, "We the People," and then all of the purposes of our government put into that one action-packed sentence: "We the People . . . in Order to form a more perfect Union, establish Justice, insure domestic Tranquility, provide for the common defense, promote the general Welfare, and [preserve] to ourselves and our Posterity" the blessings of liberty. And then, right after that first sentence—the mission statement for America, the Constitution—what happens? Article I. The Congress is created: All legislative powers herein are reserved to the Congress of the United States.

You see what just happened? The sovereign power of the people to launch the country and create the Constitution flowed right into Congress. And then you get in article I, section 8 comprehensive, vast powers that all of you know so well—the power to regulate commerce domestically and internationally, the power to declare war, the power to raise budgets and taxes and to spend money, the power to govern the seat of government, and on and on and on. And then, even in article I, section 8, clause 18, all other powers "necessary and proper" to the foregoing powers. That is all of us.

Then you get to article II, the President, four short paragraphs. And the fourth paragraph is all about what? Impeachment—how you get rid of a President who commits high crimes and misdemeanors. What is the core job of the President? To take care that the laws are faithfully executed. And our Framers were so fearful of Presidents becoming tyrants and wanting to become Kings and despots that they put the oath of office right into the Constitution. They inscribed it into the Constitution: to "preserve, protect, and defend the Constitution of the United States."

We have got the power to impeach the President. The President doesn't have the power to impeach us. Think about that. The popular branch of government has the power to impeach the President. The President does not have the power to impeach us. And, as I said before, all of us who aspire and attain a public office are nothing but the servants of the people. And the way the Framers would have it is the moment that we no longer acted as servants of the people but as masters of the people, as violators of the people's rights, that was the time to impeach, remove, convict, disqualify, start all over again, because the interests of the people are so much greater than the interests of one person—any one person, even the greatest person in the country. The interests of the people are what count.

Now, when we sit down and we close, our distinguished counterparts, the defense counsel, who have waited very patiently—and thank you—will stand up and seek to defend the President's conduct on the facts, as I think they will. It has already been decided by the Senate on Tuesday that the Senate has constitutional jurisdiction over this impeachment case brought to you by the United States House of Representatives.

So we have put that jurisdictional, constitutional issue to bed. It is over. It has already been voted on. This is a trial on the facts of what happened. And incitement, as we said, is a fact-intensive investigation and judgment that each of you will have to make. We have made our very best effort to set forth every single relevant fact that we know in the most objective and honest light. We trust and we hope that the defense will understand the constitutional gravity and solemnity of this trial by focusing like a laser beam on the facts and not return to the constitutional argument that has already been decided by the Senate. Just as a defense lawyer who loses a motion to dismiss on a constitutional basis in a criminal case must let that go and then focus on the facts which are being presented by the prosecutors in detail, they must let this constitutional jurisdictional argument go—not just because it is frivolous and wrong, as nearly every expert scholar in America opined, but because it is not relevant to the jury's consideration of the facts of the case.

So our friends must work to answer all of the overwhelming, detailed, specific, factual, and documentary evidence we have introduced of the President's clear and overwhelming guilt in inciting violent insurrection against the Union. Donald Trump, last week, turned down our invitation to come testify about his actions, and, therefore, we have not been able to ask him any questions directly as of this point.

Therefore, during the course of their sixteen-hour allotted presentation, we would pose these preliminary questions to his lawyers, which I think are on everyone's minds right now and which we would have asked Mr. Trump himself if he had chosen to come and testify about his actions and inactions when we invited him last week: One, why did President Trump not tell his supporters to stop the attack on the Capitol as soon as he learned of it? Why did President Trump do nothing to stop the attack for at least two hours after the attack began? As our constitutional Commander in Chief, why did he do nothing to send help to our overwhelmed and besieged law enforcement officers for at least two hours on January 6 after the attack began? On January 6, why did President Trump not at any point that day condemn the violent insurrection and the insurrectionists?

And I will add a legal question that I hope his distinguished counsel will address: if a President did invite a violent insurrection against our government, as, of course, we allege and think we have proven in this case—but just in general, if a President incited a violent insurrection against our government—would that be a high crime and misdemeanor? Can we all agree, at least, on that?

Senators, I have talked a lot about common sense in this trial because I think, I believe that is all you need to arrive at the right answer here. You know, when Tom Paine wrote "Common Sense," the pamphlet that launched the American Revolution, he said that common sense really meant two different things: one, common sense is the understanding that we all have without advanced learning and education. Common sense is the sense accessible to everybody. But common sense is also the sense that we all have in common, as a community. Senators, America, we need to exercise our common sense about what happened. Let's not get caught up in a lot of outlandish lawyers' theories here. Exercise your common sense about what just took place in our country. Tom Paine wasn't an American, as you know, but he came over to help us in our great revolutionary struggle against the Kings and Queens and the tyrants. And in 1776, in "The Crisis," he wrote these beautiful words.

It was a very tough time for the country. People didn't know which way things were going to go. Were we going to win, against all hope, because for most of the rest of human history it had been the Kings and the Queens and the tyrants and the nobles lording it over the common people? Could political self-government work in America was the question. And Paine wrote this pamphlet called "The Crisis," and in it he said these beautiful words. And, with your permission, I'm going to update the language a little bit, pursuant to the suggestion of Speaker Pelosi, so as not to offend modern sensibilities. Okay.

But he said: "These are the times that try men and women's souls. These are the times that try men and women's souls. The summer soldier and the sunshine patriot will shrink at this moment from the service of their cause and their country; but everyone who stands with us now will win the love and the favor and the affection of every man and every woman for all time. Tyranny, like hell, is not easily conquered, but we have this saving consolation: the more difficult the struggle, the more glorious, in the end, will be our victory." Good luck in your deliberations. We do conclude our presentation.

DAY FOUR

TRIAL OF DONALD J. TRUMP,
PRESIDENT OF THE UNITED STATES

Mr. Counsel VAN DER VEEN: The Article of Impeachment now before the Senate is an unjust and blatantly unconstitutional act of political vengeance. This appalling abuse of the Constitution only further divides our Nation when we should be trying to come together around shared priorities. Like every other politically motivated witch hunt the left has engaged in over the past four years, this impeachment is completely divorced from the facts, the evidence, and the interests of the American people. The Senate should promptly and decisively vote to reject it.

No thinking person could seriously believe that the President's January 6 speech on the Ellipse was in any way an incitement to violence or insurrection. The suggestion is patently absurd on its face. Nothing in the text could ever be construed as encouraging, condoning, or enticing unlawful activity of any kind. Far from promoting "insurrection" against the United States, the President's remarks explicitly encouraged those in attendance to exercise their rights "peacefully and patriotically."

Peaceful and patriotic protest is the very antithesis of a violent assault on the Nation's Capitol. The House Impeachment Article slanderously alleges that the President intended for the crowd at the Ellipse to "interfere with the Joint Session's solemn constitutional duty to certify the results of the 2020 Presidential election."

This is manifestly disproven by the plain text of the remarks. The President devoted nearly his entire speech to an extended discussion of how legislators should vote on the question at hand. Instead of expressing a desire that the joint session be prevented from conducting its business, the entire premise of his remarks was that the democratic process would and should play out according to the letter of the law, including both the Constitution and the Electoral Count Act. In the conclusion of his remarks, he then laid out a series of legislative steps that should be taken to improve democratic accountability going forward, such as passing universal voter ID legislation, banning ballot harvesting, requiring proof of citizenship to vote, and turning out strong in the next primaries. Not only President—these are not the words of someone inciting a violent insurrection.

Not only President Trump's speech on January 6 but, indeed, his entire challenge to the election results was squarely focused on how the proper civic process could address any concerns through the established legal and constitutional system. The President brought his case before State and Federal courts, the U.S. Supreme Court, the State legislatures, the electoral college, and, ultimately, the U.S. Congress. In the past, numerous other candidates for President have used many of the same processes to pursue their own election challenges. As recently as 2016, the Clinton campaign brought multiple postelection court cases, demanded recounts, and ridiculously declared the election stolen by Russia.

Many Democrats even attempted to persuade the electoral college delegates to overturn the 2016 results. House Manager RASKIN objected to the certification of President Trump's victory four years ago, along with many of his colleagues. You will remember, it was Joe Biden who had to gavel him down.

Mr. RASKIN, January 2017: I have an objection because ten of the twenty-nine electoral votes cast by Florida were cast by electors not lawfully certified.

Ms. JACKSON LEE: I object to the votes from the State of Wisconsin, which would not—should not—be legally certified.

Vice President BIDEN: There is no debate—

Ms. TLAIB: Mr. President, I object to the certificate from the State of Georgia on the grounds that the electoral vote was not—

Vice President BIDEN: There is no debate. There is no debate.

Mr. GRIJALVA: I object to the certification from the State of North Carolina.

Ms. JACKSON LEE: I object to the fifteen votes from the State of North Carolina.

Mr. MCGOVERN: I object to the certificate from the State of Alabama. The electors were not lawfully certified.

Vice President BIDEN: Is it signed by a Senator?

Mr. RASKIN: Not as of yet, Mr. President.

Vice President BIDEN: In that case, the objection cannot be entertained. The objection cannot be entertained. Debate is not in order.

Ms. LEE of California: Even with the—

Vice President BIDEN: There is no debate in order.

Ms. LEE of California: Even with the—

Mr. BIDEN: There is no debate.

Ms. LEE of California: Eighty-seven voting machines are—

Vice President BIDEN: There is no debate in order. Is it signed by a Senator? There is no debate. There is no debate. There is no debate by the joint session. There is no debate. There is no debate.

Ms. JACKSON LEE: Sixteen voting—

Vice President BIDEN: There is no debate.

Ms. JACKSON LEE: And the mass—

Vice President BIDEN: Please come to order.

Ms. JACKSON LEE: There is the—

Vice President BIDEN: The objection cannot be received.

Ms. JACKSON LEE: What the Russian—

Vice President BIDEN: Section 18, title 20 of the United States Code prohibits debate in the joint session.

Ms. WATERS: I do not wish to debate. I wish to ask, is there one United States Senator who will join me in this letter of objection?

Vice President BIDEN: There is no debate. There is no debate.

Ms. WATERS: Just one.

Vice President BIDEN: The gentlewoman will suspend.

Mr. Counsel VAN DER VEEN: In 2000, the dispute over the outcome was taken all the way to the Supreme Court, which ultimately rendered a decision. To litigate questions of an election integrity within this system is not incitement to insurrection. It is the democratic system working as the Founders and lawmakers have designed.

To claim that the President, in any way, wished, desired, or encouraged lawless or violent behavior is a preposterous and monstrous lie. In fact, the first two messages the President sent via Twitter, once the incursion of the Capitol began, were: stay peaceful and no violence because we are the party of law and order. The gathering on January 6 was supposed to be a peaceful event. Make no mistake about that. And the overwhelming majority of those in attendance remained peaceful.

As everyone knows, the President had spoken at hundreds of large rallies across the country over the past five years. There had never been any moblike or riotous behaviors, and, in fact, a significant portion of each event was devoted to celebrating the rule of law, protecting our Constitution, and honoring the men and women of law enforcement. Contrast the President's repeated condemnations of violence with the rhetoric from his opponents.

(video montage)

President TRUMP in June 2020: I am your President of law and order and an ally of all peaceful protesters.

. . .

Vice President BIDEN, July 2020: The vast majority of the protests have been peaceful.

. . .

President TRUMP, December 2019: Republicans stand for law and order, and we stand for justice.

. . .

Ms. PELOSI, June 2018: I just don't even know why there aren't uprisings all over the country. Maybe there will be.

. . .

President TRUMP, May 2020: My administration will always stand against violence, mayhem, and disorder.

. . .

Ms. PRESSLEY, August 2020: There needs to be unrest in the streets for as long as there is unrest in our lives.

. . .

President TRUMP, October 2020: I stand with the heroes of law enforcement.

. . .

Ms. WATERS, June 2018: And you push back on them, and you tell them they are not welcome anymore anywhere.

. . .

President TRUMP, August 2020: We will never defund our police. Together, we will ensure that America is a nation of law and order.

. . .

Vice President BIDEN, March 2018: If we were in high school, I'd take him behind the gym and beat the hell out of him.

. . .

Mr. TESTER, July 2019: But I think you need to go back and punch him in the face.

. . .

Mr. BOOKER, July 2019: I feel like punching him.

. . .

President TRUMP, October 2020: We just want law and order. Everybody wants that.

. . .

Mr. SCHUMER, March 2020: I want to tell you, Gorsuch; I want to tell you, Kavanaugh: You have released the whirlwind, and you will pay the price.

. . .

President TRUMP, October 2020: We want law and order. We have to have law and order.

. . .

Chris CUOMO, June 2020: Show me where it says that protests are supposed to be polite and peaceful.

. . .

President TRUMP, October 2020: We believe in safe streets, secure communities, and we believe in law and order.

Tragically, as we know now, the January—on January 6, a small group, who came to engage in violent and menacing behavior, hijacked the event for their own purposes. According to publicly available reporting, it is apparent that extremists of various different stripes and political persuasions preplanned and premeditated an attack on the Capitol.

One of the first people arrested was a leader of antifa. Sadly, he was also among the first to be released. From the beginning, the President has been clear: the criminals who infiltrated the Capitol must be punished to the fullest extent of the law. They should be imprisoned for as long as the law allows. The fact that the attacks were apparently premeditated, as alleged by the House managers, demonstrates the ludicrousness of the incitement allegation against the President. You can't incite what was already going to happen. Law enforcement officers at the scene conducted themselves heroically and courageously, and our country owes them an eternal debt. But there must be a discussion of the decision by political leadership regarding force posture and security in advance of the event.

As many will recall, last summer the White House was faced with violent rioters night after night. They repeatedly attacked Secret Service officers and at one point pierced a security wall, culminating in the clearing of Lafayette Square. Since that time, there has been a sustained negative narrative in the media regarding the necessity of those security measures on that night, even though they certainly prevented many calamities from occurring.

In the wake of the Capitol attack, it must be investigated whether the proper force posture was not initiated due to the political pressure stemming from the events at Lafayette Square. Consider this: On January 5, the Mayor of the District of Columbia explicitly discouraged the National Guard and Federal authorities from doing more to protect the Capitol, saying: "[T]he District of Columbia is not requesting other federal law enforcement personnel and discourages any additional deployment . . ."

This sham impeachment also poses a serious threat to freedom of speech for political leaders of both parties at every level of government. The Senate should be extremely careful about the precedent this case will set. Consider the language that the House Impeachment Article alleges to constitute incitement: "If you don't fight like hell, you're not going to have a country anymore." This is ordinary political rhetoric that is virtually indistinguishable from the language that has been used by people across the political spectrum for hundreds of years. Countless politicians have spoken of fighting for our principles. Joe Biden's campaign slogan was "Battle for the Soul" of America.

No human being seriously believes that the use of such metaphorical terminology is incitement to political violence. While the President did not engage in any language of incitement, there are numerous officials in Washington who have indeed used profoundly reckless, dangerous, and inflammatory rhetoric in recent years. The entire Democratic Party and national news media spent the last four years repeating, without any evidence, that the 2016 election had been hacked and falsely and absurdly claimed the President of the United States was a Russian spy.

Speaker PELOSI herself said that the 2016 election was hijacked and that Congress has a duty to protect our democracy. She also called the President an imposter and a traitor and recently referred to her colleagues in the House as "the enemy within." Moreover, many Democrat politicians endorsed and encouraged the riots that destroyed vast swaths of American cities last summer. When violent, leftwing anarchists conducted a sustained assault on a Federal courthouse in Portland, OR, Speaker PELOSI did not call it insurrection; instead, she called the Federal law enforcement officers protecting the building "storm troopers."

When violent mobs destroyed public property, she said: "People will do what they do." The Attorney General of the State of Massachusetts stated: "Yes, America is burning, but that's how forests grow." Representative AYANNA PRESSLEY declared: "There needs to be unrest in the streets for as long as there's unrest in our lives." The current Vice President of the United States, KAMALA HARRIS, urged supporters to donate to a fund that bailed violent rioters and arsonists out of jail. One of those was released and went out and committed another crime, assault. He beat the bejesus out of somebody. She said, of the violent demonstrations: "Everyone beware . . . they're not gonna stop before Election Day in November, and they're not gonna stop after Election Day. [T]hey're not going to let up—and they should not."

Such rhetoric continued even as hundreds of police officers across the Nation were subjected to violent assaults at the hands of angry mobs. A man claiming to be inspired by the junior Senator from Vermont came down here to Washington, D.C., to watch a softball game and kill as many Senators and Congressmen as he could. It cannot be forgotten that President Trump did not blame the junior Senator. The senior Senator from Maine has had her house surrounded by angry mobs of protesters. When that happened, it unnerved her. One of the House managers—I forget which one—tweeted "cry me a river."

Under the standards of the House Impeachment Article, each of these individuals should be retroactively censored, expelled, punished, or impeached for inciting violence by their supporters. Unlike the left, President Trump has been entirely consistent in his opposition to mob violence. He opposes it in all forms, in all places, just as he has been consistent that the National Guard should be deployed to protect American communities wherever protection is needed.

For Democrats, they have clearly demonstrated that their opposition to mobs and their view of using the National Guard depends upon the mob's political views. Not only is this impeachment case preposterously wrong on the facts, no matter how much heat and emotion is injected by the political opposition, but it is also plainly unconstitutional. In effect, Congress would be claiming the right to disqualify a private citizen, no longer a government official, from running for public office. This would transform the solemn impeachment process into a mechanism for asserting congressional control over which private citizens are and are not allowed to run for President. In short, this unprecedented effort is not about Democrats opposing political violence; it is about Democrats trying to disqualify their political opposition. It is constitutional cancel culture.

History will record this shameful effort as a deliberate attempt by the Democratic Party to smear, censor, and cancel not just President Trump but the 75 million Americans who voted for him. Now is not the time for such a campaign of retribution; it is the time for unity and healing and focusing on the interests of the Nation as a whole. We should all be seeking to cool temperatures, calm passions, rise above partisan lines. The Senate should reject this divisive and unconstitutional effort and allow the Nation to move forward.

Over the course of the next three hours or so, you will hear next from Mr. SCHOEN, who is going to talk about due process and a couple of other points you will be interested to hear. I will return with an analysis of why the First Amendment must be properly applied here, and then Mr. CASTOR will discuss the law as it applies to the speech of January 6. And then we will be pleased to answer your questions. Thank you.

. . .

Mr. Counsel SCHOEN: Leaders, Senators, throughout the course of today, my colleagues and I will explain in some detail the simple fact that President Trump did not incite the horrific, terrible riots of January 6. We will demonstrate that, to the contrary, the violence and the looting goes against the law-and-order message he conveyed to every citizen of the United States throughout his Presidency, including on January 6. First, though, we would like to discuss the hatred, the vitriol, the political opportunism that has brought us here today. The hatred that the House managers and others on the Left have for President Trump has driven them to skip the basic elements of due process and fairness and to rush an impeachment through the House, claiming "urgency."

But the House waited to deliver the Article to the Senate for almost two weeks, only after Democrats had secured control over the Senate. In fact, contrary to their claim that the only reason they held it was because Senator MCCONNELL wouldn't accept the Article, Representative CLYBURN made clear that they had considered holding the Article for over one hundred days to provide President Biden with a clear pathway to implement his agenda.

Our Constitution and any basic sense of fairness require that every legal process with significant consequences for a person's life, including impeachment, requires due process under the law, which includes factfinding and the establishment of a legitimate evidentiary record with an appropriate foundation. Even last year's impeachment followed committee hearings and months of examination and investigation by the House. Here, President Trump and his counsel were given no opportunity to review evidence or question its propriety. The rush to judgment for a snap impeachment in this case was just one example of the denial of due process. Another, perhaps even more vitally significant, example was the denial of any opportunity ever to test the integrity of the evidence offered against Donald J. Trump in a proceeding seeking to bar him from ever holding public office again and that seeks to disenfranchise some 75 million voters—American voters.

On Wednesday of this week, countless news outlets repeated the Democrat talking point about the power of never-before-seen footage. Let me ask you this: Why was this footage never seen before? Shouldn't the subject of an impeachment trial—this impeachment trial—President Trump, have the right to see the so-called new evidence against him? More importantly, the riot and the attack on this very building was a major event that shocked and impacted all Americans. Shouldn't the American people have seen this footage as soon as it was available? For what possible reason did the House managers withhold it from the American people and President Trump's lawyers? For political gain? How did they get it? How are they the ones releasing it? It is evidence in hundreds of pending criminal cases against the rioters. Why was it not released through law enforcement or the Department of Justice? Is it the result of a rushed, snap impeachment for political gain without due process?

House Manager RASKIN told us all yesterday that your job as jurors in this case is a fact-intensive job, but, of course, as several of the House managers have told you, we still don't have the facts. Speaker PELOSI herself, on February 2, called for a 9/11-style Commission to investigate the events of January 6. Speaker PELOSI says that the Commission is needed to determine the causes of the events. She says it herself. If an inquiry of that magnitude is needed to determine the causes of the riot—and it may very well be—then how can these same Democrats have the certainty needed to bring Articles of Impeachment and blame the riots on President Trump? They don't.

The House managers, facing a significant lack of evidence, turned often to press reports and rumors during these proceedings, claims that would never meet the evidentiary standards of any court. In fact, they even relied on the words of Andrew Feinberg, a reporter who recently worked for Sputnik, the Russian propaganda outlet. You saw it posted. By the way, the report they cited was completely refuted. The frequency with which House managers relied on unproven media reports shocked me as I sat in this Chamber and listened to this.

(video montage)

Mr. Manager CASTRO of Texas: And there is a lot that we don't know yet about what happened that day.

. . .

Mr. Manager RASKIN: According to those around him at the time, reportedly responded.

. . .

Mr. Manager NEGUSE: Reports across all major media outlets.

. . .

Mr. Manager NEGUSE: Reported.

. . .

Mr. Manager LIEU: Reportedly summoned.

. . .

Ms. Manager PLASKETT: Reportedly.

. . .

Mr. Manager CASTRO of Texas: Reportedly not accidental. . . . According to reports. . . .

. . .

Mr. Manager CASTRO of Texas: Who reportedly spoke to the guard.

. . .

Mr. Manager CICILLINE: It was widely reported.

. . .

Mr. Manager RASKIN: Media reports.

. . .

Mr. Manager CICILLINE: According to reports.

. . .

Mr. Manager NEGUSE: Reported.

. . .

Mr. Manager LIEU: Reportedly.

As any trial lawyer will tell you, "reportedly" is a euphemism for "I have no real evidence." "Reportedly" is not the standard in any American setting in which any semblance of due process is afforded an accused. "Reportedly" isn't even "here is some circumstantial evidence." It is exactly as reliable as "I googled this for you." And if you are worried you might ever be tried based on this type of evidence, don't be. You get more due process than this when you fight a parking ticket.

One reason due process is so important with respect to evidence offered against an accused is that it requires an opportunity to test the integrity, the credibility, the reliability of the evidence. Here, of course, former President Trump was complete-ly denied any such opportunity. And it turns out there is significant reason to doubt the evidence the House managers have put before us. Let me say this clearly. We have reason to believe the House managers manipulated evidence and selectively edited footage. If they did and this were a court of law, they would face sanctions from the judge. I don't raise this issue lightly. Rather, it is a product of what we have found in just the limited time we have had since we first saw the evidence here with you this week. We have reason to believe that the House managers cre-ated false representations of tweets, and the lack of due process means there was no opportunity to review or verify the accuracy.

Consider these facts. The House managers, proud of their work on this snap impeachment, staged numerous photo shoots of their preparations. In one of those, Manager RASKIN is seen here at his desk, reviewing two tweets side by side. The image on his screen claims to show that President Trump had retweeted one of those tweets.

Now, Members of the Senate, let's look closely at the screen because, obvi-ously, Manager RASKIN considered it important enough that he invited the *New York Times* to watch him watching it. What is wrong with this image? Actually, there are three things very wrong with it. Look at the date on the very bottom of the screen on Manager RASKIN's computer screen when we zoom into the pic-ture. The date that appears is January 3, 2020, not 2021. Why is that date wrong? Because this is not a real screenshot that he is working with. This is a recreation of a tweet. And you got the date wrong when you manufactured this graphic. You did not disclose that this is a manufactured graphic and not a real screenshot of a tweet. To be fair, the House managers caught this error before showing the image on the Senate floor. So you never saw it when it was presented to you. But that is not all. They didn't fix this one. Look at the blue checkmark next to the Twitter username of the account retweeted by the President. It indicates that this is a verified account, given the blue check by Twitter to indicate it is run by a public figure. The problem? The user's real account is not verified and has no blue checkmark, as you can see. Were you trying to make her account seem more significant or were you just sloppy? If we had due process of law in this case, we would know the truth.

But that is not all that is wrong with this one tweet. House Manager Swalwell showed you this tweet this week, and he emphasized that this tweet reflected a call to arms. He told you repeatedly that this was a promise to call in the cavalry for January 6. He expressly led you to believe that President Trump's supporter believed that the President wanted armed supporters at the January 6 speech—paramilitary groups, the cavalry—ready for physical combat. The problem is, the actual text is exactly the opposite. The tweeter promised to bring the calvary—a public display of Christ's crucifixion, a central symbol of her Christian faith with her to the President's speech—a symbol of faith, love, and peace. They just never want to seem to read the text and believe what the text means. You will see this was reported in the media last evening also.

Words matter, they told you. But they selectively edited the President's words over and over again. They manipulated video, time-shifting clips, and made it appear the President's words were playing to a crowd when they weren't. Let's take a look.

President TRUMP: After this, we're going to walk down—and I will be there with you—we're going to walk down. We are going to walk down to the Capitol. And we're going to walk down to the Capitol, and we're going cheer on our brave Senators and Congress men and women, and we're probably not going to be cheering so much for some of them because you will never take back our country with weakness. You have to show strength, and you have to be strong. We have come to demand that Congress do the right thing and only count the electors who have been lawfully slated—lawfully slated. I know that everyone here will soon be marching over to the Capitol Building to peacefully and patriotically make your voices heard.

"And we are going to walk down to the Capitol." They showed you that part. Why are we walking to the Capitol? Well, they cut that off: to "cheer on" some

Members of Congress, and not others, "peacefully and patriotically." The Supreme Court ruled in *Brandenburg* that there is a very clear standard for incitement—in short, to paraphrase, whether the speech was intended to provoke imminent lawless action and was likely to do so. "Go to the Capitol, and cheer on some Members of Congress but not others"—they know it doesn't meet the standard for incitement, so they edited it down.

We heard a lot this week about "fight like hell," but they cut off the video before they showed you the President's optimistic, patriotic words that followed immediately after.

> President TRUMP: We fight like hell. And if you don't fight like hell, you're not going to have a country anymore. Our exciting adventures and boldest endeavors have not yet begun. My fellow Americans, for our movement, for our children, and for our beloved country—and I say this despite all that has happened—the best is yet to come.

There is that famous quote, like one of the House managers said: a lie will travel halfway around the world before the truth has a chance to put its shoes on. Well, this lie traveled around the world a few times and made its way into the Biden campaign talking points and ended up on the Senate floor: the Charlottesville lie, "very fine people on both sides," except that isn't all he said. And they knew it then, and they know it now. Watch this.

> President TRUMP: But you also had people that were very fine people—on both sides. You had people in that group—excuse me, excuse me. I saw the same pictures as you did. You had people in that group that were there to protest the taking down of, to them, a very, very important statue and the renaming of a park from Robert E. Lee to another name.

> Unidentified Speaker: George Washington and Robert E. Lee are not the same.

> President TRUMP: George Washington was a slave owner. Was George Washington a slave owner? So will George Washington now lose his status? Are we going to take down—excuse me. Are we going to take down—are we going to take down statues to George Washington? How about Thomas Jefferson? What do you think of Thomas Jefferson? Do you like him? Are we going to take down the statue? Because he was a major slave owner. Now are we going to take down his statue? So you know what? It is fine. You're changing history. You're changing culture. And you had people—and I am not talking about the neo-Nazis and the white nationalists because they should be condemned totally.

But you had many people in that group other than neo-Nazis and White nationalists, okay? And the press has treated them absolutely unfairly. Now, in the other
group also, you had some fine people, but you also had troublemakers, and you see
them come with the black outfits and with the helmets and with the baseball bats.
You got—you had a lot of bad—you had a lot of bad people in the other group too.

Unidentified Speaker: Who was treated unfairly, sir? I'm sorry. I just couldn't understand what you were saying. You were saying the press treated white nationalists
unfairly? I want to understand what you're saying.

President TRUMP: No. No, there were people in that rally—and I looked the night
before. If you look, there were people protesting, very quietly, the taking down of
the statue of Robert E. Lee. I am sure in that group there were some bad ones. The
following day, it looked like they had some rough, bad people—neo-Nazis, white
nationalists—whatever you want to call them. But you had a lot of people in that
group that were there to innocently protest and very legally protest because, you
know—I don't know if you know, they had a permit. The other group didn't have a
permit.

So I only tell you this: there are two sides to a story. I thought what took place was
a horrible moment for our country, a horrible moment. But there are two sides
to the country. Does anybody have a final—does anybody have a—you have an
infrastructure—

This might be, today, the first time the news networks played those full remarks
in their context. And how many times have you heard that President Trump has
never denounced white supremacists? Now you and America know the truth. Here
is another example. One of the House managers made much of the President's supposedly ominous words of "you have to get your people to fight."

But you knew what the President really meant. He meant that the crowd should
demand action from Members of Congress and support primary challenges to
those who don't do what he considered to be right. Support primary challenges,
not violent action. I know what he meant because I watched the full video, and so
did the House managers. But they manipulated his words. You will see where they
stopped it and to give it a very different meaning from the meaning it has in full
context. Let's watch.

Mr. Manager NEGUSE: "You have to get your people to fight," he told them.

President TRUMP: You have to get your people to fight. And if they don't fight, we
have to primary the hell out of the ones that don't fight. You primary them. We are
going to. We are going to let you know who they are. I can already tell you, frankly.

The "people" who need to fight are Members of Congress. Why do we have to skip the necessary due diligence and due process of law and any—that any legal proceeding should have? It couldn't have been the urgency to get President Trump out of office. House Democrats held the Articles until he was no longer President, mooting their case. Hatred, animosity, division, political gain—and let's face it, for House Democrats, President Trump is the best enemy to attack.

[The clip played at pp. 64-65 was replayed.]

Mr. Counsel SCHOEN: That same hatred and anger has led House managers to ignore their own words and actions and set a dangerous double standard. The House managers spoke about rhetoric, about a constant drumbeat of heated language. Well, as I am sure everyone watching expected, we need to show you some of their own words.

(video montage)

Ms. PELOSI: I just don't even know why there aren't uprisings all over the country. Maybe there will be.

. . .

Ms. PRESSLEY: There needs to be unrest in streets for as long as there is unrest in our lives.

. . .

Ms. PELOSI: You've got to be ready to throw a punch. We have to be ready to throw a punch.

. . .

Mr. TESTER: Donald Trump, I think you need to go back and punch him in the face.

. . .

Ms. WALLACE: I thought he should have punched him in the face.

. . .

Mr. BOOKER: I feel like punching him.

. . .

Vice President BIDEN: I would like to take him behind the gym if I were in high school. If I were in high school, I would take him behind the gym and beat the hell out of him. You know, I wish we were in high school. I could take him behind the gym.

. . .

Ms. WATERS: I will go and take Trump out tonight.

. . .

Ms. WARREN: Take him out now.

. . .

Mr. DEPP: When was the last time an actor assassinated a President?

. . .

Mr. WILSON: They are still going to have to go out and put a bullet in Donald Trump.

. . .

Mr. Chris CUOMO: Show me where it says a protest is supposed to be polite and peaceful.

. . .

Ms. WATERS: You push back on them, and you tell them they're not welcome anymore, anywhere.

. . .

MADONNA: I have thought an awful lot about blowing up the White House.

. . .

Mr. BOOKER: Please get up in the face of some Congresspeople.

. . .

Ms. PELOSI: People will do what they do.

. . .

Mr. SCHUMER: I want to tell you, Gorsuch, I want to tell you Kavanaugh: You have released the whirlwind, and you will pay the price.

. . .

Ms. TLAIB: We're going to go in there and we're going to [bleep].

. . .

Ms. PRESSLEY: This is just a warning to you Trumpers: Be careful. Walk lightly. And for those of you who are soldiers, make them pay.

. . .

Ms. DeGENERES: If you had to be stuck in an elevator with either President Trump, Mike Pence, or Jeff Sessions, who would it be?

Ms. HARRIS: Does one of us have to come out alive?

And there is more.

(video montage)

Mr. McDONOUGH: I promise to fight every single day. One, I'm a fighter and I'm relentless. But I'm a fighter and I'm relentless. A fighter and I'm relentless. I will fight like hell.

. . .

Ms. WARREN: The way I see it now is that we pick ourselves up and we fight back; that is what it is all about. We stand up and we fight back. We do not back down, we do not compromise, not today, not tomorrow, not ever. You can lie down, you can whimper, you can pull up in a ball, you can decide to move to Canada, or you can stand your ground and fight back, and that is what it is about. We do fight back, but we are going to fight back. We are not turning this country over to what Donald Trump has sold. We are just not. Look, people are upset, and they're right to be upset. Now, we can whimper, we can whine, or we can fight back. We're up here to fight back. Me, I'm here to fight back. I'm here to fight back because we will not forget. We do not want to forget. We will use that vision to make sure that we fight harder, we fight tougher, and we fight more passionately more than ever. We still have a fight on our hands. Fight hard for the changes Americans are demanding. Get in the fight. To winning the fight. Fight. Fighting. Fighting. We'll use every tool possible to fight for this change. We'll fight. We'll fight. Fight. Fighting hard. Serious about fighting. And fight. We've got to (inaudible) and fight back. Problems—we call them out and we fight back. I'm in this fight. I am fighting. I am fighting. Get in this fight. Get in this fight. Get in this fight. And fighting. We all need to be in the fight. We all need to stay in the fight. We stay in this fight. We fought back. We fought back. I am not afraid of a fight. I am in this fight all the way. You don't get what you don't fight for. Our fight. Our fight. We are in this fight for our lives. This is the fight of our lives.

. . .

Mr. WARNER: But we are going to make sure this fight doesn't end tonight.

. . .

Mr. MENENDEZ: This is a fight for our lives, the lives of our friends and family members and neighbors. It is a fight. Fight. And it is a fight that we're going to work to make sure continues. It is a fight. It is a fight. It is a fight. And that is what this fight is for.

. . .

Mr. TESTER: Well, I'm wired to fight anyone who isn't doing their job for us. I'm Jon Tester, and you're damn right I approve this message.

. . .

Ms. ROSEN: And I'll have lots of fights ahead of us, and I'm ready to stand up and keep fighting. We're going to fight. We're going to fight. And we need to fight. Fight. We need to fight. We got a few more fights. I'm going to take the privilege of a few more fights. And we have the biggest fight of all. I will never stop fighting. I will fight like hell to fight back against anyone.

. . .

Mrs. SHAHEEN: We need to say loud and clear that we are ready to fight.

. . .

Mr. DURBIN: It's a bare knuckles fight.

. . .

Mr. WYDEN: Now they're going to actually have to fight back against people.

. . .

Mr. SCHATZ: The fight has to be conducted.

. . .

Ms. CANTWELL: It is so important that we need to fight.

. . .

Ms. MURRAY: Fight that fight.

. . .

Mr. KING: We have been fighting.

. . .

Mr. COONS: I was fighting very hard.

. . .

Mr. VAN HOLLEN: Time is of the essence both in terms of the fight.

. . .

Mr. BENNET: I think we should be fighting.

. . .

Mr. MERKLEY: I really believe we need to fight.

. . .

Mr. HEINRICH: We're simply not going to take this lying down. We're going to keep fighting.

. . .

Mr. KAINE: So I'm telling all of my colleagues, this is the fight of our life.

. . .

Ms. BALDWIN: Whose side are you on? Who are you fighting for?

. . .

Mr. HICKENLOOPER: They're fighting or I'm fighting. We're all fighting. We are both fighting.

. . .

Ms. HIRONO: We will fight back. We're not going to take this lying down.

. . .

Mr. MURPHY: I'm just going to keep the fight up.

. . .

Ms. GILLIBRAND: What we have to do right now is fight as hard as we can.

. . .

Ms. STABENOW: We have to rise up and fight back.

. . .

Mr. BLUMENTHAL: I am going to be fighting—fight like hell.

. . .

Mr. SCHUMER: Keep fighting, fighting, fighting. And we kept fighting and we did, so we're going to keep fighting.

. . .

Mr. PETERS: We have to be fighting every single day.

. . .

Mr. WHITEHOUSE: We have to fight back, and we have no choice but to do that. I think we're doing the right thing to do that.

. . .

Mr. LUJAN: Fighting.

. . .

Mr. MANCHIN: And I'm fighting.

. . .

Mr. SANDERS: Our job right now is to fight.

. . .

Ms. HASSAN: It is really important, I'm going to keep fighting.

. . .

Mr. OSSOFF: I'm asking for the support of the people across the country to fight back.

. . .

Mr. PADILLA: And you've got to be fierce in fighting.

. . .

Mr. WARNOCK: Fighting.

. . .

Ms. SMITH: Proud to have been fighting.

. . .

Mr. LEAHY: I told President Biden I will fight like mad.

. . .

Ms. CORTEZ MASTO: I will tell you what. Now more than ever, we have to fight like hell.

. . .

Mr. MARKEY: We have these battles on the floor of the Senate. I'm going to go down and battle. I'm going to be down there on the floor fighting.

. . .

Mr. SCHUMER: We Democrats are fighting as hard as we can. Democrats are fighting as hard as we can. Credit it any way, but we're fighting back.

. . .

Mr. KAINE: And what we've got to do is fight in Congress, fight in the courts, fight in the streets, fight online, fight at the ballot box.

. . .

Mr. BOOKER: Fighting and pushing around the clock. Fighting and continue to be brave and keep strong and keep fighting. We're getting people engaged in the fight. We're fighting. We've got to keep fighting and keep focused.

. . .

Ms. KLOBUCHAR: Fight. This is going to be a fight.

. . .

Mr. CASTRO: We will fight him and challenge him every way we can, in the Congress, in the courts, and in the streets.

. . .

Ms. HARRIS: To continue fighting, we each have an important role to play in fighting in this fight like so many before it. It has been a fight. The American people are going to have to fight. And about the importance of fighting. I will always fight. Fighting. But we always must fight. Joe Biden has a deep, deep seeded commitment to fight. And to fight. And about the importance of fighting. We always must fight. To fight. To fight. And to fight. As our willingness to fight. Continue the fight. As Joe Biden says, to fight. Fighting. What we are fighting for. We will tell them about what we did to fight. About a fight. Truly I do believe that we're in a fight. I believe we're in a fight. I believe we're in a fight. I believe we're in a fight. So there's a fight in front of us. A fight for all of these things. And so we're prepared to fight for that. We know how to fight. Our ongoing fight. A fight. We know how to fight. We like a good fight. We were born out of a fight. This is what is our fight right now.

. . .

Mr. RASKIN: There's the fight. There're the fight. There's the fight. And then there's the fight to defend. Back in the fight.

. . .

Ms. PELOSI: Our mission is to fight. That is the guiding purpose of House Democrats. Fighting. He has never forgotten who he is fighting for. March and fought. And we just have to fight. But this is a fight for our country.

. . .

Mr. SCHUMER: Fighting the health crisis of COVID.

. . .

Vice President BIDEN: I led the fight. And continue to fight. Never, never, give up this fight. I am a citizen fighting for it. It means not only fighting. A leader who fought for progressive change. As a lawyer who fought for people his whole life. As well as other fights he's in. I'm proud to have Tim in this fight with me. And above all, it is time for America to get back up and once again fight. Mr. Buttigieg. We will fight when we must fight.

. . .

Mr. CASTRO of Texas: What kind of America are we fighting for? We've been fighting. We need to fight. But we also need to fight. Fight for America.

. . .

Mrs. CLINTON: I am going to wake up every day and fight hard. I have been fighting. We're going to fight. We're going to fight. We're going to fight. We're going to fight. And I will fight.

. . .

Mr. BUTTIGIEG: We're in the fight of our lives right now.

. . .

Mr. O'ROURKE: We fight like hell.

. . .

Mr. WYDEN: To fight.

. . .

Ms. ROSEN: To fight.

. . .

Mr. CICILLINE: Fight against the Trump administration. Democrats are standing up to fight. We're in this fight in a serious way.

. . .

Mr. LIEU: To fight.

. . .

Ms. DEGETTE: We're eager to take on this fight. Get in this fight.

. . .

Mrs. GILLIBRAND: I have taken on the fights.

. . .

Mr. NEGUSE: As representatives for the people and legislators here in the Halls of Congress, our job is to fight.

. . .

Ms. PLASKETT: Who has led us in this fight.

. . .

Mr. SWALWELL: To fight for this. This fight.

. . .

Mr. WARNOCK: Every day I am in the United States Senate, I will fight.

. . .

Mr. BROWN: One of the things we do is fight—should fight.

. . .

Ms. OCASIO-CORTEZ: Because my constituents send me here each and every day to fight.

. . .

Ms. ABRAMS: We have been fighting this fight. And we need to be side by side to succeed. So I hope that you will all join us in our fight. And if we fight. And as the next Governor of Georgia, I will never stop fighting. We can show the old guard something new, and we can fight.

. . .

Ms. DEAN: My fight. Those fights. And to fight. To fight an administration.

. . .

Ms. HARRIS: Requiring us to fight and fight we will. Their fight. In their fight. In their fight. The fight is a fight. And so when we fight the fight that we are in. When we are fighting this fight. We fight this fight. The strength of who we are is we will fight. And we will fight. We will fight the fight. We are in a fight. The fight. Fight. Fight. It is a fight. It is a fight. And it is a fight born out of patriotism. This is a fight. Fighting. I say fight on. Fight on. Fight on. Fight on.

. . .

Ms. WARREN: I am here to say one more time in public, this is not a fight I wanted to take on, but this is the fight in front of us now.

Every single one of you and every one of you—that is okay. You didn't do anything wrong. It is a word people use. But please stop the hypocrisy. Did you tone down the rhetoric last summer when all of this was happening? Did you condemn the rioters, or did you stand with NANCY PELOSI, who said: people are going to do what they are going to do.

(video montage)

Ms. HARRIS: This is a movement. I'm telling you, they're not going to stop. And everyone beware because they're not going to stop. They're not going to stop before election day in November, and they're not going to stop after.

. . .

Mr. CUOMO: Please, show me where it says a protest is supposed to be polite and peaceful.

. . .

Ms. PELOSI: I just don't even know why there aren't uprisings all over the country. Maybe there will be.

. . .

Unidentified Speaker: It was a violent night in St. Louis. They shot and killed David in cold blood.

. . .

Ms. HANNAH-JONES: Destroying property, which can be replaced, is not violence.

. . .

Unidentified Speakers. This is an apartment complex on fire. It just collapsed. The building just collapsed. I don't know where to go now. These people did this for no reason. This is just a snapshot of some of the damage people will be waking up to.

. . .

Mr. SCHUMER: I am proud of New York, and I am proud of the protests.

. . .

Unidentified Speaker: There is damage everywhere you look. Honestly, it looks like a war zone.

. . .

Ms. PELOSI: Heartwarming to see so many people turn out peacefully.

. . .

Mr. SCHUMER: They keep doing it day after day after day. In fact, our country is a nation of protests. The patriots were protesters.

. . .

Unidentified Speaker: St. John's Church is on fire.

. . .

Unidentified Speaker: Can you disavow that was antifa?

Mr. NADLER: That is a myth.

. . .

Unidentified Speaker: I hope someone burns down your whole precinct with all y'all inside.

. . .

Mr. VELSHI: It is not, generally speaking, unruly.

. . .

Ms. WATERS; You push back on them, and you tell them they're not welcome any-more, anywhere.

. . .

Ms. HARRIS: They are not going to let up, and they should not.

Mr. Counsel SCHOEN: You claim that it is wrong to object to the certification of election results. You, along with your allies in the media, attempted to cancel and censor Members of this Chamber who voiced concerns and objected to certification.

Manager RASKIN, you had been in Congress only three days when you objected in 2017. It is one of the first things you did when you got here.

(video montage)

Mr. RASKIN: I have an objection because ten of the twenty-nine electoral votes cast by Florida were cast by electors not lawfully certified.

Vice President BIDEN: Is the objection in writing and signed not only by a Member of the House of Representatives but also by a Senator?

Mr. RASKIN: It is in writing, Mr. President.

Vice President BIDEN: Is it signed by a Senator?

Mr. RASKIN: Not as of yet, Mr. President.

Vice President BIDEN: In that case, an objection cannot be entertained.

Ms. JAYAPAL: Mr. President, I object to the certificate from the State of Georgia on the grounds that the electoral vote does not—

Vice President BIDEN: There is no debate. There is no debate.

Mr. GRIJALVA: I object to the certificate from the State of North Carolina based on violation of the—

Vice President BIDEN: There is no debate. There is no debate in the joint session.

Ms. LEE: I object because people are horrified by the overwhelming evidence—

Vice President BIDEN: Section 18, title 3 of the United States Code prohibits debate.

Ms. JACKSON LEE: I object. [. . .]

Ms. TUBBS JONES: I object to the counting of the electoral votes of the State of Ohio. [. . .]

Mr. MCGOVERN: I object to the certificate from the State of Alabama. The electors were not lawfully certified.

Ms. JACKSON LEE: I object to the fifteen votes from the State of North Carolina because of the massive voter suppression and the closing of voting booths in early voting—

Vice President BIDEN: There is no debate. There is no debate.

Ms. JACKSON LEE: Sixteen to one—

Vice President BIDEN: There is no debate.

Ms. JACKSON LEE: And the massive voting suppression that occurred—

Vice President BIDEN: The gentlewoman will suspend.

Mr. FILNER: I have an objection to the electoral votes.

Ms. WATERS: The objection is in writing, and I don't care that it is not signed by a Member of the Senate.

Ms. WATERS: I do not wish to debate. I wish to ask: Is there one United States Senator who will join me in this letter of objection?

Vice President BIDEN: There is no debate.

Ms. JAYAPAL: The objection is signed by a Member of the House but not yet by a Member of the Senate.

Vice President BIDEN: Well, it is over. (Laughter.)

Mr. Counsel SCHOEN: And when the House managers realized that the President's actual words could not have incited the riot, as you alleged in your Article of Impeachment, you attempted to pivot. You said that raising the issue of election security and casting doubt on the propriety of our elections was dangerous. One of the House managers, Mr. CICILLINE, told you that this is not about the words Mr. Trump used in isolation.

Rather, it is about the big lie, the claim that the election was stolen. The House managers told you that it is the big lie that incited the riot and that the big lie was President Trump's claim that the election was not a fair election or that the election was stolen. Claiming an election was stolen, you were told, are words that are inciteful to a candidate's followers and cause people to respond violently. Claiming an election was stolen or not legitimate is something that a candidate should never do because he or she knows or should know that such a claim and such words can actually incite violent insurrection, you were told.

Well, it seems that the House managers' position must actually be a bit narrower than that. The House managers' position really is that, when Republican candidates for office claim an election is stolen or that the winner is illegitimate, it constitutes inciting an insurrection and the candidate should know it, but Democratic Party candidates for public elective office are perfectly entitled to claim the election was stolen or that the winner is illegitimate or to make any other outrageous claim they can.

It is their absolute right to do so, and it is their absolute right to do so irrespective of whether there is any evidence to support the claim. Democratic candidates can claim that an election was stolen because of Russian collusion or without any explanation at all, and that is perfectly okay and is in no way incitement to an insurrection, and somehow, when Democratic candidates publicly decry an election as stolen or illegitimate, it is never a big lie. You have been doing it for years.

(video montage)

Mr. Manager CASTRO of Texas: But can you imagine telling your supporters that the only way you can possibly lose is if an American election was rigged and stolen from you? And ask yourself whether you have ever seen anyone at any level of government make the same claim about their own election.

. . .

Mr. BROWN: If Stacey Abrams doesn't win in Georgia, they stole it. It's clear. It's clear. And I say that publicly. It's clear.

. . .

Ms. CLINTON: You can run the best campaign—you can even become the nominee—and you can have the election stolen from you. He knows he's an illegitimate President. He knows. He knows that there were a bunch of different reasons why the election turned out the way it did.

. . .

Ms. ABRAMS: Votes remain to be counted. There are voices that are waiting to be heard. And I will not concede.

. . .

Mr. TAPPER: I respect the issues that you're raising, but you're not answering the question. Do you think it was—

Ms. ABRAMS: I am.

Mr. TAPPER: You're not using the word "legitimate."

. . .

Ms. PELOSI: There are still legitimate concerns over the integrity of our elections and of ensuring the principle of one person, one vote.

. . .

Mr. SANDERS: I agree with tens of millions of Americans who are very worried that when they cast a ballot on an electronic voting machine that there is no paper trail to record that vote.

. . .

Ms. PELOSI: But constantly shifting vote tallies in Ohio and malfunctioning electronic machines which may not have paper receipts have led to an additional loss of confidence by the public. This is their only opportunity to have this debate while the country is listening, and it is appropriate to do so.

Mr. Counsel SCHOEN: House Manager CASTRO no longer has to try to imagine it thanks to the distinguished Senator and others. It didn't have to be this way. The Democrats promised unity. They promised to deliver the very COVID relief, in the form of $2,000 stimulus checks, that President Trump called for. They should have listened to their own words of the past. I leave you with the wise words of Congressman JERRY NADLER.

Mr. NADLER, December 1998: The effect of impeachment is to overturn the popular will of the voters. We must not overturn an election and remove a President from office except to defend our system of government or our constitutional liberties against the dire threat, and we must not do so without an overwhelming consensus of the American people. There must never be a narrowly voted impeachment or an impeachment supported by one of our major political parties and opposed by the other. Such an impeachment will produce the divisiveness and bitterness in our politics for years to come and will call into question the very legitimacy of our political institutions. The American people have heard the allegations against the President, and they overwhelmingly oppose impeaching him. They elected President Clinton. They still support him. We have no right to overturn the considered judgment of the American people.

Mr. Speaker, the case against the President has not been made. There is far from sufficient evidence to support the allegations, and the allegations, even if proven true, do not rise to the level of impeachable offenses. Mr. Speaker, this is clearly a partisan railroad job. The same people who today tell us we must impeach the President for lying under oath almost to a person voted last year to re-elect a Speaker who had just admitted lying to Congress in an official proceeding. The American people are watching, and they will not forget. You may have the votes, you may have the muscle, but you do not have the legitimacy of a national consensus or of a constitutional imperative. This partisan coup d'etat will go down in infamy in the history of this Nation.

. . .

Mr. VAN DER VEEN: Good afternoon again, Senators, Mr. President. There are two fundamental questions for purposes of this free speech analysis. First, does the First Amendment to the Constitution apply in this Chamber to these impeachment proceedings? Second, if it does, do the words spoken by Mr. Trump at the Ellipse on January 6 meet the definition of "constitutional incitement" so as to void the protections afforded by the First Amendment? I will explain why the answers to both of these questions must be a resounding yes.

The Constitution and the First Amendment must certainly apply to these impeachment proceedings, and Mr. Trump's speech deserves full protection under the First Amendment, but before getting into the legal analysis, some preliminary observations about the House managers' case should be made. First, this case, unfortunately, is about political hatred. It has become very clear that the House Democrats hate Donald Trump. This type of political hatred has no place in our political institutions and certainly no place in the law. This hatred has led the House managers to manipulate and selectively edit Mr. Trump's speech to make it falsely appear that he sought to incite the crowd to violently attack the Capitol. He didn't, and we will show you why.

The hatred has also led the House managers to make some astounding legal arguments. They astoundingly urge you to disregard your oath by ignoring the First Amendment of the Constitution. They also ignore landmark binding United States Supreme Court cases, precedents—*Wood* and *Bond*—both of which unequivocally hold that elected officials have core First Amendment rights to engage in the exact type of political speech which Mr. Trump engaged in.

I was shocked the House managers not only spent a mere three pages on the First Amendment analysis in their trial memo but that, yesterday, they spent a mere ten minutes, at the end of their case, as a throwaway. What we have read and what we have heard is devoid of any constitutional analysis, far less than what I would expect from a first-year law student. They left out landmark cases—total intellectual dishonesty.

And, finally, hatred is at the heart of the House managers' frivolous attempt to blame Donald Trump for the criminal acts of the rioters based on double hearsay statements of fringe rightwing groups based on no real evidence other than rank speculation. Hatred is a dangerous thing. We all have to work to overcome it. Hatred should have no place in this Chamber, in these proceedings.

The second observation: the Senate is presented with an extraordinary task of sitting in judgment of a former President's words in a speech that he gave at a political event. The House managers accused Mr. Trump of using his words to incite the horrific events at the Capitol on January 6, but yesterday, they gave you a new and novel standard of incitement, with an element of foreseeability, a negligence concept. They cite zero case law. They made it up. This task of applying a completely made-up legal standard of incitement to an impeachment proceeding is truly an unprecedented task for the Senate, and that is something the Senate must seriously consider when deciding the issue. Do you want to create a precedent where the Senate will be tasked with sitting in judgment as to the meaning and implied intent of a President's words or words of any elected official?

Will that allow and maybe encourage a majority party to weaponize the awesome power of impeachment against the minority to suppress a point of view? Will the Senate then have to deal with constant Articles of Impeachment by a majority party accusing minority Presidents or other elected officials of so-called inciteful or false speeches? You can see where this would lead. Sadly, we have all seen the political rhetoric get ratcheted up over the last few years. We have all been witnesses to many incendiary words by our officials at political events, broadcast over the media and internet. In each of those instances, will there now be Senate impeachment hearings?

One last observation. We agree with the House managers: context does, indeed, matter. The inflammatory rhetoric from our elected officials must be considered as part of the larger context of Mr. Trump's speech at the Ellipse on January 6. The inflammatory language from both sides of the aisle has been alarming, frankly, but this political discourse must be considered as part of these proceedings to contextualize Mr. Trump's words. We have some video to play that highlights some of what I am talking about. I preface this video by noting I am not showing you this video as some excuse for Mr. Trump's speech. This is not about—this is not whataboutism. I am showing you this to make the point that all political speech must be protected.

(video montage)

Ms. PELOSI: I just don't even know why there aren't uprisings all over the country. Maybe there will be.

. . .

Ms. PRESSLEY: There needs to be unrest on the streets for as long as there is unrest in our lives.

. . .

Ms. PELOSI: We gotta be ready to throw a punch. You have to be ready to throw a punch.

. . .

Mr. TESTER: Donald Trump, I think you need to go back and punch him in the face.

. . .

Ms. WALLACE: I thought he should have punched him in the face.

. . .

Mr. BOOKER: I feel like punching him.

. . .

Vice President BIDEN: I'd like to take him behind the gym, if I were in high school. If we were in high school, I'd take him behind the gym and beat the hell out of him. You know, I wish we were in high school. I could take him behind the gym.

. . .

Ms. WATERS: I will go and take Trump out tonight.

. . .

Ms. WARREN: Take him out now.

. . .

Mr. DEPP: When was the last time an actor assassinated a President?

. . .

Mr. WILSON: They're still going to have to go out and put a bullet in Donald Trump.

. . .

Mr. CUOMO: Show me where it says that protest is supposed to be polite and peaceful.

. . .

Ms. WATERS: And you push back on them, and you tell them they are not welcome anymore, anywhere.

. . .

MADONNA: I have thought an awful lot about blowing up the White House.

. . .

Mr. BOOKER: Please, get up in the face of some Congresspeople.

. . .

Ms. PELOSI: People will do what they do.

. . .

Mr. SCHUMER: I want to tell you, Gorsuch, I want to tell you, Kavanaugh: You have released the whirlwind, and you will pay the price.

. . .

Ms. TLAIB: We are going to go in there, we are going to impeach the [bleep].

. . .

Ms. JOHNSON: This is just a warning to you Trumpers: Be careful. Walk lightly. And for those of you who are soldiers, make them pay.

. . .

Ms. DeGENERES: If you had to be stuck in an elevator with either President Trump, Mike Pence, or Jeff Sessions, who would it be?

Ms. HARRIS: Does one of us have to come out alive?

Mr. Counsel VAN DER VEEN: Again, I did not show you their robust speech to excuse or balance out the speech of my client, for I need not. I showed you the video because in this political forum, all robust speech should be protected, and it should be protected evenly for all of us. As a brief aside, we should all reflect and acknowledge the rhetoric has gotten to be too much and over the top.

It is grating on the collective well-being of the body public, the citizens. Most would like it to stop. But the point is, when you see speech such as this, you have to apply the First Amendment evenly, blindly. She is blind, Lady Justice.

Question No. 1: does the First Amendment apply to this Chamber in these proceedings? The House managers' position, as stated in their trial brief, is "The First Amendment does not apply at all to an impeachment proceeding." That is their position. This is plainly wrong. The text of the First Amendment expressly restricts Congress from regulating speech. It says: Congress shall make no law respecting an establishment of religion, or prohibiting the free exercise thereof; or abridging the freedom of speech, or of the press; or the right of the people peaceably to assemble, and to petition the Government for a redress of grievances. To ignore the Constitution would be contrary to the oath of office of a United States

Senator: "I do solemnly swear (or affirm) that I will support and defend the Constitution of the United States against all enemies, foreign and domestic; that I will bear true faith and allegiance to the same—" Well, you all know the rest.

No, the Senate cannot ignore the First Amendment. The Constitution itself limits the ability of the House to impeach to limited items, such as "high crimes and misdemeanors." The position advanced by the House managers is essentially an unlimited impeachment standard without constitutional guardrails, unmoored to any specific legal test other than the unbridled discretion of Congress. This is distinctly not the intent of the Framers. The Framers were aware of the danger of any impeachment process that would make the President "the mere creature of the Legislature," a quote directly from the Framers while debating the impeachment process on the floor of the Constitutional Convention of 1787. The Framers were fearful that any impeachment process that gave Congress full discretion on the standard for impeachment would constitute nothing less than a violation—"a violation of the fundamental principle of good Government."

One Founding Father, James Wilson, wrote extensively on the impeachment process. Mr. Wilson was a renowned legal scholar at the time, a law professor at the University of Pennsylvania in Philadelphia. He was a major force in drafting and adopting the Constitution in 1787. He served as one of the first Supreme—one of the first six Supreme Court Justices from 1789 to 1798. He was appointed by President George Washington. In fact, Wilson taught the first course on the new Constitution to President Washington and his Cabinet—the first in the Nation's history—in Philadelphia at the University of Pennsylvania in 1789. Wilson, in his law lectures, the first of their kind under the Constitution, plainly states that the Senate may not ignore the Constitution in impeachment proceedings. He states that lawful and constitutional conduct may not be used as an impeachable offense.

Let me say that again. He states that lawful and constitutional conduct may not be used as an impeachable offense. Read along with me: "The doctrine of impeachments is of high import in the constitutions of free states. On one hand, the most powerful magistrates should be amenable to the law: on the other hand, elevated characters should not be sacrificed merely on account of their elevation. No one should be secure while he violates the constitution and the laws: everyone should be secure while he observes them."

To be clear, James Wilson is saying that the Constitution does indeed apply when judging whether to convict an official by impeachment. If the complained-of conduct is constitutional, it cannot be impeachable. Are we to ignore the words and teachings of James Wilson? The House managers surely want you to. The House managers have made several references to this letter signed by 140 partisan "law professors" calling Mr. Trump's First Amendment defense "legally frivolous."

This is really an outrageous attempt to intimidate Mr. Trump's lawyers. Whenever a lawyer advances a truly "frivolous" argument, they may violate professional, ethical rules and could be subject to discipline. This letter is a direct threat to my law license, my career, and my family's financial well-being.

These "law professors" should be ashamed of themselves, and so should the House managers. How dare you? Do you really hate Donald Trump so much that you are willing to destroy good, hard-working people's lives, people that are only doing their jobs, and, frankly, as counsel for an accused fulfilling a constitutional role? It is astounding, really. I am a citizen, not a politician. I know these First Amendment arguments are not anywhere close to frivolous. They are completely meritorious.

Interestingly, the law professors' letter was issued on February 5—three days before we even filed our legal brief in this matter—and they ignored landmark, bedrock Supreme Court cases directly addressing this issue. In our brief, we have a direct quote from James Wilson, the Founding Father, supporting our position. The direct quote was documented in the Founding Father's original legal papers on the subject. He was the primary draftsman of the Constitution who taught the new Constitution to President Washington. He says so long as acts of elected officials like Mr. Trump are constitutionally protected, he should not be impeached. We have landmark U.S. Supreme Court decisions—*Wood* and *Bonds*, which I will explain in detail—supporting our position. All of this the House managers and the partisan law professors completely and misleadingly ignore. Frivolous? Hardly.

The letter is a bully tactic, and I think evidence is the House managers know they have a problem with the First Amendment defense on the merits, so they are resorting to such tactics. The House managers' suggestion that the First Amendment does not apply to this impeachment process is completely untenable. Ignoring the First Amendment would conflict with the Senators' oath of office. It would also conflict with well-settled Supreme Court precedent and ignore the intent of the Framers of the Constitution, such as James Wilson. Above all else, ignoring the Constitution would adopt the new Raskin "common-sense" doctrine we heard yesterday, eroding hundreds of years of First Amendment protections.

We are here under the Constitution. It is illogical what the House managers said. The Constitution does apply to this constitutional impeachment process. It is double-talk. Nonsense. Illogical. If the House managers had their way, they would ignore all of the Constitution. Does that include the Sixth Amendment? The right to counsel? They would have Mr. Trump sitting here without lawyers. And who would be next? It could be anyone—one of you or one of you.

You must reject this invitation to ignore the First Amendment. It is anti-American and would set dangerous precedent forever. The law has developed over the years to clearly establish elected officials have the right to engage in protected speech. Mr. Trump is not just a guy on the street or a guy at a bar or a fire chief or a police officer—there were a few of them in there—all analogies given by the House managers.

These sideways analogies are wrong. Mr. Trump was an elected official, and there is an entire body of law, Supreme Court landmark cases, supporting the conclusion that Mr. Trump actually has enhanced free speech rights because he is an elected official. These cases are ignored by the House managers and the law professors, and that, too, is total intellectual dishonesty. The Supreme Court has long held that the First Amendment's right to freedom of speech protects elected officials.

Two important, on-point decisions from the Supreme Court—*Wood v. Georgia* and *Bond v. Floyd*—expressly contradict the House managers' position. The House managers do not even cite those cases in their brief. They barely acknowledge them in their reply, and they were mum on them yesterday. In *Wood v. Georgia*, the Supreme Court addressed the case involving a sitting sheriff whose reelection was being investigated by a grand jury impaneled by a judge based on allegations of irregular "Negro bloc voting." It was in the Sixties.

The sheriff spoke publicly in multiple press releases calling the grand jury investigations "racist," "illegitimate," and an attempt to "intimidate" voters. He even urged the grand jurors on how to decide the issues and "not let its high office be a party to any political attempt to intimidate" voters. The sheriff viewed the grand jury's challenging the legitimacy of his election. The sheriff even sent a letter to the grand jurors with these allegations, which is an extraordinary step since laws in most States, including Georgia, prohibit attempts to influence or intimidate jurors. The sheriff was charged and convicted of contempt of court and obstruction of the grand jury. But the Supreme Court, in a decision written by Justice Brennan, reversed.

The Court held that the First Amendment protected an elected public official's speech because the voting controversy directly affected the sheriff's political career: the petitioner was an elected official and had the—Read with me, please, everybody. The petitioner was an elected official and had the right to enter the field of political controversy, particularly where his political life was at stake. The role that elected officials play in our society makes it all the more imperative that they be allowed freely to express themselves on matters of current public importance. *Wood* thus stands for the proposition that a difference of political opinion, expressed in speech on an issue of voting irregularity, cannot be punishable where all that was done was to encourage investigation and peaceful political speech—just like Mr. Trump has done here. The legal scholars call that directly on point.

A second case, *Bond v. Floyd*, involved a State legislature punishing an elected official for protected political speech. Bond is particularly instructive here, too. In *Bond*, the Supreme Court squarely addressed a question of an elected official's punishment by a legislature for statements alleged to have incited public violation of law—the burning of draft cards. The Court unequivocally rejected the idea— advanced here by the House managers—that an elected official is entitled to no protection under the First Amendment. The Supreme Court held that the Georgia House of Representatives was in fact forbidden by the First Amendment from punishing *Bond*, by not seating him, for advocating against the policy of the United States.

There are three fundamental holdings in *Bond*. No. 1: the manifest function of the First Amendment in a representative government requires that legislators be given the widest latitude to express their views on issues of policy. No. 2: just as erroneous statements must be protected to give freedom of expression the breathing space it needs to survive, so statements criticizing public policy and the implementation of it must be similarly protected. Third holding: legislators have an obligation to take positions on controversial political questions so that their constituents can be fully informed by them, and be better able to assess their qualifications—Please, read along with me—their qualifications for office; also so they may be represented in governmental debates by the person they have elected to represent them.

Mr. Trump enjoys this same First Amendment protection from Congress. The First Amendment's protections guarantee free speech addressing the electoral integrity issues essential to his career that Mr. Trump has consistently advocated. The House managers argue that "the First Amendment"—and I quote—"does not shield public officials who occupy sensitive policymaking positions from adverse actions when their speech undermines important government[al] interests."

That is flat wrong. They are in essence attempting to treat Mr. Trump as their employee. This is not the law under *Wood* and *Bond*. Mr. Trump was elected by the people. He is an elected official. The Supreme Court says elected officials must have the right to freely engage in public speech. Indeed, the Supreme Court expressly rejected the House managers' argument in *Wood v. Georgia*, holding that the sheriff was "not a civil servant," but an elected official who had "core" First Amendment rights which could not be restricted. That is *Wood v. Georgia*, page 395, footnote 21. The House managers do not mention *Wood* or *Bond* in the trial brief or anywhere else. Why? Why not? Because it does not fit their narrative or their story. They want to punish Mr. Trump for engaging in constitutionally protected free speech and they do not want you to consider the issue. But you must.

Question 2: does Mr. Trump's speech deserve protection under the First Amendment? There is no doubt Mr. Trump engaged in constitutionally protected political speech that the House has, improperly, characterized as "incitement of insurrection." The fatal flaw of the House's arguments is that it seeks to mete out governmental punishment—impeachment—based on First Amendment political speech. Speech for political purposes is the kind of activity to which the First Amendment offers its strongest protection. These are bedrock principles recognized by our Supreme Court for decades.

The Court has stated in no uncertain terms the importance of these principles to our democratic principles: the general proposition that freedom of expression upon public questions is secured by the First Amendment has long been settled by our decisions. The constitutional safeguard, we have said, "was fashioned to assure unfettered interchange of ideas for the bringing about of political and social changes desired by the people." *New York Times v. Sullivan.* Our First Amendment decisions have created a rough hierarchy in the constitutional protection of speech. Core political speech occupies the highest, most protected position. . . . Even political speech that may incite unlawful conduct is protected from the reach of government punishment.

The Court has said: every idea is an incitement, and if speech may be suppressed whenever it might inspire someone to act unlawfully, then there is no limit to the State's censorial power. The government may not prohibit speech because it increases the chances of an unlawful act will be committed "at some indefinite time" in the future. The House managers showed you a series of tweets going all the way back to 2015 in an effort to prove "incitement." All of that evidence is totally irrelevant under the constitutional definition of incitement.

Brandenburg v. Ohio is really the landmark case on the issue of incitement speeches. The applicable case was mentioned yesterday. In the *Brandenburg v. Ohio* case, another landmark, the Court held the government may only—the government may only—suppress speech for advocating the use of force or a violation of law if "such advocacy is directed to inciting or producing imminent lawless action and is likely to incite or produce such action." The *Brandenburg* holding has been interpreted as having three basic prongs to determine if speech meets the definition of "incitement." The *Brandenburg* test precludes speech from being sanctioned as incitement to a riot unless—this is one, the speech explicitly or implicitly encouraged use of violence or lawless action; two, the speaker intends that his speech will result in use of violence or lawless action, and; three, the imminent use of violence or lawless action is the likely result of the speech.

The House managers cannot get past the first prong of the *Brandenburg* test. They have not and cannot prove Mr. Trump explicitly or implicitly encouraged use of violence or lawless action—period. *Brandenburg* requires a close examination of the words themselves. The words are either important or they are not. The House managers admitted that the incitement issue is not about the words. Why not? Because on the face of it, Mr. Trump's words are no different than the figurative speech used by every one of the Senators assembled here today. If it is not about the words but about the "Big Lie" of a "stolen election" then why isn't House Manager RASKIN guilty, since he tried to overturn the 2016 election?

The more the House managers speak, the more hypocrisy gets revealed—hypocrisy. Even though they say it is not about the words, the law under *Brandenburg* requires a close analysis of the words to determine incitement. So we need to look at those words. Mr. Trump did the opposite of advocating for lawless action—the opposite. He expressly advocated for peaceful action at the Save America rally. He explicitly stated—these are the words: I know that everyone here will soon be marching over to the Capitol building to peacefully and patriotically make your voices heard. "To peacefully and patriotically make your voices heard"—that is how this President has spoken for years when he condemns violence, lawlessness, and rioters. The House managers have played manipulated, selectively edited parts of Mr. Trump's speech. They focus heavily on the word "fight." The President used the word "fight" twenty times in his speech. They picked only two. Why? Why not the other eighteen? Because they don't tell the story in the way they want to tell it. Here are all of them. Listen to the context.

President TRUMP: And, Rudy, you did a great job. He's got guts. You know what? He's got guts unlike a lot of people in the Republican Party. He's got guts. He fights. He fights. I'll tell you.

Thank you very much, John. Fantastic job. I watched. That is a tough act to follow, those two. There's so many weak Republicans. And we have great ones. Jim Jordan and some of these guys—they're out there fighting. The House guys are fighting. But it's—it's incredible. Many of the Republicans, I helped them get in. I helped them get elected. Did you see the other day where Joe Biden said: I want to get rid of the America First policy? What's that all about? Get rid of. How do you say I want to get rid of America First? Even if you're going to do it, don't talk about it, right?

Unbelievable what we have to go through. What we have to go through. And you have to get your people to fight. And if they don't fight, we have to primary the hell out of the ones that don't fight. You primary them. We're going to. We're going to let you know who they are. I can already tell you, frankly. Republicans are constantly fighting like a boxer with his hands tied behind his back. It's like a boxer. And we want to be so nice. We want to be so respectful of everybody, including bad people.

And we're going to have to fight much harder. And Mike Pence is going to have to come through for us, and if he doesn't, that will be a, a sad day for our country, because you're sworn to uphold our Constitution. And the accountability says if we see somebody in there that doesn't treat our vets well or they steal, they rob, they do things badly, we say: Joe you're fired.

Get out of here. Before you couldn't do that. You couldn't do that before. So we've taken care of things. We've done things like nobody's ever thought possible. And that's part of the reason that many people don't like us, because we've done too much. But we've done it quickly. And we were going to sit home and watch a big victory, and everybody had us down for a victory. It was going to be great and now we're out here fighting. I said to somebody, I was going to take a few days and relax after our big electoral victory. 10 o'clock it was over. The American people do not believe the corrupt, fake news anymore. They have ruined their reputation.

But you know, it used to be that they'd argue with me. I'd fight. So I'd fight, they'd fight, I'd fight, they'd fight. Pop pop. You'd believe me, you'd believe them. Somebody comes out. You know, they had their point of view; I had my point of view. But you'd have an argument. Now what they do is they go silent. It's called suppression, and that's what happens in a Communist country. That's what they do. They suppress. You don't fight with them anymore unless it's a bad story. They have a little bad story about me. They make it 10 times worse, and it's a major headline.

But Hunter Biden, they don't talk about him. What happened to Hunter? Where's Hunter? With your help over the last four years, we built the greatest political movement in the history of our country and nobody even challenges that. I say that over and over, and I never get challenged by the fakeness, and they challenge almost everything we say. But our fight against the big donors, big media, big tech, and others is just getting started. This is the greatest in history. There's never been a movement like that. Our brightest days are before us. Our greatest achievements, still away. I think one of our great achievements will be election security. Because nobody until I came along had any idea how corrupt our elections were. And again, most people would stand there at 9 o'clock in the evening and say I want to thank you very much, and they go off to some other life.

But I said something's wrong here, something is really wrong, can have happened. And we fight. We fight like hell. And if you don't fight like hell, you're not going to have a country anymore. Our exciting adventures and boldest endeavors have not yet begun. My fellow Americans, for our movement, for our children, and for our beloved country. And I say this despite all that's happened. The best is yet to come.

"A boxer fighting with his hand tied behind his back"? "Members of Congress fighting"? "Rudy being Rudy." These are the metaphorical, rhetorical uses of the word "fight." We all know that, right? Suddenly, the word "fight" is off limits. Spare us the hypocrisy and false indignation. It is a term used over and over and over again by politicians on both sides of the aisle. And, of course, the Democrat House Managers know that the word "fight" has been used figuratively in political speech forever. But don't take it from me. It is best to listen to them.

[The clip played at pp. 398-400 was replayed.]

Hypocrisy. The reality is, Mr. Trump was not in any way, shape, or form instructing these people to fight or to use physical violence. What he was instructing them to do was to challenge their opponents in primary elections, to push for sweeping election reforms, to hold Big Tech responsible—all customary and legal ways to petition your government for redress of grievances, which, of course, is also protected constitutional speech.

But the House Managers don't want you to focus on those things because, again, it does not fit their story. In the end, I leave you with this quote from Benjamin Franklin: "Freedom of speech is a principal pillar of a free government; when this support is taken away, the constitution of a free society is dissolved, and tyranny is erected on its ruins." Thank you.

. . .

Mr. Counsel CASTOR: Mr. President, Members of the Senate, good afternoon. It has been my great privilege over the past couple of weeks to lead this outstanding

team of lawyers and dedicated professionals in the defense of the 45th President of the United States. One of the most difficult things in leading such a talented group is deciding who is responsible for what and the strategy and the order in which we will present our evidence. You have heard from Mr. van der Veen and Mr. Schoen on the importance of the First Amendment and the importance of due process of law, and because I had the opportunity to set out the schedule, I decided that I would take the last substantive part of the case for myself.

You can take that two ways. The first, perhaps, is the best, and that would be that it is almost over. The second is that perhaps you have to wait another hour for it to be over. The reason why I chose this section—and believe me, it was a very difficult decision to make because I thought that the other arguments presented by Mr. Schoen and Mr. van der Veen were outstandingly researched, thoroughly vetted, and wonderfully and articulately presented by them.

But the critical issue in this case is the very narrow issue that is charged against the 45th President, and that issue is, did the 45th President engage in incitement of—they continue to say "insurrection"? Clearly, there was no insurrection. "Insurrection" is a term of art defined in the law, and it involves taking over a country, a shadow government, taking the TV stations over, and having some plan on what you are going to do when you finally take power. Clearly, this is not that.

What our colleagues here across the aisle meant is incitement to violence, to riot. So the word "incitement" is the critical case and the critical issue in the case. Now, the first time that you heard from us, I told you that you would never hear from our side that what happened on January 6 was anything other than horrific and that the 45th President of the United States and his lawyers and his entire team adamantly denounce that violence by those criminals that occurred in this very Chamber, this very building. There was a reason why we started our presentation back on Tuesday in that way, because I did not want the Senators to consider that there was any challenge to that particular fact.

Yet the House managers, knowing it was not contested at all, chose to spend fourteen-plus hours showing you pictures of how horrific the attack on the United States Capitol was. They spent no time at all in connecting legally the attack on the Capitol to the 45th President of the United States, which is the only question that needs to be answered, is, was Donald Trump responsible for inciting the violence that came to this building on January 6? Now, by any measure, President Trump is the most pro-police, anti-mob rule President this country has ever seen. His real supporters know this. He made it clear throughout his Presidency. He made it clear during the violence this past summer. He made it clear on January 6.

But politics changes things. Politics has created and interposed an element that should not be here. It has interposed the element of hatred. And the political world changes when hatred becomes part of the dynamic. As we wrote in our answer to the original charging document—and I hope that this is a phrase that lives on long after we are all departed, and I hope someday this becomes the mantra by which all of us operate who work for the benefit of the public—that political hatred has no place in the American justice system and most certainly no place in the Congress of the United States. To illustrate the contrast that I am speaking of, we have a video.

[The clip played at pp. 369-371 was replayed.]

Is there truly anyone in this Chamber who disagrees with the words as spoken by President Trump on that video? Surely not. Surely not. This contrast and in this context, I ask you to keep that in mind. My colleagues here—actually, my colleague here, Mr. RASKIN, hopes that you don't. They have used selective editing and manipulated visuals to paint a picture far different from this truth. Make no mistake, and I will repeat it now and anytime I am ever asked, January 6 was a terrible day for our country.

The attack on this building shocked us all. President Trump did not incite or cause the horrific violence that occurred on January 6, 2021. They know that. We know the President did not incite the riot because of his plain words that day, as Mr. van der Veen elucidated on a few moments ago. We know the President could not have incited the riots because of the timeline of the events of that day. We heard a great deal from the House managers about their prosecutorial bona fides and their ability to analyze evidence, apply it to statutes, use timelines, and figure out what happened based on circumstantial evidence and direct evidence and testimony and forensic analysis.

I can't recall any of the House managers who got up that didn't make some reference to prosecutorial bona fides. Well, I spent more than three decades locking up killers. And I do know a little bit about applying facts to the law. We know that the President would never have wanted such a riot to occur because his longstanding hatred for violent protesters and his love for law and order is on display, worn on his sleeve every single day that he served in the White House.

But if we are going to apply the facts to the statute, it has to be done systematically. It has to be done with precision, the way a court would expect us to do that. Let's look at the letter of the law. Again, Mr. van der Veen gave you an overview of the *Brandenburg* case and some of the related cases. You notice that when Mr. Van der Veen listed the elements that he took verbatim or close to verbatim right out of *Brandenburg*, they bore no reference whatsoever to the elements that flashed up by the Democratic managers the other day repeatedly. He actually used the Supreme Court's case. He didn't make it up. Let's look at the letter of the law.

The Supreme Court of the United States, over 50 years ago, laid out a clear test to determine whether speech is incitement. Under that test, the *Brandenburg v. Ohio* test, there are three elements that must be proven beyond a reasonable doubt, by a preponderance of the evidence—whatever the Senate considers—I suggest beyond a reasonable doubt.

First, the speech in question must explicitly or implicitly encourage the use of violence or lawless action. But here the President's speech called for peaceful protests.

Second, the speaker must intend that his speech will result in the use of violence or lawless action. And, again, as Mr. van der Veen pointed out, the President clearly deplores rioters and political violence and did so throughout his term as President and never hesitated to express his admiration for the men and women that protect this country.

Finally, the third element under the *Brandenburg* test is the imminent use of violence—imminent use of violence—in other words, right then. The imminent use of violence or lawless action must be the likely result of the speech—the likely result of the speech.

Well, that argument is completely eviscerated by the fact that the violence was preplanned, as confirmed by the FBI, Department of Justice, and even the House managers—not the result of the speech at all. Several of my colleagues of the House managers got up and spoke about the proceeding in the House being like a grand jury proceeding. Well, I have been in grand jury proceedings. I have run grand juries. In grand jury proceedings, you call witnesses; you hear evidence; you make transcripts; you take affidavits; you develop physical evidence; you hear reports from police officers; you hear forensic analysis from scientists; in fact, you invite the target of the grand jury to come in and testify if he or she pleases to be heard by the grand jury. Which one of those things happened in the House prior to the Impeachment Article? I don't believe any of them happened.

So the suggestion that what happened in the House was anything at all like a grand jury investigating a case and referring it for prosecution is complete nonsense. And if the House managers are trying to fool you about that, you must ask yourself: what else are they trying to fool you about? Let's look more closely at the President's speech. We have mentioned this lie before, but it is so critical, we need to talk about it again. The President asked that the attendees at his rally peacefully make their voices heard.

President TRUMP: I know that everyone here will soon be marching over to the Capitol Building to peacefully and patriotically make your voices heard.

The managers would have you believe that the President's supporters usually follow his every word but, in this case, imputing some imaginary meaning to them while ignoring his most clear instructions.

President Trump said "peacefully and patriotically make your voices heard." And the House managers took from that "go down to the Capitol and riot." So you are supposed to put yourselves in the heads of the people who hear "peacefully and patriotically make your voices heard" and conclude that those words do not mean what the President said. More than that, the President criticized the destruction wrought by leftwing anarchists and rioters. He told his supporters that they build; they don't destroy.

> President TRUMP: If this happened to the Democrats, there'd be hell all over the country going on. There'd be hell all over the country. But just remember this: You're stronger. You're smarter. You've got more going than anybody. And they try and demean everybody having to do with us. And you're the real people. You're the people that built this Nation. You're not the people that tore down our Nation.

Is it possible, listening to those words in the proper cadence without them being edited or the sound changed so that they are indistinguishable or sounds as though the crowd is right there, but listening to it here as you have here, unedited by us— is it possible that President Trump's disdain for political violence could be any clearer to the persons listening as he was speaking? Is it possible his words could have been misunderstood? I suggest to you that is the possibility.

Now, the House managers said the President told the crowd: "You have to get [out] your people to fight." The House managers' claim is that the President of the United States was telling the audience to get each other to physically fight, but that is not what the President said. The people who should fight, he said, were Members of Congress. If they don't fight, what the President said is, what should the rally attendees do? If Members of Congress wouldn't fight for the principles they held dear, what was it that the President specifically told his supporters at that rally he wanted them to do? He wanted them to support primary challenges.

Now, nobody in this Chamber is anxious to have a primary challenge. That is one truism I think I can say with some certainty. But that is the way we operate in this country. When the people of a State want to change their Representatives and their Senators, they use the electoral process. President Trump told his listeners that if their Members of Congress won't fight for their views, then go back home and find others that will. That is what President Trump said—the people who should fight were the Members of Congress.

> Mr. Manager NEGUSE: "You have to get your people to fight," he told them.

. . .

President TRUMP: You have to get your people to fight. And if they don't fight, we
have to primary the hell out of the ones that don't fight. You primary them. We're
going to let you know who they are. I can already tell you, frankly.

It is pretty stark contrast when you watch that video, isn't it?

When you see the House manager tell you—and I don't know if we're under
oath here, but when I walked into this room, I sure as heck felt as if I was under
oath and felt like I was speaking not only to Senators of the United States but
before the entire world and with God watching. And a House manager got up
here and told you that the President of the United States, on January 6, 2021, told
the crowd that they had to go and fight. And the implication that they wanted you
to draw was that he was sending them down to Capitol Hill to go and breach the
building and trash the very sacred Halls of Congress.

But we now know that is not at all anything near what the President said. What
the President said was: if you can't get your Members of Congress to do as you
would like them to do, you primary them. That is the American way. The first way
that the House managers presented and wanted you to conclude, that is the criminal way. But what the President said was the American way. Again, the House
managers manipulated President Trump's words. I can't stand here and pretend
to tell you that I know every time from all those videos that the House managers
manipulated what the President said, put up evidence that was not with the foundation of correctness and admissibility we expect.

I can't tell you that I picked up every one. I don't think Mr. van der Veen or Mr.
Schoen or any of the others who worked with us can tell you that. But what I can
tell you is there were an awful lot of times. And I know at least some of you were
judges in previous lives. If one of the lawyers was able to create the impression that
one side intentionally presented false or misleading evidence, that judge would
give an instruction called *falsus in uno, falsus in omnibus*: false in one thing, false
in everything. In other words, if they are trying to fool you about one thing, not
only might they be trying to fool you in something else, but under that maxim of
the law, you may conclude they are trying to fool you in everything else.

President Trump was immediate in his calls for calm and respect for law
enforcement. The House managers emphasized President Trump's tweet in the
6 p.m. hour where he told the crowds: go home with love & in peace. Remember
this day. What is it they left out? Well, the House starts their recitation of what
President Trump said as far as the aftermath of when the Capitol was breached at
roughly 6 p.m. What they don't tell you and didn't tell you—and which you probably don't know because I think I am the first one to say it in this forum—is at

2:38, President Trump urged protesters at the U.S. Capitol to stay peaceful: "Please support our Capitol Police and Law Enforcement. They are truly on the side of our Country. Stay peaceful!" Before we run the graphic, I just want to point out to you, President Trump's speech ended at 1:11 p.m. So at 2:38 p.m., by the time word reaches the President that there is a problem down here, he is out urging people to support the police, stay peaceful, support our Capitol Police and law enforcement. They are on the side of the country. Stay peaceful.

At 3:13 p.m., President Trump urged protesters at the U.S. Capitol to remain peaceful: "no violence. Remember, WE are the Party of Law and Order. Respect the law and our great men and women in blue." 3:13 p.m. President Trump's words couldn't have incited the riot at the Capitol. The day's events make this clear. Let's walk through the actual timeline.

At 11:15 a.m. police security camera videos show crowds forming at First Street, near the Capitol Reflecting Pool. This is a full 45 minutes before President Trump even took the stage on January 6. Let me repeat that. Violent criminals were assembling at the Capitol, over a mile away, almost an hour before the President uttered a single word on the Ellipse. You did not hear that fact during the hours and hours of the House managers' presentation, did you? When the President spoke, what did he call for? He called for rally attendees to peacefully and patriotically make their voices heard, for them to walk down Pennsylvania Avenue to cheer on Members of Congress. President Trump went on for more than an hour, ending at 1:11.

Now, why is this important? Because of all of the events that I am about to describe, they all occurred before—before—President Trump's remarks concluded.

At 12:49 p.m., the first barriers at the U.S. Capitol Grounds were pushed over, and the crowd entered the restricted area. At 1:05 p.m., Acting Defense Secretary Christopher Miller received open source reports of demonstrator movements to the U.S. Capitol. At 1:09 p.m., U.S. Capitol Police Chief Steven Sund called the House and Senate Sergeant at Arms, telling them he wanted an emergency declared, and he wanted the National Guard called. The point: Given the timeline of events, the criminals at the Capitol were not there at the Ellipse to even hear the President's words. They were more than a mile away, engaged in their preplanned assault on this very building. This was a preplanned assault—make no mistake—and that is a critical fact. Watch this.

Mr. Manager CICILLINE: Does anyone in this Chamber honestly believe that but for the conduct of President Trump that that charge in the Article of Impeachment, that that attack on the Capitol would have occurred? Does anybody believe that?

. . .

Mr. BLITZER: It was not some sort of spontaneous decision by a bunch of "protesters" to go up to Capitol Hill and storm Capitol Hill. This was all planned out.

. . .

Mr. TAPPER: How much of it was planned? How much of this was strategized ahead of time?

. . .

Mr. PEREZ: They are getting indications, some evidence that indicates that there was some level of planning.

. . .

Ms. QUIJANO: There appears to be premeditation.

. . .

Mr. MUIR: An FBI internal report the day before the siege, warning of a violent war at the Capitol.

. . .

Ms. QUIJANO: The FBI issued a warning of a "war" at the Capitol.

. . .

Mr. COLBERT: The FBI warned law enforcement agencies about this specific attack.

. . .

[Unidentified Speaker]: Be ready to fight. Congress needs to hear glass breaking, doors being kicked in.

. . .

Mr. D'ANTUONO: We developed some intelligence that a number of individuals were planning to travel to the D.C. area with intentions to cause violence. We immediately shared that information.

Ms. HERRIDGE: And they pushed out that information through this JTTF structure.

Mr. D'ANTUONO: It was immediately disseminated through a written product and briefed to our command post operation to all levels of law enforcement.

. . .

Unidentified Speakers: The FBI says two pipe bombs discovered near the Capitol on January 6 were placed there the night before. New video appears to show a person suspected of planting pipe bombs near the U.S. Capitol the night before. The FBI now says the bombs were planted the night before the Capitol siege, between 7:30 and 8:30 p.m.

. . .

Mr. MUIR: They were planted the day before.

. . .

Ms. HERRIDGE: It all goes to the idea of premeditation and coordination among individuals.

. . .

Mr. COMEY: This was a planned assault of people going after a castle.

Mr. Counsel CASTOR: So, to answer the question of the House manager, "Does anybody believe that this would have occurred but for the speech of Donald Trump?" I do. All of these facts make clear that the January 6 speech did not cause the riots. The President did not cause the riots. He neither explicitly nor implicitly encouraged the use of violence or lawless action but, in fact, called for the peaceful exercise of every American's First Amendment right to peacefully assemble and petition their government for redress of grievances. In other words, the *Brandenburg* standard is not made out.

The House managers admitted many facts are unknown. Even Speaker PELOSI admitted not knowing the real cause of the violence when she called for a 9/11-style Commission to examine the facts and causes that led to the violence.*

Let's touch now on the second absurd and conflated allegation in the House managers' single Article. President Trump's phone call to Georgia Secretary of State Brad Raffensperger—surreptitiously recorded, by the way—included multiple attorneys and others on the call. Let me point out the very obvious fact that the House managers ignored.

The private call that was made public by others cannot really be the basis to claim that the President intended to incite a riot, because he did not publicly disclose the contents of the call. How could he have hoped to use this call to invite his followers if he had no intent to make the conversation public and, indeed, had nothing to do with its being secretly recorded? The House managers told you that the President demanded that the Georgia Secretary of State "find" just over 11,000 votes. The word "find," like so many others the House managers highlighted, is taken completely out of context. The word "find" did not come out of thin air.

Based on an analysis of publicly available voter data that the ballot rejection rate in Georgia in 2016 was approximately 6.42 percent, and even though a tremendous amount of new, first-time mail-in ballots were included in the 2020 count, the

---

* Senators saw this text highlighted on screen: "It is also clear that we need to establish a 9/11-type commission to examine and report on the facts, causes, and security relating to the terrorist mob attack on January 6."

Georgia rejection rate in 2020 was a mere four-tenths of one percent—a drop-off from 6.42 percent to .4 percent. President Trump wanted the signature verification to be done in public. How can a request for signature verifications to be done in public be a basis for a charge for inciting a riot?

With that background, it is clear that President Trump's comments and the use of the word "find" were solely related to his concerns with the inexplicable dramatic drop in Georgia's ballot rejection rates. Let's examine how the word "find" was used throughout that conversation. Mr. Trump's first use of the word "find" was as follows: "we think that, if you check the signatures, a real check of the signatures going back in Fulton County, you'll find at least a couple hundred thousand of forged signatures of people who have been forged, and we are quite sure that's going to happen." President Trump also used "find" as follows: "Now, why aren't we doing signature, and why can't it be open to the public, and why can't we have professionals do it instead of rank amateurs who will never find anything and don't want to find anything? They don't want to find—you know, they don't want to find anything. Someday, you'll tell me the reason why, because I don't understand your reasoning, but, someday, you'll tell me the reason why, but why don't you want to find?"

President Trump echoed his previous sentiments again in the context of pursuing a legitimate and robust investigation into the lack of signature verification for mail-in and absentee ballots. "And why can't we have professionals do it instead of rank amateurs who will never find anything and don't want to find anything? They don't want to find anything. You know, they don't want to find anything. They don't want to find—you know, they don't want to find anything. Someday, you'll tell me why, because I don't understand your reasoning, but, someday, you'll tell me why, but why don't you want to find?"

"We can go through signature verification, and we'll find hundreds of thousands of signatures, and you could let us do it, and the only way you can do it, as you know, is to go to the past, but you didn't do that in Cobb County. You just looked at one page compared to another. The only way you could do a signature verification is to go from one that's signed on November 'whatever,' recently, and compare it to two years ago, four years ago, six years ago, you know, or even one, and you'll find that you have many different signatures, but in Fulton, where they dumped ballots, you will find that you have many that aren't even signed and that you have many forgeries."

Mr. Trump continued to use the word "find" throughout the conversation, each and every other time in the context of his request that Mr. Raffensperger undertake a review of signature verifications and his concerns, generally, with ballot integrity and his reported electoral deficit. Here are a few examples. "But why wouldn't you want to find the right answer, Brad? Instead of keep saying that the numbers are right, because those numbers are so wrong."

Another example: "We think that, if you check the signatures—a real check of the signatures—going back in Fulton County, you will find at least a couple hundred thousand of forged signatures of people who have been forged, and we are quite sure that's going to happen." Moreover, there was nothing untoward with President Trump or any other candidate, for that matter, speaking with the lead elections officer of the State. That is why the Georgia Secretary of State took a call, along with members of his team, one of whom decided to record it and release it to the press. The only reason this conversation is being discussed in this Chamber is because, once again, the media and their Democratic allies distorted the true conversation to mislead you and the American public. So we have a complete lack of evidence to the Article of Impeachment presented by the House managers. So why are we here? Politics. Their goal is to eliminate a political opponent, to substitute their judgment for the will of the voters.

(video montage)

Mr. CAPEHART: Why bother with a Senate trial of Donald Trump? He's no longer President.

. . .

Mr. PELLEY: He will be out of office anyway.

. . .

Ms. WALLACE: Is it to keep him from ever running again?

. . .

Ms. DEGETTE: To make sure he may never run for office again.

. . .

Mr. CASTRO of Texas: To keep him from running for office again.

. . .

Mr. KAINE: So Donald Trump will not be able to run for office again.

. . .

Ms. BALDWIN: Barring him from running for office again.

. . .

Mr. VAN HOLLEN: To disqualify him from running for office.

. . .

Ms. CLARK of Massachusetts: To disqualify him from ever running for office again.

. . .

Mr. SCHIFF: To disqualify him from running for office again.

. . .

Mr. EMANUEL: It's about focusing so that he can never run again.

. . .

Mr. SCHUMER: To remove him from ever running for office again.

. . .

Mr. POCAN: To never be able to run for office again.

. . .

Ms. KLOBUCHAR: To ban former President Trump from running again.

. . .

Mr. GREEN of Texas: If we don't impeach this President, he will get reelected.

Mr. Counsel CASTOR: The goal is to eliminate a political opponent, to substitute their judgment for the will of the voters. Members of the Senate, our country needs to get back to work. I know that you know that, but, instead, we are here. The majority party promised to unify and deliver more COVID relief, but, instead, they did this. We will not take most of our time today—us of the defense—in the hopes that you will take back these hours and use them to get delivery of COVID relief to the American people.

Let us be clear. This trial is about far more than President Trump. It is about silencing and banning the speech the majority does not agree with. It is about canceling 75 million Trump voters and criminalizing political viewpoints. That is what this trial is really about. It is the only existential issue before us. It asks for constitutional cancel culture to take over in the United States Senate. Are we going to allow canceling and banning and silencing to be sanctioned in this body?

To the Democrats, who view this as a moment of opportunity, I urge you instead to look to the principles of free expression and free speech. I hope, truly, that the next time you are in the minority, you don't find yourself in this position. To the Republicans in this Chamber, I ask when you are next in the majority, please resist what will be an overwhelming temptation to do this very same thing to the opposing party. Members of the Senate, this concludes the formal defense of the 45th President of the United States to the Impeachment Article filed by the House of Representatives. I understand that there is a procedure in place for questions, and we await them; thereafter, we will close on behalf of President Trump.

SENATORS' QUESTIONS

Mr. SCHUMER: Mr. President, I send a question to the desk. Isn't it the case that the violent attack and siege on the Capitol on January 6 would not have happened if not for the conduct of President Trump?

. . .

Mr. Manager CASTRO of Texas: To answer your question very directly, Donald Trump assembled the mob. He assembled the mob, and he lit the flame. Everything that followed was because of his doing, and although he could have immediately and forcibly intervened to stop the violence, he never did. In other words, this violent, bloody insurrection that occurred on January 6 would not have occurred but for President Trump. The evidence we presented in trial makes this absolutely clear.

This attack, as we said, didn't come from one random speech, and it didn't happen by accident, and that mob didn't come out of thin air. Before the election, Donald Trump spread lie after lie about potential fraud—an election, remember, that hadn't even happened yet. Months before the election took place, he was saying it was rigged and that it was going to be stolen. All of his supporters believed that the only way he was going to lose is if the election was stolen, if the election was rigged. And when he did lose, he spent week after week inciting his supporters to believe that their votes had been stolen and that the election was fraudulent and it was their patriotic duty to fight like hell to stop the steal and take their country back.

And, remember, this is in the United States, where our vote is our voice. You tell somebody that an election victory is being stolen from them, that is a combustible situation. And he gave them clear direction on how to deal with that. For example, on December 19, eighteen days prior to January 6, President Trump told them how and where to fight for it. He first issued his call to action for January 6. This was a "save the date" sent eighteen days before the event on January 6, and it wasn't just a casual one-off reference or a singular invitation.

For the next eighteen days, he directed all of the rage he had incited to January 6; and that was, for him, what he saw as his last chance to stop the transfer of power, to stop from losing the Presidency. And he said things like, "Fight to the death" and January 6 will be a "wild" and "historic day." And this was working. They got the message.

In the days leading to the attack, report after report, social media post after social media post, confirmed that these insurgents were planning armed violence, but they were planning it because he had been priming them, because he had been amping them up. That is why they were planning it. And these posts, confirmed by reports from the FBI and Capitol Police, made clear that these insurgents were planning to carry weapons, including guns, to target the Capitol itself. And yet Donald Trump, from January 5 to the morning of his speech, tweeted thirty-four times, urging his supporters to get ready to stop the steal. He even, on the eve of the attack, warned us that it was coming. He warned us that thousands were descending into D.C. and would not take it anymore.

When they got here at the Save America March, he told them again in that speech exactly what to do. His lawyer opened with: "Let's have trial by combat." That was Rudy Giuliani. And Donald Trump brought that message home. In fact, he praised Rudy Giuliani as a fighter, and President Trump used the words "fight" or "fighting" twenty times in that speech. Remember, you have just told these people—these thousands of people—that somebody has stolen your election, your victory; you are not going to get the President that you love.

Senators, that is an incredibly combustible situation when people are armed and they have been saying that they are mad as hell and they are not going to take it anymore. He looked out to a sea of thousands, some wearing body armor, helmets, holding sticks and flag poles, some of which they would later use to beat Capitol Police; and he told them that they could play by different rules—play by different rules. He even, at one point, quite literally, pointed to the Capitol as he told them to "fight like hell."

After the attack, you know, we have shown clearly, well, that once the attack began, insurgent after insurgent made clear they were following the President's orders. You saw us present that evidence of the insurgents who were there that day who said: I came because the President asked me to come. I was here at his invitation. You saw that of the folks that were in the Capitol that day.

. . .

Mr. GRAHAM: I send a question to the desk on behalf myself, Senators CRUZ, MARSHALL, and CRAMER to counsel for Donald Trump. Does a politician raising bail for rioters encourage more rioting?

. . .

Mr. Counsel CASTOR: Yes.

. . .

Mr. WARNOCK: I send a question to the desk. Is it true or false that in the months leading up to January 6th, dozens of courts, including State and Federal courts in Georgia, rejected President Trump's campaign's efforts to overturn his loss to Joe Biden?

. . .

Mr. Manager RASKIN: Mr. President, Senators, that is true. That is true. I want to be clear, though, that we have absolutely no problem with President Trump having pursued his belief that the election was being stolen or that there was fraud or corruption or unconstitutionality. We have no problem at all with him going to court to do it, and he did, and he lost in sixty-one straight cases. In Federal court and State court, in the lowest courts in the land, in the U.S. Supreme Court, he lost it. He lost in courts in Pennsylvania, Arizona, Georgia, Michigan, Minnesota, Nevada, and Wisconsin.

All of them said the same thing; they couldn't find any corruption; they couldn't find any fraud, certainly nothing rising to a material level that would alter the outcome of any of the elections; and there was no unconstitutionality. That is the American system. So, I mean, it is hard to imagine him having gotten more due process than that in pursuing what has come to be known popularly as the big lie, the idea that somehow the election was being stolen from him. We have no problem with the fact that he went to court to do all those things.

But notice, number one, the big lie was refuted, devastated, and demolished in Federal and State courts across the land, including by eight judges appointed by President Donald Trump himself. We quoted earlier in the case what happened in Pennsylvania, where U.S. District Court Judge Matthew Brann said: "In the United States, this can—that this Court has been presented with strained legal arguments without merit and speculative accusations . . . In the [United States of America], this cannot justify the disenfranchisement of a single voter, let alone all the voters of its sixth most populated state. Our people, laws, and institutions demand more."

Then it went up to Judge Stephanos Bibas, who is a Trump appointee, who is part of the appeals court panel. He said: "The Campaign's claims have no merit. The number of ballots it specifically challenges is far smaller than the [roughly] 81,000-vote margin of victory. And it never claims fraud or that any votes were cast by illegal voters. Plus, tossing out millions of mail-in ballots would be drastic and unprecedented, disenfranchising a huge swath of the electorate and upsetting all down-ballot races too." Which, incidentally, they weren't being challenged, even though it was the exact same ballot that had been brought.

So the problem was when the President went from his traditional combat, which was fine, to intimidating and bullying State election officials and State legislators, and then finally, as Representative CHENEY said, summoning a mob, assembling a mob, and then lighting the match for an insurrection against the Union. When he crossed over from nonviolent means, no matter how ridiculous or absurd—that is fine. He is exercising his rights—to inciting violence, that is what this trial is about. We heard very little of that from the presentation of the President's lawyers. They really didn't address the facts of the case at all. There were a couple of propaganda reels about Democratic politicians that would be excluded in any court in the land. They talked about the Rules of Evidence. All of that was totally irrelevant to the case before us. Whatever you think about it, it is irrelevant, and we will be happy, of course, to address the First Amendment argument too.

. . .

Ms. COLLINS: Mr. President, I send a question to the desk from Senator COL-LINS and Senator MURKOWSKI for the counsel for the former President. Exactly when did President Trump learn of the breach of the Capitol, and what specific actions did he take to bring the rioting to an end, and when did he take them? Please be as detailed as possible.

. . .

Mr. Counsel VAN DER VEEN: Is it possible to read the question again?

. . .

The PRESIDENT pro tempore: The clerk will read the question again. [The question was read a second time.]

. . .

Mr. Counsel VAN DER VEEN: The House Managers have given us absolutely no evidence, one way or the other, on that question. We are able to piece together a timeline, and it goes all the way back to December 31; January 2, there is a lot of interaction between the authorities and getting folks to have security beforehand on the day.

We have a tweet at 2:38, so it was certainly sometime before then. With the rush to bring this impeachment, there has been absolutely no investigation into that. And that is the problem with this entire proceeding. The House Managers did zero investigation, and the American people deserve a lot better than coming in here with no evidence, hearsay on top of hearsay on top of reports that are hearsay. Due process is required here, and that was denied.

. . .

Ms. ROSEN: Mr. President, I send a question to the desk for the House managers. On January 6, the anti-Semitic Proud Boys group that President Trump had told to stand by, laid siege to the Capitol alongside other rioters, including one wearing a "Camp Auschwitz" shirt. Is there evidence that President Trump knew or should have known that his tolerance of anti-Semitic hate speech, combined with his own rhetoric, could incite the kind of violence we saw on January 6?

. . .

Ms. Manager PLASKETT: Mr. President, Senators, Donald Trump has a long history of praising and encouraging violence, as you saw. He has espoused hateful rhetoric himself. He has not just tolerated it, but he has encouraged hateful speech by others. He has refused, as you saw in the September debate—that interview—to condemn extremists and white supremacist groups, like the Proud Boys, and he has, at every opportunity, encouraged and cultivated actual violence by these groups.

Yes, he has encouraged actual violence, not just the word "fight." He told groups like the Proud Boys, who had beaten people with baseball bats, to stand by. When his supporters in the fifty-car caravan tried to drive a bus of Biden campaign workers off the road, he tweeted a video of that incident with fight music attached to it and wrote: "I LOVE TEXAS!"

When his supporters sent death threats to the Republican Secretary of State Raffensperger in Georgia, he responded by calling Mr. Raffensperger an enemy of the state, after he knew of those death threats. And in the morning of the second Million MAGA March, when it erupted in violence and burned churches, he began that day with the tweet: "We have just begun to fight."

I want to be clear that Donald Trump is not on trial for those prior statements—however as hateful and violent and inappropriate as they may be. But his statements, the President's statements make absolutely clear three important points for our case. First, President Trump had a pattern and practice of praising and encouraging violence, never condemning it. It is not a coincidence that those very same people—Proud Boys, organizers of the Trump caravan, supporters and speakers of the second Million MAGA March—all showed up on January 6 to an event that he had organized with those same individuals who had organized that violent attack.

Second, his behavior is different. It is not just that it was a comment by an official to fight for a cause. This is months of cultivating a base of people who were violent—not potentially violent but were violent—and that their prior conduct both helped him cultivate the very group of people that attacked us; it also shows clearly that he had that group assembled, inflamed, and, in all the public reports, ready to attack. He deliberately encouraged them to engage in violence on January 6. President Trump had spent months calling supporters to a march on a specific day, at a specific time, for a specific purpose. What else were they going to do to stop the certification of the election on that day but to stop you—but to stop you physically? There was no other way, particularly after his Vice President said that he would refuse to do what the President asked.

The point is this: that by the time he called the cavalry—not calvary but cavalry—of his thousands of supporters on January 6, an event he had invited them to, he had every reason to know that they were armed, violent, and ready to actually fight. He knew who he was calling and the violence they were capable of, and he still gave his marching orders to go to the Capitol and "fight like hell" to stop the steal. How else was that going to happen? If they had stayed at the Ellipse, maybe it would have just been to violently—to fight in protest with their words. But to come to the Capitol? That is why this is different, and that is why he must be convicted and acquitted—and disqualified.

. . .

Mr. HAGERTY: Mr. President, on behalf of Senator SCOTT of South Carolina and myself, I would like to submit a question to the desk. Given that more than 200 people have been charged for their conduct at the Capitol on January 6, that our justice system is working to hold the appropriate persons accountable, and that President Trump is no longer in office, isn't this simply a political show trial that is designed to discredit President Trump and his policies and shame the 74 million Americans who voted for him?

. . .

Mr. Counsel CASTOR: Thank you, Senators, for that question. That is precisely what the 45th President believes this gathering is about. We believe in law and order and trust that the Federal authorities that are conducting investigations and prosecutions against the criminals that invaded this building will continue their work and be as aggressive and thorough as we know them to always be and that they will continue to identify those that entered the inner sanctum of our government and desecrated it.

The 45th President no longer holds office, and there is no sanction available under the Constitution, in our view, for him to be removed from the office that he no longer holds. The only logical conclusion is that the purpose of this gathering is to embarrass the 45th President of the United States and in some way try to create an opportunity for Senators to suggest that he should not be permitted to hold office in the future or, at the very least, publicize this throughout the land to try to damage his ability to run for office when and if he is acquitted and, at the same time, tell the 74 million people who voted for him that their choice was the wrong choice. I believe that this is a divisive way of going about handling impeachment, and it denigrates the great solemnity that should attach to such proceedings. I yield the remainder of my time, Mr. President.

. . .

Mr. MARKEY: Mr. President, I send a question for the House managers to the desk because the President's counsel did not answer the question which was posed to them.

The question is from Senator MARKEY, with Senator DUCKWORTH, to the managers on the part of the House of Representatives. Exactly when did the President learn of the breach at the Capitol, and what steps did he take to address the violence? Please be as detailed as possible.

. . .

Ms. Manager PLASKETT: Yes. Mr. President, Senators, this attack was on live TV, on all major networks, in real time. The President, as President, has access to intelligence information, including reports from inside the Capitol. He knew the violence that was underway. He knew the severity of the threats. And, most importantly, he knew that Capitol Police were overwhelmingly outnumbered and in a fight for their lives against thousands of insurgents with weapons. We know he knew that. We know that he did not send any individuals. We did not hear any tweets. We did not hear him tell those individuals: "Stop. This is wrong. You must go back." We did not hear that. So what else did the President do? We are unclear.

But we believe it was a dereliction of his duty, and that was because he was the one who had caused them to come to the Capitol, and they were doing what he asked them to do. So there was no need for him to stop them from what they were engaged in. But one of the things I would like to ask is we still have not heard and pose to you all the questions that were raised by Mr. RASKIN, Manager RASKIN, in his closing argument: Why did President Trump not tell the protesters to stop as soon as he learned about it? Why did President Trump do nothing to stop the attack for two hours after the attack began? Why did President Trump do nothing to help protect the Capitol and law enforcement battling the insurgents?

You saw the body cam of a Capitol Police officer at 4:29, still fighting—4:29 after since what time?—one, two in the afternoon. Why did he not condemn the violent insurrection on January 6? Those are the questions that we have, as well, and the reason this question keeps coming up is because the answer is nothing.

The Senator from Utah, Mr. ROMNEY, on behalf of himself and Senator COLLINS, submits a question: The question is for both sides, and the time will be evenly divided. When President Trump sent the disparaging tweet at 2:24 p.m. regarding Vice President Pence, was he aware that the Vice President had been removed from the Senate by the Secret Service for his safety?

. . .

Mr. Manager RASKIN: I'm sorry. Could the question be read again, Mr. President?

. . .

The PRESIDENT pro tempore: Of course. [The question was read again.]

. . .

The PRESIDENT pro tempore: The House managers are recognized for two and a half minutes.

. . .

Mr. Manager CASTRO of Texas: Thank you. Well, let me tell you what he said at 2:24 p.m. He said: "Mike Pence didn't have the courage to do what should have been done to protect our Country and our Constitution . . . USA demands the truth!" And you know by now what was all over the media. You couldn't turn on the television, you couldn't turn on the radio, you couldn't consume any media or probably take any phone calls or anything else without hearing about this and also hearing about the Vice President. And here is what Donald Trump had to know at that time because the whole world knew it. All of us knew it.

Live television had, by this point, shown that the insurgents were already inside the building and that they had weapons and that the police were outnumbered. And here are the facts that are not in dispute. Donald Trump had not taken any measures to send help to the overwhelmed Capitol Police. As President, at that point, when you see all this going on and the people all around you are imploring you to do something and your Vice President is there, why wouldn't you do it?

Donald Trump had not publicly condemned the attack, the attackers, or told them to stand down despite multiple pleas to do so, and Donald Trump hadn't even acknowledged the attack. And, after Wednesday's trial portion concluded, Senator TUBERVILLE spoke to reporters and confirmed the call that he had with the President and did not dispute Manager CICILLINE's description in any way that there was a call between he and the President around the time that Mike Pence was being ushered out of the Chamber, and that was shortly after 2 p.m.

And Senator TUBERVILLE specifically said that he told the President: Mr. President, they just took the Vice President out; I have got to go. That was shortly after 2 p.m. There were still hours of chaos and carnage and mayhem, and the Vice President and his family were still in danger at that point. Our Commander in Chief did nothing.

. . .

The PRESIDENT pro tempore: Counsel for the former President.

. . .

Mr. Counsel VAN DER VEEN: The answer is no. At no point was the President informed the Vice President was in any danger. Because the House rushed through this impeachment in seven days with no evidence, there is nothing at all in the record on this point because the House failed to do even a minimum amount of due diligence. What the President did know is that there was a violent—there was a violent riot happening at the Capitol. That is why he repeatedly called via tweet and via video for the riots to stop, to be peaceful, to respect Capitol Police and law enforcement, and to commit no violence and to go home.

But to be clear, this is an Article of Impeachment for incitement; this is not an Article of Impeachment for anything else. It is one count. They could have charged anything they wanted. They chose to charge incitement. So that the question—although answered directly no, it is not really relevant to the charges for the impeachment in this case. And I just wanted to clear up one more thing. Mr. CASTRO, in his first answer, may have misspoke, but what he said was Mr. Trump had said "fight to the death." That is false. I am hoping he misspoke. Thank you.

. . .

Ms. KLOBUCHAR: Mr. President, on behalf of myself and Senators CASEY and BROWN, I send a question to the desk.

In presenting your case, you relied on past precedents from impeachment trials, such as William Belknap's impeachment. After what you have presented in the course of this trial, if we do not convict former President Trump, what message will we be sending to future Presidents and Congresses?

. . .

Ms. Manager PLASKETT: As we have shown, President Trump engaged in a course of conduct that incited an armed attack on the Capitol. He did so while seeking to overturn the results of the election and thwart the transfer of power. And when the attack began, he further incited violence aimed to his own Vice President, even demonstrating his state of mind by failing to defend us and the law enforcement officials who protect us.

The consequences of his conduct were devastating on every level. Police officers were left overwhelmed, unprotected. Congress had to be evacuated; our staff barricaded in this building, calling their families to say goodbye. Some of us, like Mr. RASKIN, had children here. And these people in this building, some of whom were on the FBI's watch list, took photos, stole laptops, destroyed precious statues, including one of John Lewis, desecrated the statue of a recently deceased Member of Congress who stood for nonviolence. This was devastating. And the world watched us, and the world is still watching us to see what we will do this day and will know what we did this day one hundred years from now. Those are the immediate consequences, and our actions will reverberate as to what are the future consequences. The extremists who attacked the Capitol at the President's provocation will be emboldened.

All our intelligence agencies have confirmed this; it is not House managers saying that. They are quite literally standing by and standing ready. Donald Trump told them: this is only the beginning. They are waiting and watching to see if Donald Trump is right that everyone said this was totally appropriate.

Let me also bring something else up. I will briefly say that defense counsel put a lot of videos out in their defense, playing clip after clip of Black women talking about fighting for a cause or an issue or a policy. It was not lost on me, as so many of them were people of color and women and Black women, Black women like myself, who are sick and tired of being sick and tired for our children—your children, our children.

This summer, things happened that were violent, but there were also things that gave some of us Black women great comfort: seeing Amish people from Pennsylvania standing up with us, Members of Congress fighting up with us. And so I thought we were past that. I think maybe we are not. There are longstanding consequences, decisions like this that will define who we are as a people, who America is. We have in this room made monumental decisions. You all have made monumental decisions. We have declared wars, passed civil rights acts, ensured that no one in this country is a slave. Every American has the right to vote, unless you live in a territory. At this time, some of these decisions are even controversial, but history has shown that they define us as a country and as a people. Today is one of those moments, and history will wait for our decision.

The Senator from Utah, Mr. LEE, sends a question on behalf of himself, Senator HAWLEY, Senator CRAPO, Senator BLACKBURN, and Senator PORTMAN, and the question is for the counsel for the former President:

Multiple State constitutions enacted prior to 1787—namely, the constitutions of Delaware, Virginia, Pennsylvania, and Vermont—specifically provided for the impeachment of a former officer. Given that the Framers of the U.S. Constitution would have been aware of these provisions, does their decision to omit language specifically authorizing the impeachment of former officials indicate that they did not intend for our Constitution to allow for the impeachment of former officials?

. . .

Mr. Counsel VAN DER VEEN: Good question, and the answer is yes, of course they left it out. The Framers were very smart men, and they went over draft after draft after draft on that document, and they reviewed all the other drafts of all of the State constitutions, all of them. They picked and chose what they wanted, and they discarded what they did not. What they discarded was the option for all of you to impeach a former elected official. I hope that is answering your question. Thank you.

. . .

PADILLA, the Senator from California, submits a question for the House managers:

Having been on the frontlines of combatting the "big lie" over the past four years as California's chief elections officer, it is clear that President Trump's plot to undermine the 2020 election was built on lies and conspiracy theories. How did this plot to unconstitutionally keep President Trump in power lead to the radicalization of so many of President Trump's followers and the resulting attack on the Capitol?

. . .

Mr. Manager CASTRO: Senators, Donald Trump spent months inciting his base to believe that their election was stolen, and that was the point—that was the thing that would get people so angry. Think about that, what it would take to get a large group of thousands of Americans so angry to storm the Capitol. That was the purpose behind Donald Trump saying that the election had been rigged and that the election had been stolen.

To be clear, when he says the election is stolen, what he is saying is that the victory—and he even says one time, the election victory—has been stolen from them. Think about how significant that is to Americans. Again, you are right, over 70 million—I think 74 million people voted for Donald Trump. And this wasn't a one-off comment. It wasn't one time. It was over and over and over and over and over again, with a purpose.

We are not having this impeachment trial here because Donald Trump contested the election. As I said during the presentation, nobody here wants to lose an election. We all run our races to win our elections. But what President Trump did was different. What our Commander in Chief did was the polar opposite of what we are supposed to do. We let the people decide the elections, except President Trump. He directed all of that rage that he had incited to January 6, the last chance—again, to him, this was his last chance. This was certifying the election results. He needed to whip up that mob, amp them up enough to get out there and try to stop the election results, the certification of the election. And, you all, they took over the Senate Chamber to do that. They almost took over the House Chamber.

There were fifty or so or more House Members who were literally scared for their lives up in the Gallery. A woman who bought into that big lie died because she believed the President's big lie. This resulted in a loss of one of his supporter's lives. A Capitol Police officer died that day—other of President Trump's supporters. Two Capitol Police officers ended up taking their own lives. Defense counsel—their defense is basically everything President Trump did is okay, and he could do it again. Is that what we believe; that there is no problem with that, that it is perfectly fine if he does the same thing all over again?

This is dangerous. He is inciting his base. He was using the claim of a rigged election. We have never seen somebody do that over and over and over again—tell a lie, say six months ahead of time that it is a rigged election. There is a dangerous consequence to that when you have millions of followers on Twitter and millions of followers on Facebook and you have that huge bully pulpit of the White House and you are the President of the United States. There is a cost to doing that. People are listening to you in a way that, quite honestly, they are not listening to me and they are not listening to all of us in this room. I just want to clear up—the defense counsel made a point about something that I read earlier.

The defense counsel suggested I misspoke. I just want to clarify for the record that the tweet I referenced—let me read you the tweet directly: "If a Democrat Presidential Candidate had an Election Rigged & Stolen, with proof of such acts at a level never seen before, the Democrat Senators would consider it an act of war, and fight to the death. Mitch & the Republicans do NOTHING, just want to let it pass. NO FIGHT!"

So Donald Trump was equating what Democrats would do if their election was stolen. He said they'd fight to the death. Why do you think he sent that tweet? Because he is trying to say: hey, the other side would fight to the death; so you should fight to the death. I mean, do we read that any other way?

. . .

Senator HAWLEY, on behalf of himself and Senator CRAMER, sends a question for the counsel and House managers:

If the Senate's power to disqualify is not derivative of the power to remove a convicted President from office, could the Senate disqualify a sitting President but not remove him or her?

. . .

Mr. Counsel VAN DER VEEN: Would you read that question again, if you would please?

. . .

[The question was read again.]

. . .

Mr. Counsel VAN DER VEEN: No. But I can't let this rest. Mr. CASTRO attributed a statement the time before last that he was up here that Donald Trump had told his people to fight to the death. I am not from here. I am not like you guys. I was being very polite in giving an opportunity to correct the record, and I thought that is exactly what he would do.

But instead, what he did is he came up and illustrated the problem with the presentation of the House case. It has been smoke and mirrors, and, worse, it has been dishonest. He came up and tried to cover when he got caught, as they were caught earlier today with all of the evidence, checking tweets, switching dates—everything they did. And bear in mind, I had two days to look at their evidence.

And when I say two days, I mean they started putting in their evidence. So I started being able to get looking at it. That is not the way this should be done. But what we discovered was, he knew what he was doing. He knew that the President didn't say that to his people. What he said was, if it happened to the Democrats, this is what they would do. In his speech that day, you know what he said? He said, if this happened to the Democrats, if the election were stolen from the Democrats, all hell would break loose.

But he said to his supporters: we are smarter. We are stronger. And we are not going to do what they did all summer long. So what he did was he misrepresented a tweet to you to put forth the narrative that is wrong. It is wrong. It is dishonest, and the American people don't deserve this any longer. You must acquit.

. . .

Mr. Manager RASKIN: Thank you, Mr. President. That was profoundly inaccurate and irrelevant to what the question is. So I am going to get back to the question. So under article II, section 4, a President who is in office must be convicted before removal and then must be removed before disqualification. Okay. But if the President is already out of office, then he can be separately disqualified, as this President is. But these powers have always been treated as separate issues, which is why I think there have been eight people who have been convicted and removed, and just three of them disqualified.

And, as you know, there is a totally separate process within the Senate for doing this. The Constitution requires a two-thirds vote for conviction. But for disqualification, it is a majority vote. It is a separate thing. So people could vote to convict and then vote not to disqualify. If they felt that the evidence demonstrated the President was guilty of incitement to insurrection, they could vote to convict. If they felt they didn't want to exercise the further power established by the Constitution to disqualify, they wouldn't even have to do that. And that could be something that is taken up separately by the Senate and by a majority vote.

. . .

Ms. WARREN: Mr. President, I send a question to the desk.

The defense's presentation highlighted the fact that Democratic Members of Congress raised objections to the counting of electoral votes in past joint sessions of Congress. To your knowledge, were any of those Democratic objections raised after insurrectionists stormed the Capitol in order to prevent the counting of electoral votes and after the President's personal lawyer asked Senators to make these objections specifically to delay the certification?

. . .

Mr. Manager RASKIN: The answer is no, we are not aware that any other objections were raised in the counting of electoral college votes, either by Democrats or Republicans. This has been kind of a proud bipartisan tradition under the electoral college because the electoral college is so arcane and has so many rules to it. I think that my co-counsel on the other side had some fun because I was one of the people who took, I think, about thirty seconds in 2016 to point out that the electors from Florida were not actually conforming to the letter of the law because they have a rule in Florida that you can't be a dual officeholder. In other words, you can't be a State legislator and also be an elector. That was improper form. I think then-Vice President Biden properly gaveled me down and said: "Look, we are going to try to make the electoral college work, and we are going to vindicate the will of the people." And that is pretty much what happened.

Nobody has stormed the Capitol before or, as Representative CHENEY, the secretary of the Republican conference said, gone out and summoned a mob, assembled a mob, incited a mob, and lit a match. As Representative CHENEY said, all of this goes to the doorstep of the President. None of it would have happened without him and everything is due to his actions. This would not have happened. That is the chair of the House Republican conference, who was the target of an effort to remove her, which was rejected on a vote of by more than two to one in the House Republican conference, when there was an attempt to remove her for voting for impeachment and becoming a leader for vindicating our constitutional values.

So please don't mix up what Republicans and Democrats have done, I think, in every election for a long time, to say there are improprieties going on in terms of conforming with State election laws, with the idea of mobilizing a mob insurrection against the government that got five people killed, 140 Capitol officers wounded, and threatened the actual peaceful succession of power and transfer of power in America. If you want to talk about reforming the electoral college, we can talk about reforming the electoral college. You don't do it by violence.

. . .

Mr. CRAMER: I send a question to the desk for the former President's attorneys.

Given the allegations of the House manager that President Trump has tolerated anti-Semitic rhetoric, has there been a more pro-Israel President than President Trump?

. . .

Mr. Counsel VAN DER VEEN: No. But it is apparent that nobody listened to what I said earlier today, because the vitriolic speech needs to stop. You need to stop. There was nothing funny here, Mr. RASKIN. We aren't having fun here. This is about the most miserable experience I have had down here in Washington, D.C. There is nothing fun about it. And in Philadelphia, where I come from, when you get caught doctoring the evidence, your case is over, and that is what happened. They got caught doctoring the evidence, and this case should be over.

. . .

The Senator from Vermont, Mr. SANDERS, has a question for both the counsel for the former President and the House managers:

The legislative clerk read as follows: the House prosecutors have stated over and over again that President Trump was perpetrating a big lie when he repeatedly claimed that the election was stolen from him and that he actually won the election by a landslide. Are the prosecutors right when they claim that Trump was telling a big lie or, in your judgment, did Trump actually win the election?

. . .

Ms. Manager PLASKETT: As we all know, President Trump did lose the election by 7 million votes, 306 electoral votes. By the time of the January 6 attack, the courts, the Justice Department, all fifty States across the country had done—agreed that the votes were counted. The people had spoken, and it was time for the peaceful transfer of power as our Constitution and the rule of law demands. Sixty-one courts—sixty-one courts—the President went to. That is fine, appropriate. He lost. He lost. He lost the election. He lost the court case.

As Leader MCCONNELL recognized the day after the electors certified the votes on December 14, he said: "Many millions of us had hoped that the Presidential election would yield a different result, but our system of government has processes to determine who will be sworn in on January 20. The electoral college has spoken." Patriotism. Sometimes, there is a reason to dispute an election. Sometimes, the count is close. Sometimes, we ask for a recount, go to courts. All of that is appropriate. I lost my first election. I stayed in bed for three days. We do what we need to do, and we move on.

This was not that because, when all of these people confirmed that Donald Trump had lost, when the courts, his—his—Department of Justice, State officials, Congress, his Vice President were ready to commit to the peaceful transfer of power—the peaceful transfer of power—Donald Trump was not ready, and we are all here because he was not ready. Day after day, he told his supporters false, outlandish claims of why this election was rigged. Now, let's be clear: President Trump had absolutely no support of these claims, but that wasn't the point of what he was doing. He did it to make his supporters frustrated, to make them angry.

. . .

Mr. Counsel VAN DER VEEN: Thank you. May I have the question read again and not have it count against my time?

. . .

[The question was read again.]

. . .

Mr. Counsel VAN DER VEEN: Who asked that?

. . .

Mr. SANDERS: I did.

. . .

Mr. Counsel VAN DER VEEN: My judgment is irrelevant in this proceeding. It absolutely is. What is supposed to happen here is the Article of Impeachment—

. . .

Mr. Counsel VAN DER VEEN: May I have the question read again, please?

. . .

[The question was read again.]

. . .

Mr. Counsel VAN DER VEEN: In my judgment, it is irrelevant to the question before this body. What is relevant in this Impeachment Article is, were Mr. Trump's words inciteful to the point of violence and riot? That is the charge. That is the question; and the answer is, no, he did not have speech that was inciteful to violence or riot.

Now, what is important to understand here is the House managers have completely, from the beginning of this case to right now, done everything except answer that question—the question they brought before you, the question they want my client to be punished by. That is the question that should be getting asked. The answer is, he advocated for peaceful, patriotic protest. Those are his words.

The House managers have shown zero—zero—evidence that his words did anything else. Remember, all of the evidence is this was premeditated; the attack on the Capitol was preplanned. It didn't have anything to do with Mr. Trump in any way, what he said on that day on January 6 at that Ellipse, and that is the issue before this Senate. Now, on the issue of contesting elections and the results, the Democrats have a long, long history of just doing that. I hope everybody was able to see the video earlier today. Over and over again, it has been contested. When Mr. Trump was elected President, we were told that it was hijacked.

. . .

Mr. JOHNSON: Mr. President, I send a question to the desk for both parties.

The House managers assert that the January 6 attack was predictable, and it was foreseeable. If so, why did it appear that law enforcement at the Capitol were caught off guard and unable to prevent the breach? Why did the House Sergeant at Arms reportedly turn down a request to activate the National Guard, stating that he was not comfortable with the optics?

. . .

Mr. Counsel VAN DER VEEN: Would you read the question again, please?

. . .

[The question was read again.]

. . .

Mr. Counsel VAN DER VEEN: Holy cow. That is a really good question. Had the House managers done their investigation, maybe somebody would have an answer to that, but they didn't. They did zero investigation. They did nothing. They looked into nothing. They read newspaper articles. They talked to their friends—you know, a TV reporter or something or something or another. But, Jiminy Cricket, there is no due process in this proceeding at all, and that question highlights the problem. When you have no due process, you have no clear-cut answers, but we do know that there was, I think, a certain level of foreseeability. It looks like, from the information they were presenting, some law enforcement knew that something could be happening. In my presentation, we knew that the mayor, two days before—before—had been offered to have Federal troops or National Guard deployed, beef up security here, and Capitol Police. It was offered. So somebody had to have an inkling of something. My question is, Who ignored it and why? If an investigation were done, we would know the answer to that too. Thank you.

. . .

Ms. Manager PLASKETT: First, if defense counsel has exculpatory evidence, you are welcome to give it to us. We would love to see it. You have had an opportunity to give us evidence that would exculpate the President. Haven't seen it yet. Everyone—the defense counsel wants to blame everyone else except the person who was most responsible for what happened on January 6, and that is President Trump, Donald Trump. He is the person who foresaw this the most because he had the reports; he had access to the information. He, as well, had—we all know how he is an avid cable news watcher. He knew what was going to happen. He cultivated these individuals.

These are the undisputed facts. The National Guard was not deployed until over two hours after the attack. I heard reference to Mayor Bowser in the defense's presentation. Mayor Bowser does not have authority over the Capitol or Federal buildings. She could not deploy the National Guard to the Capitol. That is outside of the jurisdiction of the Mayor of the District of Columbia. At no point in that entire day did the President of the United States, our Commander in Chief, tell anyone—law enforcement struggling for their lives, insurgents who felt empowered by the sheer quantity of them, any of us in this building, or the American people—that he was sending help. He did not defend the Capitol. The President of the United States did not defend the Capitol of this country. It is indefensible.

. . .

Senator MERKLEY submits a question for the House managers: If a President spins a big lie to anger Americans and stokes the fury by repeating the lie at event after event and invites violent groups to D.C. the day and hour necessary to interrupt the electoral college count and does nothing to stop those groups from advancing on the Capitol and fails to summon the National Guard to protect the Capitol and then expresses pleasure and delight that the Capitol was under attack, is the President innocent of inciting an insurrection because in a speech he says "be peaceful"?

. . .

Mr. Manager CASTRO of Texas: You all ask a very important question, which is, given everything that the President did leading up to the election, after the election, and leading up to January 6, all of the incitement of his supporters, whom he convinced with a big lie over and over that the election had been stolen from them and from him, and then once the mob had stormed the Capitol, the Vice President was in danger, the Speaker was in danger, the Members of the House and the Senate and all the staff here—the janitorial staff, the cafeteria workers, everybody—and all of the hot rhetoric that he spoke with and then simply a few times said "stay peaceful"—remember, he said "stay peaceful" when they had already gotten violent, when they had already brought weapons, when they had already hurt people. What he never said was: "Stop the attack. Leave the Capitol. Leave immediately."

Let me be clear. The President's message in that January 6 speech was incendiary. So in the entire speech, which was roughly 1,100 words, he used the word "peaceful" once, and using the word "peaceful" was the only suggestion of nonviolence. President Trump used the word "fight" or "fighting" twenty times. Now, again, consider the context. He had been telling them a big lie over and over, getting them amped up, getting them angry because an election had been stolen from them. There are thousands of people in front of him. Some of them are carrying weapons and arms. They are angry. He is telling them to fight. President Trump's words in that speech, just like the mob's actions, were carefully chosen. His words incited their actions.

Now, how do we know this? For months, the President had told his supporters his big lie that the election was rigged, and he used the lie to urge his supporters not to concede and to stop the steal.

. . .

Mr. Manager RASKIN: If you rob a bank, and on the way out the door, you yell "respect private property," that is not a defense to robbing the bank.

. . .

Mr. CRUZ: Mr. President, I send a question to the desk directed at both sides.

The Senator from Texas has a question for both sides.

Out of their sixteen hours, the House managers devoted all of fifteen minutes to articulating a newly created legal standard for incitement: one, was violence foreseeable; two, did he encourage violence; three, did he do so willfully? Is this new standard derived from the Criminal Code or any Supreme Court case? While violent riots were raging, KAMALA HARRIS said on national TV: they're not gonna let up—and they should not. And she also raised money to bail out violent rioters. Using the managers' proposed standard, is there any coherent way for Donald Trump's words to be incitement and KAMALA HARRIS' words not to be incitement?

. . .

Mr. Manager RASKIN: Thank you, Mr. President and Senators. I am not familiar with the statement that is being referred to with respect to the Vice President, but I find it absolutely unimaginable that Vice President HARRIS would ever incite violence or encourage or promote violence. Obviously, it is completely irrelevant to the proceeding at hand, and I will allow her to defend herself.

The President's lawyers are pointing out that we have never had any situation like this before in the history of the United States, and it is true. There has never been a President who has encouraged a violent insurrection against our own government. So we really have nothing to compare it to. So what we do in this trial will establish a standard going forward for all time.

Now, there are two theories that have been put before you, and I think we have got to get past all of the picayune, little critiques that have been offered today about this or that. Let's focus on what is really at stake here. The President's lawyers say, echoing the President, his conduct was totally appropriate; in other words, he would do it again. Exactly what he did is the new standard for what is allowable for him or any other President who gets into office. Our point is that his incitement so overwhelmed any possible legal standard we have that we have got the opportunity now to declare that Presidential incitement to violent insurrection against the Capitol and the Congress is completely forbidden to the President of the United States under the impeachment clauses.

So we set forth for you the elements of encouragement of violence, and we saw it overwhelmingly. We know that he picked the date of that rally. In fact, there was another group that was going to have a rally at another date, and he got it moved to January 1.* He synchronized exactly with the time that we would be in joint session, and as Representative CHENEY said: he summoned that mob, he assembled that mob, he incited that mob, he lit the match.

Come on, get real. We know that this is what happened. The second thing is the foreseeability of it. Was it foreseeable? Remember Lansing, Michigan, and everything we showed you. They didn't mention that, of course. Remember the MAGA 2 march, the MAGA 2 rally. They didn't mention that. The violence all over the rally, the President cheering it on, delighting in it, reveling in it, exalting in it. Come on. How gullible do you think we are? We saw this happen. We just spent eleven or twelve hours looking at all that.

. . .

Mr. Counsel VAN DER VEEN: Senator CRUZ, I believe the first part of your question refers to the newly-created Raskin doctrine on the First Amendment,

---

*   It appears that Rep. Raskin intended to say "January 6."

and he just—his answer actually gave you a new one: appropriateness. The standard that this body needs to follow for law is *Brandenburg v. Ohio*, and the test really—the three-part test really comes out of *Bible Believers v. Wayne County*, to be specific. The speech has to be explicitly or implicitly encouraged, the use of "violence." In other words, it has to be in the words itself, which is—clearly, it is not in the words itself.

That is step one. They don't get past it. Two, the speaker intends that his speech will result in use of violence or lawless action. There is no evidence of that, and it is ludicrous to believe that that would be true. Third, the imminent use of violence or lawless action is likely to result from speech. Also, they fail on all three points of the law as we know it and needs to be applied here. I don't know why he said he never heard KAMALA HARRIS say about the riots and the people rioting and ruining our businesses and our streets that they are not going to let up and they should not because we played it three times today. We gave it to you in audio, I read it to you, and you got it in video. That is what she said. But it is protected speech. Her speech is protected also, Senator. That is the point.

You all have protections as elected officials, the highest protections under the First Amendment, and that First Amendment applies here in this Chamber to this proceeding. And that is what you need to keep focused on. You need to keep focused on what is the law and how do we apply it to this set of facts. It is your duty. You can't get caught up in all of the rhetoric and the facts that are irrelevant. You need to keep focused on what is the issue before you decided based on the law— *Brandenburg* and *Bible Believers*—and apply it to the facts, and that requires you to look at the words, and there were no words of incitement of any kind.

. . .

[The PRESIDENT pro tempore:] The Senator from Washington, Senator MURRAY, has a question for the House managers:

At 6:01 p.m. eastern time on January 6, President Trump tweeted: "These are the things that happen when a sacred landslide election victory is so unceremoniously & viciously stripped away from great patriots who have been badly and unfairly treated for so long." Adding for rioters to "go home with love and in peace." What is the relevance of this tweet to President Trump's guilt?

. . .

Mr. Manager CASTRO of Texas: Senators, this was a key quote and a key statement by the President that day—that horrific day. Remember, the Capitol had been stormed. It had been attacked. People had yelled, "Hang Mike Pence." People had gone after Speaker PELOSI. People brought baseball bats and other weapons. Many Members of Congress in the Senate and the House were fearful for their own lives. The President didn't call the National Guard. His own administration didn't list him as somebody who they had spoken with to activate the Guard. And he said: remember this day forever.

So if he was not guilty of inciting insurrection, if this is not what he wanted, if it wasn't what he desired, by that time the carnage had been on television for hours. He saw what was going on. Everybody saw what was going on. If it wasn't what he wanted, why would he have said, "Remember this day forever"?

Why commemorate a day like that, an attack on the U.S. Capitol, for God's sake? Why would you do that, unless you agreed that it was something to praise, not condemn; something to hold up and commemorate? No consoling the Nation, no reassuring that the Government was secure, not a single word that entire day condemning the attack or the attackers or the violent insurrection against Congress. This tweet is important because it shows two key points about Donald Trump's state of mind. First, this was entirely and completely foreseeable, and he foresaw it, and he helped incite it over many months. He's saying: I told you this was going to happen if you certified the election for anyone else besides me, and you got what you deserve for trying to take it away from me. And we know this because that statement was entirely consistent with everything he said leading up to the attack.

Second, this shows that Donald Trump intended and reveled in this. Senators, he reveled in this. He delighted in it. This is what he wanted. "Remember this day forever," he said—not as a day of disgrace, as it is to all of us, but as a day of celebration and commemoration, and if we let it, if we don't hold him accountable and set a strong precedent, possibly a continuation later on. We will, of course, all of us, remember this day but not in the same way that Donald Trump suggested. We will remember the bravery of our Capitol and Metro police forces. We will remember the officer who lost his life and sadly the others who did as well, and the devastation that was done to this country because of Donald Trump.

. . .

[The PRESIDENT pro tempore:] The Senator from Louisiana, Mr. CASSIDY, has a question for both counsel for the former President and counsel for the House:

Senator TUBERVILLE reports that he spoke to President Trump at 2:15 p.m. He told the President that the Vice President had just evacuated. I presume it was understood at this time that rioters had entered the Capitol and threatened the safety of Senators and the Vice President. Even after hearing of this, at 2:24 p.m. President Trump tweeted that Mike Pence "lacked courage," and he did not call for law enforcement backup until then. This tweet and lack of response suggests President Trump did not care that Vice President Pence was endangered, or that law enforcement was overwhelmed. Does this show that President Trump was tolerant of the intimidation of Vice President Pence?

. . .

Mr. Counsel VAN DER VEEN: Directly, no. But I dispute the premise of your facts. I dispute the facts that are laid out in that question and, unfortunately, we are not going to know the answer to the facts in this proceeding because the House did nothing to investigate what went on. We are trying to get hearsay from Mr. TUBERVILLE. There was hearsay from Mr. LEE—I think it was two nights ago—and we ended where Mr. LEE was accused of making a statement that he never made.

But it was a report from a reporter from a friend of somebody who had some hearsay that they heard the night before at a bar somewhere. I mean, that is really the kind of evidence that the House has brought before us. And so I have a problem with the facts in the question because I have no idea, and nobody from the House has given us any opportunity to have any idea. But Mr. Trump and Mr. Pence have had a very good relationship for a long time, and I am sure Mr. Trump very much is concerned and was concerned for the safety and well-being of Mr. Pence and everybody else who was over here. Thank you.

. . .

Mr. Manager RASKIN: Counsel said before: this has been my worst experience in Washington. For that, I guess we are sorry, but, man, you should have been here on January 6. The counsel for the President keeps blaming the House for not having the evidence that is within the sole possession of their client, who we invited to come and testify last week. We sent a letter on February 4. I sent it directly to President Trump, inviting him to come and to explain and fill in the gaps of what we know about what happened there. And they sent back a contemptuous response just a few hours later. I think they, maybe, even responded more quickly to my letter than President Trump did as Commander in Chief to the invasion and storming of the Capitol of the United States.

But in that letter I said: you know, if you decline this invitation, we reserve all rights, including the right to establish at trial that your refusal to testify supports a strong adverse inference. What's that? Well, Justice Scalia was the great champion of it. If you don't testify in a criminal case, it can't be used against you. Everybody knows that. That is the Fifth Amendment privilege against self-incrimination. But if it is a civil case and you plead the Fifth or you don't show up, then, according to Justice Scalia and the rest of the Supreme Court, you can interpret every disputed fact against the defendant. That is totally available to us.

So, for example, if we say the President was missing in action for several hours and he was derelict in his duty and he deserted his duty as Commander in Chief, and we say that, as inciter-in-chief, he didn't call this off and they say: Oh, no, he was really doing whatever he can." If you are puzzled about that, you can resolve that dispute—that factual dispute—against the defendant who refuses to come to a civil proceeding. He will not spend one day in jail if you convict him. This is not a criminal proceeding. This is about preserving the Republic, dear Senate. That is what this is about—setting standards of conduct for the President of the United States so this never happens to us again.

So rather than yelling at us and screaming about how "we didn't have time" to get all of the facts about what your client did, bring your client up here and have him testify under oath about why he was sending out tweets denouncing the Vice President of the United States while the Vice President was being hunted down by a mob that wanted to hang him and was chanting in this building: "Hang Mike Pence. Hang Mike Pence." "Traitor. Traitor. Traitor."

. . .

Mr. MANCHIN: Mr. President, I send a question to the desk directed to the House managers.

Would the President be made aware of the FBI and intelligence information of a possible attack and would the President be responsible for not preparing to protect the Capitol and all elected officials of government with National Guard and law enforcement as he did when he appeared in front of the Saint John's Episcopal Church?

. . .

Ms. Manager PLASKETT: It is the responsibility of the President to know. The President of the United States, our Commander in Chief, gets daily briefings on what is happening in the country that he has a duty to protect. Additionally, the President would have known, just like the rest of us know, all of the reports that were out there and publicly available.

How many of you received calls saying to be careful on January 6, to be careful that day? I'm not—I'm seeing reports. It doesn't seem safe. How much more would the President of the United States? Donald Trump, as our Commander in Chief, absolutely had a duty and a sworn oath to preserve, protect, and defend us and to do the same for the officers under his command. And he was not just our Commander in Chief. He incited the attack.

The insurgents were following his commands, as we saw when we read aloud his tweets attacking the Vice President. And with regard to the Vice President, I'm sure they did have a good relationship, but we all know what can happen to one who has a good relationship with the President when you decide to do something that he doesn't like. I am sure some of you have experienced that when he turns against you after you don't follow his command. You heard from my colleagues that, when planning this attack, the insurgents predicted that Donald Trump would command the National Guard to help them.

Well, he didn't do much better. He may not have commanded the Guard to help them, but it took way, way too long for him to command the Guard to help us. This is all connected. We're talking about free speech? This was a pattern and practice of months of activity. That was the incitement. That is the incitement—the activity he was engaged in for months before January 6, not just the speech on January 6. All of it, in its totality, is a dereliction of duty of the President of the United States against the people who elected him—all of the people of this country.

. . .

Mr. SULLIVAN: Mr. President, I send a question to the desk for the former President's counsel.

The House manager said yesterday that due process is discretionary, meaning the House is not required to provide and, indeed, did not provide in this snap impeachment any constitutional protection to a defendant in the House impeachment proceedings. What are the implications for our constitutional order of this new House precedent combined with the Senate's power to disqualify from public office a private citizen in an impeachment trial?

. . .

Mr. Counsel VAN DER VEEN: Mr. President, that is a complicated question. Could I have that read again?

. . .

[The question was read again.]

. . .

Mr. Counsel VAN DER VEEN: Mr. President, well, first of all, due process is never discretionary. Good Lord, the Constitution requires that the accused have the right to due process because the power that a prosecutor has to take somebody's liberty when they are prosecuting them is the ultimate thing that we try to save. In this case, just now, in the last two hours, we have had prosecutorial misconduct. What they just tried to do was say that it is our burden to bring them evidence to prove their case, and it is not. It is not our burden to bring any evidence forward at all.

What is the danger? Well, the danger is pretty obvious. If the majority party doesn't like somebody in the minority party and they are afraid they may lose the election or if it is somebody in the majority party and there is a private citizen who wants to run against somebody in the majority party, well, they can simply bring impeachment proceedings. And, of course, without due process, they are not going to be entitled to a lawyer. They are not going to be entitled to have notice of the charges against them.

It puts us into a position where we are the kind of judicial system and governing body that we are all very, very afraid of. From what we left hundreds of years ago, and when regimes all around this world that endanger us—that is how they act; that is how they conduct themselves: without giving the accused due process, taking their liberty, without giving them just a basic fundamental right, under the 5th to the 14th applied to the States, due process. If you take away due process in this country from the accused, if you take that away, there will be no justice and nobody, nobody will be safe.

But it is patently unfair for the House managers to bring an impeachment proceeding without any—again, without any investigation at all and then stand up here and say: one, they had a chance to bring us evidence; and, two, let's, let's, let's see what we can do about flipping around somebody's other constitutional rights to having a lawyer or to having a—to see the evidence at all. It just gets brought in without anybody, as it was here, without anybody having an opportunity to review it beforehand. They actually sent it to us on the 9th, the day after we started this. So it is a really big problem. The due process clause applies to this impeachment hearing, and it has been severely and extremely violated. This process is so unconstitutional because it violates due process. I am not even going to get into the jurisdiction part. The due process part should be enough to give anybody who loves our Constitution and loves our country great pause to do anything but acquit Donald Trump. Thank you.

. . .

Mr. BLUMENTHAL: Mr. President, I send a question to the desk for the House managers.

Former President Trump and his attorneys have cited the *Brandenburg v. Ohio* case in support of their argument that the First Amendment protects Trump. Did the *Brandenburg* case prohibit holding public officials accountable, through the impeachment process, for the incitement of violence?

. . .

Mr. Manager RASKIN: Thank you, Mr. President, Senators. So let's start with the letter of more than 140 constitutional law professors, which I think they described as partisan in nature. That is a slur on the law professors, and I hope that they would withdraw that. There are very conservative luminaries on that list, including the cofounder of the Federalist Society, Ronald Reagan's former Solicitor General, Charles Fried; as well as prominent law professors across the intellectual, ideological, and First Amendment spectrum. And they all called their First Amendment arguments frivolous, which they are. Now, they have retreated to the position of *Brandenburg v. Ohio*. They want their client to be treated like a guy at the mob, I think they said, a guy in the crowd who yells something out.

Even on that standard, this group of law professors said there is a very strong argument that he is guilty even under the strict *Brandenburg* standard. Why?

Because he incited imminent, lawless action and he intended to do it and he was likely to cause it. How did we know he was likely to cause it? He did cause it. They overran the Capitol, right? So even if you want to hold the President of the United States of America to that minimal standard and forget about his constitutional oath of office, as I said before, that would be a dereliction of legislative duty on our part if we said all we are going to do is treat the President of the United States like one of the people he summoned to Washington to commit an insurrection against us. Okay.

The President swore to preserve, protect, and defend the Constitution of the United States. That is against all comers, domestic or foreign. That is what ours says, right? Did he do that? No. On the contrary. He is like the fire chief. He doesn't just say 'go ahead and shout "fire" inside a theater. He summons the mob and sends the mob to go burn the theater down, and when people start madly calling him and ringing alarm bells, he watches it on TV. And he takes his sweet time for several hours and turns up the heat on the deputy fire chief, whom he is mad at because he is not making it possible for him to pursue his political objectives. And then, when we say, "We don't want you to be fire chief ever again," he starts crying about the First Amendment.

Brandenburg was a case about a bunch of Klansmen who assembled in a field, and they weren't near anybody such that they could actually do violent damage to people, but they said some pretty repulsive, racist things. But the Supreme Court said they weren't inciting imminent lawless action because you couldn't have a mob, for example, break out, the way that this mob broke out and took over the Capitol of the United States of America. And, by the way, don't compare him to one of those Klansmen in the field asserting their First Amendment rights. Assume that he were the chief of police of the town who went down to that rally and started calling for, you know, a rally at the city hall and then nurturing that mob, cultivating that mob, pulling them in over a period of weeks and days, naming the date and the time and the place, riling them up beforehand, and then just say: "Be my guest. Go and stop the steal." Come on. Back to Tom Paine. Use your common sense. Use your common sense. That is the standard of proof we want.

They are already treating their client like he is a criminal defendant. They are talking about beyond a reasonable doubt. They think that we are making a criminal case here. My friends, the former President is not going to spend one hour or one minute in jail. This is about protecting our Republic and articulating and defining the standards of Presidential conduct, and if you want this to be a standard for totally appropriate Presidential conduct going forward, be my guest, but we are headed for a very different kind of country at that point.

. . .

The PRESIDENT pro tempore: The Senator from Kansas, Mr. MARSHALL, has a question for the counsel for the former President.

The House Managers' single Article of Impeachment is centered on the accusation that President Trump singularly incited a crowd into a riot. Didn't the House managers contradict their own charge by outlining the premeditated nature and planning of this event and by also showing the crowd was gathered at the Capitol even before the speech started and barriers were pushed over some twenty minutes before the conclusion of President Trump's speech?

. . .

Mr. Counsel VAN DER VEEN: Yes. The House managers contradicted their own charge by outlining the premeditated nature and planning of this event and by also showing the crowd gathered at the Capitol, even before the speech started, and barriers were pushed over some twenty minutes before the conclusion of President Trump's speech. The answer is yes. And I want to take the rest of my time to go back to the last question because it was completely missed by the House managers. *Brandenburg v. Ohio* is an incitement case. It is not an elected official case. That is *Wood* and *Bond*. And the whole problem that the House managers have in understanding the First Amendment argument here is that elected officials are different than anybody else. He is talking about fire chiefs. Fire chiefs are not elected officials. Police officers aren't elected officials.

Elected officials have a different, a higher standard on the holdings that I gave you—the highest protections, I should say. It is not a higher standard. It is a higher protection to your speech because of the importance of political dialogue. Because of what you all say in your public debate about policy, about the things that affect all of our lives, that is really important stuff, and you should be free to talk about that in just about any way that you can.

Brandenburg comes into play, from a constitutional analysis perspective, when you are talking about incitement. Is the speech itself inciteful to riot or lawlessness—one of the two—and the answer here is no. In *Brandenburg*, through—again, *Bible Believers* require you to look at the words of the speech. You actually can't go outside the words of the speech. You are not allowed to in the analysis. So all the time they are trying to spend on tweets going back to 2015 or everything they want to focus on that was said in the hours and the days afterward are not applicable or relevant to the scholastic inquiry as to how the First Amendment is applied in this Chamber in this proceeding.

So, again, we need to be focused on what is the law and then how do we apply it to this set of facts. So it is important to have that understanding that elected officials and fire chiefs are treated differently under First Amendment law, and that is to the benefit of you all, which is to the benefit of us all because we do want you to be able to speak freely without fear that the majority party is going to come in and impeach you or come in and prosecute you to try to take away your seat where you sit now. That is not what the Constitution says should be done. But, yes, they do. They do contradict themselves, of course. Thank you.

. . .

Mr. VAN HOLLEN: Mr. President, I send a question to the desk for the House managers.

Would you please respond to the answer that was just given by the former President's counsel?

. . .

Mr. Manager RASKIN: Mr. President, thank you. I am not sure which question the Senator was referring to, but let me quickly just dispense with the counsel's invocation again of *Bond v. Floyd*. This is a case I know well, and I thank him [for] raising it. Julian Bond was a friend of mine. He was a colleague of mine at American University. He was a great civil rights hero. In his case, he got elected to the Georgia State Legislature and was a member of SNCC, the Student Non-violent Coordinating Committee, the great committee headed up by the great Bob Moses for a long time. He got elected to the Georgia Legislature, and they didn't want to allow him to be sworn in. They wouldn't allow him to take his oath of office because SNCC had taken a position against the Vietnam war. So the Supreme Court said that was a violation of his First Amendment rights not to allow him to be sworn in.

That is the complete opposite of Donald Trump. Not only was he sworn in on January 20, 2017, he was President for almost four years before he incited this violent insurrection against us, and he violated his oath of office. That is what this impeachment trial is about—his violation of his oath of office and his refusal to uphold the law and take care that the laws are faithfully executed. Please don't desecrate the name of Julian Bond, a great American, by linking him with this terrible plot against America that just took place in the storming of the U.S. Capitol. I am going to turn it over to my colleague Ms. PLASKETT.

. . .

Ms. Manager PLASKETT: Thank you. Let's just be clear. President Trump summoned the mob, assembled the mob, lit the flame. Everything that followed was his doing. Although he could have immediately and forcefully intervened to stop the violence, he didn't. In other words, this attack would not have happened without him. This attack is not about one speech. Most of you men would not have your wives with one attempt of talking to her. (Laughter.) It took numerous tries. You had to build it up. That is what the President did as well. He put together the group that would do what he wanted, and that was to stop the certification of the election so that he could retain power to be President of the United States, in contravention of an American election.

. . .

Mr. RUBIO: Mr. President, I send a question to the desk.

Voting to convict the former President would create a new precedent that a former official can be convicted and disqualified by the Senate. Therefore, is it not true that under this new precedent, a future House, facing partisan pressure to "Lock her up," could impeach a former Secretary of State and a future Senate be forced to put her on trial and potentially disqualify from any future office?

. . .

Mr. Manager RASKIN: Mr. President, Senators, three quick points here. First of all, I don't know how many times I can say it. The jurisdictional issue is over. It is gone. The Senate settled it. The Senate entertained jurisdiction exactly the way it has done since the very beginning of the Republic in the *Blount* case, in the *Belknap* case, and you will remember, both of them, former officials. In this case, we have a President who committed his crimes against the Republic while he was in office. He was impeached by the House of Representatives while he was in office. So the hypothetical suggested by the gentleman from Florida has no bearing on this case because I don't think you are talking about an official who was impeached while they were in office for conduct that they committed while they were in office.

. . .

Mr. Counsel VAN DER VEEN: Thank you. Could I have the question read again to make sure I have it right and can answer it directly?

. . .

[The question was read again.]

. . .

Mr. Counsel VAN DER VEEN:. If you see it their way, yes. If you do this the way they want it done, that could happen to, the example there, a former Secretary of State. But it could happen to a lot of people, and that is not the way this is supposed to work. Not only could it happen to a lot of people, it would become much more regular too. But I want to address that, and I want you to be clear on this. Mr. RASKIN can't tell you on what grounds you acquit. If you believe—even though there was a vote that there is jurisdiction, if you believe jurisdiction is unconstitutional, you can still believe that. If you believe that the House did not give appropriate due process in this, that can be your reason to acquit. If you don't think they met their burden in proving incitement, that these words incited the violence, you can acquit.

Mr. RASKIN doesn't get to give you under what grounds you can acquit. So you have to look at what they have put on in its totality and come to your own understanding as to whether you think they have met their burden to impeach. But the original question is an absolutely slippery slope that I don't really think anybody here wants to send this country down. Thank you.

. . .

Mr. BENNET: Mr. President, I send a question to the desk.

The Senator from Colorado, Senator BENNET, has a question for the House managers: Since the November election, the Georgia Secretary of State, the Vice President, and other public officials withstood enormous pressure to uphold the lawful election of President Biden and the rule of law. What would have happened if these officials had bowed to the force President Trump exerted or the mob that attacked the Capitol?

. . .

Mr. Manager CASTRO of Texas: I want to take a minute and remind everybody about the incredible pressure that Donald Trump was putting on election officials in different States in this country and the intimidation that he was issuing, and I want to remind everyone of the background of Donald Trump's call to one Secretary of State, the Secretary of State from Georgia, Mr. Raffensperger.

Donald Trump tried to overturn the election by any means necessary. He tried again and again to pressure and threaten election officials to overturn the election results. He pressured Michigan officials, calling them late at night and hosting them at the White House. He did the same thing with officials in Pennsylvania. He called into a local meeting of the Pennsylvania Legislature, and he also hosted them at the White House, where he pressured them. In Georgia, it was even worse. He sent tweet after tweet attacking the Secretary of State until Mr. Raffensperger got death threats to him and his family.

His wife got a text that said: "Your husband deserves facing a firing squad." A firing squad for doing his job. Mr. Raffensperger stood up to him. He told the world that elections are the bedrock of this society and the votes were accurately counted for Donald Trump's opponent.

Officials like Mr. Sterling warned Trump that if this continued, someone is going to get killed, but Donald Trump didn't stop. He escalated it even further. He made a personal call. He made a personal call. You heard that call because it was recorded. The President of the United States told the Secretary of State that if he does not find votes, he will face criminal penalties.

Please, Senators, consider that for a second, the President putting all of this public and private pressure on elected officials, telling them that they could face criminal penalties if they don't do what he wants. And not just any number of votes that he was looking for—Donald Trump was asking the Secretary of State to somehow find the exact number of votes Donald Trump lost the State by. Remember, President Biden won Georgia by 11,779 votes. In his own words, President

Trump said: "All I want to do is this. I just want to find 11,780 votes." He wanted the Secretary of State to somehow find the precise number, plus one, of votes that he needed to win.

As a Congress and as a nation, we cannot be numb to this conduct. If we are and if we don't set a precedent against it, more Presidents will do this in the future. This will be a green light for them to engage in that kind of pressure and that kind of conduct. This could have gone a very different way if those elected officials had bowed to the intimidation and the pressure of the President of the United States. It would have meant that, instead of the American people deciding this election, President Trump alone would have decided this American election. That is exactly what was at stake, and that is exactly what he was trying to do.

He intended, wanted to, and tried to overturn the election by any means necessary. He tried everything else that he could do to win. He started inciting the crowd; issuing tweet after tweet; issuing commands to stop the count, stop the steal. He worked up the crowd, sent a "save the date." So it wasn't just one speech or one thing; he was trying everything. He was pressuring elected officials. He was riling up his base, telling them the election had been stolen from them, that it had been stolen from him. It was a combination of things that only Donald Trump could have done. For us to believe otherwise is to think that somehow a rabbit came out of a hat and this mob just showed up here on their own, all by themselves. This is dangerous, Senators, and the future of our democracy truly rests in your hands.

. . .

The PRESIDENT pro tempore: The Senator from Texas, Mr. CORNYN, has a question for both counsel for the former President and the House managers.

The House managers have argued that if the Senate cannot convict former officers, then the Constitution creates a January exception pursuant to which a President is free to act with impunity because he is not subject to impeachment, conviction, and removal and/or disqualification. But isn't a President subject to criminal prosecution after he leaves office for acts committed in office, even if those acts are committed in January?

. . .

Mr. Counsel CASTOR: The Senator from Texas's question raises a very, very important point. There is no such thing as a January exception to impeachment. There is only the text of the Constitution, which makes very clear that a former President is subject to criminal sanction after his Presidency for any illegal acts he commits. There is no January exception to impeachment. There is simply a way we treat high crimes and misdemeanors allegedly committed by a President when he is in office—impeachment—and how we treat criminal behavior by a private citizen when they are not in office.

. . .

Mr. Manager RASKIN: Wouldn't a President who decides to commit his crimes in the last few weeks in office, like President Trump by inciting the insurrection against the counting of electoral college votes, be subject to criminal prosecution by the U.S. attorney for the District of Columbia, for example, the Department of Justice?

Well, of course he would be, but that is true of the President regardless of when he commits his offense in office. In other words, that is an argument for prosecuting him if he tried to stage an insurrection against the Union in his third year in office or his second year in office. You could say, well, he could be prosecuted afterwards.

The reason that the Framers gave Congress—the House the power to impeach; the Senate the power to try, convict, remove, and disqualify—was to protect the Republic. It is not a vindictive power. I know a lot of people are very angry with Donald Trump about these terrible events that took place. We don't come here in anger, contrary to what you heard today. We come here in the spirit of protecting our Republic, and that is what it is all about. But their January exception would essentially invite Presidents and other civil officers to run rampant in the last few weeks in office on the theory that the House and the Senate wouldn't be able to get it together in time—certainly according to their demands for months and months of investigation—wouldn't be able to get it together in time in order to vindicate the Constitution. That can't be right. That can't be right. We know that the peaceful transfer of power is always the most dangerous moment for democracies around the world. Talk to the diplomats. Talk to the historians. They will tell you that is a moment of danger. That is when you get the coups. That is when you get the insurrections. That is when you get the seditious plots. And you know what, you don't even have to read history for that. You don't even have to consult the Framers. You don't have to look around the world. It just happened to us.

The moment when we were just going to collect the already-certified electoral college votes from the States by the popular majorities within each State—except for Maine and Nebraska, which do it by congressional district as well as statewide, but otherwise, it is just the popular majorities in the States. And we were about to certify it, and we got hit by a violent, insurrectionary mob. Don't take our word for it. Listen to the tapes, unless they are going to claim those are fabricated too. And the people are yelling: "This is our house now" and "Where are the 'blank' votes at?" and "Show us the votes," et cetera.

. . .

Mr. SCHUMER: I ask unanimous consent that the time for questions and answers be considered expired.

DAY 5

THE **PRESIDENT** PRO TEMPORE: THE SENATE WILL BEGIN AS A COURT OF
Impeachment.

Motion to Subpoena Witnesses

Mr. Manager RASKIN: Thank you, Mr. President. Good morning, Senators. Over the last several days, we have presented overwhelming evidence that establishes the charges in the Article of Impeachments. We have shown you how President Trump created a powder keg, lit a match, and then continued his incitement, even as he failed to defend us from the ensuing violence. We have supported our position with images, videos, affidavits, documents, tweets, and other evidence, leaving no doubt that the Senate should convict. We believe we have proven our case.

But last night, Congresswoman Jaime Herrera Beutler of Washington State issued a statement confirming that in the middle of the insurrection, when House Minority Leader Kevin McCarthy called the President to beg for help, President Trump responded: "Well, Kevin, I guess these people are more upset about the election than you are."

Needless to say, this is an additional critical piece of corroborating evidence, further confirming the charges before you, as well as the President's willful dereliction of duty and desertion of duty as Commander in Chief of the United States, his state of mind, and his further incitement of the insurrection on January 6.

For that reason, and because this is the proper time to do so under the resolution that the Senate adopted to set the rules for the trial, we would like the opportunity to subpoena Congresswoman Herrera regarding her communications with House Minority Leader Kevin McCarthy and to subpoena her contemporaneous notes that she made regarding what President Trump told Kevin McCarthy in the middle of the insurrection.

We would be prepared to proceed by Zoom deposition of an hour or less just as soon as Congresswoman Herrera Beutler is available and to then proceed to the next phase of the trial, including the introduction of that testimony shortly thereafter.

Congresswoman Beutler further stated that she hopes other witnesses to this part of the story—other patriots, as she put it—would come forward. And if that happens, we would seek the opportunity to take their depositions via Zoom, also for less than an hour, or to subpoena other relevant documents as well.

. . .

Mr. Counsel VAN DER VEEN: The first thing I want to say on the issue of witnesses is that the House manager just got up here and described the Articles of Impeachment and the charges. There is no plural here. That is wrong. There is one Article of Impeachment, and there is one charge, and that is incitement of violence and insurrection. What you all need to know and the American people need to know is, as of late yesterday afternoon, there was a stipulation going around that there weren't going to be any witnesses. But after what happened here in this Chamber yesterday, the House managers realized they did not investigate this case before bringing the impeachment. They did not give the proper consideration and work.

They didn't put the work in that was necessary to impeach the former President. But if they want to have witnesses, I am going to need at least over one hundred depositions, not just one. The real issue is incitement. They put into their case over one hundred witnesses, people who have been charged with crimes by the Federal Government, and each one of those, they said that Mr. Trump was a coconspirator with. That is not true, but I have the right to defend that.

The only thing that I ask, if you vote for witnesses, do not handcuff me by limiting the number of witnesses that I can have. I need to do a thorough investigation that they did not do. I need to do the 9/11-style investigation that Nancy Pelosi called for. It should have been done already. It is a dereliction of the House managers' duty that they didn't. And now, at the last minute, after a stipulation had apparently been worked out, they want to go back on that. I think that is inappropriate and improper. We should close this case out today. We have each prepared our closing arguments.

We each—I mean, I had eight days to get ready for this thing, but we each had those eight days equally, together, to prepare ourselves. And the House managers need to live with the case that they brought. But if they don't, please, in all fairness and in all due process, do not limit my ability to discover, discover, discover the truth. That would be another sham. And that is the President's position, my position.

. . .

Mr. Manager RASKIN: Mr. President.

. . .

The PRESIDENT pro tempore: Mr. Raskin.

. . .

Mr. Manager RASKIN: Thank you, Mr. President. First of all, this is the proper time that we were assigned to talk about witnesses. This is completely within the course of the rules set forth by the Senate. There is nothing remotely unusual about this. I think we have done an exceedingly thorough and comprehensive job with all the evidence that was available. Last night, this was breaking news, and it responded directly to a question that was being raised by the President's defense counsel, saying that we had not sufficiently proven to their satisfaction—although I think we have proven to the satisfaction of the American people, certainly—that the President, after the breach and invasion took place, was not working on the side of defending the Capitol but, rather, was continuing to pursue his political goals.

And the information that came out last night by Congresswoman Beutler, apparently backed up by contemporaneous notes that she had taken, I think, will put to rest any lingering doubts raised by the President's counsel, who now says he wants to interview hundreds of people. There is only one person the President's counsel really needs to interview, and that is their own client, and bring him forward, as we suggested last week, because a lot of this is matters that are in his head. Why did he not act to defend the country after he learned of the attack? Why was he continuing to press the political case? But this piece of evidence is relevant to that.

Finally, I wasn't—I was a little bit mystified by the point about the Article of Impeachment, which I referred to. The dereliction of duty, the desertion of duty, is built into the incitement charge, obviously. If the President of the United States is out inciting a violent insurrection, he is, obviously, not doing his job at the same time. Just like, if a police officer is mugging you, yeah, he is guilty of theft and armed robbery, whatever it might be, but he is also not doing his job as a police officer. So it is further evidence of his intent and what his conduct is.

. . .

Mr. Counsel VAN DER VEEN: First of all, it is my understanding it has been reported that Mr. McCarthy disclaims the rumors that have been the basis of this morning's antics but, really, the rumors that have been the basis of this entire proceeding. This entire proceeding is based on rumor, report, innuendo. There is nothing to it, and they didn't do their work. Just like what happened with Mr. Lee two or three nights ago, some supposed conversation that happened, and they had to withdraw that. They had to back off of that because it was false. It was a false narrative. But it is one Article of Impeachment. Yeah, they threw a lot of stuff in it in violation of rule XXIII. Rule XXIII says you cannot combine counts. It is a defect in their entire case. It is one of the four reasons why you can vote to acquit in this case: jurisdiction, rule XXIII, due process, and the First Amendment. They all apply in this case.

Let me take my own advice and cool the temperature in the room a little bit. It is about the incitement. It is not about what happened afterwards. That is actually the irrelevant stuff. That is the irrelevant stuff. It is not the things that were said from the election to January 6. It is not relevant to the legal analysis of the issues that are before this body. It doesn't matter what happened after the insurgence into the Capitol Building because that doesn't have to do with incitement. Incitement is—it is a point in time, folks. It is a point in time when the words are spoken, and the words say, implicitly say, explicitly say "commit acts of violence or lawlessness." And we don't have that here.

So for the House managers to say we need depositions about things that happened after, it is just not true. But—but if he does, there are a lot of depositions that need to be happening. Nancy Pelosi's deposition needs to be taken. Vice President Harris's deposition absolutely needs to be taken, and not by Zoom. None of these depositions should be done by Zoom. We didn't do this hearing by Zoom. These depositions should be done in person, in my office, in Philadelphia. That is where they should be done. (Laughter.)

I don't know how many civil lawyers are here, but that is the way it works, folks. When you want somebody's deposition, you send a notice of deposition, and they appear at the place where the notice says. That is civil process. I don't know why you are laughing. It is civil process. That is the way lawyers do it. We send notices of deposition.

I haven't laughed at any of you, and there is nothing laughable here. He mentioned my client coming in to testify. That is not the way it is done. If he wanted to talk to Donald Trump, he should have put a subpoena down, like I am going to slap subpoenas on a good number of people if witnesses are what is required here for them to try to get their case back in order, which has failed miserably for four reasons: there is no jurisdiction here. There has been no due process here. They have completely violated and ignored and stepped on the Constitution of the United States. They have trampled on it like people who have no respect for it. And if this is about nothing else, it has to be about the respect of our country, our Constitution, and all of the people that make it up.

So that I ask, when considering or voting on this witness matter—and, to be clear, this may be the time to do it, but, again, everybody needs to know—all of the backroom politics, I am not so much into it all, and I am not too adept at it either. But there was a stipulation. They felt pretty comfortable after day two, until their case was tested on day three. Now is the time to end this. Now is the time to hear the closing arguments. Now is the time to vote your conscience. Thank you.

. . .

Mr. Manager RASKIN: We were involved in no discussions about a stipulation, and I have no further comment. Thank you, Mr. President.

. . .

Mr. Counsel VAN DER VEEN: I am going to require a deposition on that.

Vote on Motion

So the question is, shall it be in order to consider and debate, under the Rules of Impeachment, any motion to subpoena witnesses or documents?

. . .

[Vote and discussion omitted, because the question was resolved by stipulation.]

Stipulation

Mr. Counsel CASTOR: Senators, Donald John Trump, by his counsel, is prepared to stipulate that if Representative Herrera Beutler were to testify under oath as part of these proceedings, her testimony would be consistent with the statement she issued on February 12, 2021, and the former President's counsel is agreeable to the admission of that public statement into evidence at this time.

. . .

The PRESIDENT pro tempore: Thank you, Mr. Castor. Mr. Raskin.

. . .

Mr. Manager RASKIN: Thank you, Mr. President. The managers are prepared to enter into the agreement. I will now read the statement. This is the statement of Congresswoman Jaime Herrera Beutler, February 12, 2021: "In my January 12 statement in support of the article of impeachment, I referenced a conversation House Minority Leader Kevin McCarthy relayed to me that he had with President Trump while the January 6 attack was ongoing.

"Here are the details: When McCarthy finally reached the president on January 6 and asked him to publicly and forcefully call off the riot, the president initially repeated the falsehood that it was antifa that had breached the Capitol. McCarthy refuted that and told the president that these were Trump supporters. That's when, according to McCarthy, the president said: 'Well, Kevin, I guess these people are more upset about the election than you are.'

"Since I publicly announced my decision to vote for impeachment, I have shared these details in countless conversations with constituents and colleagues, and multiple times through the media and other public forums. I told it to the *Daily News* of Longview on January 17. I've shared it with local county Republican executive board members, as well as other constituents who asked me to explain my vote. I shared it with thousands of residents on my telephone town hall on February 8."

Mr. President, I now move that the Senate admit the statement into evidence.

. . .

The PRESIDENT pro tempore: Is there objection? Without objection, the statement will be admitted into evidence. And does either party wish to make any further motions related to witnesses or documents at this time?

. . .

Mr. Counsel CASTOR: Mr. President, the President's counsel have no further motions.

. . .

Mr. Manager RASKIN: And, Mr. President, we have no further motions either.

Admission of Evidence

[The evidence was admitted without objection.]

Closing Arguments

Pursuant to the provisions of S. Res. 47, the Senate has provided for up to four hours in closing arguments. They will be equally divided between the managers on the part of the House of Representatives and the counsel for the former President. And pursuant to rule XXII of the Rules of Procedure and Practice in the Senate When Sitting on Impeachment Trials, the argument shall be opened and closed on the part of the House of Representatives. The Chair recognizes Mr. Manager Raskin to begin the presentation on the part of the House of Representatives. Mr. Raskin, under rule XXII, you may reserve time if you wish.

. . .

Mr. Manager RASKIN: Thank you, Mr. President. Members of the Senate, before I proceed, it was suggested by defense counsel that Donald Trump's conduct during the attack, as described in Congresswoman Beutler's statement, is somehow not part of the constitutional offense for which former President Trump has been charged. I want to reject that falsehood and that fallacy immediately.

After he knew that violence was underway at the Capitol, President Trump took actions that further incited the insurgence to be more inflamed and to take even more extreme, selective, and focused action against Vice President Mike Pence. Former President Trump also, as described by Congresswoman Beutler's notes, refused requests to publicly, immediately, and forcefully call off the riots.

And when he was told that the insurgents inside the Capitol were Trump supporters, the President said: "Well, Kevin, I guess these people are more upset about the election than you are." Think about that for a second. This uncontradicted statement that has just been stipulated as part of the evidentiary record, the President said: Well, Kevin, I guess these people—meaning the mobsters, the insurrectionists—are more upset about the election than you are.

That conduct is obviously part and parcel of the constitutional offense that he was impeached for: namely, incitement to insurrection; that is, continuing incitement to the insurrection. The conduct described not only perpetuated his continuing offense but also provides to us here, today, further decisive evidence of his intent to incite the insurrection in the first place. When my opposing counsel says that you should ignore the President's actions after the insurrection began, that is plainly wrong, and it, of course, reflects the fact that they have no defense to his outrageous, scandalous, and unconstitutional conduct in the middle of a violent assault on the Capitol that he incited. Senators, think about it for a second.

Say you light a fire, and you are charged with arson. And the defense counsel says: everything I did after the fire started is irrelevant. And the court would reject that immediately and say: that is not true at all. It is extremely relevant to whether or not you committed the crime. If you run over and try to put out the flames, if you get lots of water and say, "Help, help, there is a fire," and you call for help, a court will infer that—could infer that you didn't intend for the fire to be lit in the first place. They would accept your defense, perhaps, that it was all an accident. It was all an accident. Accidents happen with fire.

But if, on the other hand, when the fire erupts, you go and you pour more fuel on it, you stand by and you watch it, gleefully, any reasonable person will infer that you not only intended the fire to start but that once it got started and began to spread, you intended to continue to keep the fire going. And that is exactly where we are, my friends. Of course, your conduct, while a crime is ongoing, is relevant to your culpability, both to the continuation of the offense but also directly relevant, directly illuminating to what your purpose was originally; what was your intent? And any court in the land would laugh out any—would laugh out of court any criminal defendant who said: "What I did after I allegedly killed that person is irrelevant to whether or not I intended to kill them." I mean, come on.

Donald Trump's refusal not only to send help but also to continue to further incite the insurgence against his own Vice President—his own Vice President—provides further decisive evidence of both his intent to start this violent insurrection and his continued incitement once the attack had begun to override the Capitol. All right. Senators, that was in response to this new evidentiary particle that came in.

But in my closing, I want to thank you for your remarkable attention and your seriousness of purpose befitting your office. We have offered you overwhelming and irrefutable and certainly unrefuted evidence that former President Trump incited this insurrection against us. To quote the statement Representative Liz Cheney made in January: on January 6, 2021, a violent mob attacked the United States Capitol to obstruct the process of our democracy and stop the counting of presidential electoral votes.

This insurrection caused injury, death and destruction in the most sacred space in our Republic. She continued—Representative Cheney continued: much more will become clear in coming days and weeks, but what we know now is enough. The President of the United States summoned this mob, assembled the mob, and lit the flame of this attack. Everything that followed was his doing. None of this would have happened without the President. The President could have immediately and forcefully intervened to stop the violence. He did not. There has never been a greater betrayal by the President of the United States of his office and his oath to the Constitution. I will vote to impeach the President.

Representative Cheney was right. She based her vote on the facts, on the evidence, and on the Constitution. And the evidence—video, documentary, eyewitness—has only grown stronger and stronger and more detailed right up to today, right up to ten minutes ago, over the course of this Senate trial. And I have no doubt that you all noticed that, despite the various propaganda reels and so on, President Trump's lawyers have said almost nothing to contest or overcome the actual evidence of former President Trump's conduct that we presented, much less have they brought their client forward to tell us his side of the story. We sent him a letter last week, which they rejected out of hand. The former President of the United States refused to come and tell us.

And I ask any of you: if you were charged with inciting violent insurrection against our country and you were falsely accused, would you come and testify? I know I would. I would be there at seven in the morning waiting for the doors to open. I am sure that is true of one hundred Senators in this room. I hope it is true of hundred Senators in this room. The Senate was lectured several times yesterday about cancel culture.

Well, not even two weeks ago the President's most reliable supporters in the House—I am sorry; not the President. The former President's most reliable supporters in the House tried to cancel out Representative Cheney because of her courageous and patriotic defense of the Republic and the truth and the Constitution. They tried to strip her of her leading role as chair of the House Republican Confer-

ence. But, you know what—I hope everybody takes a second to reflect on this—
the conference rejected this plainly retaliatory and cowardly attempt to punish her
for telling the truth to her constituents and her country in voting for impeachment.

Who says you can't stand up against bullies? Who says? In my mind, Liz Cheney
is a hero for standing up for the truth and resisting this retaliatory cancel culture
that she was subjected to. But she beat them on a vote of 145 to 61, more than a two-
to-one vote. You know, Ben Franklin, a great champion of the Enlightenment, an
enemy of political fanaticism and cowardice, and, of course, another great Philadelphian, once wrote this: I have observed that wrong is always growing more
wrong until there is no bearing it anymore and that right, however opposed, comes
right at last. Comes right at last. Think about that. This is America, home of the
brave, land of the free—the America of Ben Franklin, who said: If you make yourself a sheep, the wolves will eat you.

Don't make yourself a sheep. The wolves will eat you. The America of Thomas
Jefferson, who said at another difficult moment: A little patience, and we shall see
the reign of witches pass over, their spirits dissolve, and the people, recovering
their true sight, restore their government to its true principles. The America of
Tom Paine, who said: the mind once enlightened cannot again become dark.

Now, we showed you hour after hour of real time evidence demonstrating every
step of Donald Trump's constitutional crime. We showed you how he indoctri-
nated the mob with his Orwellian propaganda about how the election he lost by
more than 7 million votes and 306 to 232 in the electoral college—which he had
described as a landslide when he won by the exact same margin in 2016—was
actually a landslide victory for him being stolen away by a bipartisan conspiracy
and fraud and corruption. We showed you how sixty-one courts and eighty-eight
judges—Federal, State, local, trial, appellate—from the lowest courts in the land
to the United States Supreme Court across the street and 8 Federal judges he himself named to the bench, all found no basis in fact or law for his outlandish and
deranged inventions and concoctions about the election.

In the meantime, President Trump tried to bully State-level officials to commit
a fraud on the public by literally "finding" votes. We examined the case study of
Georgia, where he called to threaten Republican Brad Raffensperger to find him
11,780 votes. That is all he wanted, he said, 11,780 votes—don't we all—11,780
votes, that is all he wanted to nullify Biden's victory and to win the election.
Raffensperger ended up with savage death threats against him and his family, telling him he deserved a firing squad.

Another election official urged Trump to cut it out or people would get hurt and
killed, a prescient warning indeed. Raffensperger ended up saying that he and
his family supported Donald Trump, gave him money, and now Trump "threw us

under the bus." We saw what happened in Lansing, Michigan, with the extremist mob he cultivated, which led to two shocking Capitol sieges and a criminal conspiracy by extremists to kidnap and likely assassinate Governor Whitmer. We saw him trying to get State legislatures to disavow and overthrow their popular election results and replace them with Trump electors. We showed you the process of summoning the mob, reaching out, urging people to come to Washington for a "wild" time.

As we celebrate Presidents Day on Monday, think, imagine: is there another President in our history who would urge supporters to come to Washington for a "wild" time? You saw how he embraced the violent extremist elements like the Proud Boys, who were told in a nationally televised Presidential candidate debate to "stand back and stand by," which became their official slogan as they converged on Washington with other extremist and seditious groups and competed to be the lead storm troopers of the attack on this building. You saw the assembly of the mob on January 6.

And how beautiful that angry mob must have looked to Donald Trump as he peered down from the lectern with the seal of the President of the United States of America emblazoned on it. That crowd was filled with extremists in tactical gear, armed to the teeth and ready to fight, and other brawling MAGA supporters, all of them saying: Stop the steal right now. And he said he was going to march with them to the Capitol, even though the permit for the rally specifically forbade a march. But he said he would march with them, giving them more comfort that what they were doing was legitimate, it was okay.

But, of course, he stayed back, as he presumably didn't want to be too close to the action at the Capitol, as the lawyers called it—not an insurrection, they urged us yesterday; it is an action. He didn't want to be too close to the action when all hell was about to break loose. Now, incitement, as we have discussed, requires an inherently fact- based evidentiary inquiry, and this is what we did. We gave you many hours of specific, factual details about, to use Congresswoman Cheney's words, how the President summoned the mob, assembled the mob, incited it, lit the match, sending them off to the Capitol where they thought, as they yelled out, that they had been invited by the President of the United States. And then, of course, they unleashed unparalleled violence against our overwhelmed and besieged but heroic police officers, who you thoughtfully honored yesterday, when the officers got in their way as they entered the Capitol at the behest of the President of the United States to stop the steal.

Now, I am convinced most Senators must be convinced by this overwhelming and specific detail, because most Americans are. But say you still have your doubts; you think the President really thought that he was sending his followers to participate in a peaceful, nonviolent rally, the kind that might have been organized by Julian Bond, who my distinguished opposing counsel brought up; Ella Baker; Bob Moses; our late, beloved colleague John Lewis, for the Student Nonviolent Coordinating Committee.

Maybe the President really thought this was going to be like the March on Washington organized by Bayard Rustin and Dr. Martin Luther King, who said: nonviolence is the answer to the crucial moral and political questions of our time. So let's say you are still flirting with the idea that Donald Trump's conduct was totally appropriate, as he proclaimed right off the bat, and he is the innocent victim of a mass accident or catastrophe, like a fire or a flood—as we were invited to frame it on our opening day by distinguished cocounsel or opposing counsel—and you think maybe we are just looking for somebody to blame for this nightmare and catastrophe that has befallen the Republic. We are just looking for someone to blame.

Well, here is the key question, then, in resolving your doubts if you are in that category: how did Donald Trump react when he learned of the violent storming of the Capitol and the threats to Senators, Members of the House, and his own Vice President, as well as the images he saw on TV of the pummeling and beating and harassment of our police officers? Did he spring into action to stop the violence and save us? Did he even wonder about his own security since an out-of-control, anti-government mob could come after him too? Did he quickly try to get in touch with or denounce the Proud Boys, the Oath Keepers, the rally organizers, the Save America rally organizers, and everyone on the extreme right to tell them that this was not what he had in mind, it was a big mistake, call it off, call it off, call it off— as Representative Gallagher begged him to do on national television?

No. He delighted in it. He reveled in it. He exalted in it. He could not understand why the people around him did not share his delight. And then a long period of silence ensued while the mob beat the daylights out of police officers and invaded this building, as you saw on security footage, and proceeded to hunt down Vice President Mike Pence as a traitor and denounced and cursed Speaker Pelosi, both of whom you heard mob members say that they wanted to kill. They were both in real danger, and our government could have been thrown into absolute turmoil without the heroism of our officers and the bravery and courage of a lot of people in this room. Here is what Republican Representative Anthony Gonzalez of Ohio said. He is a former pro football player: we are imploring the president to help, to stand up, to help defend the U.S. Capitol and the United States Congress, which was under attack. We are begging, essentially, and he was nowhere to be found. *Nowhere to be found.*

And as I have emphasized this morning, that dereliction of duty, that desertion of duty was central to his incitement of insurrection and inextricable from it—inextricable, bound together. It reveals his state of mind that day, what he was thinking as he provoked the mob to violence and further violence. It shows how he perpetuated his continuing offense on January 6, his course of conduct charged in the Article of Impeachment as he further incited the mob during the attack, aiming it at Vice President Mike Pence himself, while failing to quell it in either of his roles as Commander in Chief or his real role that day: "inciter in chief." And it powerfully demonstrates that the ex-President knew, of course, that violence was foreseeable, that it was predictable and predicted that day since he was not surprised and not horrified.

No. He was delighted. And through his acts of omission and commission that day, he abused his office by siding with the insurrectionists at almost every point, rather than with the Congress of the United States, rather than with the Constitution. In just a moment, my colleague Mr. Cicilline will address President Trump's conduct, his actions and inactions, his culpable state of mind during the attack, as he will establish yesterday's explosive revelations about House Minority Leader Kevin McCarthy's desperate call to Trump—and Trump's truly astounding reaction—confirming that Trump was doing nothing to help the people in this room or this building. It is now clear beyond a doubt that Trump supported the actions of the mob, and so he must be convicted. It is that simple.

JANUARY 6, 2021

- 1:11pm – President Trump Ends Speech
- 1:34pm – Mayor Bowser Formally Requests Assistance
- 1:49pm – Capitol Police Request National Guard
- 1:49pm – President Trump Tweets A Video Of His Speech
- 2:12pm – Insurgents Enter The Building
- 2:12pm – Vice President Pence Is Ushered Off Senate Floor
- 2:13pm – Senate Is Declared In Recess
- 2:15pm – The Insurgents Chant "Hang Mike Pence!"
- 2:16pm – Capitol Police Announce Capitol Breach
- 2:18pm – Capitol Police Lockdown The Capitol
- 2:24pm – President Trump Tweets Attack On Vice President (Played On Bullhorn At Capitol)
- 2:25-2:26pm – Vice President Further Evacuated

When he took the stage on January 6, he knew exactly how combustible the situation was. He knew there were many people in the crowd who were ready to jump into action, to engage in violence at any signal that he needed them to fight like hell to stop the steal. And that is exactly what he told them to do. Then he aimed them straight here, right down Pennsylvania, at the Capitol, where he told them the steal was occurring; that is, the counting of the electoral college votes.

And we all know what happened next. They attacked this building. They disrupted the peaceful transfer of power. They injured and killed people, convinced that they were acting on his instructions and with his approval and protection. And while that happened, he further incited them while failing to defend us. If that is not ground for conviction, if that is not a high crime and misdemeanor against the Republic and the United States of America, then nothing is. President Trump must be convicted for the safety and security of our democracy and our people. Mr. Cicilline.

. . .

Mr. Manager CICILLINE: Mr. President, distinguished Senators, as we have demonstrated, there is overwhelming evidence that President Trump incited the violence and knew violence was foreseeable on January 6. He knew that many in the crowd were posed for violence at his urging and, in fact, many in the sea of thousands in the crowd were wearing body armor and helmets and holding sticks and flagpoles.

And then he not only provoked that very same crowd but aimed them at the Capitol. He literally pointed at this building, at us, during his speech. He pointed to the building where Congress was going to certify the election results and where he knew the Vice President himself was presiding over the process. No one is suggesting that President Trump intended every detail of what happened on January 6, but when he directed the sea of thousands before him—who, reportedly, were ready to engage in real violence—when he told that crowd to fight like hell, he incited violence targeted at the Capitol, and he most certainly foresaw it.

My colleague, Manager Dean, will stand up after and walk you through the overwhelming evidence that supports those claims. I want to start, though, by talking about what happened after that. There was a lot of discussion yesterday about what the President knew and when he knew it. There are certain things that we do not know about what the President did that day, because the President—that is, former President Trump—has remained silent about what he was doing during one of the bloodiest attacks on our Capitol since 1812.

Despite a full and fair opportunity to come forward, he has refused to come and tell his story. As Manager Raskin said, we would all do that. In fact, I would insist on it. If I were accused of a grave and serious crime that I was innocent of, I would demand the right to tell my side of the story. President Trump declined. But there are certain facts that are undisputed, that we know to be true despite the President's refusal to testify; which is, counsel either ignored entirely or didn't and couldn't dispute. Before I go to those facts, let me quickly just touch on a few things. First, President Trump and his counsel have resorted to arguments that the evidence presented was somehow manufactured or hidden from them.

I want to be very clear about this because this is important. In terms of the timing of when they received the materials here, defense counsel had access to all materials when they were entitled to have them under S. Res. 47, and they cannot and have not alleged otherwise. As to their desperate claim that evidence was somehow manufactured, they have not alleged that one tweet from their client was actually inaccurate—nor can they.

We got these tweets—which are, of course, statements from the former President—from a public archive, and they are all correct. We also know the President's claims about evidence being manipulated also are untrue because they didn't even object to the introduction of the evidence when they had the opportunity to do so. So I hope we can now set those issues aside and turn to the facts of this case and really set the record straight about the undisputed facts in this case, about what the President knew that day and when he knew it.

At the outset, let me say this. As you may recall, in direct response to a question yesterday, President Trump's counsel stated, and I quote: "At no point was the President informed the Vice President was in any danger." As we walk through these undisputed facts, you will see, quite clearly, that is simply not true.

As you can see here, from just after 12 p.m. to just before 2 p.m., President Trump delivered his statements at the rally, which incited an initial wave of protesters coming down to the Capitol, and his speech was still ongoing, and you saw the evidence of people broadcasting that on their phones.

He finished his speech at 1:11 p.m., at which point a much larger wave surged toward us here at the Capitol, ripping down scaffolding and triggering calls for law enforcement assistance.

Thirty minutes later, at 1:49 p.m., as the violence intensified, President Trump tweeted a video of his remarks at the rally with the caption: "Our country has had enough, we will not take it anymore, and that's what this is all about." During the half-hour following that tweet, the situation here drastically deteriorated. Insurrectionists breached the Capitol barriers, then its steps, then the complex itself.

By 2:12, the insurrectionist mob had overwhelmed the police and started their violent attack on the Capitol. And as you all know, this attack occurred and played out on live television. Every major network was showing it. We have shown you, during the course of this trial, side-by-side exactly what the President would have seen on TV or his Twitter account. We have also shown you that he would have seen around 2:12 p.m. images of Vice President Pence being rushed off the Senate floor. I won't replay all of that for you, but for timing purposes, here is the footage reacting to Vice President Pence leaving the floor.

Unidentified Speakers on MSNBC: No audio. They just cut out. It looks—and sometimes the Senate. It seemed like they just ushered Mike Pence out really quickly.
Yes, they did. That is exactly what just happened there. They ushered Mike Pence
out. They moved him fast. There was—I saw the motions too.

Defense counsel seems to suggest that somehow the President of the United
States was not aware of this; that the President had no idea that his Vice President
had been evacuated from the Senate floor for his safety because violent rioters had
broken into the Capitol with thousands more coming and with the Capitol Police
completely overwhelmed. This was on live television. So defense counsel is suggesting that the President of the United States knew less about this than the American people—this is just not possible—that the Secret Service failed to mention
that his Vice President was being rushed from the Senate for his own protection,
but nobody in the White House thought to alert him; that none of our law enforcement agencies raised a concern to the Commander in Chief that the Vice President
was being evacuated from the Senate floor as a violent mob assaulted the Capitol.
It simply cannot be.

And with each passing minute on the timeline of events on January 6, it grows
more and more inconceivable. Let's continue forward in time. Between 2:12 to
2:24, the Senate recessed. Speaker Nancy Pelosi was ushered off the floor. The
Capitol Police announced a breach and a lockdown, and the insurrectionist mob
began chanting: "Hang Mike Pence." And it was unfolding on live TV in front of
the entire world.

So, again, let me ask you: does it strike you as credible that nobody, not a single
person, informed the President that his Vice President had been evacuated or that
the President didn't glance at the television or his Twitter account and learn about
the events that were happening?

Remember, this was the day of the electoral college. Remember his obsession
with stopping the certification. It is just not credible that the President at no point
knew his Vice President was in this building and was in real danger.

Senators, I submit to you these facts, this timeline is undisputed. At 2:24 p.m.,
after rioters breached the barriers, after calls for assistance, after rioters stormed
the building, after Vice President Pence was rushed from the Senate floor, and just
before Vice President Pence was further evacuated for his safety, President Trump
decided to attack his own Vice President on Twitter. The undisputed facts confirmed that not only must President Trump have been aware of the Vice President's
danger but he still sent out a tweet attacking him, further inciting the very mob
that was in just a few feet of him, inside of this very building.

The Vice President was there with his family, who was in danger for his life.
They were chanting, "Hang Mike Pence," and had erected a noose outside. And

as we have shown, the mob responded to President Trump's attack instantly. The tweet was read aloud on a bullhorn, if you remember that video. Insurrectionists began chanting again about Mike Pence. And in those critical moments, we see President Trump engaging in a dereliction of his duty by further inciting the mob, in real-time, to target the Vice President, with knowledge that the insurrection was ongoing.

And that's, of course, included in the conduct charged in this Article of Impeachment. The former President's counsel's suggestion otherwise is completely wrong. His further incitement is impeachable conduct that continued during the course of this assault itself, and it is part of a constitutional crime and was entirely and completely a part of his indefensible failure to protect the Congress. Now there's been some confusion as to the phone call I referenced with Senator Lee. So I want to be clear about certain facts that are not in dispute.

First, Senator Lee has confirmed that the call occurred at 2:26 p.m. So I added that to the timeline above. Remember, by this phone call, the Vice President has just been evacuated on live television for his own safety. And Donald Trump had, after that, tweeted an attack on him, which the insurgents read on a bullhorn. And a few minutes after Donald Trump's tweet, he didn't reach out to check on the Vice President's safety.

The call was interrupted. Senator Tuberville has since explained, and I quote: "I looked at the phone and it said the White House on it, [and] I said hello, the President said a few words. I said 'Mr. President they're taking the Vice President out, and they want me to get off the phone, and I've got to go.'" That was his second evacuation that day. A minute later, live feeds documented the insurgents chanting: "Mike Pence is a traitor."

At this point, even if somehow he had missed it earlier, it is inconceivable that the President—the former President—was unaware that the Vice President was in danger. And what does the President do after hearing that? Does he rush to secure the Capitol? Does he do anything to quell the mob? Does he call his Vice President to check on his safety? We all know the answers to those questions too. There can be no dispute. He took none of those steps, not a single one.

Even after learning that Senators were being evacuated and that Vice President Pence had also been evacuated, he did nothing to help the Vice President. And here is some more evidence that we have since learned. At some point over the following thirty minutes, President Trump spoke to Minority Leader Kevin McCarthy. And as Representative Jaime Herrera Beutler has revealed—evidence that now has been stipulated as part of the evidentiary record—in that conversation, Kevin McCarthy is pleading with the former President to do something. He first tries to assign the blame to another group, and Leader McCarthy says: "No, these are your supporters, Mr. President." What does the President say in response? Not "I'll send people right away; I didn't realize you were in danger." He says: "Well, Kevin—" And I quote. I quote: "Well, Kevin, I guess these people are more upset about the election than you are." *I guess these people are more upset about the election than you are.*

The President, just as he conveyed in that tweet at 6:01, was essentially saying: "You got what you deserve." Let me say that again. Not only was the President fully aware of the Vice President's situation and the situation that we were all in, when he was asked for help, when he was asked to defend the Capitol less than thirty minutes after inciting this violence against his own Vice President, President Trump refused that request for assistance, and he told us why—his singular focus: stopping the certification of the election of his opponent. He incited the violence to stop the certification. He attacked the Vice President and further incited the insurrection to pressure the Vice President to stop the certification of the election. He called Senator Tuberville to stop the certification, and he refused to send help to Congress. This Congress and the Vice President of the United States were in mortal danger because he wanted to stop the certification.

He did these things—attacking the Vice President, calling Senator Tuberville, refusing Senator McCarthy's request—with full knowledge of the violent attack that was underway at that point. He chose retaining his own power over the safety of Americans. I can't imagine more damning evidence of his state of mind. The call ended with a screaming match interrupted by violent rioters breaking through the windows of Representative McCarthy's office. Senators, the President knew this was happening. He didn't do anything to help his Vice President or any of you or any of the brave officers and other employees serving the American people that day. His sole focus was stealing the election for himself. He apparently has still not thought of anyone else.

Senators, remember, as one of you said, during this attack, they could have killed us all—our staff, the officers protecting all of us, everyone. President Trump not only incited it but continued inciting it as it occurred with attacks on his Vice President and then willfully refused to defend us, furthering his provocation and incitement by the mob, siding with the mob, siding with the violent insurrectionists, criminals who killed and injured police officers sworn to protect us, because they were "more upset about the election" than Leader McCarthy. Those facts are undisputed. President Trump has not offered any evidence or any argument to disprove them. His lawyers almost entirely ignored these facts in their short presentation.

We have only his counsel's false claim yesterday that "at no point was the President informed that the Vice President was in any danger," a claim that is refuted not just by common sense but by the timeline you have seen and also the Vice President's legal team. So there can be no doubt, at the moment we most needed a President to preserve, protect, and defend us, President Trump instead willfully betrayed us. He violated his oath. He left all of us and officers like Eugene Goodman to our own devices against an attack he had incited and he alone could stop. That is why he must be convicted.

I would like to conclude by making one final point that follows directly from what I discussed. Our case and the Article of Impeachment before you absolutely includes President Trump's dereliction of duty on January 6, his failure as "inciter in chief" to immediately quell or call off the mob, his failure as Commander in Chief to immediately do everything in his power to secure the Capitol. That is a further basis on which to convict, and there can be no doubt of that. The ongoing constitutional misconduct is like any continuing offense, and the proof of that is overwhelming. Most directly, his dereliction of duty offers conclusive, irrefutable evidence that he acted willfully, as we charge. He wasn't furious or sad or shocked, like virtually everyone else in America. He was reported by those around him as "delighted."

Rather than rush to our aid or demand his mob retreat, he watched the attack on TV and praised the mob to Leader McCarthy as more loyal to him, more upset about the election. That was all that mattered. His reaction is also further evidence of his intent. He acted exactly the way a person would act if they had indeed incited the mob to violence to stop the steal. Moreover, as I have shown, President Trump's dereliction and desertion of duty includes his decision to further incite the mob even as he failed to protect us. While the mob hunted Vice President Pence in these very halls, he attacked Vice President Pence. While he tried to stop the steal, he spread the big lie.

We all saw how his mob responded in real time. This further incitement was part of his dereliction of duty. It was also part of his course of conduct encouraging and provoking the mob to violence. President Trump's dereliction of duty also highlights how foreseeable the attack was to him. In his tweet just after 6 p.m., he said: "These are the things and events that happen when a sacred landslide election victory is so unceremoniously & viciously stripped away from great patriots who have been badly & unfairly treated for so long." This tweet continued his endorsement of the attack, his failure to condemn it, his desertion of duty, but it also reveals his view this was of course what would happen when Congress refused his demand to reject the election that he continued to tell his supporters was stolen and he had actually won in a landslide.

Again, he wasn't surprised. He saw this as a predictable result of his repeated demands that his followers stop the steal by any means possible. This was all connected. His dereliction of duty, his desertion of duty was part and parcel of the crime charged in the impeachment, and it is certainly a basis on which to vote for conviction. If you believe that he willfully refused to defend us and the law enforcement officers fighting to save us and that he was delighted by the attack and that he saw it as a natural result of his call to stop the steal and that he continued to incite and target violence as the attack unfolded, we respectfully submit you must vote to convict and disqualify so that the events on January 6 can never happen again in this country.

. . .

Ms. Manager DEAN: We are grateful for your kind attention this week as we engaged in a process formulated and put to paper by the Founders in my home city of Philadelphia, which is getting its fair share of attention this week, in 1787—234 years ago. My colleague Mr. Cicilline addressed the importance of the President's dereliction of duty.

I will focus on three specific aspects of this case which the defense has raised questions about. First, the defense suggests that this was just one speech and one speech cannot incite insurrection, and the defense suggested, because the attack was preplanned by some insurrectionists, Donald Trump is somehow not culpable. Both of these things are, mainly, not true nor are they what we allege.

So let's be clear. We are not suggesting that Donald Trump's January 6 speech by itself incited the attack. We have shown that his course of conduct leading up to and including that speech incited the attack. The defense is correct that the insurrection was preplanned. That supports our point. We argue and the evidence overwhelmingly confirms that Donald Trump's conduct over many months incited his supporters to believe, one, his big lie, that the only way he could lose was if the election were rigged; two, that, to ensure the election would not be stolen to prevent the fraud, they had to stop the steal; and, three, they had to fight to stop the steal or they would not have a country anymore.

This conduct took time, and it culminated in Donald Trump's sending a "save the date" on December 19, eighteen days before the attack, telling his base exactly when, where, and who to fight. While he was doing this, he spent $50 million from his legal defense fund to simultaneously broadcast his message to "stop the steal" over all major networks. Donald Trump invited them; he incited them; then he directed them. Here are a few clips that will help bring that story to light.

(video montage)

Mr. WALLACE: Can you give a direct answer you will accept the election?

President TRUMP: I have to see. Look, I have to see. No, I'm not going to just say yes.

. . .

President TRUMP: This election will be the most rigged election in history.

. . .

President TRUMP: This is going to be the greatest election disaster in history.

. . .

President TRUMP: The only way they can take this election away from us is if this is a rigged election. We're going to win this election.

. . .

President TRUMP: It's a rigged election. That's the only way we are going to lose.

. . .

Unidentified Speaker: Do you commit to making sure that there's a peaceful transfer of power?

. . .

President TRUMP: Get rid of the ballots, and you'll have a very trans—you'll have a very peaceful—there won't be a transfer, frankly. There'll be a continuation.

. . .

President TRUMP: That's the only way we're going—that's the only way we're going to lose is if there's mischief, mischief, and it'll have to be on a big scale, so be careful.

. . .

President TRUMP: But this will be one of the greatest fraudulent—most fraudulent elections ever.

. . .

President TRUMP: I'm not going to let this election be taken away from us. That's the only way they're going to win it.

. . .

President TRUMP: This is a fraud on the American public.

(People chanting: Yeah.)

This is an embarrassment to our country.

(People chanting: Yeah.)

We were getting ready to win this election. Frankly, we did win this election.

(People chanting: Yeah.)

. . .

President TRUMP: We were winning in all the key locations by a lot, actually, and then our numbers started miraculously getting whittled away in secret, and this is a case where they're trying to steal an election. They're trying to rig an election, and we can't let that happen.

. . .

President TRUMP: You can't let another person steal that election from you. All over the country, people are together in holding up signs: "Stop the steal."

. . .

President TRUMP: If we don't root out the fraud—the tremendous and horrible fraud—that has taken place in our 2020 election, we don't have a country anymore.

. . .

President TRUMP: We cannot allow a completely fraudulent election to stand.

. . .

President TRUMP: We're going to fight like hell, I'll tell you right now.

(People chanting: Yeah.)

President TRUMP: If you don't fight to save your country with everything you have, you're not going to have a country left.

. . .

President TRUMP: We will not bend. We will not break. We will not yield. We will never give in. We will never give up. We will never back down. We will never ever surrender.

. . .

President TRUMP: All of us here today do not want to see our election victory stolen. We will never give up. We will never concede. It doesn't happen. You don't concede when there's theft involved.

(People chanting: Yeah.)

President TRUMP: And to use a favorite term that all of you people really came up with: we will stop the steal.

President TRUMP: Because you'll never take back our country with weakness. You have to show strength, and you have to be strong.

Make no mistake, this election was stolen from you, from me, from the country. And we fight. We fight like hell, and if you don't fight like hell, you're not going to have a country anymore.

Our point is this: this was not one speech. This was a deliberate, purposeful effort by Donald Trump, over many months, that resulted in the well-organized mob attack on January 6. That brings me to my second point, the violence. Defense counsel argues that there is no way that Donald Trump could have known what would happen. Yet we are not suggesting nor is it necessary for us to prove that Donald Trump knew every detail of what would unfold on January 6 or even how horrible and deadly the attack would become, but he did know, as he looked out on that sea of thousands in front of him—some wearing body armor and helmets, others carrying weapons—that the result would be violence. The evidence over-whelmingly demonstrates this.

A few points on this. Donald Trump knew the people he was inciting leading up to January 6. He saw the violence they were capable of. He had a pattern and practice of praising and encouraging supporters of violence, never condemning it. It is not a coincidence that those same people—the Proud Boys, the organizer of the Trump caravan, the supporters and speakers at the second Million MAGA March—all showed up on January 6.

And Donald Trump's behavior was different. This was not just a comment by an official or a politician fighting for a cause; this was months of cultivating a base of people who were violent, praising that violence, and then leading them—leading that violence, that rage straight to a joint session of Congress, where he knew his Vice President was presiding. And Donald Trump had warnings about the crowd in front of him on January 6. There were detailed posts online of attack plans. Law enforcement warned that these posts were real threats and even made arrests in the days leading up to the attack. There were credible reports that many would be armed and ready to attack the Capitol.

Despite these credible warnings of serious, dangerous threats to our Capitol, when the crowd was standing in front of the President, ready to take orders and attack, he said: We're going to the Capitol. And we fight. We fight like hell. And if you don't fight like hell, you're not going to have a country anymore. Here is a short clip.

President TRUMP: What do you want to call them? Give me a name. Give me a name. Who would you like me to condemn? Who would you like me to condemn?

Mr. WALLACE: White supremacists and—

President TRUMP: Proud Boys? Stand back and stand by.

. . .

President TRUMP: It is something. Do you see the way our people, they—you know, they were protecting his bus yesterday because they are nice. So his bus—they had hundreds of cars: "Trump, Trump." Trump and the American flag. That's what—you see Trump and American flag.

. . .

At the first Million MAGA March we promised that if the GOP would not do everything in their power to keep Trump in office, that we would destroy the GOP. And as we gather here in Washington, DC, for a second Million MAGA March, we are done making promises. It has to happen now. We are going to destroy the GOP.

(People chanting: Destroy the GOP.)

. . .

President TRUMP: Because you'll never take back our country with weakness. You have to show strength and you have to be strong.

Senators, the violence on January 6 was demonstrably foreseeable. Trump even said so himself at 6:01 p.m. the day of the attack. The last thing he said before he went to sleep, "These are the things that happen." He foresaw this, and he admitted as much. That brings me to my final point, the insurrectionists. Defense counsel has suggested these people came here on their own. The defense brief states that the insurrectionists "did so [for] their own accord and for their own reasons and are being criminally prosecuted."

It is true that some insurrectionists are being prosecuted, but it is not true that they did so of their own accord and for their own reasons. The evidence makes clear the exact opposite—that they did this for Donald Trump at his invitation, at his direction, at his command. They said this before the attack, during the attack. They said it after the attack. Leading up to January 6, in post after post, the President's supporters confirmed this was for Donald Trump; it was at his direction. One supporter wrote: "If Congress illegally [certified] Biden, . . . Trump would have absolutely no choice but to demand us to storm the Capitol and kill/beat them up for it." They even say publicly, openly, and proudly that President Trump would help them commandeer the National Guard so all they have to do is overwhelm 2,000 Capitol Police officers. During his speech on January 6, Trump supporters chanted his words back to him. They even live-tweeted his commands, as Ms. DeGette showed you.

During the attack, the insurrectionists at the Capitol chanted Donald Trump's words from his tweets, rallies, and from the speech of the 6th. They held signs that said—and chanted—"Fight for Trump." "Stop the steal." They read his tweets over bullhorns, amplifying his demands. Another rioter, while live-streaming the insurrection from the Capitol, said: "He'll be happy. We're fighting for Trump." What is more, the insurrectionists were not hiding. They believed they were following the orders from our Commander in Chief. They felt secure enough in the legitimacy of their actions to take selfies, to post photos and videos on social media. After the attack, rioter after rioter confirmed this too. Jenna Ryan, who was later accused for her role in the insurrection, said: I thought I was following my President. "I thought we were following what we were called to do. President Trump requested that we be in D.C. on the 6th."

When it became clear that Donald Trump would not protect them, some of his supporters said they felt "duped"; they felt "tricked." Listen to some of this evidence.

> Ms. PIERSON: And even if they think for a second that they're going to get away with this today, they got another thing coming because today is just a day, and today is just the beginning. They haven't seen a resistance until they have seen a patriot fight for their country. If you die today—

Ms. Manager DEAN: They told you themselves: they were following the President's orders. And you'll see something clearly: Donald Trump knew who these people were. As the slides show, the people he cultivated, whose violence he praised, were all there on January 6—the Proud Boys, who Donald Trump told to "stand back and stand by" in September of 2020; Keith Lee, the organizer of the Trump caravan that tried to drive the Biden campaign bus off the road; Katrina Pierson, the speaker at the second Million MAGA March—they were all there. Here is one final clip, also submitted in the Record.

> Unidentified Speaker 1 in front of the Capitol, as Confederate flag blows in the background, January 6, 2021: That's what we fuckin' need to have, 30,000 guns up here.

> Unidentified Speaker 2: Next trip.

Senators, some of the insurrectionists are facing criminal charges. Donald Trump was acting as our Commander in Chief; he was our President. He used his office and the authority it commands to incite an attack, and when Congress and the Constitution were under attack, he abandoned his duties, violated his oath, failing to preserve, protect, and defend. That is why we are here—because the President of the United States, Donald J. Trump, incited and directed thousands of people to attack the legislative branch.

He knew what his supporters were capable of. He inflamed them, sent them down Pennsylvania Avenue, not on any old day but on the day we were certifying the election results. As they were banging on our doors, he failed to defend us because this is what he wanted. He wanted to remain in power. For that crime against the Republic, he must be held accountable. Senators, the insurrectionists are still listening.

Before I end, I must admit, until we were preparing for this trial, I didn't know the extent of many of these facts. I witnessed the horror, but I didn't know. I didn't know how deliberate the President's planning was, how he had invested in it, how many times he incited his supporters with these lies, how carefully and consistently he incited them to violence on January 6. While many of us may have tuned out his rallies, I also did not know the extent that his followers were listening, were hanging on his every word, and honestly, I did not know how close the mob actually came to their violent end, that they were just steps away from all of us, that the death toll could have been much higher but for the bravery of men and women who protect us.

But now we know. We know the bravery of people like Officer Goodman and all the men and women of the Capitol Police, of the custodians who with pride and a sense of duty in their work cleaned up shattered glass, splintered wood, and blood-stained floors. We know the sacrifice of life and limb. We know what Donald Trump did. We know what he failed to do. Though it is difficult to bear witness and face the reality of what happened in these halls, what happens if we don't confront these facts? What happens if there is no accountability?

For those who say we need to get past this, we need to come together, we need to unify, if we don't set this right and call it what it was—the highest constitutional crime by the President of the United States—the past will not be past. The past will become our future for my grandchildren and for their children. Senators, we are in a dialogue with history, a conversation with our past with a hope for our future. Two hundred and thirty-four years from now, it may be that no one person here among us is remembered. Yet, what we do here, what is being asked of each of us here in this moment, will be remembered. History has found us. I ask that you not look the other way.

. . .

Mr. Manager NEGUSE: Mr. President, distinguished Senators, there is an old quote from Henry Clay, a son of Kentucky, that "courtesies of a small and trivial character are the ones [that] strike deepest in the grateful and appreciating heart." I want to say on behalf of all the House managers that we are very grateful for the courtesies that you have extended to us and the President's counsel during the course of this trial. You have heard my colleague Manager Dean go through the overwhelming evidence that makes clear that President Trump must be convicted and disqualified for his high crime. I am not going to repeat that evidence; it speaks for itself.

Earlier in this trial, you might recall a few days ago that I mentioned my expectation that President Trump's lawyers might do everything they could to avoid discussing the facts of this case, and I can understand why. I mean, the evidence that all of us presented, that Manager Dean has summarized, is pretty devastating. So rather than address it, the President has offered up distractions, excuses, anything but actually trying to defend against the facts. They said things like President Trump is now a private citizen, so the criminal justice system can deal with it, or that we haven't set a clear standard for incitement—we talked a lot about due process—and that all politicians say words like "fight."

I would like to take a minute to explain why each of those distractions are precisely that—distractions—and why they do not prevent in any way this Senate from convicting President Trump. Number one, every President is one day a private citizen, so the argument that because President Trump has left office, he shouldn't be impeached for conduct committed while he was in office doesn't make sense. I mean, why would the Constitution include the impeachment power at all if the criminal justice system serves as a suitable alternative once a President leaves office? It wouldn't.

Impeachment is a remedy separate and apart from the criminal justice system, and for good reason. The Presidency comes with special powers, extraordinary powers not bestowed on ordinary citizens, and if those powers are abused, they can cause great damage to our country, and they have to be dealt with in a separate forum, this forum. It would be unwise to suggest that, going forward, the only appropriate response to constitutional offenses committed by a President are criminal charges when the President returns to private life. That is not the kind of political system any of us want, and it is not the kind of constitutional system the Framers intended. Second, it is true we have not cited criminal statutes establishing elements of incitement because, again, this isn't a criminal trial. It is not a criminal case. President Trump is charged with a constitutional offense, and you are tasked with determining whether or not he committed that high crime as understood by our Framers.

So the relevant question, which President Trump's lawyers would have you ignore, is: would our Framers have considered a President inciting a violent mob to attack our government while seeking to stop the certification of our elections—would they have considered that an impeachable offense? Who among us, who among us really thinks the answer to that question is no? Third, due process. So just to be absolutely clear, the House, with the sole power of impeachment, determines what the process looks like in the House, and the Senate does the same for the trial. During this trial, the President has counsel. They have argued very vigorously on his behalf. We had a full presentation of evidence, adversarial presentations, motions.

The President was invited to testify. He declined. The President was invited to provide exculpatory evidence. He declined. You can't claim there is no due process when you won't participate in the process.

And we know this case isn't one that requires a complicated legal analysis. You all—you lived it. The managers and I, we lived it. Our country lived it. The President, in public view, right out in the open, incited a violent mob, a mob that temporarily, at least, stopped us from certifying an election. If there were ever an exigent circumstance, this is it. Number four, we all know that President Trump's defense, as we predicted, spent a lot of time—all the time comparing his conduct to other politicians using words like "fight." Of course, you saw the hours of video. As I said on Thursday, we trust you to know the difference because what you will not find in those video montages that they showed you is any of those speeches, those remarks culminating in a violent insurrection on our Nation's Capitol. That is the difference.

The President spent months inflaming his supporters to believe that the election had been stolen from him, from them, which was not true. He summoned the mob, assembled the mob, and when the violence erupted, he did nothing to stop it; instead, inciting it further. Senators, all of these arguments offered by the President have one fundamental thing in common—one. They have nothing to do with whether or not—factually, whether or not the President incited this attack. They have given you a lot of distractions so they don't have to defend what happened here on that terrible day, and they do that because they believe those distractions are going to work, that you will ignore the President's conduct instead of confronting it. I think they are wrong.

Some of you know this already. I am the youngest member of our manager team by quite a few years, so perhaps I am a bit naive, but I just don't believe that. I really don't. I don't believe their effort is going to work, and here is why: because I know what this body is capable of. I may not have witnessed it, but I have read about it in the history books. I have seen the C-SPAN footage, archives, sometimes have watched them for hours—yes, I have actually done that—and the history of our country in those books and in those tapes, the history of this country has been defined right here on this floor. The 13th Amendment, the amendment abolishing slavery, was passed in this very room. In this room—not figuratively, literally where you all sit and where I stand.

In 1964, this body, with the help of Senators like John Sherman Cooper and so many others, this body secured passage of the Civil Rights Act. We made the decision to enter World War II from this Chamber. We have certainly had our struggles, but we have always risen to the occasion when it mattered the most, not by ignoring injustice or cowering to bullies and threats but by doing the right thing, by trying to do the right thing, and that is why so many nations around the world aspire to be like America. They stand up to dictators and autocrats and tyrants because America is a guiding light for them, a North Star.

They do so, they look to us because we have been a guiding light, a North Star in these moments because the people who sat in your chairs, when confronted with choices that define us, rose to the occasion. I want to offer one more example of a decision made in this room by this body that resonated with me. The first day I stood up in this trial, I mentioned that I was the son of immigrants, like many of you, and many Senators graciously approached me after my presentation and asked me where my parents were from, and I told folks who asked that my folks were from East Africa.

In 1986, this body considered a bill to override President Reagan's veto of legislation opposing sanctions on South Africa during apartheid. Two Senators who are sitting in this room, one Democrat and one Republican, voted to override that veto. That vote was not about gaining political favor. In fact, it was made despite potentially losing political favor. And I have to imagine that that vote was cast, like the decisions before it, because there are moments that transcend party politics and that require us to put country above our party because the consequences of not doing so are just too great. Senators, this is one of those moments. Many folks who are watching today's proceedings may not know this, but House Members like me, Manager Raskin, and fellow managers, we are not allowed on the Senate floor without express permission. No one is.

Certainly, the Senators are aware of that. This floor is sacred. It is one of the reasons why I, like so many of you, were so offended to see it desecrated by that mob and to see those insurrectionists diminishing it and devaluing it and disrespecting these hallowed Halls that my whole life I held in such awe. Because of those rules that I just mentioned, this will be the only time I have the privilege to stand before you like this. When the trial is over, I will go back to being not impeachment manager but to being just a House Member. The trial will end, and we will resume our lives and our work. But for some, there will be no end—no end to the pain of what happened on January 6. The officers who struggled to recover from the injuries they sustained to protect us, they struggle to recover today, and the families who continue to mourn those whom they lost on that terrible, tragic day. I was struck yesterday by defense counsel's continued references to hate.

One of my favorite quotes of Dr. Martin Luther King, Jr.—it is one that has sustained me during times of adversity, and I suspect it has sustained some of you: "I have decided to stick with love. Hate is too great a burden to bear." This trial is not born from hatred—far from it. It is born from a love of country—our country— and our desire to maintain it and our desire to see America at its best. And in those moments that I spoke of—the Civil Rights Act and so much more—we remember those moments because they helped define and enshrine America at its best. I firmly believe that our certification of the electoral college votes in the early hours of January 7, our refusal to let our Republic be threatened and taken down by a violent mob, will go down in history as one of those moments too.

And I believe that this body can rise to the occasion once again today by convicting President Trump and defending our Republic. And the stakes—the stakes—could not be higher, because the cold, hard truth is that what happened on January 6 can happen again. I fear, like many of you do, that the violence we saw on that terrible day may be just the beginning. We have shown you the ongoing risks and the extremist groups that grow more emboldened every day. Senators, this cannot be the beginning. It can't be the new normal. It has to be the end. That decision is in your hands.

. . .

Mr. Manager RASKIN: Mr. President, Senators, my daughter Hannah said something to me last night that stopped me cold and brought me up short. The kids have been very moved by all the victims of the violence, the officers and their families, but Hannah told me last night she felt really sorry for the kid of the man who said goodbye to his children before he left home to come and join Trump's actions. Their father had told them that their dad might not be coming home again, and they might never see him again.

In other words, he was expecting violence and he might die, as insurrectionists did. And that shook me. Hannah said: "How can the President put children and people's families in that situation and then just run away from the whole thing?" That shook me, and I was filled with self-reproach because, when I first saw the line about "your father going to Washington and you might not see him again," I just thought about it, well, like a prosecutor, like a manager. I thought: what damning evidence that people were expecting lethal violence at a protest called by the President of the United States in saying their final goodbyes to their kids.

But Hannah—my dear Hannah—thought of it like a human being. She thought of it—if you will forgive me—like a patriot, someone who just lost her brother and doesn't want to see any other kids in America go through that kind of agony and grief. Senators, when I say all three of my kids are better than me, you know that I am not engaged in idle flattering. Maybe some of you feel the same way about your kids. They are literally better people. They have got a lot of their mom inside of them. They are better than me.

And Hannah saw through the legality of the situation. She saw through the politics of the situation, all the way to the humanity of the situation and the morality of the situation. That was one of the most patriotic things I ever heard any-body say. The children of the insurrectionists, even the violent and dangerous ones—they are our children too. They are Americans, and we must take care of them and their future. We must recognize and exorcise these crimes against our Nation, and then we must take care of our people and our children—their hearts and their minds.

As Tommy Raskin used to say: "It's hard to be human." Many of the Capitol and Metropolitan police officers and Guards men and women who were beaten up by the mob also have kids. You remember Officer Fanone, who had a heart attack after being tased and roughed up for hours by the mob, and then begging for his life telling the insurrectionists that he had four daughters, and that just about broke my heart all over again. We talked about this for a long time last night. My kids felt terrible that other kids' fathers and mothers were pulled into this nightmare by a President of the United States.

Senators, we proved to you he betrayed his country. We proved he betrayed his Constitution. We proved he betrayed his oath of office. The startling thing to recognize now is that he is even betraying the mob. He told them he would march with them, and he didn't. They believed the President was right there with them, somewhere in the crowd, fighting the fantasy conspiracy—steal the election and steal their country away from them. They thought they were one big team working together. He told them their great journey together was just beginning, and now there are hundreds of criminal prosecutors getting going all over the country and people getting set to say goodbye to members of their family.

And the President who contacted them, solicited them, lured him, invited them, and incited them, that President has suddenly gone quiet and dark, nowhere to be found. He cannot be troubled to come here to tell us what happened and tell us why this was the patriotic and the constitutional thing to do. Senators, this trial, in the final analysis, is not about Donald Trump. The country and the world know who Donald Trump is. This trial is about who we are—who we are.

My friend, Dar Williams, said that sometimes the truth is like a second chance. We have got a chance here with the truth. We still believe in the separation of powers. President Trump tried to sideline or run over every other branch of gov-ernment, thwart the will of the people at the State level, and usurp the people's choice for President. This case is about whether our country demands a peaceful, nonviolent transfer of power to guarantee the sovereignty of the people.

Are we going to defend the people who defend us, not just honor them with medals, as you rightfully did yesterday, but actually back them up against savage, barbaric insurrectionary violence? Will we restore the honor of our Capitol and the people who work here? Will we be a democratic nation that the world looks to for understanding democratic values and practices and constitutional government and the rights of women and men? Will the Senate condone the President of the United States inciting a violent attack on our Chambers, our offices, our staff, and the officers who protect us?

When you see the footage of Officer Hodges stuck in the doorway, literally being tortured by the mob—if the government did that to you, that would be torture. And when you see that footage, and he is shouting in agony for his dear life, it is almost unwatchable. When the Vice President of the United States escapes a violent mob that has entered this Capitol Building seeking to hang him and calling out "traitor, traitor, traitor," and when they shut down the counting of the electoral college votes, is this the future you imagined for our kids? Is it totally appropriate, as we have been told? Or as Representative Cheney said, is it the greatest betrayal of the Presidential oath of office in the history of our country?

And if we can't handle this together as a people—all of us—forgetting the lines of party and ideology and geography and all of those things, if we can't handle this, how are we ever going to conquer the other crises of our day? Is this America? Is this what we want to bequeath to our children and our grandchildren?

I was never a great Sunday school student. Actually, I was pretty truant most of the time. But one line always stuck with me from the Book of Exodus as both beautiful and haunting, even as a kid, after I asked what the words meant. Thou shalt not follow a multitude to do evil. Thou shalt not follow a multitude to do evil. The officer who got called the N-word fifteen times and spent hours with his colleagues battling insurrectionists who had metal poles and baseball bats and hockey sticks, bear spray, and Confederate battle flags posed the right question to the Senate and to all of us: Is this America?

Dear Senators, it is going to be up to you, and whatever committees and subcommittees you are on, whatever you came to Washington to do to work on—from defense to agriculture, to energy, to aerospace, to healthcare—this is almost certainly how you will be remembered by history. That might not be fair. It really might not be fair, but none of us can escape the demands of history and destiny right now. Our reputations and our legacy will be inextricably intertwined with what we do here and with how you exercise your oath to do impartial justice—impartial justice. I know and I trust you will do impartial justice, driven by your meticulous attention to the overwhelming facts of the case and your love for our Constitution, which I know dwells in your hearts. "The times have found us," said Tom Paine, the namesake of my son. "The times have found us."

Is this America? What kind of America will we be? It's now literally in your hands. Godspeed to the Senate of the United States. We reserve any remaining time.

. . .

Mr. Counsel VAN DER VEEN: I will promise that I will be the only one talking, and it will not be so long. Before I start my prepared closing, I really want to clean up a few things from the mess that was the closing of the House managers. I do not want to ruin my closing because I think the ending is pretty good. What they didn't—they started off by misstating the law, and they started off by misstating the intent of our stipulation. What we did today was stipulate to an article that was published in a magazine, apparently, they have had for weeks, according to the documents they produced today, but for some reason this morning popped up with it. The stipulation was that they can put that in. We did not stipulate to its contents for truthfulness, and they tried to portray that in their closing as the stipulation. The stipulation was read into the Record. The proponents of that conversation— the real ones—have denied its content, its veracity.

With respect to—and I am not going to talk much about the tortured analysis of our arson wars that started off or the truly sideways analogies that were used with fires. What I do want to talk about, though, is the doctoring of evidence. First of all, they sent us their evidence on Tuesday the 9th at 2:32 p.m. by email. I was in the room trying the case already when they sent their evidence—due process. They used evidence that was flat wrong two or three nights ago with Senator Lee and had to withdraw it. They tried to use it again today. They tried to use evidence that they had never presented in the case in their closing argument. That is a very desperate attempt by a prosecuting team—nine of them—by a prosecuting team that knew that their case has collapsed. Their closing did not mention one piece of law. They didn't talk about the Constitution once. They didn't talk about the First Amendment and its application. They didn't talk about due process and how it applies to this proceeding for my client.

The basic rule of any court is that when you close a case out, you close on the facts that were admitted in the trial. It is a basic, fundamental principle of due process and fairness. And that was violently breached today on multiple occasions. And you have to ask yourself why? Why did they resort to those tactics at this moment in time?

Senators, good afternoon. Mr. President. What took place here at the U.S. Capitol on January 6 was a grave tragedy. Over the course of this trial, you have heard no one on either side of this debate argue that the infiltration of the Capitol was anything less than a heinous act on the home of American democracy. All of us, starting with my client, are deeply disturbed by the graphic videos of the Capitol attack that have been shown in recent days. The entire team condemned and have repeatedly condemned the violence and law breaking that occurred on January 6 in the strongest possible terms. We have advocated that everybody be found and punished to the maximum extent of the law.

Yet the question before us is not whether there was a violent insurrection of the Capitol. On that point, everyone agrees. Based on the explicit text of the House Impeachment Article, this trial is about whether Mr. Trump willfully engaged in an incitement of violence and even insurrection against the United States, and that question they have posed in their Article of Impeachment has to be set up against the law of this country. No matter how much truly horrifying footage we see of the conduct of the rioters and how much emotion has been injected into this trial, that does not change the fact that Mr. Trump is innocent of the charges against him. Despite all of the video played, at no point in their presentation did you hear the House managers play a single example of Mr. Trump urging anyone to engage in violence of any kind. At no point did you hear anything that could ever possibly be construed as Mr. Trump encouraging or sanctioning an insurrection.

Senators, you did not hear those tapes because they do not exist, because the act of incitement never happened. He engaged in no language of incitement whatsoever on January 6 or any other day following the election. No unbiased person honestly reviewing the transcript of Mr. Trump's speech on the Ellipse could possibly believe that he was suggesting violence. He explicitly told the crowd that he expected the protest outside the Capitol to be peaceful and patriotic. They claim that is not enough. His entire premise was that the proceedings of the joint session should continue. He spent nearly the entire speech talking about how he believes the Senators and Members of Congress should vote on the matter. It is the words. The Supreme Court ruled in Brandenburg that there is a very clear standard for incitement. In short, you have to look at the words themselves. The words have to either explicitly or implicitly call for—the words—call for lawlessness or violence. Whether the speech—you have to determine whether the speech was intended to provoke the lawlessness and whether the violence was the likely result of the word itself. They fail on all three prongs.

The false and defamatory claim that Mr. Trump gave a speech encouraging his supporters to go attack the Capitol has been repeated so often, uncritically, without any examination of the underlying facts, that the American—the Americans—listening at home were probably surprised to learn it is not true. Furthermore, some of the people in this room followed Mr. Trump's statements and tweets in the weeks leading up to January 6 very closely. We know that he was not trying to foment an insurrection during the time because no one—from the Speaker of the House to the Mayor of Washington, D.C.—behaved in a fashion consistent with the belief that violence was being advocated for. Mr. Trump did not spend the weeks prior to January 6 inciting violence. He spent those weeks pursuing his election challenge through the court system and other legal procedures, exactly as the Constitution and the Congress prescribe.

To believe based on the evidence you have seen that Mr. Trump actually wanted and, indeed, willfully incited an armed insurrection to overthrow the U.S. Government would be absurd. The gathering on January 6 was supposed to be an entirely peaceful event. Thousands and thousands of people, including Mr. Trump, showed up that day with that intention. A small percentage—a small fraction of those people—then engaged in truly horrible behavior. But as we now know, that those actors were preplanned and premeditated and acted even before this speech was completed, to which is the basis of the Article of Impeachment. It was preplanned and premeditated by fringe—left and right—groups. They hijacked the event for their own purposes.

The House managers' false narrative is a brazenly dishonest attempt to smear, to cancel—constitutional canceled culture—their Number one political opponent, taking neutral statements, commonplace political rhetoric, removing words and facts from context and ascribing to them the most sinister and malevolent intentions possible. Their story was based not on evidence but on the sheer personal and political animus. The flimsy theory of incitement you heard from the House managers could be used to impeach, indict, or expel countless other political leaders. Many leading figures in other parties have engaged in far more incendiary and dangerous rhetoric, and we played some of them. I am not going to replay it. I am not going to replay you the words.

You all saw the evidence. I am not going to replay mob scenes. I don't want to give those people another platform, any more view from the American people as to what they did. They should be canceled. Democrat politicians spent months prior to January 6 attacking the very legitimacy of our Nation's most cherished institutions and traditions. They didn't just question the integrity of one election; they challenged the integrity of our entire Nation—everything from our Founding Fathers, our Constitution, the Declaration of Independence, law enforcement officers, and the United States Military. They said that our society was rooted in hatred. They even said that America deserved—and I will quote—"a reckoning."

As you heard yesterday, throughout the summer, Democrat leaders, including the current President and Vice President, repeatedly made comments that provided moral comfort to mobs attacking police officers. During that time, many officers across the country were injured. As we all know, two sheriff's deputies in Los Angeles were ambushed and shot at point-blank range. Members of this very body have been in danger. Senators from Maine to Kentucky, and most points in between, have been harassed by mobs. Last August, a menacing leftwing mob swarmed Senator Rand Paul and his wife as they left the White House, and they had to be rescued by police. For months, our Federal courthouse in Portland was placed under siege by violent anarchists who attacked law enforcement officers daily and repeatedly and tried to set fire to the building. Speaker Pelosi did not call the violent siege of the Federal building an insurrection. She called the Federal agents protecting the courthouse "stormtroopers." The White House complex was besieged by mobs that threw bricks, rocks, and bottles at Secret Service agents, set fire to a historic structure, and breached a security fence to infiltrate the Treasury grounds. When my client's administration sent in the National Guard to secure the Nation's Capital City amidst the violence, Democrat leaders demanded that the forces be withdrawn. The Washington, D.C., Mayor said the presence of the National Guard was an affront to the safety of the District. It must be fully investigated whether political leadership here in Washington, D.C., took an inadequate and irresponsible force posture on January 6 because of their commitment to the false narrative of what happened last June.

Hopefully we can all now agree that the administration acted properly by taking action to stop a riotous mob, establishing an appropriate security perimeter, and preventing the White House from potentially being overrun. The House managers argued this week that an alleged brief delay in issuing a public statement from Mr. Trump on January 6 was somehow evidence that he committed incitement or supported the violence. Yet for months last year Joe Biden and Vice President Harris and countless other Democrats repeatedly refused to condemn the extremists as riots were occurring daily, as businesses were being ramshackled, as neighborhoods were being burned, as bombs were exploding. They repeatedly refused to tell their violent supporters to stand down. Some even suggested that the mobs' actions were justified. Vice President Harris literally urged her followers to donate money to a fund to bail out the violent, extreme rioters so that they could get out and continue to do it over and over again. She later said that those folks were not going to let up and that they should not. All of this was far closer to the actual definition of "incitement" than anything President Trump has ever said or done, never mind what he said on the 6th.

It is a hypocrisy. It is a hypocrisy that the House managers have laid at the feet of this Chamber. The House managers suggested that this recent history is irrelevant to the current proceedings, but not only is Democrats' behavior surrounding last year's riots highly relevant as precedent and not only does it reveal the dishonesty and insincerity of this entire endeavor, it also provides crucial context that should inform our understanding of the events that took place on January 6. Many of the people who infiltrated the Capitol took pictures of themselves and posted them on social media. To some, it seems, they thought that it was all a game. They apparently believed that violent mobs, destruction of property, rioting, assaulting police, and vandalizing historic treasures was somehow now acceptable in the United States.

Where might they have gotten that idea? I would suggest to you that it was not from Mr. Trump. It was not Mr. Trump. It was not anyone in the Republican Party that spent the six months immediately prior to the Capitol assault giving rhetorical aid and comfort to mobs, making excuses for rioters, celebrating radicalism, and explaining that angry, frustrated, and marginalized people were entitled to blow off steam like that.

Let me be very clear. There can be no excuse for the depraved actions of the rioters here at the Capitol or anywhere else across this country. One hundred percent of those guilty of committing crimes deserve lengthy prison sentences for their shameful and depraved conduct. But this trial has raised the question about words, actions, and consequences. As a nation, we must ask ourselves, how did we arrive at this place where rioting and pillaging would become commonplace? I submit to you that it was month after month of political leaders and media personalities, bloodthirsty for ratings, glorifying civil unrest and condemning the reasonable law enforcement measures that are required to quell violent mobs. Hopefully we can all leave this Chamber in uniform agreement that all rioting—all rioting—is bad and that law enforcement deserves our respect and support. That has been Mr. Trump's position from the very beginning.

The real question in this case is, who is ultimately responsible for such acts of mayhem and violence when they are committed? The House Democrats want two different standards—one for themselves and one for their political opposition. They have carried out a grossly unconstitutional effort to punish Mr. Trump for protected First Amendment speech. It is an egregious violation of his constitutional rights. Since he uttered not a single word encouraging violence, this action can only be seen as an effort to censor disfavored political speech and discriminate against a disapproved viewpoint. It is an unprecedented action with the potential to do grave and lasting damage to both the Presidency and the separation of powers and the future of democratic self-government.

Yesterday we played you a video of countless Democrat Members of the Senate urging their supporters to fight. We showed you those videos not because we think you should be forcibly removed from office for saying those things but because we know you should not be forcibly removed from office for saying those things. But recognize the hypocrisy yesterday in questioning, House Manager Raskin admitted that the House Democrats had invented an entirely new legal standard. In fact, they have created a new legal theory: the Raskin doctrine. The Raskin doctrine is based on nothing more than determining protected speech based on the party label next to your name. Regardless of what you have heard or what you have seen from the House managers, if you pay close attention, you will see that any speech made by Democrat elected officials is protected speech, while any speech made by

Republican elected officials is not protected. The creation of the Raskin doctrine actually reveals the weakness of the House managers' case.

Elected officials—and we reviewed this in-depth yesterday—under Supreme Court precedent *Wood* and *Bond*—by the way, *Bond* didn't burn his draft card; he actually still had it. It was part of his defense. But in *Bond* and in *Wood*, the Court clearly directed all to know that elected officials hold the highest protections of speech, the highest protections, and I remind you why: because you all need to be free to have robust political discussion because your discussion is about how our lives are going to go, and that shouldn't be squelched by any political party on either side of the aisle, no matter who is the majority party at the time.

Why would the House managers make up their own legal standard? I will tell you why. Because they know they cannot satisfy the existing constitutional standard set forth by the United States Supreme Court that has existed for more than half a century. They argue Mr. Trump, as an elected official, has no First Amendment rights. It is the complete opposite of the law. We have shown you, without contradiction, that is wrong. They also know that they cannot satisfy the three-part test of *Brandenburg*, as elucidated in the *Bible Believers* case. There was absolutely no evidence that Mr. Trump's words were directed to inciting imminent lawless action. There was no evidence that Mr. Trump intended his words to incite violence. And the violence was preplanned and premeditated by a group of lawless actors who must be prosecuted to the fullest extent of the law, but it proves that his words weren't what set this into motion, what was the incitement.

With no ability and no evidence to satisfy the existing constitutional standard, what are the House managers to do? They had to make up their own law. This is not only intellectually dishonest, folks; it is downright scary. What type of precedent would be set if the Senate did vote to convict? Can Congress now ignore Supreme Court precedent on the contours of protected free speech? Will Congress be permitted to continually make up their own legal standards and apply those new standards to elected officials' speech? This would allow Congress to use the awesome impeachment power as a weapon to impeach their fellow colleagues in the opposing party.

This is not a precedent that this Senate can set here today. If the Senate endorses the House Democrats' absurd new theory, you will set a precedent that will trouble leaders from both parties literally for centuries to come, but that will not be the only disgraceful precedent to come from this case. This has been perhaps the most unfair and flagrantly unconstitutional proceeding in the history of the United States Senate. For the first time in history, Congress has asserted the right to try and punish a former President who is a private citizen. Nowhere in the Constitution is the power enumerated or implied. Congress has no authority, no right, and no business holding a trial of Citizen Trump, let alone a trial to deprive him of some fundamental civil rights.

There was mention of a January exception argument. The January exception argument is a creation of the House managers' own conduct by delaying. They sat on the Article. They could have tried the President while he was still in office if they really believed he was an imminent threat. They didn't. The January exception is a red herring. It is nonsense because Federal, State, and local authorities can investigate. Their January exception always expires on January 20.

House Democrats and this deeply unfair trial have shamefully trampled every tradition, norm, and standard of due process in a way I have never ever seen before. Mr. Trump was given no right to review the so-called evidence against him at trial. He was given no opportunity to question its propriety. He was given no chance to engage in factfinding. Much of what was introduced by the House was unverified second- or thirdhand reporting cribbed from a biased news media, including stories based on anonymous sources whose identities are not even known to them, never mind my client. They manufactured and doctored evidence, so much so that they had to withdraw it.

We only had—we had the evidence after we started the trial. They went on for two days, so in the evening, I was able to go back and take a really close look at the stuff. Myself and Mr. Castor and Ms. Bateman and Mr. Brennan, we all worked hard and looked at the evidence, four volumes of books in little, tiny print. We started—we literally had twelve, fourteen hours to really look at the evidence before we had to go on, and just in that short time of looking at the evidence, we saw them fabricating Twitter accounts. We saw the masked man sitting at his desk with the *New York Times* there. And when we looked closely, we found that the date was wrong; the check had been added.

They fabricated evidence. They made it up. They never addressed that in their closing—as though it were acceptable, as though it were all right, as though that is the way it should be done here in the Senate of the United States of America. Fraud—flat-out fraud. Where I come from, in the courts I practice in, there are very harsh repercussions for what they pulled in this trial. As we have shown, the House managers were caught creating false representations of tweets, manipulating videos, and introducing into the Record completely discredited lies, such as the "fine people" hoax, as factual evidence.

Most of what the House managers have said and shown you would be inadmissible in any respectable court of law. They were not trying a case; they were telling a political tale—a fable—and a patently false one at that. House Democrats have denied due process and rushed the impeachment because they know that a fair trial would reveal Mr. Trump's innocence of the charges against him. The more actual evidence that comes out, the clearer it is that this was a preplanned and pre-meditated attack, which his language in no way incited. Because their case is so weak, the House managers have taken a kitchen-sink approach to the supposedly single Article of Impeachment. They allege that Mr. Trump incited the January 6 violence. They allege that he abused power by attempting to pressure Georgia Secretary of State Raffensperger to undermine the results of the 2020 election, and they allege that he gravely endangered the democratic system by interfering with the peaceful transition of power.

There are at least three things there. Under the Senate rules, each of these allegations must have been alleged in a separate Article of Impeachment. I need not remind this Chamber that rule XXIII of the Rules of Procedure and Practice in the Senate when Sitting on Impeachment Trials provides, in pertinent part, that an Article of Impeachment "shall not be divisible . . . thereon." Why is that? Because the Article at issue here alleges multiple wrongs in the single Article, it would be impossible to know if two thirds of the Members agreed on the entire Article or just on parts of it as the basis for a vote to convict. Based on this alone, the Senate must vote to acquit Mr. Trump. You have got to at least obey your own rules if it is not the Constitution you are going to obey. In short, this impeachment has been a complete charade from beginning to end. The entire spectacle has been nothing but an unhinged pursuit of a longstanding political vendetta against Mr. Trump by the opposition party.

As we have shown, Democrats were obsessed with impeaching Mr. Trump from the very beginning of his term. The House Democrats tried to impeach him in his first year. They tried to impeach him in his second year. They did impeach him in his third year. And they impeached him again in his fourth year. And now they have conducted a phony impeachment show trial when he is a private citizen out of office. This hastily orchestrated and unconstitutional circus is the House Democrats' final, desperate attempt to accomplish their obsessive desire of the last five years. Since the moment he stepped into the political arena, my client—since my client stepped in, they have been possessed by an overwhelming zeal to vanquish an independent-minded outsider from their midst and to shame, demean, silence, and demonize his supporters in the desperate hope that they will never, ever pose an electoral challenge. We heard one of the Congressmen on the screen: if you don't impeach him, he might be elected again. That is the fear. That is what is driving this impeachment.

When you deliberate over your decision, there are four distinct grounds under which you must acquit my client. First is jurisdiction. There is no jurisdiction. And if you believe that, you still get to say it. Two, rule XXIII—it had to be divisible. Each allegation had to be singularly set out in front of you so it could be voted on and to see if two thirds of you think that they proved that case or not. They didn't do that. You have got to ask yourself why. They know the Senate rules. They got them, and so did I. Why did they do it? Because they hadn't investigated, first of all. But, also, what they found out is when they were preparing all this, they couldn't do it. So if they threw in as much as they could and made as many bold, bald allegations as they could, then maybe two thirds of you would fall for it. That is why the rules don't allow it to go that way. Due process—I have exhausted that subject. It is a really good reason for all of you—all of you—in this Chamber to stop the politics, to read the Constitution and apply it to this proceeding and acknowledge that the lack of due process—way over the top, shocking. And you must not stand for it. And, of course, the First Amendment—the actual facts of this case. There were no words of incitement.

Four grounds. Nobody gets to tell you which ground to pick, and nobody gets to tell you how many grounds to consider. Senators, do not let House Democrats take this maniacal crusade any further. The Senate does not have to go down this dark path of enmity and division. You do not have to indulge the impeachment lust, the dishonesty, and the hypocrisy. It is time to bring this unconstitutional political theater to an end. It is time to allow our Nation to move forward. It is time to address the real business pressing this Nation—the pandemic, our economy, racial inequality, economic and social inequality. These are the things that you need to be thinking and working on for all of us in America—all of us. With your vote, you can defend the Constitution. You can protect due process. And you can allow America's healing to begin. I urge the Senate to acquit and vindicate the Constitution of this great Republic. Thank you.

. . .

Mr. Manager RASKIN: Mr. President, Senators, I understand—I am told we have around twenty-seven minutes, but I will return all of that but perhaps five back to you. There are just a few things I need to address. In an extraordinary and perhaps unprecedented act of self-restraint on my part, I will resist the opportunity to rebut every single false and illogical thing that you just heard. And I am going to be able to return to you, you know, perhaps twenty-two, twenty-three minutes.

A few points: one, we have definitely made some progress in the last few days because a few days ago, the President's team—although I think it was perhaps a member who has since left the team—lectured us that this was not an insurrection and said that impeachment managers were outrageous in using the word "insurrection." Today, counsel, in his closing statement, said it was a violent insurrection, and he denounced it. And I would certainly love to see President Trump also call it a violent insurrection and denounce it too. And I believe—although, I don't have a verbatim text—that counsel called for long sentences for the people who were involved. Again, I would love to hear that come from the President as well.

The distinguished counsel complains that there is no precedent with the developed body of law that the Senate has for impeaching and convicting a President who incites violent insurrection against the Congress and the government of the United States. Well, I suppose that is true because it never occurred to any other President of the United States—from George Washington, to John Adams, to Thomas Jefferson, to James Madison, to James Monroe, to Abraham Lincoln, to Ronald Reagan, to George W. Bush, to Barack Obama—to incite a violent insurrection against the Union. You are right. We have got no precedent for that, and so they think that that somehow is a mark in their favor—that is a score for them— that this Senate has to be the first one to define incitement of violent insurrection against the Union.

And so the gentleman puts it on me. He says: ". . . a President . . . committing incitement to violent insurrection against the Union is the new Raskin doctrine." We have tried to convince them that there are well-known principles and elements of incitement, which we have talked to you about ad nauseam, and that this is an intrinsically, inherently fact-based judgment. But if that is the Raskin doctrine— that a President of the United States cannot incite violent insurrection against the Union and the Congress—then I embrace it, and I take it as an honor.

Most law professors never even get a doctrine named after them, so I will accept that. And, finally, the counsel goes back to Julian Bond's case because, I think, in the final analysis, their best argument—as pathetically weak as it is—is really about the First Amendment. But, remember, they keep talking about stifling President Trump's speech.

Someone tell me when his speech has ever been stifled. He says exactly what he wants whenever he wants. If and when you convict him for incitement of insurrection, he will continue to say whatever he wants on that day. Remember, they referred yesterday to interference with his liberty, which I found absolutely bizarre because everybody knows he will not spend one minute in prison or jail from conviction on these charges. It is a civil remedy to protect all of us—to protect the entire country, our children, our Constitution, our future. That is what impeachment trial convictions are all about—are all about. Julian Bond—see, I knew Julian Bond, so forgive me. Most people say: "don't even respond to this stuff." I have got to respond to this. Julian Bond was a civil rights activist who decided to go into politics, like the people in this room, like all of us who are in politics. And they tried to keep him out. He was a member of SNCC, the Student Nonviolent Coordinating Committee, which really launched the voting rights movement in America. It is a great story that Bob Moses tells in his book called

Radical Equations about—you know, he was a graduate student, mathematics, at Harvard.

He was a graduate student in mathematics at Harvard. He went to Mississippi. You know why? Because he saw a picture in the *New York Times* of Black civil rights protesters, college students, I think, North Carolina A&T. He saw a picture of them on the cover of the *New York Times*, and they were sitting in at a lunch counter. He looked at the picture, and he said: "They looked the way that I felt." They looked the way that I felt. He said he had to go down south to Mississippi, and they launched the voting rights movement. That is where the phrase "One-person, one-vote" comes from. It was not invented by the Supreme Court. They would go door-to-door to try to register people to vote. But anyway, Julian Bond was a part of that movement, the Student Nonviolent Coordinating Committee—nonviolence. It was the end, and it was the means—nonviolence. And he ran for the State legislature in Georgia, a path other civil rights activists followed, like our great, late, beloved colleague John Lewis, who is in our hearts today. And when he got elected, they wanted to try to keep him from being sworn in to the Georgia Legislature. And so they said the Student Nonviolent Coordinating Committee is taking a position against the Vietnam war. You are a member of SNCC. We are not going to admit you because you took a position against the Vietnam war.

And the Supreme Court, in its wisdom, said you cannot prevent someone from swearing an oath to become a member of a legislative body because of a position that they took or a group they were part of—took before they got sworn in. That is the exact opposite of Donald Trump. He got elected to office. He swore an oath to the Constitution to preserve, protect, and defend the Constitution. He served as President for four years, right up until the end, when he wanted to exercise his rights under the imaginary January exception, and he incited a violent mob and insurrection to come up here, and we all know what happened.

He is being impeached and convicted for violating his oath of office that he took. He is not being prevented from taking his oath in the first place. The First Amendment is on our side. He tried to overturn the will of the people, the voice of the people. He lost that election by more than 7 million votes. Some people don't want to admit it. Counsel for the President could not bring themselves to admit that the election is over in answer to the question from the distinguished gentleman from Vermont. He refused to answer that. He said it was irrelevant, despite all of the evidence you have heard about the big lie and how that set the stage for his incitement of the insurrectionary violence against us.

The First Amendment is on our side. We are defending the Bill of Rights. We are defending the constitutional structure. We are defending the separation of powers. We are defending the U.S. Senate and the U.S. House against a President who acted no better than a marauder and a member of that mob by inciting those people to come here. And in many ways, he was worse. He named the date; he named the time; and he brought them here; and now he must pay the price. Thank you, Mr. President.

. . .

Mr. SCHUMER: Mr. President, the Senate is now ready to vote on the Article of Impeachment. And after that is done, we will adjourn the Court of Impeachment.

. . .

The PRESIDENT pro tempore: The clerk will read the Article of Impeachment. The senior assistant legislative clerk read as follows:

ARTICLE I: INCITEMENT OF INSURRECTION

The Constitution provides that the House of Representatives "shall have the sole Power of Impeachment" and that the President "shall be removed from Office on Impeachment for, and Conviction of, Treason, Bribery, or other high Crimes and Misdemeanors". Further, section 3 of the 14th Amendment to the Constitution prohibits any person who has "engaged in insurrection or rebellion against" the United States from "hold[ing] any office . . . under the United States". In his conduct while President of the United States—and in violation of his constitutional oath faithfully to execute the office of President of the United States and, to the best of his ability, preserve, protect, and defend the Constitution of the United States, and in violation of his constitutional duty to take care that the laws be faithfully executed—Donald John Trump engaged in high Crimes and Misdemeanors by inciting violence against the Government of the United States, in that:

On January 6, 2021, pursuant to the 12th Amendment to the Constitution of the United States, the Vice President of the United States, the House of Representatives, and the Senate met at the United States Capitol for a Joint Session of Congress to count the votes of the Electoral College. In the months preceding the Joint Session, President Trump repeatedly issued false statements asserting that the Presidential election results were the product of widespread fraud and should not be accepted by the American people or certified by State or Federal officials. Shortly before the Joint Session commenced, President Trump, addressed a crowd at the Ellipse in Washington, DC. There, he reiterated false claims that "we won this election, and we won it by a landslide." He also willfully made statements that, in context, encouraged—and foreseeably resulted in—lawless action at the Capitol, such as: "if you don't fight like hell you're not going to have a country anymore."

Thus incited by President Trump, members of the crowd he had addressed, in an attempt to, among other objectives, interfere with the Joint Session's solemn constitutional duty to certify the results of the 2020 Presidential election, unlawfully breached and vandalized the Capitol, injured and killed law enforcement personnel, menaced Members of Congress, the Vice President, and Congressional personnel, and engaged in other violent, deadly, destructive, and seditious acts. President Trump's conduct on January 6, 2021, followed his prior efforts to subvert and obstruct the certification of the results of the 2020 Presidential election.

Those prior efforts included a phone call on January 2, 2021, during which President Trump urged the Secretary of State of Georgia, Brad Raffensperger, to "find" enough votes to overturn the Georgia Presidential election results and threatened Secretary Raffensperger if he failed to do so. In all this, President Trump gravely endangered the security of the United States and its institutions of Government. He threatened the integrity of the democratic system, interfered with the peaceful transition of power, and imperiled a coequal branch of Government. He thereby betrayed his trust as President, to the manifest injury of the people of the United States.

Wherefore, Donald John Trump, by such conduct, has demonstrated that he will remain a threat to national security, democracy, and the Constitution if allowed to remain in office, and has acted in a manner grossly incompatible with self-governance and the rule of law. Donald John Trump thus warrants impeachment and trial, removal from office, and disqualification to hold and enjoy any office of honor, trust, or profit under the United States.

Vote on Article I

The PRESIDENT pro tempore: Each Senator, when his or her name is called, will stand in his or her place and vote guilty or not guilty, as required by rule XXIII of the Senate Rules on Impeachment.

Article I, section 3, clause 6 of the Constitution regarding the vote required for conviction of impeachment provides that "no person shall be convicted without the concurrence of two thirds of the Members present."

The question is on the Article of Impeachment. Senators, how say you? Is the respondent, Donald John Trump, guilty or not guilty? A rollcall vote is required. The clerk will call the roll. The senior assistant legislative clerk called the roll. The result was announced—guilty fifty-seven, not guilty forty-three, as follows:

YEAS—57 Baldwin Bennet Blumenthal Booker Brown Burr Cantwell Cardin Carper Casey Cassidy Collins Coons Cortez Masto Duckworth Durbin Feinstein Gillibrand Hassan Heinrich Hickenlooper Hirono Kaine Kelly King Klobuchar Leahy Lujan Manchin Markey Menendez Merkley Murkowski Murphy Murray Ossoff Padilla Peters Reed Romney Rosen

Sanders Sasse Schatz Schumer Shaheen Sinema Smith Stabenow Tester Toomey Van Hollen Warner Warnock Warren Whitehouse Wyden

NAYS—43 Barrasso Blackburn Blunt Boozman Braun Capito Cornyn Cotton Cramer Crapo Cruz Daines Ernst Fischer Graham Grassley Hagerty Hawley Hoeven Hyde-Smith Inhofe Johnson Kennedy Lankford Lee Lummis Marshall McConnell Moran Paul Portman Risch Rounds Rubio Scott (FL) Scott (SC) Shelby Sullivan Thune Tillis Tuberville Wicker Young

The PRESIDENT pro tempore: On this vote, the yeas are fifty-seven, the nays are forty-three.

Two thirds of the Senators present not having voted guilty, the Senate adjudges that the respondent Donald John Trump, former President of the United States, is not guilty as charged in the Article of Impeachment.

The Presiding Officer directs the judgment to be entered in accordance with the judgment of the Senate, as follows: The Senate, having tried Donald John Trump, former President of the United States, upon one Article of Impeachment exhibited against him by the House of Representatives, and two thirds of the Senators present not having found him guilty of the charge contained therein, it is, therefore, ordered and adjudged that the said Donald John Trump be, and is hereby, acquitted of the charge in said Article.

PUBLISHING IN THE PUBLIC INTEREST

Thank you for reading this book published by The New Press. The New Press is a nonprofit, public interest publisher. New Press books and authors play a crucial role in sparking conversations about the key political and social issues of our day.

We hope you enjoyed this book and that you will stay in touch with The New Press. Here are a few ways to stay up to date with our books, events, and the issues we cover:

- Sign up at www.thenewpress.com/subscribe to receive updates on New Press authors and issues and to be notified about local events
- Like us on Facebook: www.facebook.com/newpressbooks
- Follow us on Twitter: www.twitter.com/thenewpress
- Follow us on Instagram: www.instagram.com/thenewpress

Please consider buying New Press books for yourself; for friends and family; or to donate to schools, libraries, community centers, prison libraries, and other organizations involved with the issues our authors write about.

The New Press is a 501(c)(3) nonprofit organization. You can also support our work with a tax-deductible gift by visiting www.thenewpress.com/donate.